DICTIONARY OF
LITURGICAL
LATIN

WILFRID DIAMOND

DICTIONARY OF
LITURGICAL LATIN

DICTIONARY OF
LITURGICAL LATIN

WILFRID DIAMOND, Joseph 1913-

THE BRUCE PUBLISHING COMPANY
MILWAUKEE

Library of Congress Catalog Card Number: 61–7491

© 1961 The Bruce Publishing Company

Made in the United States of America

(Second printing — 1962)

DICTIONARY OF
LITURGICAL LATIN

A

ábacus –i, *m.*, a small table for cruets, the credence, a table or shelf in the wall at the epistle side of the altar

abaliénor –ári, *dep. 1*, to be estranged, depart

abávus –i, *m.*, a forefather

Abba (Aramaic), Father

ábbas –átis, *m.*, an abbot

abbátia –ae, *f.*, an abbey, abbacy, an abbey governed by an abbot

abbatiális –e, *adj.*, pertaining to an abbey or an abbot

abbatíssa –ae, *f.*, a superior of a monastery of nuns, an abbess

abbreviátor –óris, *m.*, one who makes abstracts from papal bulls

abbrévio –are, *1*, to shorten, cut off

abdicátio –ónis, *f.*, a renouncing, disowning

ábdico –áre, *1*, to renounce, abandon, give up

abdíco –ere –díxi –díctum, *3*, to disapprove of

ábditum –i, *n.*, a hidden place, lair, secret

ábditus –a –um, *adj.*, hidden, concealed

ábdo –ere –didi –ditum, *3*, to conceal, hide, secrete

abecetuórium, *n.*, the act of tracing Greek and Latin alphabets on the floor while consecrating a church

aberrátio –ónis, *f.*, relief from anything irksome

abérro –are, *1*, to go astray, wander

abhórreo –ére, *2*, to shrink back or away from

abiégnus –a –um, *adj.*, of fir

ábies –étis, *f.*, a fir tree

abietárius –ii, *m.*, a carpenter, worker in wood

abígo –ere –égi –áctum, *3*, to banish, drive away

ábitus –us, *m.*, a going away, departure

abjécte, *adv.*, cowardly

abjéctio –ónis, *f.*, an outcast

abjício –ere –jéci –jéctum, *3*, to refuse, cast off, debase, degrade

abjúdico –are, *1*, to take away by judgment, deny on oath

abjúngo –ere –júnxi –júnctum, *3*, to unlock, unloose

abjurátio –ónis, *f.*, an abjuration

abjúro –áre, *1*, to deny on oath

ablácto –áre, *1*, to wean

ablegátio –ónis, *f.*, a sending away

áblego –áre, *1*, to send away

ábluo –ere –lui –lútum, *3*, to wash away, cleanse

ablútio –ónis, *f.*, the act of washing, a washing away; the mixture of wine and water taken by the priest at Mass

ábnego –áre, *1*, to refuse or deny

abnórmis –e, *adj.*, unconventional, irregular

abnúo –ere –ui, *3*, to deny, refuse by a motion of the head

abnúto –áre, *1*, to deny repeatedly, deny by a nod of the head

abóleo –ére –évi –itum, *2*, to destroy, abolish

abolésco –ere –évi, *3*, to decay, vanish

abolítio –ónis, *f.*, a removing, abolition

abólla –ae, *f.*, a thick woolen cloak

abominábilis –e, *adj.*, hateful, worthy of destruction

abominátio –ónis, *f.*, abomination, aversion, loathing

abóminor –ári, *dep. 1*, to abhor, hate, detest, loathe

abórior –órtus sum, *dep. 4*, to set, disappear

abortívus –a –um, *adj.*, prematurely born, abortive

ábra –ae, *f.*, a maid

Abrahámus –i, *m.*, Abraham. *The word is indeclinable in the Psalms.*

abrenunciátio –ónis, *f.*, a repudiation, renouncing

abrenúncio –áre, *1*, to renounce

abrípio –ere –ripui –réptum, *3*, to drag away, tear away

abrogátio –ónis, *f.*, a repealing

ábrogo –áre, *1*, to revoke, abrogate

abrúmpo –ere –rúpi –rúptum, *3*, to loosen, separate, break

abrúptio –ónis, *f.*, a tearing away

abrúptus –a –um, *adj.*, steep, precipitous

abscédo –ere –céssi –céssum, *3*, to retire, depart

abscéssio –ónis, *f.*, a going away, separation

abscéssus –us, *m.*, death

abscído –ere –cidi –císsum, *3*, to cut off

abscíndo –ere –scidi –scíssum, *3*, to cut off, tear away

abscóndite, *adv.*, secretly

abscónditum –i, *n.*, a hidden place or thing; *in abscóndita*, in secret

abscóndo –ere –didi –ditum, *3*, to hide, conceal

abscónsio –ónis, *f.*, a shelter

abscónsus –a –um, *adj.*, hidden, secret

ábsens –éntis, *adj.*, absent

abséntia –ae, *f.*, absence

absída –ae, *f.*, an apse, apsis

absidiále –is, *n.*, a smaller apse flanking a larger one

absidióla –ae, *f.*, a smaller apse flanking a larger one

absímilis –e, *adj.*, unlike, dissimilar

absínthium –ii, *n.*, absynth, wormwood

ábsis –idis, *f.*, an apse

absísto –ere –stiti –stitum, *3*, to be exiled, cease, depart, withdraw

ábsit, far be it! God forbid!

absolúte *adv.*, completely, absolutely

absolútio –ónis, *f.*, absolution, the sacramental remission of sin; the short prayer before the lessons in Matins

absólvo –ere –sólvi –solútum, *3*, to absolve, pardon, release

absórbeo –ére –ui, *2*, to swallow, gulp down, absorb

abstémius –a –um, *adj.*, temperate, abstaining from wine

abstérgeo –ére –térsi –térsum, *2*, to blot out, wipe away

ábstinens –éntis, *adj.*, temperate, abstinent

abstinéntia –ae, *f.*, abstinence, moderation, an abstaining from certain foods

abstíneo –ére –ui –téntum, *2*, to abstain, hold back, keep away from

abstráctio –ónis, *f.*, removal, detachment

ábstraho –ere –tráxi –tráctum, *3*, to drag away, to bring forth

abstrúdo –ere –úsi –úsum, *3*, to hide, conceal

ábsum –esse –fui, to be absent

absúmo –ere –súmpsi –súmptum, *3*, to consume, take away

absúrde, *adv.*, absurdly

absúrditas –átis, *f.*, absurdity, incongruity

absýnthium –ii, *n.*, wormwood

abúndans –ántis, *adj.*, abundant, rich, overflowing, abounding in

abundánter, *adv.*, abundantly, fully

abundántia –ae, *f.*, abundance, plenty, prosperity

abundántius, *adv.*, more frequently

abúnde, *adv.*, abundantly

abúndo –áre, *1*, to abound, have abundance of, be rich, overflow

abúsio –ónis, *f.*, scorn, contempt

abútor –úti –úsus sum, *dep. 3*, to use, destroy

abýssus –i, *f.*, an abyss, depths, the deep

académia –ae, *f.*, an academy, college

académicus –a –um, *adj.*, academic

acathólicus –a –um, *adj.*, non-Catholic

accédit, *impers.*, it is added

accédo –ere –céssi –céssum, *3*, to approach, draw nigh, come near, accede, approve

accelerátio –ónis, *f.*, hastening

accélero –áre, *1*, to hasten

accéndo –ere –di –cénsum, *3*, to inflame, kindle, set on fire

accénseo –ere –ui –cénsum, *2*, to reckon in addition, add to

accensíbilis –e, *adj.*, burning

accéntus –us, *m.*, an accent; the parts sung by the celebrant at Mass

acceptábilis –e, *adj.*, pleasing, acceptable

accéptio –ónis, *f.*, respect, distinction

accépto –áre, *1*, to accept, receive with pleasure

accéptus –a –um, *adj.*, acceptable, worthy, agreeable

accérso –ere –sívi –sítum, *3*, to summon, call

accéssus –us, *m.*, an approach, access

áccidens –éntis, *n.*, accident

accidéntia –órum, *n.*, appearance, accidents

áccido –ere –cidi, *3*, to happen, arrive, fall upon

accíngo –ere –cínxi –cínctum, *3*, to equip, gird

áccio –íre –ívi *or* –ii –ítum, *4*, to summon, call to, procure, take

accípio –ere –cépi –céptum, *3*, to accept, receive, take

accípiter –tris, *m.*, a hawk

acclamátio –ónis, *f.*, an exclamation, a ceremonial greeting

acclámo –áre, *1*, to cry out at

acclínis –e, *adj.*, leaning, bowing

acclíno –áre, *1*, to lean on

acclívis –e, *adj.*, inclined upward

áccola –ae, *c.*, a sojourner

áccolo –ere –ui, *3*, to dwell by or near

accómodo –áre, *1*, to accommodate, adjust, put on, fit, incline

accrédo –ere –crédidi –créditum, *3*, to believe

accrésco –ere –crévi –crétum, *3*, to grow

accúbitus –us, *m.*, prostration, repose

áccubo –áre, *1*, to lie down

accúmbo –ere, –cubui –cubitum, *3,* to sit at table, recline

accúmulo –are, *1,* to heap up

accuráte, *adv.,* accurately

accurátio –ónis, *f.,* carefulness, accuracy

accurátus –a –um, *adj.,* accurate, correct, careful

accúrro –ere –cúrri *or* –cúcurri –cúrsum, *3,* to occur, run to meet

accusátio –ónis, *f.,* an accusation

accusátor –óris, *m.,* an accuser

accúso –áre, *1,* to accuse

acédior –ári, *dep. 1,* to be pained, wearied

acéphalus –a –um, *adj.,* without a head

acérbe, *adv.,* bitterly, harshly

acérbitas –átis, *f.,* bitterness, evil, sinfulness

acérbus –a –um, *adj.,* sour, bitter, sharp

acérra –ae, *f.,* an incense boat

acérvo –áre, *1,* to heap up, amass

acérvus –i, *m.,* a heap

acescéntia –ae, *f.,* acidity, sourness

acésco –ere, ácui, *3,* to become or turn sour

acetábulum –i, *n.,* a dish, bowl

acétum –i, *n.,* vinegar, an acid

achátes –ae, *m.,* agate

acícula –ae, *f.,* a pin

ácies –éi, *f.,* army, line of battle, keenness, the pupil of the eye

ácinum –i, *n.,* a grape, the stone of a grape

ácinus –i, *m.,* a grape, the stone of a grape

acistárium –ii, *n.,* a monastery

acolythátus –us, *m.,* the order of acolyte

acólythus –i, *m.,* an acolyte

acquiésco –ere –quiévi –quiétum, *3,* to repose, rest, follow again, agree

acquíro –ere –quisívi –quisítum, *3,* to procure, acquire

acquisítio –ónis, *f.,* purchase, acquisition

acquisítus –a –um, *adj.,* acquired

ácriter, *adv.,* keenly, sharply, violently

Act., *abbrev.* of *Actus Apostolorum,* the Acts of the Apostles

Acta Apostólicae Sedis, the *Acts of the Apostolic See,* official Vatican publication

Acta Mártyrum, the Acts of the Martyrs

Acta Sanctae Sedis, the *Acts of the Holy See,* now called *Acta Apostolicae Sedis*

Acta Sanctórum, the Acts of the Saints

áctio –ónis, *f.,* a deed, action; *gratiarum actio,* thanksgiving

Actio sacrífica, the Eucharistic Sacrificial action

actor –óris, *m.,* governor, steward, agent, guardian

actuális –e, *adj.,* actual

actuálitas –átis, *f.,* reality, existence

actuárius –ii, *m.,* a clerk, actuary

actuósus –a –um, *adj.,* active

actus –us, *m.,* a deed, act, work, office

actus nóxius, sin

acúleus –i, *m.,* a sharp point, sting

acúmen –inis, *n.,* a sharp point, keenness

acúo –ere –ui –útum, *3,* to sharpen, exercise

acupictúra –ae, *f.,* embroidery

acus, acus, *f.,* a pin, needle

acutále, *adv.,* somewhat sharply

acútus –a –um, *adj.,* sharp, sharpened, keen, pointed, acute

acystérium –ii, *n.,* a monastery

Adam, Adae, *m.,* Adam, the man God created in the Garden of Eden

adamantínus –a –um, *adj.,* unconquered, of a diamond

adámas –ántis, *m.,* a diamond, steel

adámo –áre, *1,* to fall in love, love greatly

Adamus –i, *m.,* Adam. (*This form is found outside the Vulgate.*)

adapério –íre –pérui –pértum, *4,* to open

adapértio –ónis, *f.,* an explanation, opening

adáquo –áre, *1,* to give a drink, water

adaúgeo –ere –aúxi –aúctum, *2,* to increase

addécimo –áre, *1,* to levy, tithe, tax

addíco –ere –díxi –díctum, *3,* to judge, condemn

addítio –ónis, *f.,* addition

additítius –a –um, *adj.,* additional

addúco –ere –dúxi –dúctum, *3,* to bring, provoke, escort

ádeo –íre –ívi *or* –ii –itum, *4,* to go to, approach

adeps –ipis, *m.* and *f.,* marrow, fat, the best

ádfero –férre –tuli, allátum, *3,* to bring together, carry

adhaéreo –ére –haési –haésum, *2,* to cling to, adhere, cleave to

adhíbeo –ére –ui –itum, *2,* to apply, add to, make use of

ad hóminem arguméntum, an argument

based on the principles admitted by an opponent

adhórtor –ári, *dep. 1,* to encourage, exhort

ádigo –ere –égi –áctum, *3,* to drive, impel, drive to

adímo –ere –émi –émptum, *3,* to take away, remove

adímpleo –ére –plévi –plétum, *2,* to fill, fulfill

adínflo –flúre, *1,* to swell up

adinvénio –íre –véni –véntum, *4,* to find

adinvéntio –ónis, *f.,* work, device, invention, plan

ad ínvicem, one with another, among themselves

adipíscor –písci, adéptus sum, *3,* to obtain, acquire, gain, achieve

áditus –us, *m.,* an approach, entry, access, report, gate

adjício –ere –jéci –jéctum, *3,* to grant, add, direct one's thoughts

adjúdico –áre, *1,* to judge, sentence

adjuméntum –i, *n.,* help, aid, assistance

adjúnctio –ónis, *f.,* restriction, limitation

adjúngo –ere –júnxi –júnctum, *3,* to join, attach

adjuraméntum –i, *n.,* an adjuration, oath

adjúro –áre, *1,* to adjure

adjútor –óris, *m.,* a helper

adjutórium –ii, *n.,* help, assistance

adjútrix –icis, *f.,* a female helper

ádjuvo –áre –júvi –jútum, *1,* to help

adlabóro –áre, *1,* to work, labor, toil

adléctus –i, *m.,* one elected into a college

ad líbitum, at one's pleasure, referring to the choice of a prayer in the Office or in the Mass

ad límina Apostolórum, to the threshold of the Apostles

adminículum –i, *n.,* a support or prop

adminíster –tri, *m.,* an assistant

administrátio –ónis, *f.,* administration, administering, governing

administrátor –óris, *m.,* one who administers or conducts; the bishop or priest appointed to administer a parish or diocese which is vacant

administratórius –a –um, *adj.,* ministering

adminístro –áre, *1,* to administer, minister, manage

admirábilis –e, *adj.,* wonderful, admirable, worthy of admiration

admirátio –ónis, *f.,* surprise, disapproval of an unusual or improper action

admíror –ári, *dep. 1,* to admire, wonder at

admísceo –ere –míscui –míxtum, *2,* to mix

admissúra –ae, *f.,* admission

admítto –ere –mísi –míssum, *3,* to admit, join

admíxtio –ónis, *f.,* a mixture, mixing

ádmodum, *adv.,* exceedingly, very

admóneo –ere –ui –itum, *2,* to admonish, warn

admónitus –a –um, *adj.,* warned, admonished

admóveo –ére –móvi –mótum, *2,* to move, move near, bring

adnéxus –a –um, *adj.,* connected

adnotátio –ónis, *f.,* annotation, comment

adnóto –áre, *1,* to note

ad nutum sanctae sedis, at the will (nod) of the Holy See

adóleo –ére –ui, *2,* to burn, consume, honor, incense

adoléscens –éntis, *m.,* a young man

adolescéntia –ae, *f.,* youth, adolescence

adolescéntior –óris, *m.,* a young man

adolescéntula –ae, *f.,* a very young maiden

adolescéntulus –i, *m.,* a very young man

adolésco –ere –évi, adúltum, *3,* to grow up

Adonái, *m., indecl.,* Adonai (Lord, God). The Hebrew substitute for Jahweh, rendered in the Vulgate as *Dominus* and in the Douay Bible as "Lord."

adóptio –ónis, *f.,* adoption

ádor –oris, *n.,* a species of grain

adorábilis –e, *adj.,* adorable, worthy of adoration

adorándus –a –um, *adj.,* adorable

adorátio –ónis, *f.,* adoration

adorátor –óris, *m.,* a worshiper, adorer

adórior –órtus sum, *dep. 4,* to rise up

Adórna thálamum, an antiphon chanted on Candlemas Day

adórno –áre, *1,* to provide, furnish, prepare, adorn

adóro –áre, *1,* to adore, worship

Adóro Te, a hymn frequently sung at Benediction of the Blessed Sacrament

adpertinére, to appertain to

adscísco –ere –scívi –scítum, *3,* to receive, admit

adscríbo –ere –scrípsi –scríptum, *3*, to ascribe to, write, enroll

adscríptus –a –um, *adj.*, approved

adsédeo –ere –sédi –séssum, *2*, to be near, sit by

adséntior –iri, *dep. 4*, to assent, approve

adsído –ere –sédi, *3*, to sit down

adspérgo –ere –spérsi –spérsum, *3*, to scatter, bespatter

adspersórium –ii, *n.*, a sprinkler

adspício –ere –spéxi –spéctum, *3*, to look on

adspíro –áre, *1*, to breathe upon, inspire

adstípulor –ári, *dep. 1*, to strengthen, agree to

adstríngo –ere –strínxi –stríctum, *3*, to bind, fetter, draw close

ádsum –ésse, ádfui (áffui), to be present, attend

adulátio –ónis, *f.*, flattery

aduléscens –éntis, *m.*, youth

adúlter –i, *m.*, an adulterer

adúltera –ae, *f.*, an adultress

adulterínus –a –um, *adj.*, not genuine

adultérium –ii, *n.*, adultery

adúltero –áre, *1*, to commit adultery

adúltus –i, *m.*, an adult

adúltus –a –um, *adj.*, adult

adúno –áre, *1*, to unite

adúro –ere –ússi –ústum, *3*, to burn up, set on fire

ádvena –ae, *c.*, a stranger

advénio –íre –véni –véntum, *4*, to come

adventéntia –ae, *f.*, knowledge, warning

Advéntus, the season of Advent, a period of prayer and fasting in preparation for Christmas. It marks the beginning of the ecclesiastical year.

advéntus –us, *m.*, arrival, advent

advérsa –órum, *n.*, adversity

adversárius –ii, *m.*, adversary

advérsitas –átis, *f.*, adversity, calamity

advérsor –ári, *dep. 1*, to oppose, resist

advérsum –i, *n.*, harm

advérsus –a –um, *adj.*, adverse

adverténtia –ae, *f.*, awareness, noticing, attending

advérto –ere –vérti –vérsum, *3*, to advert to

advocáta –ae, *f.*, advocate

advocátio –ónis, *f.*, the function of a patron, the right of presentation to a vacant benefice

advocátus –i, *m.*, advocate

Advocátus Diáboli, the Devil's Advocate, a slang name given to the Pro-

moter of the Faith in the process of beatification or canonization

ádvoco –áre, *1*, to call, call to

advólo –áre, *1*, to fly to

advólvo –ere –vólvi –volútum, *3*, to roll

ádytum –i, *n.*, a sanctuary, the Holy of Holies. *In the plural*, the inmost recesses.

aedes –is, *f.*, a dwelling, church, temple, palace

aedícula –ae, *f.*, a little building, chapel, the tabernacle

aedíficans –ántis, *m.*, a builder

aedificátio –ónis, *f.*, a building, edification, good example

aedificátor –óris, *m.*, a repairer

aedificátus –a –um, *adj.*, constructed, built

aedífico –áre, *1*, to build

aedítuus –i, *m.*, a caretaker, caretaker of a temple, janitor, trustee of a church

aeger –gra –grum, *adj.*, sick, ill

aegre, *adv.*, ill, badly

aegritúdo –inis, *f.*, illness, sickness

aegrotátio –ónis, *f.*, illness, sickness

aegróto –áre, *1*, to be sick, grow sick

aegrótus –a –um, *adj.*, sick, ill

aémula –ae, *f.*, a rival

aemulátio –ónis, *f.*, envy, emulation

aemulátor –óris, *m.*, an eager imitator

aémulor –ári, *dep. 1*, to envy

aémulus –a –um, *adj.*, emulating, rivaling. (Takes the dative.)

Aenária –ae, *f.*, the island of Ischia in the Mediterranean Sea

Aenéas –ae, *m.*, the paralytic healed by St. Peter

aéneus –a –um, *adj.*, brazen, of bronze

aenígma –atis, *n.*, a difficult question, riddle, obscurity

aequális –e, *adj.*, equal

aequálitas –átis, *f.*, equality

aequáliter, *adv.*, evenly, equally

aequanímiter, *adv.*, calmly

aeque, *adv.*, equally; *aeque ac*, as well as

aequinóctium –ii, *n.*, the equinox

aequíparo –áre, *1*, to compare

aéquitas –átis, *f.*, justice, equality, righteousness

aequo –áre, *1*, to make level, make equal

aequor –óris, *n.*, the sea

aequus –a –um, *adj.*, equal right

aër, áëris, *m.*, the air

aerárium –ii, *n.*, treasury

aéreus –a –um, *adj.*, of copper, bronze, or brass

aérius –a –um, *adj.*, sky-colored, azure, light blue, of or pertaining to the air, windy, raging

aerúgino –áre, *1*, to rust

aerúgo –inis, *f.*, rust, mildew, blight

aerúmna –ae, *f.*, affliction, hardship, trial, trouble

aerumnósus –a –um, *adj.*, sorrowing

aes, aeris, *n.*, bronze, copper, a copper coin

aestas –átis, *f.*, summer

aestimátio –ónis, *f.*, evaluation, count

aestimátor –óris, *m.*, one who esteems

aéstimo –áre, *1*, to esteem, consider

aestivális –e, *adj.*, pertaining to summer

aestívus –a –um, *adj.*, of summer

aéstuo –áre, *1*, to kindle, scorch, be hot, rage

aestus –us, *m.*, heat, rage

aetas –átis, *f.*, age; *aetátem habére*, to be of age

aeternális –e, *adj.*, eternally

Aetérna Simplícitas, Christ (*Conf.* of St. Augustine)

aetérnitas –átis, *f.*, eternity

aetérnus –a –um, *adj.*, eternal; *in aetérnum*, forever

aether –eris, *m.* (*acc.*, aéthera), the sky, the upper air

aethérius –a –um, *adj.*, airy, ethereal

aevum –i, *n.*, time, eternity, an age

affátim, *adv.*, earnestly, completely, sufficiently

affectátus –a –um, *adj.*, voluntary

afféctus –us, *m.*, affection, love, devotion

áffero –érre, áttuli, allátum, *3*, to give, bring to, bring forth

affício –ere –féci –féctum, *3*, to attach to, affect, do something to

affínis –e, *adj.*, allied, related

affínitas –átis, *f.*, relationship by marriage, union of any kind

affirmátio –ónis, *f.*, affirmation

affírmo –áre, *1*, to affirm, prove, strengthen, support a statement

affíxio –ónis, *f.*, nailing, fastening

afflátus –us, *m.*, a breathing upon, spirit, breath

afflictátio –ónis, *f.*, misery, suffering, punishment, chastisement

afflíctio –ónis, *f.*, affliction

afflígo –ere –flíxi –flíctum, *3*, to afflict, punish, chastise

afflo –áre, *1*, to teach, inspire, breathe on

áffluo –ere –flúxi –flúxum, *3*, to flow to, abound, be wealthy

affor, affári, *dep. 1*, to say, speak

affúlgeo –ére –fúlsi –fúlsum, *2*, to shine forth

agénda –ae, *f.*, a ritual

agénda –órum, *n.*, the Mass

agens –éntis, *m.*, a doer, agent, actor

ager –gri, *m.*, a field, country

agger, ággeris, *m.*, a mound, wall

aggéstus –us, *m.*, a mound, heap

aggrávo –áre, *1*, to be heavy

aggrédior –íri –gréssus sum, *dep. 3*, to go to, approach

ággrego –áre, *1*, to join with, add to

ágito –áre, *1*, to shake, agitate

agmen –inis, *n.*, a throng, multitude, host

agnéllus –i, *m.*, a little lamb

agnómen –inis, *n.*, a surname

agnósco –ere –nóvi –nitum, *3*, to know, recognize, understand, perceive

agnus –i, *m.*, a lamb

Agnus Dei, a part of the Mass, designation of Christ, a sacramental of wax stamped with the image of the Lamb of God

ago –ere, egi, actum, *3*, to do, make, give, express, return

agon –ónis, *m.*, a struggle, combat, contest, agony; *in agóne*, for mastery

agónia –ae, *f.*, agony, death struggle

agonízo –áre, *1*, to struggle, suffer agony

agonósticus –a –um, *adj.*, pertaining to a contest

agréstis –e, *adj.*, wild

agrícola –ae, *m.*, a farmer

agricultúra –ae, *f.*, agriculture

ala –ae, *f.*, a wing

alabástrum –i, *n.*, alabaster, an alabaster box

alácer –cris –cre, *adj.*, active, quick, cheerful

alácris –cris –cre, *adj.*, active, quick, cheerful

alácritas –átis, *f.*, cheerfulness, eagerness

alácriter, *adv.*, eagerly, with alacrity

álapa –ae, *f.*, a slap, blow, light blow on the cheek

alátus –a –um, *adj.*, winged

alba –ae, *f.*, the alb

albárius –a –um, *adj.*, white

alba Romána, a surplice

álbeo –ére –ui, *2*, to become white

albésco –ere, *3*, to grow white, become bright

albúgo –inis, *f.*, a film, white spot
album –i, *n.*, a list, tablet
albus –a –um, *adj.*, white
ales –itis, *adj.*, winged
alga –ae, *f.*, seaweed
algésco –ere, *3*, to catch cold, become cold
álgidus –a –um, *adj.*, cold
algor –óris, *m.*, cold, coldness
alienátus –a –um, *adj.*, strange
alienígena –ae, *m.*, a foreigner, stranger
aliéno –áre, *1*, to estrange, alienate
aliénus –a –um, *adj.*, strange
aliméntum –i, *n.*, nourishment
alimónium –ii, *n.*, nourishment
alióqui, *adv.*, otherwise, in other respects
alióquin, *adv.*, otherwise
aliquámdiu, *adv.*, for a little while
aliquándo, *adv.*, at last, at times, at any time, heretofore
aliquántisper, *adv.*, for a while
aliquántulum, *adv.*, a little
aliquátenus, *adv.*, to a certain degree
aliquómodo, *adv.*, in some manner, somehow
áliter, *adv.*, otherwise; *áliter atque*, otherwise than
alitúrgicus –a –um, *adj.*, without the liturgy
aliúnde, *adv.*, another way, hence
allabóro –áre, *1*, to work, labor
allegória –ae, *f.*, a figure, allegory
allegórice, *adv.*, allegorically
allegóricus –a –um, *adj.*, allegoric
alleluiáticus –a –um, *adj.*, pertaining to alleluia
    antíphona alleluiática, an antiphon consisting of repetitions of the word alleluia
    tempus alleluiáticum, the season in which alleluia is said
    versus alleluiáticus, verses consisting of or containing alleluia
állevo –áre, *1*, to lift up
allício –ere –léxi –léctum, *3*, to allure, attract, charm
allído –ere –lísi –lísum, *3*, to strike against, dash upon
álligo –áre, *1*, to bind, tie
allocútio –ónis, *f.*, speech, discourse, address, encouragement
allóphylus –i, *m.*, a foreigner, stranger. (Used for the Philistines in the Greek text.)
allóquium –ii, *n.*, exhortation, conversation

álloquor –qui, allocútus sum, *dep.* 3, to converse with, address, speak
almárium –ii, *n.*, a sacristy
almúcia –ae, *f.*, an amice
almus –a –um, *adj.*, kind, gracious, dear, cherished, propitius, forgiving, indulgent
almútium –ii, *n.*, a mozetta
alo –ere, alui, altum *or* alitum, *3*, to nourish, support, sustain
áloe –es, *f.*, aloes, bitterness
altáre –is, *n.*, an altar
altáre fixum, a permanent altar
altáre majus, a high altar
altáre minus, a side altar
altáre portátile, a portable altar, altar stone
altáre privilegiátum, a privileged altar
altáre viáticum, a portable altar
altarísta –ae, *m.*, an assistant priest
altárium –ii, *n.*, a sanctuary, altar, the table on which the Mass is offered
alterátio –ónis, *f.*, alteration, change
altércor –ári, *dep.* 1, to dispute
altérius, of one another
alternátim, *adv.*, alternately
altérno –áre, *1*, to change
altérnus –a –um, *adj.*, alternate
áltero –áre, *1*, to change
alterúter –tra –trum, one toward another; *ad alterútrum*, one to another
altília, fatlings
áltilis –e, *adj.*, fatted, fattened
Altíssimus –i, *m.*, the Most High
altitúdo –inis, *f.*, depth, height, high place
altrínsecus, *adv.*, on opposite sides
altum –i, *n.*, the deep
altum domínium, supreme dominion
altus –a –um, *adj.*, exalted, deep, high
alumnáticum –i, *n.*, an annual tax for the maintenance of a seminary
alumnátus –us, *m.*, a seminary
alúmnus –i, *m.*, a student, pupil, one nourished and brought up
alvéolus –i, *m.*, a bowl
álveus –i, *m.*, a channel, the bed of a river
alvus –i, *f.*, womb
ama –ae, *f.*, a cruet
amánter, *adv.*, lovingly
amára, *n. pl.*, bitterness
amáre, *adv.*, bitterly
amarésco –ere, *3*, to become bitter
amarícor –ári, *dep.* 1, to grow bitter
amaritúdo –inis, *f.*, anguish, bitterness

amárus –a –um, *adj.*, bitter, unkind, severe

amátor –oris, *m.*, a lover

amatórium –ii, *n.*, a hymn of love

amátrix –ícis, *f.*, a lover

ámbigo –ere, *3*, to doubt

ámbio –íre, *4*, to go around, canvas

ambitiósus –a –um, *adj.*, ambitious

ámbitus –us, *m.*, a cope, circle, corridor, cloister, the act of walking about

ambo –ónis, *m.*, a pulpit

ambolágium –ii, *n.*, the amice

ambon –ónis, *m.*, a pulpit

ámbulo –áre, *1*, to walk

amens –éntis, *adj.*, insane

amethystus –i, *f.*, an amethyst

amíca mortis, things pertaining to death

amício –íre –ícui (–íxi) –íctum, *4*, to wrap about, clothe

amicítia –ae, *f.*, friendship

amictórium –ii, *n.*, covering for the body

amíctus –a –um, *adj.*, clothed

amíctus –us, *m.*, vesture, garment, the amice

amícus –i, *m.*, friend

amítto –ere –mísi –míssum, *3*, to send away, disperse

amo –áre, *1*, to love

amoénus –a –um, *adj.*, pleasant

amor –óris, *m.*, love

amphitheátrum –i, *n.*, amphitheater

ámphora –ae, *f.*, a pitcher, jug, bottle

ample, *adv.*, richly, amply

ampléctor –plécti –pléxus sum, *dep. 3*, to embrace

ampléxus –us, *m.*, an embrace

amplificátor –óris, *m.*, one who increases

amplífico –áre, *1*, to increase

ámplior, *adj.*, greater

ámplius, *adv.*, any more, yet more

amplus –a –um, *adj.*, more, large, spacious, ample

ampóla –ae, *f.*, a cruet

ampolláta –ae, *f.*, a cruet

ampúlla –ae, *f.*, a cruet

ámputo –áre, *1*, to cut off, amputate, remove, take away

ámula –ae, *f.*, a small hook

amulétum –i, *n.*, an amulet

ámulum –i, *n.*, starch

amússis –is, *f.*, a rule, level; *ad amússim,* exactly, accurately

amýgdala –ae, *f.*, an almond

amygdalínus –a –um, *adj.*, pertaining to the almond tree, of almonds

amýgdalus –i, *f.*, an almond tree

ámylum –i, *n.*, starch

anabolárium –ii, *n.*, a veil, covering

anachoréta –ae, *m.*, an anchorite

anachoréticus –a –um, *adj.*, eremitical

anaglýphum –i, *n.*, sculpture in relief

anaglýptum –i, *n.*, an image in relief

anagnósis –eos, *f.*, a lectionary

anagnóstes –ae, *m.*, a lector, reader

analógia –ae, *f.*, harmony, resemblance, analogy

analógium –ii, *n.*, a lectern, reader's desk, pulpit

análogus –a –um, *adj.*, appropriate, suitable

anamnésis –is, *f.* (Greek), a commemoration

anáphora –ae, *f.*, the offertory in the Greek Mass

anástasis –is, *f.*, the resurrection

anáthema –atis, *n.*, anathema, denunciation, thing given over to evil

anáthema sit, let him be accursed

anathematísmus, *n.*, anathema

anathematízo –áre, *1*, to curse, denounce, anathematize

anceps –cípitis, *adj.*, two-edged, two-headed

ánchora –ae, *f.*, an anchor

ancílla –ae, *f.*, a handmaid, maidservant

ancus –i, *m.*, a group of musical notes

anéthum –i, *n.*, a dill, anise

anfráctus –us, *m.*, winding, bending

angária –ae, *f.*, compulsory service for the public

angário –áre, *1*, to exact service, compel, force, requisition

angélicus –a –um, *adj.*, angelic

ángelus –i, *m.*, an angel, messenger, spiritual being created by God, superior in nature and intelligence to man

ango –ere, *3*, to press together, distress, trouble

angor –óris, *m.*, distress

angório –áre, *1*, to compel, force

anguis –is, *c.*, a snake

anguláris –e, *adj.*, corner, angular

ángulus –i, *m.*, a corner, stay

angústa –ae, *f.*, a narrow place, narrowness

angústia –ae, *f.*, want, anguish

angústiae –árum, *f.*, tribulations, necessities, difficulty

angustiátus –a –um, *adj.*, narrow

anhélo –áre, *1*, to desire, grasp, pant for

ánima –ae, *f.*, mind, soul, life, breath of life

animadvérto –ere –vérti –vérsum, *3,* to take notice of, observe, mark

animaéquus –a –um, *adj.,* calm, undisturbed in mind

ánimal –ális, *n.,* animal, beast

ánimans –antis, *adj.,* living

animátus –a –um, *adj.,* inspired, animated, living

animósitas –átis, *f.,* high spirits, ardor, enthusiasm, ambition

ánimus –i, *m.,* soul, mind

annális –is, *n.,* annals, record

annículus –a –um, *adj.,* one year old

anniversárium –ii, *n.,* anniversary

anniversárius –a –um, *adj.,* pertaining to an anniversary

annóna –ae, *f.,* grain, crop, yearly produce

annótinus –a –um, *adj.,* annual, a year's duration

annuláris –e, *adj.,* annual, a year's duration

annuláris –e, *adj.,* pertaining to a ring

annúllo –áre, *1,* to destroy, annihilate

ánnulus –i, *m.,* a ring

Ánnulus Piscatóris, a ring worn by the Pope on which is represented St. Peter casting a net

annumerábilis –e, *adj.,* can be added to

annúmero –áre, *1,* to number

annunciátor –óris, *m.,* a herald, one who announces

annuntiátio –ónis, *f.,* annunciation, declaration

annuntiátor –óris, *m.,* a herald, announcer

annúntio –áre, *1,* to announce, declare, relate

ánnuo –ere –ui, *3,* to beckon, nod, wink, assent, *also* to mock

annus –i, *m.,* a year

ánnuus –a –um, *adj.,* yearly, annual

anónymus –a –um, *adj.,* name unknown, without a name

ansa –ae, *f.,* opportunity, a handle

anstrúo –ere –xi –ctum, *3,* to support

ánsula –ae, *f.,* a loop, hook

anteáctus –a –um, *adj.,* past

antecédo –ere –céssi –céssum, *3,* to surpass, go before, go ahead

antecéllo –ere (no perfect), *3,* to excel, surpass, rise

antecéssor –óris, *m.,* predecessor

anteéo –íre –ívi *or* –ii –ítum, *4,* to go before

antelucánum –i, *n.,* dawn, the period between 4 and 6 o'clock in the morning

antelucánus –a –um, *adj.,* before dawn, before daybreak

antemurále –is, *n.,* a bulwark, outside wall

anténna –ae, *f.,* the transverse beam of a cross, a sail yard

antepéndium –ii, *n.,* a hanging in front of an altar, a frontal

ántequam, *adv.,* before

antérior –óris, *adj.,* prior, before, previous

antésto –áre –stiti, *1,* to stand before

antevérto –ere –vérti –vérsum, *3,* to come before, precede

Anthológion, a book in the Greek rite containing the offices for feasts

antícipo –áre, *1,* to anticipate, prevent, forestall, act before a specified time

antiménsium –i, *n.,* the consecrated cloth used for an altar in the Eastern Church; there is also an *antiménsium Latínum*

antipéndium –ii, *n., see* antepéndium

antíphona –ae, *f.,* an antiphon

antiphonális –e, *adj.,* antiphonal, pertaining to an antiphon

antiphonárium –ii, *n.,* a book of the antiphons, the Gradual, the antiphoner

Antiphonárium Missae, an early designation for the Gradual

Antiphonárium Offícii, a book containing the antiphons for the Divine Office

antiphonárius –a –um, *adj.,* pertaining to an antiphon

antiphonátim, *adj.,* antiphonally

Antíphones Majóres, the "O" antiphons of Vespers from Dec. 17 to 23 inclusive

antíphonus –a –um, *adj.,* antiphonal

antiquárius –ii, *m.,* an old scribe, antiquary

antiquátus –a –um, *adj.,* archaic

antíquus –a –um, *adj.,* of old, former, ancient, antique

antístes –itis, *m.,* a bishop, priest, presiding officer

antístes sacrórum, *m.,* a bishop

antístita –ae, *f.,* superioress

antísto –áre –stiti, *1,* to stand before

antrum –i, *n.,* a cave, den

ánulus –i, *m.,* a ring

anus –us, *f.,* an old woman

anxíetas –átis, *f.,* anxiety

ánxior –ári, *dep. 1,* to be in anguish, troubled

ánxius –a –um, *adj.*, afflicted, dejected, uneasy, anxious

aper, apri, *m.*, a wild boar

apério –íre –pérui –pértum, *4,* to open

aperítio –ónis, *f.*, an opening

apérnor –ári, *dep. 1,* to scorn

apérte, *adv.*, openly, plainly, sharply

apértus –a –um, *adj.*, open

apex –icis, *m.*, a point, summit, top

apis –is, *f.*, a bee

apíscor, apísci, áptus sum, *dep. 3,* to seize, attack

Apocalýpsis –is, *f.*, the book of Revelations or the Apocalypse of St. John

apocalýpticus –a –um, *adj.*, pertaining to the Apocalypse

apocatástasis –is, *f.*, a restoration, reestablishment

apocrisiárius –ii, *m.*, an envoy, nuntio, delegate

apócrypha –órum, *n.*, apocryphal gospels. They lack genuineness and canonicity and are not included in the Bible.

apócryphus –a –um, *adj.*, apocryphal

apologéticus –a –um, *adj.*, apologetic

apológia –ae, *f.*, an apology, defense, justification, explanation

apoplécticus –a –um, *adj.*, apoplectic

apopléxia –ae, *f.*, apoplexy

apório –ári, *dep. 1,* to be in need, perplexed, waver, pressed

apostásia –ae, *f.*, apostasy

apóstata –ae, *m.*, an apostate

apostáticus –a –um, *adj.*, apostate, rebel

apóstato –áre, *1,* to fall away from, fall off, apostatize

apostátrix –ícis, *f.*, an apostate

a posterióri, reasoning from experience. Opposed to *a priori.*

apóstola –ae, *f.*, a female apostle

apostolátus –us, *m.*, an apostleship

Apostólicae Curae, a bull of Pope Leo XIII, 1896, in which Anglican Orders are declared invalid

Apostólicae sedis grátia, by favor of the Apostolic See

Apostólicum –i, *n.*, the book of Epistles

Apostólicus, a title applied to the Pope

apostólicus –a –um, *adj.*, apostolic

Apostólicus Rex, a title given to the kings of Hungary

Apostolórum commemorátio, a former feast in honor of all the Apostles

apóstolus –i, *m.*, one who is sent, an apostle

apothéca –ae, *f.*, a storeroom, cellar

appáreo –ére –ui –itum, *2,* to be evident, appear, shine forth

apparítio –ónis, *f.*, an apparition, appearance, manifestation

appáritor –óris, *m.*, servant, usher

appellátio –ónis, *f.*, appellation

appéllo –áre, *1,* to call

appéllo –ere –puli –púlsum, *3,* to bring, drive to, direct

appéndo –ere –péndi –pénsum, *3,* to balance, weigh out

appensórius –a –um, *adj.*, with a handle

appetítor –óris, *m.*, a coveter

appetítus –us, *m.*, appetite, hunger, passion

appetivítus –a –um, *adj.*, having an appetite for

áppeto –ere –ívi *or* –ii –ítum, *3,* to pursue, fall upon, attack, reach to, wish for, hunger after

ápplico –áre, *1,* to add to, join, bring, apply, place

appóno –ere –pósui –pósitum, *3,* to proceed, put to, add to, do unto, put near to, set, place

appósitus –a –um *adj.*, placed near

apprehéndo –ere –héndi –hénsum, *3,* to take hold of, seize, apprehend, lay hands on, press to, embrace

apprétio –áre, *1,* to put a price on, value, prize

ápprimo –ere –préssi –préssum, *3,* to press to

approbátio –ónis, *f.*, approbation, approval, sanction

appropínquo –áre, *1,* to draw near, approach

apprópio –áre, *1,* to be at hand, approach

appropriátio –ónis, *f.*, appropriation

appróximo –áre, *1,* to approach, draw near to

aprílis –is, *m.*, the month of April

a prióri, reasoning based on reason. Opposed to *a posteriori.*

aptitúdo –inis, *f.*, aptitude

apto –áre, *1,* to prepare, adapt to, fit to

aptus –a –um, *adj.*, fitting, suitable, appropriate

aqua –ae, *f.*, water

aquadúctus –us, *m.*, aqueduct, water course

aquamaníle –is, *n.*, a basin for use at the Lavabo at Mass

aquamánus –us, *m.*, a dish for washing the hands

áquila –ae, *f.*, an eagle

aquílo –ónis, *m.*, the north wind

ara –ae, *f.*, an altar, an altar stone

ara gestatória, *f.*, a portable altar

aránea –ae, *f.*, a spider

aratiúncula –ae, *f.*, a furrow

arátor –óris, *m.*, a plowman

arátrum –i, *n.*, a plow

árbiter –tri, *m.*, a judge

arbitrátus –us, *m.*, choice, will

arbítrium –ii, *n.*, free will, free choice

árbitror –ari, *dep. 1,* to think

arbor –óris, *f.*, a tree

arbústa, *n. pl.*, branches

arbústum –i, *n.*, an orchard

arcánum –i, *n.*, a secret place, secret, mystery

arcánus –a –um, *adj.*, secret, sacred

arcárius –ii, *m.*, a treasurer

árceo –ere –ui, *2,* to prevent, enclose, shut up

arcésso –ere –ívi –ítum, *3,* to summon, call

arceuthínus –a –um, *adj.*, pertaining to a fir tree

archaeológia –ae, *f.*, the science of antiquities

archaeológicus –a –um, *adj.*, pertaining to the science of antiquities

archángelus –i, *m.*, an archangel

archibasílica –ae, *f.*, an archbasilica, cathedral church

archicántor –óris, *m.*, leader of a choir of cantors

archicapellánus –i, *m.*, an almoner

archiconfratérnitas –átis, *f.*, archconfraternity

archidiaconátus –us, *m.*, a deanery, the office of archdeacon

archidiáconus –i, *m.*, an archdeacon

archidiocésis –is, *f.*, an archdiocese

archiepiscopális –e, *adj.*, archepiscopal

archiepiscopátus –us, *m.*, an archbishopric

archiepíscopus –i, *m.*, an archbishop

archimímus –i, *m.*, a player, a leading actor

archipraésul –is, *m.*, an archbishop

archiprésbyter –eri, *m.*, an archpriest

archisodálitas –átis, *f.*, an archsodality or confraternity

archistérium –ii, *n.*, a monastery

archisynagógus –i, *m.*, the ruler of a synagogue

architéctus –us, *m.*, an architect

architriclínus –i, *m.*, a chief steward

archívium –ii, *n.*, archives

archívum –i, *n.*, archives

arcosólium –ii, *n.*, an arched recess forming a burial place in the Catacombs

árctius, *adv.*, more closely, more firmly

arctus –us, *m.*, a bow, rainbow

arcus –us, *m.*, a bow, rainbow

árdeo –ére, arsi, arsum, *2,* to burn, glow, be on fire

ardésco –ere, arsi, *3,* to kindle, take fire

ardor –óris, *m.*, burning

árduus –a –um, *adj.*, difficult, steadfast

área –ae, *f.*, a floor, threshing floor, courtyard

área mártyrum, a burial place

arefácio –ere –féci –fáctum, *3,* to parch

aréna –ae, *f.*, an arena, ground, sand, space in front of a house

arenária –ae, *f.*, a sand pit, catacomb

áreo –ere, árui, *2,* to dry up, be dry, wither

aréola –ae, *f.*, a small plot, garden, small open place

arésco –ere, árui, *3,* to become dry, dry up, pine away

argénteus –i, *m.*, a piece of silver

argénteus –a –um, *adj.*, silver

argéntum –i, *n.*, money, silver

argumentátio –ónis, *f.*, argument, debate

argumentósus –a –um, *adj.*, rich in material, busy

arguméntum –i, *n.*, an argument, reproof

árguo –ere –ui, *3,* to accuse, rebuke, convince

árida –ae, *f.*, dryness, dry land

áridus –a –um, *adj.*, dry, parched, arid, withered

áries –etis, *m.*, a ram

aríolus –i, *m.*, a soothsayer, cunning man

Arma Christi, an emblem formed by the instruments of the Passion

armamentárium –ii, *n.*, an armory

armaríolum –i, *n.*, a small chest

armárium –ii, *n.*, a locker, wardrobe, vault

armatúra –ae, *f.*, armor

armátus –a –um, *adj.*, armed

armellínum –i, *n.*, ermine

arméntum –i, *n.*, a herd, cattle

ármiger –gera –gerum, *adj.*, bearing arms or armor

armúlla –ae, *f.*, a bracelet

Armórum Christi, a feast formerly celebrated in honor of the instruments of the Passion

armus –i, *m.*, a shoulder

aro, aráre, *1*, to plough

aróma –atis, *n.*, aroma, spice, perfume, aromatic substance

aromatízans –tis, *adj.*, fragrant, aromatic

aromatízo –áre, *1*, to make sweet or fragrant, make aromatic

arreptítius –a –um, *adj.*, raving mad

arrha –ae, *f.*, a pledge, a wedding gift

árrhabo –ónis, *m.*, a pledge, a wedding gift

arrídeo –ére –rísi –rísum, *2*, to laugh, smile

árrigo –ere –réxi –réctum, *3*, to rouse, excite, stir up

arrípio –ere –rípui –réptum, *3*, to seize, snatch, take, lay hold of

ars, artis, *f.*, art, knowledge, trade, scheme

arthrítis –ídis, *f.*, gout

articulátus –a –um, *adj.*, distinct

artículo mortis, at the moment of death

artículus –i, *m.*, a finger, joint, moment of time, point

ártifex –icis, *m.*, artificer, maker, author

artificiális –e, *adj.*, artificial

artifícium –ii, *n.*, a craft, handicraft, skill

artophórion, *n.*, the vessel in which the Blessed Sacrament is kept in the Greek churches

artus –us, *m.*, limb, joint

arundinétum –i, *n.*, a growth of reeds, thicket of rushes

arúndo –inis, *f.*, a reed, staff for the three candles formerly used on Holy Saturday

arúspex –icis, *m.*, a soothsayer

arvína –ae, *f.*, fat

arvum –i, *n.*, a field

arx, arcis, *f.*, a throne, fortress, castle

as, assis, *m.*, a copper coin, farthing

ascélla –ae, *f.*, a pinion or wing, armpit

ascéndo –ere, ascéndi, ascénsum, *3*, to ascend, go up, climb up

ascénsio –ónis, *f.*, ascension

ascénsor –óris, *m.*, a rider, climber, one who mounts

ascénsus –us, *m.*, ascent, means of ascent

ascésis –eos, *f.*, discipline, training

ascéta –ae, *m.*, a hermit, ascetic, penitent

ascetárium –ii, *n.*, a monastery

ascéticus –a –um, *adj.*, ascetical

áscia –ae, *f.*, a hatchet, carpenter's ax

áscio –íre, *4*, to take, to get

ascopéra –ae, *f.*, a satchel, wallet

ascéllus –i, *m.*, a donkey, young ass

ásina –ae, *f.*, a she ass

asinárius –a –um, *adj.*, pertaining to an ass

ásinus –i, *m.*, an ass

ascísco –ere –scívi –scítum, *3*, to receive

aspéctus –us, *m.*, countenance, vision, sight, appearance, aspect, look

asper –a –um, *adj.*, sharp, rough, difficult

aspergíllum –i, *n.*, a sprinkler

aspérgo –ere –spérsi –spérsum, *3*, to sprinkle

aspérgo –inis, *f.*, a sprinkling

aspernátor –óris, *m.*, a contemner

aspérnor –ári, *dep. 1*, to despise

áspero –áre, *1*, to make rough

aspérsio –ónis, *f.*, a sprinkling, aspersion

aspersórium –ii, *n.*, a sprinkler

aspérsus –a –um, *adj.*, sprinkled, rough

aspício –ere –spéxi –spéctum, *3*, to look at, regard, behold

aspíro –áre, *1*, to assist, be favorable to, aspire to, breathe

aspis –idis, *f.*, an asp, adder

aspórto –áre, *1*, to bring

assécla –ae, *m.*, a follower

asséntior –iri –sénsus sum, *dep. 4*, to agree

ássequor –qui –secútus sum, *dep. 3*, to observe, follow

asser –eris, *m.*, a plank, board, lath

ássero –ere –sérui –sértum, *3*, to declare, assert, remark, justify

assértor –oris, *m.*, a champion, defender

assérvo –áre, *1*, to protect, guard, preserve

asséssio –ónis, *f.*, a sitting as an assessor

asséssor –óris, *m.*, a member of a board in the Curia

asseveránter, *adv.*, emphatically, absolutely

assérvo –áre, *1*, to guard, watch over

assídeo –ére –sédi –séssum, *2*, to sit, be seated

assídue, *adv.*, assiduously

assidúitas –átis, *f.*, custom

assíduus –a –um, *adj.*, continual, unceasing

assígno –áre, *1*, to assign, designate

assímilo –áre, *1*, to compare

assímilor –ári, *dep. 1*, to be compared, become like

assisténtia –ae, *f.*, assistance, attendance

assísto –ere –ástiti, *3,* to stand near, take a stand, be present

assístrix –icis, *f.,* attendant, assistant

associátio –ónis, *f.,* association, accompaniment, an escort

assócio –áre, *1,* to escort, associate, come over

assóleo –ére, *2,* to be usual, be accustomed to

assuetúdo –inis, *f.,* custom, habit

assuméntum –i, *n.,* a patch

assúmo –ere –súmpsi –súmptum, *3,* to receive, assume, take, take unto oneself, raise, lift up

assúmptio –ónis, *f.,* assumption, the act of being taken up

assus –a –um, *adj.,* roasted, broiled

asto –áre, ástiti, *1,* to stand by or near

astríngo –ere –strínxi –stríctum, *3,* to tighten, draw together, bind together, contract

astrum –i, *n.,* a star

ástruo –ere –strúxi –strúctum, *3,* to teach, form, build, establish, support

astus –us, *m.,* cleverness, cunning

astútia –ae, *f.,* subtlety, craftiness

astútus –a –um, *adj.,* wise, prudent

asýlum –i, *n.,* a refuge, a place of sanctuary

ater –tra –trum, *adj.,* dark, black

athenaéum –i, *n.,* a high school

athenaéum majus, a university

athléta –ae, *m.,* a wrestler, a champion athlete

atramentárium –ii, *n.,* an inkwell

atraméntum –i, *n.,* ink

átrium –ii, *n.,* a hall, court, the vestibule of a church

atrox –ócis, *adj.,* fierce, horrible, terrible, atrocious

áttamen, *conj.,* nevertheless

atténdo –ere –téndi –téntum, *3,* to attend, hearken, consider, mind, look to, beware

atténte, *adv.,* attentively

atténtius, *adv.,* more attentively

atténto –áre, *1,* to attempt

atténuo –áre, *1,* to weaken

áttero –ere –trívi –trítum, *3,* to bruise, destroy

attestátio –ónis, *f.,* evidence, proof, the act of attesting

attéxo –ere –téxui –téctum, *3,* to weave or plait, to add

attíneo –ére –tínui –téntum, *2,* to pertain to

attíngo –ere –tigi –táctum, *3,* to draw on, manage

attóllo –ere, *3,* to support, lift up

attónitus –a –um, *adj.,* astonished, stunned

attrácto –áre, *1,* to lay hands on, feel, touch

attríbuo –ere –ui –útum, *3,* to bestow, grant, attribute

attribútio –ónis, *f.,* a giving

attrítus –a –um, *adj.,* hard

átvero, *conj.,* however

auctor –óris, *m.,* author, creator, founder

auctóritas –átis, *f.,* authority, the right of someone to impose the duty of obedience on others

auctrix –ícis, *f.,* authoress, mother

audácter, *adv.,* boldly

aúdeo –ére, ausus sum, *2,* to dare

Audiéntes, *m. pl.,* the hearers, the lowest class of public penitents in the early Church

audiéntia –ae, *f.,* hearing, attention, an audience

aúdio –íre, *4,* to hear

audítor –óris, *m.,* a hearer, listener, disciple, one who examines accounts

aúditus –a –um, *adj.,* heard, audible

audítus –us, *m.,* a hearing

aúfero –férre, ábstuli, ablátum, *3,* to take away

aufúgio –ere –fúgi, *3,* to flee

aúgeo –ére, auxi, auctum, *2,* to increase, enlarge

augésco –ere, auxi, *3,* to increase

auguméntum –i, *n.,* increase, advancement

augur –úris, *c.,* a soothsayer

augurátrix –ícis, *f.,* a sorceress

aúguror –ári, *dep. 1,* to prophesy

augústus –i, *m.,* the month of August

aula –ae, *f.,* a temple, court, dwelling

aúlaeum –i, *n.,* a hanging, curtain, canopy

aula transvérsa, a transept

aura –ae, *f.,* breath, air, breeze

auréola –ae, *f.,* a halo, nimbus, auriole, a symbolic oval of light placed over the heads of saints in Christian art to symbolize their special honor in heaven

aúreus –a –um, *adj.,* of gold, golden

aúreus –i, *m.,* a piece of gold

aurichálcum –i, *n.,* brass, fine brass

aurícula –ae, *f.,* an ear

auriculáris –e, *adj.*, auricular, pertaining to the ear

auriculárius –ii, *m.*, a secret adviser

aurifrisiátus –a –um, *adj.*, embroidered with gold

aurifrísius –a –um, *adj.*, gold-embroidered

auriphrygiátus –a –um, *adj.*, embroidered with gold

auris –is, *f.*, an ear

auróra –ae, *f.*, dawn, morning

aurúgo –inis, *f.*, a burning wind, paleness

aurum –i, *n.*, gold

ausculátor –óris, *m.*, a listener

auscúlto –áre, *1*, to listen

auspicátus –a –um, *adj.*, auspicious, happy

auspícium –ii, *n.*, an omen, divination, idolatry, divination by means of birds, heathen worship in general

auśpico –áre, *1*, to foretell

auśpicor –ári, *dep. 1*, to begin

auster –ari, *m.*, the south, wind, the south

austéritas –átis, *f.*, rigor, austerity

austérus –a –um, *adj.*, austere

austrális –e, *adj.*, south

authentícitas –átis, *f.*, genuineness, authenticity

authénticum –i, *n.*, a document certifying to the genuineness of a relic

authénticus –a –um, *adj.*, authentic, genuine

autógraphum –i, *n.*, an original written document

autumnális –e, *adj.*, autumn, withered

autúmnus –i, *m.*, autumn

auxiliárius –a –um, *adj.*, assistant, auxiliary

auxiliátor –óris, *m.*, a helper

auxiliátrix –icis, *f.*, a female helper

auxílior –ári, *dep. 1*, to help, aid, assist, support

auxílium –ii, *n.*, aid, help

avarítia –ae, *f.*, covetousness, avarice

avárus –a –um, *adj.*, covetous, avaricious

avéllo –ere –vélli *or* –vúlsi –vúlsum, *3*, to separate, tear away, withdraw

áveo –ére, *2*, to crave, pant after

aversátrix –ícis, *f.*, one who rebels or oppresses

avérsio –ónis, *f.*, apostasy, aversion, turning away

avérso –áre, *1*, to turn away from

avérto –ere –vérti –vérsum, *3*, to turn away, ward off, avert, pervert

ávia –ae, *f.*, a grandmother

ávide, *adv.*, eagerly

avídius, *adv.*, more eagerly

avis –is, *f.*, a bird

avítus –a –um, *adj.*, ancestral

ávoco –áre, *1*, to withdraw oneself

avólo –áre, *1*, to fly away

avúnculus –i, *m.*, an uncle

avus –i, *m.*, a grandfather

axílla –ae, *f.*, side, armpit

Azarías –ae, *m.*, Sidrach, one of the three youths cast into the fiery furnace by Nabuchodonosor

ázyma –órum, *n. pl.*, unleavened bread, the Jewish feast of unleavened bread **Azymes,** the feast of Azymes, which lasted seven days. Azyme bread was unleavened prescribed for the Passover. Unleavened bread is a type of sincerity, truth, and freedom from the corrupting leaven of sin.

azymíta –ae, *m.*, one who uses unleavened bread for the Eucharist

ázymus –a –um, *adj.*, unleavened, unfermented

B

bacca –ae, *f.*, a berry, the fruit of the olive

baccalaúreus –i, *m.*, a bachelor (academic)

bácile –is, *n.*, a basin

bácilis –e, *adj.*, low, base

bacíllum –i, *n.*, a staff

báculum –i, *n.*, a staff

báculus –i, *m.*, a staff, stick

báculus pastorális, a crozier

bájulo –áre, *1*, to carry, bear

balbútio –íre, *4*, to babble, stammer, stutter

baldachínum –i, *n.*, a canopy

bálneum –i, *n.*, a bath

bálsamum –i, *n.*, balsam, balm

bálteus –i, *m.*, a belt

bancále –is, *n.*, a cushion

bannum –i, *n.*, a ban

baptísma –atis, *n.*, baptism, the sacrament of initiation and regeneration

baptismális –e, *adj.*, baptismal

baptísmus –i, *m.,* baptism, washing, sprinkling

Baptísta –ae, *m.,* John the Baptist, precursor of the Lord

baptistérium –ii, *n.,* baptistry

baptizátor –óris, *m.,* the minister of baptism

baptízo –áre, *1,* to baptize

Barábbas –ae, *m.,* Barabbas, the murderer preferred to Christ

Barachías –ae, *m.,* Barachias, mentioned in Mt. 23:35

baráthrum –i, *n.,* the lower world, abyss, bottomless pit

barba –ae, *f.,* a beard

barbáricus –a –um, *adj.,* foreign

bárbarus –a –um, *adj.,* foreign

barbátus –a –um, *adj.,* bearded

bárbitos –i, *m.* and *f.,* a lute, lyre

barbitónsor –óris, *m.,* a barber

bardus –a –um, *adj.,* dull, stupid

baríle –is, *n.,* a cask

Barjésus –i, *m.,* otherwise Elymas, a false prophet who opposed Barnabas and Paul at Paphos

Bárnabas –ae, *m.,* Barnabas the Apostle, originally known as Joseph, a rich levite, a native of Cyprus, journeyed with St. Paul to Asia Minor

baro –ónis, *m.,* a baron

Barsábas –ae, *m.,* Barsabas, nominated with Matthias to succeed Judas; also the name of a disciple sent with Silas to Antioch with letters from the Apostles

Bartimaéus –i, *m.,* Bartimaeus, the son of Timaeus, a beggar in Jericho who received sight

basílica –ae, *f.,* a basilica, church, originally the form of building used for early Christian churches

basilíscus –i, *m.,* a basilisk, a kind of lizard, a kind of venemous serpent

basis –is, *f.,* foundation, base, pedestal

bassus –a –um, *adj.,* low, base

batállum –i, *n.,* the clapper of a bell

batíllum –i, *n.,* a shovel, brazier

bátuo –ere, *3,* to beat or strike

batus –i, *m.,* a liquid measure

bdéllium –ii, *n.,* resin, gum

beatificátio –ónis, *f.,* beatification, the act of beatifying

beatífico –áre, *1,* to beatify, make happy

beatitúdo –inis, *f.,* happiness, bliss, beatitude, blessedness

beátus –a –um, *adj.,* blessed, happy

behmoth (Hebr.), some large animal. It is uncertain whether this is the elephant or the hippopotamus

bekah (Hebr.), half a shekel

bellátor –óris, *m.,* a warrior

belligerátor –óris, *m.,* warrior

bello –áre, *1,* to fight against, make war

béllua –ae, *f.,* a savage beast

béllulus –a –um, *adj.,* pretty, elegant, beautiful

bellum –i, *n.,* war

bema –tis, *n.,* the sanctuary, a bishop's chair

Benedícite, the ordinary salutation in a monastery

Benedícite, first word of the Canticle of the Three Children, sung at Lauds on Sundays

Benedíctus, the first word of the Canticle of Zachary, also of the Canticle of David

benefácio –ere –féci –fáctum, *3,* to do good to, do well

benefáctor –óris, *m.,* benefactor

benefáctum –i, *n.,* favor, good deed, benefit

beneficéntia –ae, *f.,* liberality

beneficiárius –ii, *m.,* the holder of a benefice, a prebendary

beneficiátus –i, *m.,* the holder of a benefice, a prebendary

benefícium –ii, *n.,* a benefit, favor, benifice

beneficus –a –um, *adj.,* beneficent

beneplácens –éntis, *adj.,* acceptable

benepláceo –ére, *2,* to be pleasing to

beneplácitum –i, *n.,* approval, pleasure, favor, gracious purpose

beneplácitus –a –um, *adj.,* acceptable, agreeable, well-pleasing

benesónans –antis, *adj.,* sweet-sounding, melodious, loud

benévolens –entis, *adj.,* well-wishing, obliging

benévolus –a –um, *adj.,* kind, benevolent

benígne, *adv.,* favorably

benígnitas –átis, *f.,* goodness, benignity, favor

benígnus –a –um, *adj.,* merciful, loving, good, benign, gracious, kindly, favoring

beo –áre, *1,* to bless

berýllus –i, *m.,* the beryl, a precious stone

béstia –ae, *f.,* a beast

Bethánia –ae, *f.,* Bethany, a village at

the Mount of Olives, about two miles from Jerusalem

Béthlehem (Hebr.), Bethlehem, a town about six miles south of Jerusalem. The birthplace of Jesus Christ.

Bethphánia –ae, *f.*, a former name for Epiphany

Bethséda, a pool in Jerusalem near the sheep-market gate

Bíblia –ae, *f.*, the Bible

Bíblia Paúperum, a picture book much used for religious instruction in the fifteenth century

bíblicus –a –um, *adj.*, biblical, pertaining to the Bible

bibliothéca –ae, *f.*, a library

bibliothecárius –ii, *m.*, a librarian

bibo –ere, bibi, bíbitum, *3,* to drink

biceps –cípitis, *adj.*, two-edged, two-handed

bícolor –óris, *adj.*, of two colors

bidens –éntis, *f.*, sheep, an animal for sacrifice

biduánus –a –um, *adj.*, for a period of two days

bíduum –i, *n.*, a space of two days

bíduus –a –um, *adj.*, for a period of two days

biénnium –ii, *n.*, a space of two years

bifaciátus –a –um, *adj.*, two-faced

bifrons –tis, *adj.*, two-faced

bigámia –ae, *f.*, bigamy

bígamus –i, *m.*, a bigamist

bilínguis –e, *adj.*, double-tongued

bilis –is, *f.*, hypochondria

bilocátio –ónis, *f.*, being in more than one place at the same time

bimátus –us, *m.*, two years of age

binátio –ónis, *f.*, a duplication, bination, the celebration of Mass twice in one day by the same priest

bini –ae –a, *adj.*, two, two of a kind, in pairs

bino –áre, *1,* to duplicate

bipertítus –a, –um, *adj.*, double, with two parts

birétum (birrétum) –i, *n.*, a biretta, a stiff square cap with a number of ridges on top worn by clerics

bis, twice

bísomus –a –um, *adj.*, for two bodies

bissextílis annus, a leap year

bístropha –ae, *f.*, two notes of the same pitch (mus.)

bitúmen –inis, *n.*, cement, slime, pitch

bivírga –ae, *f.*, two square, tailed notes (mus.)

blande, *adv.*, softly, tenderly, caressingly

blandiméntum –i, *n.*, allurement, flattery, fawning

blándior –íri –ítus sum, *dep. 4,* to coax, caress, flatter

blandítia –ae, *f.*, flattery

blandus –a –um, *adj.*, soothing, soft, smooth

Blásius –ii, *m.*, St. Blaise, a bishop in Armenia, martyred under the Roman Emperor Licinius, A.D. 316. Invoked by those suffering from throat diseases. Feast Feb. 3

blasphémia –ae, *f.*, blasphemy, reviling, evil, contumelious language directed at or concerning God

blasphémo –áre, *1,* to blaspheme

blasphémus –i, *m.*, a blasphemer

Boanérges, the "sons of thunder," James and John, sons of Zebedee

bolis –idis, *f.*, a sounding lead

bombácium –ii, *n.*, cotton

bombyx –cis, *m.*, cotton, wadding, a silkworm

Bonipórtus –us, *m.*, "fair havens" (Acts 27:8)

bónitas –atis, *f.*, goodness, kindness

bonum –i, *n.*, good

bonus –a –um, *adj.*, good: *in bonum,* for good

boreália, *n.*, northern parts

boreális –e, *adj.*, northern

borith, *indecl.*, soap, a cleanser

bos, bovis, *m.*, an ox

botrus –i, *m.*, a bunch, cluster of grapes

bracca –ae, *f.*, a coat; *in the plural,* breeches

brácchium –ii, *n.*, arm

brachiále –is, *n.*, a bracelet

brachíolum –i, *n.*, the arm of a chair

bráchium –ii, *n.*, arm

bractéola –ae, *f.*, a golden spangle

bránchia –ae, *f.*, the gill of a fish

brándeum –i, *n.*, a handkerchief, a sheet, the silk or cloth covering for relics

brávium –ii, *n.*, a prize in a contest

breve –is, *n.*, a list, brief

breviárium –ii, *n.*, an abridgment or summary, a condensed copy, a book containing the Divine Office, called a Breviary. The present Roman Breviary is divided into four volumes, Pars Verna, Pars Aestiva, Pars Autumnalis, and Pars Hiemalis.

Breviárum Pinánum, the Breviary prescribed by Pope Pius V

Breviárum Sanctae Crucis, the Breviary of the Holy Cross, compiled by Cardinal Quinonez about 1535

brévio –áre, *1*, to shorten, abridge, condense

brevículus –a –um, *adj.*, somewhat short; *in bревículo*, after a little while

brevis –e, *adj.*, short, in a short space

brévitas –átis, *f.*, shortness

bréviter, *adv.*, shortly, briefly

bruchus –i, *m.*, a locust, grasshopper

bruma –ae, *f.*, winter

brumális –e, *adj.*, wintry, pertaining to winter

búbulus –i, *m.*, a buffalo, ox; *in the feminine*, a wild cow

bucále –is, *n.*, a water jug, pitcher

búccino –áre, *1*, to sound a trumpet

bucélla –ae, *f.*, a fragment, morsel, small mouthful

búcina –ae, *f.*, a trumpet

bufo –ónis, *m.*, a toad

búgia –ae, *f.*, a hand candlestick

bulbus –i, *m.*, an onion

bulla –ae, *f.*, a bull, papal document

bullárium –ii, *n.*, a collection of papal bulls; that of Cocquelines, containing the bulls of all the Popes from Leo the Great to Benedict XIII, is the most famous

búllio –íre, *4*, to bubble

burdo –ónis, *f.*, burden, beast of burden, mule

bursa –ae, *f.*, a burse, case for the corporal

búrsula –ae, *f.*, a small case for the corporal

bútyrum –i, *n.*, butter, cheese

byssínus –a –um, *adj.*, of linen or silk

byssus –i, *m.*, fine linen, silk

C

cabus –i, *m.*, a kettle, measure of corn

cacúmen –inis, *n.*, tip, highest point, summit, peak

cadáver –eris, *n.*, carcass, dead body, corpse

Cades (Hebr.), a city in Edom, to the south of Palestine. Here the Jews were twice turned back from entering the Promised Land. Here also Moses struck the rock and brought forth the miraculous flow of water

cado –ere, cécidi, casum, *3*, to fall, fall down, fall into sin, fall prostrate, beat

caducárius –a –um, *adj.*, epileptic

cadúcitas –átis, *f.*, weakness, frailty, perishableness

cadúcus –a –um, *adj.*, perishable, weak, frail

cadus –i, *m.*, a large vessel, jug, barrel, cask

caecátus –a –um, *adj.*, blinded

caécitas –átis, *f.*, darkness, blindness, spiritual blindness

caecus –a –um, *adj.*, blind

caecus –i, *m.*, a blind man

caecútio –íre, *4*, to see badly, be dim

caedes –is, *f.*, slaughter

caedo –ere, cecídi, caesum, *3*, to cut down, hew in pieces, strike, beat, kill

caelebs –ibis, *adj.*, angelic, heavenly, unmarried, celibate

caeles –itis, *adj.*, heavenly

caeléstis –e, *adj.*, heavenly, divine, celestial

caeli –órum, *n. pl.*, heaven

caelibátus –us, *m.*, celibacy

caelícola –ae, *m.*, one in heaven

caélicus –a –um, *adj.*, angelic, heavenly

caélitus, *adv.*, divinely, by divine instruction

caelum –i, *n.*, heaven, sky

caementárius –ii, *m.*, a mason

caeménto –áre, *1*, to fasten with mortar, cement, fasten with cement

caeméntum –i, *n.*, cement, mortar

caenum –i, *n.*, dirt, filth, mud, mire

caereiále –is, *n.*, a book of ceremonies, a book giving instructions for ceremonies

caeremónia –ae, *f.*, a ceremony

Caeremoniále Episcopórum, the Ceremonial of Bishops

Caeremoniále Románum, the Roman Ceremonial

caeremoniális –e, *adj.*, ceremonial

caeremoniárius –ii, *m.*, a master of ceremonies

caerúleus –a –um, *adj.*, light blue

Caesar –aris, *m.*, Caesar. Always in the New Testament the Roman Emperor

caesar –aris, *m.*, emperor

Caesaraéa –ae, *f.*, Caesarea, a seaport on the Mediterranean, 70 miles N.W. of Jerusalem, and now entirely desolate

Caesaraéa Philíppi, a town in the extreme north of Canaan, near the source of the river Jordan. The most northerly point of Christ's journeys.

Caesariénsis –e, *adj.*, pertaining to Caesarea

caesáries –ei, *f.*, a head of hair

caetus –us, *m.*, an assemblage

calámitas –átis, *f.*, distress, calamity

calamitósus –a –um, *adj.*, calamitous

cálamus –i, *m.*, a pen, fishing rod, reed, sweet cane

cálathus –i, *m.*, a flat basket

calcábilis –e, *adj.*, something that can be trod upon

calcáneum –ei, *n.*, a heel

calcar –áris, *n.*, a spur

calcátor –óris, *m.*, a treader

calceaméntum –i, *n.*, a shoe

calceátus –a –um, *adj.*, shod, with shoes on

calcedónius –ii, *m.*, a precious stone, chalcedony

cálceo –áre, *1*, to put shoes on

cálcitro –áre, *1*, to kick

calco –áre, *1*, to trample on, tread upon

cálculus –i, *m.*, a pebble, stone, coal

caldária –ae, *f.*, a caldron

calefácio –ere –féci –fáctum, *3*, to warm

calefáctio –ónis, *f.*, heat, heating

calefácto –áre, *1*, to heat, make warm

calefío –fíeri –fáctus sum, *pass. of* calefácio, *3*, to grow warm

caléndae –árum, *f. pl.*, the first day of the month, the kalends

calendárium –ii, *n.*, a calendar

cáleo –ere –ui, *3*, to become warm, to glow

cálidus –a –um, *adj.*, hot

cáliga –ae, *f.*, a sandal, boot, buskin, a stocking worn by bishops

caliginósus –a –um, *adj.*, dark, misty

calígo –áre, *1*, to be in darkness, be misty, waste away

calígo –inis, *f.*, darkness, cloud, mist, dark cloud, a thick atmosphere

cálipha –ae, *m.*, caliph

calix –icis, *m.*, a chalice, goblet, cup

cálleo –ére –ui, *2*, to be hardened, know by experience, understand

cállide, *adv.*, craftily

callíditas –átis, *f.*, craftiness

cállidus –a –um, *adj.*, crafty, subtle

callis –is, *m.* and *f.*, a narrow way, footpath

callus –i, *m.*, hard skin

calor –óris, *m.*, heat

calóta –ae, *f.*, a skull cap

calúmnia –ae, *f.*, oppression, false accusation, calumny

calumniátor –óris, *m.*, oppressor, calumniator

calúmnio –áre, *2*, to oppress, calumniate, accuse falsely

calumniósus –a –um, *adj.*, calumnious

calvária –ae, *f.*, a skull

Calváriae Locus, Mount Calvary, the hill near Jerusalem where Christ was crucified. There is no sanction for the term "Mount Calvary" as it is only 18 feet high.

cálveo –ére, *2*, to be bald

calvus –a –um, *adj.*, bald

calx –cis, *f.*, lime

calybíta –ae, *m.*, a cabin dweller, hermit

camaúra –ae, *f.*, a close-fitting cap

camelaúcium –i, *n.*, a red velvet hood worn on certain occasions by the pope

camelopárdulus –i, *m.*, a giraffe

camelóttum –i, *n.*, a kind of cloth

camélus –i, *m.* and *f.*, a camel

cámera –ae, *f.*, a chamber, room, vault, small room

camerális –e, *adj.*, pertaining to a small room or chamber

camerárius –ii, *m.*, a chamberlain

camínus –i, *m.*, a furnace, forge, fire

camísia –ae, *f.*, an alb

camísium –ii, *n.*, an alb

campána –ae, *f.*, a bell

campanárium –ii, *n.*, a belfry

campanárius –ii, *m.*, a bell ringer

campaníle –is, *n.*, a belfry

campánula –ae, *m.*, a little boy

campéster –tris –tre, *adj.*, flat, pertaining to a plain

campus –i, *m.*, a field, plain

camus –i, *m.*, a bit for a horse, curb

Cana –ae, *f.*, Cana of Galilee, a village where Christ performed his first miracle. It was also the native place of Nathaniel.

Canaan. The name denotes the people who sprang from Canaan and the county in which they dwelt. It lay chiefly in the low districts along the east coast of the Mediterranean, north of the Philistines. In New Testament times it was divided into the following provinces: Iturea, Gualanitis, Trachonitis, Batanaea, Auranitis, Galilee, Samaria, and Judea.

cancellária –ae, *f.*, a chancery

cancellárius –ii, *m.*, a chancellor

cancellátio –ónis, *f.*, folding, crossing

cancellátus –a –um, *adj.*, crossed, canceled

cancéllo –áre, *2*, to fold crosswise

cancéllus –i, *m.*, a grating, lattice, enclosure, the partition between the sanctuary and nave of a church

candéla –ae, *f.*, a candle, lamp

candelábrum –i, *n.*, a candlestick, the name applied to a chandelier for lamps

candélula –ae, *f.*, a small taper

candens –éntis, *adj.*, red-hot, glowing hot

cándeo –ére –ui, *2*, to shine, glitter

candésco –ere, cándui, *3*, to become glittering white, shine

candidátio –ónis, *f.*, whiteness

candidátus –a –um, *adj.*, white-robed, dressed in white. The Blessed are represented as being clothed with white robes.

candidátus –i, *m.*, a candidate

cándidus –a –um, *adj.*, white

candífico –áre, *1*, to make dazzling white

candor –óris, *m.*, brightness

cáneo –ére –ui, *2*, to be white, gray, hoary

canis –is, *m.* and *f.*, a dog

canístrum –i, *n.*, a basket

caníties, *f.*, old age

canna –ae, *f.*, an ell, yard

cánnabis –is, *f.*, linen

cano –ere, cécini, cantum, *3*, to sing, to celebrate in song

canon –ónis, *m.*, a canon, norm, rule, the Canon of the Mass, a catalog or list of books or saints

canónia –ae, *f.*, the prebend of a canon

canonicális –e, *adj.*, pertaining to a canon

canonicátus –us, *m.*, the office of a canon

canónicus –a –um, *adj.*, canonical

canónicus –i, *m.*, a canon

canonisátio –ónis, *f.*, canonization. A Papal declaration that one already beatified is to be regarded as a saint.

canoníssa –ae, *f.*, a canoness

canonísta –ae, *m.*, one learned in canon law

canonízo –áre, *1*, to canonize

canórus –a –um, *adj.*, melodius, harmonious

cantábilis –e, *adj.*, worthy of song

canthárus –i, *m.*, a large pitcher, a well

canthus –i, *m.*, the rim or tire of a wheel

Cántica Gráduum, *n.*, a name for the Gradual Psalms

cantículum –i, *n.*, a brief song

cánticum –i, *n.*, a song, a canticle, a sacred scriptural chant or prayer differing from the Psalms, used in the Divine Office

cantiléna –ae, *f.*, music, song

cantíllo –áre, *1*, to warble, chirp

cántio –ónis, *f.*, a song

canto –áre, *1*, to sing, play, crow

cantor –óris, *m.*, a singer, chanter

cantus –us, *m.*, a song, crowing

Cantus Gregoriánus, plain chant

canus –a –um, *adj.*, gray, hoary

capax –ácis, *adj.*, fit for, capable

capélla –ae, *f.*, a chapel, a choir

capéllae magíster, a choir master

capellánus –i, *m.*, a chaplain

capelláris –e, *adj.*, pertaining to a chapel

capéllus –i, *m.*, a hat

capésso –ere –ívi *or* –ii –itum, *3*, to seize, lay hold of, to gain

Caphárnaum, *indecl.*, Capharnaum, a city in the land of Gennesaret, on the western shore of the Sea of Galilee, near the northern end

capillaméntum –i, *n.*, hair, wig

capíllus –i, *m.*, hair, a beard

cápio –ere, cepi, captum, *3*, to take, catch, contain, receive, obtain, understand

capitális –e, *adj.*, capital

capitáneus –ei, *m.*, a captain, leader

capitéllum –i, *n.*, the head of a column, the capitulum or short lesson of the Little Hours

capitilávium –ii, *n.*, the washing of the head

capítium –ii, *n.*, the collar of a tunic, a hood

Capituláre –is, *n.*, a list of initial and concluding words of the Epistles and Gospels of the Missal, a book containing the Collects

capituláris –e, *adj.*, pertaining to a chapter

capítulum –i, *n.*, the little chapter, a cathedral chapter, a chapter of the Bible cappa –ae, *f.*, a large cloak

Cáppadox –ócis, *n.*, a Cappadocian. Cappadocia was an elevated tableland in the east of Asia Minor.

cápparis –is, *f.*, a caper tree

cappélla –ae, *f.*, a chapel

cappellánia –ae, *f.*, a chaplaincy

cappellánus –i, *m.*, a chaplain

caprínus –a –um, *adj.*, pertaining to a ghost

capsa –ae, *f.*, a small case for relics

capsélla –ae, *f.*, a small box, a coffer

cápsula –ae, *f.*, a round metal vessel in which the Host is reserved in the tabernacle for Exposition and Benediction

cáptio –ónis, *f.*, a trap, net, prey, booty

captívitas –átis, *f.*, captivity

captívo –áre, *1*, to lead into captivity

captívus –a –um, *adj.*, captive

capto –áre, *1*, to seek after

captúra –ae, *f.*, a catch of fish

captus –us, *m.*, capture

capulátus –a –um, *adj.*, hooded

caput –itis, *n.*, head, chapter

capútium –ii, *n.*, a hood

carbasínus –a –um, *adj.*, green

carbo –ónis, *m.*, coal

carbonárius –ii, *n.*, a collier, coal burner

carcer –eris, *m.*, a prison

carcerális –e, *adj.*, pertaining to a prison

cardinalátus –us, *m.*, cardinalate

cardinális –is, *m.*, a cardinal, principal, chief

cardinalítius –a –um, *adj.*, pertaining to a cardinalship

caréna –ae, *f.*, a fast of forty days

caréntia –ae, *f.*, lack

cáreo –ére –ui –itum, *2*, to lack, be wanting in

cárica –ae, *f.*, a dried fig

carína –ae, *f.*, ship, keel

cáritas –átis, *f.*, charity, love

carmen –inis, *n.*, a song, canticle

carnális –e, *adj.*, bodily, carnal, fleshy, sensual

carnálitas –átis, *f.*, sensuality

carnáliter, *adv.*, sensually

cárneus –a –um, *adj.*, carnal, pertaining to the flesh

cárnifex –icis, *m.*, an executioner

carníficus –a –um, *adj.*, corporal, pertaining to the flesh

Carnis prívium novem, the Sunday before Lent

caro, carnis, *f.*, flesh, meat, the lower appetites or passions

carpo –ere –psi –ptum, *3*, to seize, pluck

carrúca –ae, *f.*, a carriage or coach

cartállus –i, *m.*, a basket

carus –a –um, *adj.*, dear, beloved

cáseum –i, *n.*, cheese

cásia –ae, *f.*, cassia, wild cinnamon

cassídile –is, *n.*, a wallet, satchel

cassis –ídis, *f.*, a helmet

cassus –a –um, *adj.*, useless, vain, empty

castéllum –i, *n.*, a town, walled town, village

castífico –áre, *1*, to cleanse, purify, render chaste

castigátio –ónis, *f.*, reproof, chastisement, punishment

castígo –áre, *1*, to chastise, punish, reprove

castimónia –ae, *f.*, chastity

castra –órum, *n.*, army, camp

castramétor –ári, *dep. 1*, to pitch camp, encamp

castro –áre, *1*, to castrate

castrum –i, *n.*, a camp, fort, castle

castrum dolóris, a catafalque

cásula –ae, *f.*, a chasuble, cottage

casus –us, *m.*, peril, misfortune, chance, case

catábulum –i, *n.*, a stable, place where animals are kept, menagerie

cataclýsmus –i, *m.*, a deluge, flood

catacúmba –ae, *f.*, an underground room, catacomb

catálogus –i, *m.*, a list

catarácta –ae, *f.*, a cataract, waterfall, floodgate, rushing waters, grating

cataráctes –ae, *m.*, a waterfall, floodgate

catásta –ae, *f.*, a platform, scaffold, the rack

catástrophe –es, *f.*, catastrophe, disaster

catechésis –is, *f.*, instruction to catechumens, catechetical instruction, an interrogation

catechéticus –a –um, *adj.*, catechetical

catechisátio –ónis, *f.*, questioning, catechizing

catechísmus –i, *m.*, a catechism

catechísta –ae, *m.*, a catechist, one who teaches catechism

catechísticus –a –um, *adj.*, pertaining to the catechism

catechízo –áre, *1*, to teach, instruct, teach by question and answer

catechumátus –us, *m.*, the time of instruction before baptism

catechúmena –ae, *f.*, a female catechumen

catechúmenus –i, *m.*, a male catechumen

catéllus –us, *m.*, a little dog

caténa –ae, *f.*, a chain, small chain

catérva –ae, *f.*, a crowd, congregation

cáthedra –ae, *f.*, a chair, seat, pulpit, professorship, the episcopal office; *ex cathedra*, officially

cathedrális –e, *adj.*, pertaining to an official see; *Ecclésia Cathedrális*, a cathedral.

cathedráticum –i, *n.*, an annual tribute paid to a bishop

cathólicus –a –um, *adj.*, universal, Catholic

cathúrnus, *m.*, pride, majesty, haughtiness

catínum –i, *n.*, a vessel, dish

catínus –i, *m.*, a vessel, dish

cátulus –i, *m.*, a cub, whelp

caucus –i, *m.*, a cruet

cauda –ae, *f.*, a tail, trail of a garment

caudatárius –ii, *m.*, a trainbearer

caula –ae, *f.*, a fold, sheepfold

cauma –átis, *n.*, heat

causa –ae, *f.*, cause, means, matter, case, occasion, reason

Causae Majóres, greater cases

causo –áre, *1*, to cause

caute, *adv.*, carefully

caútio –ónis, *f.*, caution, warning

cautum –i, *n.*, concern

cáveo –ére, cavi, cautum, *2*, to beware, take care

cavérna –ae, *f.*, a cave, cavern, hollow place

cavíllor –ári, *dep. 1*, to jest

Cedar, *indecl.*, the second son of Ismael

cedo –ere, cessi, cessum, *3*, to withdraw, yield, allow, grant

cedrínus –a –um, *adj.*, pertaining to cedar

cedrus –i, *f.*, the cedar tree

celatúra –ae, *f.*, the canopy over an altar

céleber –bris –bre, *adj.*, solemn

célebrans –tis, *m.*, the officiating minister, the celebrant

celebrátio –ónis, *f.*, a celebration, the performance of a sacred function

celébritas –átis, *f.*, feast, celebration

célebro –áre, *1*, to celebrate

celériter, *adv.*, quickly, swiftly

célero –áre, *1*, to hasten

cella –ae, *f.*, a cellar

cellárium –ii, *n.*, a chamber, pantry, storeroom

cellerárius –ii, *m.*, the cellarer

céllula –ae, *f.*, a hut

celo –áre, *1*, to conceal, hide

celsitúdo –inis, *f.*, height, highness, exaltation

celsus –a –um, *adj.*, high, sublime, noble

celtis –is, *f.*, a chisel, tool, instrument

celúma –átis, *n.*, a song, shout

cenodóxia –ae, *f.*, vainglory

cenotáphium –ii, *n.*, a cenotaph, catafalque

cénseo –ére –sui –sum, *2*, to approve, estimate, think, call

censúra –ae, *f.*, blame, censure, criticism

census –us, *m.*, cost, expense, tribute, rating, appraisal, census

centenárius –a –um, *adj.*, a hundredfold

centésimus –a –um, *adj.*, hundredth

centrum –i, *n.*, middle, center

céntuplum, *adv.*, a hundredfold

centúrio –ónis, *m.*, a centurion

cera –ae, *f.*, wax

cerástes –ae, *m.*, a horned serpent

cérebrum –i, *n.*, the brain

ceremónia, *also* cerimónia –ae, *f.*, ceremony

ceremoniále, *also* cerimoniále –is, *n.*, the direction of ceremonies

ceréolus –i, *m.*, a small wax candle

cereostátum –i, *n.*, a candelabrum, a candlestick

céreus –a –um, *adj.*, made of wax

céreus –i, *m.*, a wax candle or taper

cerevísia *or* cervísia –ae, *f.*, beer

cerno –ere, crevi, cretum, *3*, to discern

cérnuus –a –um, *adj.*, prostrate, falling down, with bowed heads

ceroferárium –ii, *n.*, a candlestick

ceroferárius –ii, *m.*, a torchbearer

certámen –inis, *n.*, fight, struggle, strife

certátim, *adv.*, eagerly

certe, *adv.*, certainly

cértior fíeri, to be informed

certitúdo –inis, *f.*, certainly

certo –áre, *1*, to fight, contend, struggle

certus –a –um, *adj.*, fixed, certain, determined

cervícal –ális, *n.*, a pillow

cervicátus –a –um, *adj.*, stiff-necked

cervix –ícis, *f.*, neck

cervus –i, *m.*, a stag, hart, deer; *f.*, –a –ae, a doe, hind

céspes –itis, *m.*, turf

cessátio –ónis, *f.*, cessation, ceasing

cessátio a divínis, suspension of divine service

cesso –áre, *1,* to cease, delay, loiter

cete –ion, *n. pl.,* a whale, dolphin

céterus –a –um, *adj.,* the other, rest; *de cétero,* finally; as for the rest

cetus –i, *m.,* a whale

chalcedónius –ii, *f.,* chalcedony

chameunía –ae, *f.,* sleeping on the ground

Chánaan, *indecl.,* Canaan, the promised land, Palestine west of the Jordan and the Dead Sea

Chananaéus –a –um, *adj.,* Canaanite

charácter –eris, *n.,* character, spiritual mark

charísma –atis, *n.,* a spiritual gift

charismáticus –a –um, *adj.,* charismatic, pertaining to a spiritual gift

cháritas –átis, *f.,* charity, love; also *cáritas*

charitatívus –a –um, *adj.,* charitable

charta –ae, *f.,* paper

chartáceus –a –um, *adj.,* pertaining to paper

charta-glóriae, *f.,* an altar card

chártula –ae, *f.,* a small piece of paper

charus –a –um, *adj.,* dear

cherub, *indecl.,* plural *cherubim,* cherub; cherubim, the second among the nine choirs of angels

chiánter –tri, *m.,* a choirboy

chirógraphum –i, *n.,* handwriting

chirothéca –ae, *f.,* a glove

chlamys –idis, *f.,* a cloak

Chloes, Chloe, a female disciple at the place (perhaps Philippi) whence St. Paul sent his first epistle to the Corinthians

choerogríllus –i, *m.,* a hare

chorális –e, *adj.,* choral

choraúlis –is, *m.,* a young chorister

chorda –ae, *f.,* a cord, string, cincture, a stringed instrument

chórdula –ae, *f.,* a tape or ribbon, cord or string

chórea –ae, *f.,* choir, dancing

chorepíscopus –i, *m.,* an auxiliary bishop

chóricus –a –um, *adj.,* pertaining to a choir

chorísta –ae, *m.,* a chorista, member of a choir

chorus –i, *m.,* choir, singing; the sanctuary or occupants of the sanctuary

chrisma –atis, *n.,* chrism, a mixture of olive oil and balm, blessed by the bishop and used in confirmation, baptism, and other ceremonies

chrismále –is, *n.,* a linen cloth used at baptism, a vessel for oils, the pyx, the corporal or pall, a cerecloth laid upon a consecrated altar

chrismális –e, *adj.,* pertaining to chrism

chrismárium –ii, *n.,* a vessel for chrism

chrismátio –ónis, *f.,* anointing with chrism

chrismatórium –ii, *n.,* a linen cloth used at baptism, a vessel for oils, the pyx, the corporal or pall, a cerecloth laid upon a consecrated altar

Christiádes –um, *c.,* Christians

Christiádum –i, *n.,* Christendom

Christiánitas –átis, *f.,* the Christian religion, Christianity

Christiánus –a –um, *adj.,* Christian

Chrístifer –fera –ferum, *adj.,* Christ-bearing

Christifidélis –e, *c.,* a follower or believer in Christ, one faithful to Christ

Christus –i, *m.,* Christ, the Messias

chrónicon –i, *n.,* a chronicle

chronológia –ae, *f.,* chronology

chronológicus –a –um, *adj.,* chronological

chrysólithus –i, *m.* and *f.,* topaz, chrysolite

chrysoprásus –i, *m.,* the chrysoprase (a precious stone)

Chusi, *m.,* an unknown Benjamite

chytrópus –ódis, *m.,* a pot with feet

cibária –órum, *n.,* food, sustenance, victuals

cibo –áre, *1,* to give to eat, feed

cibórium –ii, *n.,* ciborium, the vessel in which the Sacred Hosts are kept, a tabernacle, a canopy

cibus –i, *m.,* food, meat, fuel

cicátrix –ícis, *f.,* a wound, scar, mark, bruise

cicindéle –is, *n.,* a lamp made of glass

cicónia –ae, *f.,* a crane, stork

cicúta –ae, *f.,* hemlock

cidáris –is, *f.,* a Persian miter

cíeo, ciére, civi, citum, *2,* to invoke, call by name, rouse, set in action

cilícinus –a –um, *adj.,* made of haircloth

cilícium –ii, *n.,* sackcloth, haircloth

cimélium –ii, *n.,* treasure

cimitérium –ii, *n.,* cemetery

cinctículus –i, *m.,* an apron

cinctórium –ii, *n.,* a girdle

cinctúra –ae, *f.,* a cincture, belt

cinctus –us, *m.,* a girdle

cingo –ere, cinxi, cinctum, *3*, to gird
cíngulum –i, *n.*, a girdle, cincture, belt
cíngulus –us, *m.*, a girdle, cincture, belt
cínifes –um, *m. pl.*, a gnat, kind of fly
cinis –eris, *m.*, ashes, cinders; *dies cínerum*, Ash Wednesday
cinnamómun –i, *n.*, cinnamon
cinýra –ae, *f.*, a lute, kind of harp
circitórium –ii, *n.*, a curtain, veil
circúeo –íre, *4*, to go about, compass
circúitor –óris, *m.*, an inspector
circúitus –us, *m.*, circuit; *in circúitu*, round about
círculus –i, *m.*, a circle
circumamíctus –a –um, *adj.*, clothed about
circumcído –ere –cídi –císum, *3*, to circumcise
circumcíngo –ere –cínxi –cinctum, *3*, to gird about
circumcísio –ónis, *f.*, circumcision
circumcursátio –ónis, *f.*, attention
circumdátio –ónis, *f.*, putting on, wearing
circúmdo –are –dedi –datum, *1*, to surround, encompass, put around, go around
circumdólo –áre, *1*, to hew around with an ax
circumdúco –ere –dúxi –dúctum, *3*, to lead about
circúmeo –íre, *4*, to go around
circúmfero –férre –tuli –látum, *3*, to carry about
circumfluéntia –ae, *f.*, a superabundance
circumfódio –ere –fódi –fóssum, *3*, to dig a ditch or trench around
circumfúlgeo –ére –fúlsi –fúlsum, *2*, to shine round about
circumgésto –áre, *1*, to carry around
circúmligo –áre, *1*, to bind up or around
circumornátus –a –um, *adj.*, adorned round about, decorated around
circumpédes –um, *m.*, foot gear, sandals
circumpléctor –plécti –pléxus sum, *3*, to clasp around, surround, compass about
circumpóno –ere –pósui –pósitum, *3*, to place upon, put upon
circumquáque, *adv.*, all around
circumscríptio –ónis, *f.*, circumscribing
circumsédeo –sédi, *2*, to sit around
circumséptus –a –um, *adj.*, covered on all sides
circumsísto –ere –steti, *3*, to surround
circumspéctor –óris, *m.*, one who sees all
circumspício –ere –spéxi –spéctum, *3*, to look around, seek for

circumstántia –ae, *f.*, a circumstance, detail
circúmsto –stáre –steti, *1*, to stand around, be present
circumtéctus –a –um, *adj.*, covered about
circumvénio –íre –véni –véntum, *4*, to approach, circumvent
circumvéntio –ónis, *f.*, a surrounding
circúmvolo –áre, *1*, to fly about
Cisiojánus –i, *m.*, a metrical calendar
Cisson (Kishon)), a river in northern Palestine
cistérna –ae, *f.*, a pit, ditch
citátus –a –um, *adj.*, swift
citérior –ius, *adv.*, hither, on this side
cíthara –ae, *f.*, a harp, stringed instrument
citharízo –áre, *1*, to play the harp
citharoédus –i, *m.*, a harper, one who plays the harp
cito, *adv.*, quickly, speedily
cívicus –a –um, *adj.*, civic
civílis –e, *adj.*, civil
civílitas –átis, *f.*, citizenship
civis –is, *m.* and *f.*, citizen
cívitas –átis, *f.*, city, state, citizenship
clades –is, *f.*, defeat, disaster
clámito –áre, *1*, to shout loudly
clamo –áre, *1*, to proclaim, shout, call, cry out
clamor –óris, *m.*, shout, cry, crying, clamor
clandestínitas –átis, *f.*, secrecy
clandestínus –a –um, *adj.*, secret
clango –ere, *3*, to shout, clang
clangor –óris, *m.*, noise, sound
clarésco –ere, clárui, *3*, to shine forth, become clear, be visible
clarificátio –ónis, *f.*, glorification
clarífico –áre, *1*, to glorify, praise, extol
cláritas –átis, *f.*, clarity, brightness, light, glory
clarus –a –um, *adj.*, clear, well-known
clássicus –a –um, *adj.*, classic
classis –is, *f.*, rank, order, class
clathri –órum, *n.*, a grating
claúdico –áre, *1*, to limp, be halt or lame
claudo –ere, clausi, clausum, *3*, to close
claudus –a –um, *adj.*, lame
clausa –ae, *f.*, a cell
claustrális –e, *adj.*, pertaining to the cloister
claustrum –i, *n.*, a monastery, cloister
claúsula –ae, *f.*, a sentence, enclosure
clava –ae, *f.*, a cudgel, mace
clavícula –áre, *f.*, a small key

cláviger –eri, *m.,* a key or mace bearer
clavis –is, *f.,* a key
clavus –i, *m.,* a nail
clemens –éntis, *adj.,* merciful, clement, loving
cleménter, *adv.,* graciously, mercifully
cleméntia –ae, *f.,* clemency
Cléophas –ae, *m.,* Cleophas, or Klopas
clericális –e, *adj.,* clerical, priestly
clericátus –us, *m.,* the clerical state
cléricus –i, *m.,* a cleric, clerk
clerus –i, *m.,* clergy, an assignment by lot
clíbanus –i, *m.,* an oven, furnace
clímacus –i, *m.,* a group of three musical notes in descending scale
clínicus –i, *m.,* a patient confined to bed, physician
clinsa –ae, *f.,* a small hand bell
clípeum –i, *n., or* clípeus, *m.,* a shield, buckler
clivis –is, *f.,* two musical notes the second of which is lower than the first
clivósus –a –um, *adj.,* hilly, ridged
clivus –i, *m.,* a hill
clúeo –ére, *2,* to be named, be called
clusor –óris, *m.,* a smith
clýpeum –i, *n., see* clípeum
clýpeus –i, *m., see* clípeum
Cnidus, a city on a promontory of Caria (Acts 27:7)
coacérvo –áre, *1,* to heap up, collect
coácte, *adv.,* by restraint
coáctio –ónis, *f.,* compulsion
coadjúto –áre, *1,* to urge
coadjútor –óris, *m.,* a helper
coadúno –áre, *1,* to unite, knit together
coaedífico –áre, *1,* to build together
coaequális –e, *adj.,* coequal
coaéquo –áre, *1,* to make equal, fill up
coaetáneus –a –um, *adj.,* equal, equal in age, contemporary
coaetérnus –a –um, *adj.,* coequal, co-eternal
coaévus –i, *m.,* one equal in age
coágito –áre, *1,* to shake together
coagménto –áre, *1,* to join together
coagulátus –a –um, *adj.,* curdled
coágulo –áre, *1,* to curdle
coalésco –ere –álui –álitum, *3,* to grow together
coangústo –áre, *1,* to hem in, straighten
coapóstolus –i, *m.,* a fellow apostle
coárcto –áre, *1,* to straighten, force, constrain
coassístens –éntis, *m.,* a coassistant

coccíneus –a –um, *adj.,* of scarlet
cóccinum –i, *n.,* scarlet
cóchlea –ae, *f.,* a screw
cóchlear –áris, *n.,* a spoon
cóctilis –e, *adj.,* bake, crooked
coctória –ae, *f.,* a kiln
cocus –i, *m.,* a cook
codex –icis, *m.,* a book, document, scroll
coeles –itis, *m.,* a saint
coeléstis –a, *adj.,* heavenly, celestial
Coeléstis aulae jánua, Gate of Heaven
coelibátus –us, *m.,* celibacy
coelícola –ae, *c.,* a dweller in heaven
coélicus –a –um, *adj.,* heavenly, celestial
coélitus, *adv.,* from heaven
coelum –i, *n.,* heaven; *plural,* coeli
coemetérium –ii, *n.,* a cemetery
coémo –ere –émi –émptum, *3,* to buy, purchase together
coena –ae, *f.,* supper, feast, dinner
coenáculum –i, *n.,* a refectory, dining room
coeno –áre, *1,* to have supper, sup, dine
coenobiárcha –ae, *m.,* an abbot
coenobíta –ae, *m.,* a monk
coenobíticus –a –um, *adj.,* pertaining to monastic life
coenóbium –ii, *n.,* a monastery, convent
coepíscopus –i, *m.,* a fellow bishop
coérceo –ere –cui –citum, *2,* to restrain, check, prune, enclose
coetus –us, *m.,* host, assembly
Coetus coélicus omnis, the whole heavenly host
coexténdo –ere –téndi –ténsus *or* –téntus, *3,* to have the same expansion
cogitátio –ónis, *f.,* thought, plans, designs
cogitátum –i, *n.,* care
cogitátus –us, *m.,* counsel, thought, thinking
cógito –áre, *1,* to think, take counsel, cogitate, take thought
cognáta –ae, *f.,* a cousin
cognátio –ónis, *f.,* kindred, kinship, progeny, descendant
cognátus –i, *m.,* a kinsman
cognítio –ónis, *f.,* knowledge, idea
cógnitor –óris, *m.,* a witness
cognoméntum –i, *n.,* a name
cognómino –áre, *1,* to name
cognóminor –ári, *dep. 1,* to be surnamed
cognoscíbilis –e, *adj.,* knowable
cognoscíbiliter, *adv.,* knowingly, recognizably
cognoscitívus –a –um, *adj.,* cognizant, aware

cognósco –ere –nóvi –nitum, *3,* to get acquainted with, learn, perceive

cogo –ere, coégi, coáctum, *3,* to compel, gather together

cohabitátio –ónis, *f.,* cohabitation

cohábito –áre, *1,* to live together

cohaéreo –ére –haési –haésum, *2,* to cleave to

cohéres –édis, *m.,* coheir

cohíbeo –ére –ui –itum, *2,* to restrain, hinder, confine, hold together

cohibítio –ónis, *f.,* a checking, restraint

cohors –tis, *f.,* cohort, guard, band

cohortátio –ónis, *f.,* exhortation

cohórtor –ári, *dep. 1,* to encourage, exhort

coinquíno –áre, *1,* to defile

cola –ae, *f.,* a strainer

colaphízo –áre, *1,* to buffet, strike, box one's ears

cólaphus –i, *m.,* a cuff, blow, blow with the fist or hand, box on the ear

colatórium –ii, *n.,* a strainer

collábor –i –lápsus sum, *dep. 3,* to collapse, fall

collactáneus –i, *m.,* a foster brother

colláre –is, *n.,* a collar

collárium –ii, *n.,* a Roman collar, a collar

collátio –ónis, *f.,* a meeting, gathering, assembly, collection, conference, discussion, contribution, present

collátus, *m.,* conferring

collaudátio –ónis, *f.,* praise

collaudátor –óris, *m.,* one who joins in praises

collaúdo –áre, *1,* to praise very much, praise together

collécta –ae, *f.,* a collection, assembly, the Collect at Mass

collectáneum –i, *n.,* a book of Collects

collectárium –ii, *n.,* a book of Collects

colléctor –óris, *m.,* a fellow student

colléctus –a –um, *adj.,* shut

colléga –ae, *m.,* a companion

collegiáliter, *adv.,* in a body

collegiáta –ae, *f.,* an institution, collegiate church

collegiátus –a –um, *adj.,* corporate, collegiate

collégium –ii, *n.,* a college, body of clergy

Collégium sacrum, the college of cardinals

collído –ere –lísi –lísum, *3,* to cast down, strike together, bruise, crush, clash

colligátio –ónis, *f.,* a band

cólligo –ere –légi –léctum, *3,* to gather up, take in, pack up, bring together, collect

collíneo –áre, *1,* to direct in a straight line

collínus –a –um, *adj.,* hilly, on a hill, pertaining to a hill

colliquefácio –féci –fáctum, *3,* to melt

colliquésco –ere, *3,* to melt

collis –is, *m.,* a hill

cólloco –áre, *1,* to place, set, put

cólloquor –qui –cútus *or* –quétus sum, *dep. 3,* to converse together, negotiate with

collucátio –ónis, *f.,* wrestling

collúceo –ére, *2,* to shine on all sides, burn, be illuminated

collúctor –óris, *m.,* an interlocutor

collum –i, *n.,* neck

collústro –áre, *1,* to illuminate

collýrida –ae, *f.,* a cake

collýrium –ii, *n.,* a salve, a paste

colo –áre, *1,* to refine

colo –ere, cólui, cultum, *3,* to celebrate, worship, till

colóbium –ii, *n.,* a cowl-like habit or tunic

colónia –ae, *f.,* city

colónus –i, *m.,* a dweller, inhabitant

colorátus –a –um, *adj.,* colored

cóloro –áre, *1,* to color, give tone to, gloss over

Colóssae –árum, *f.,* Colosse, a city in Asia Minor

Colossénses –ium, *m.,* Colossians

Colossénsis –e, *adj.,* pertaining to Colossae

colum –i, *n.,* a strainer

colúmba –ae, *f.,* a dove, symbol of innocence and purity. *Also* a dove-shaped vessel in which the Eucharist was preserved in the early Church

cólumen –inis, *n.,* a support, pillar, column

Colúmnae Flagellátio, the Scourging at the Pillar. Feast on the Tuesday after Quinquagesima Sunday.

columnélla –ae, *f.,* a small column

coma –ae, *f.,* hair

cómbino –áre, *1,* to unite, combine, associate with, be joined with

combúro –ere –ússi –ústum, *3,* to burn, consume

combústio –ónis, *f.,* burning

combustúra –ae, *f.,* a burning

comédo –ere –édi –ésum or –éstum, 3, to eat, devour, consume entirely

comes –itis, m., a companion, count

comessátio –ónis, f., a feasting, reveling, banquet

comessátor –óris, m., a banqueter

comestábilis –e, adj., eatable

coméstio –ónis, f., eating

coméstor –óris, m., an eater

cóminus, adv., in close combat

comitátus –us, m., company, escort, an imperial count, the reception of the Holy Eucharist

comitíssa –ae, f., a countess

comitíva –ae, f., retinue, an escort

cómitor –ári, dep. 1, to accompany, be together

commártyr –is, c., a fellow martyr

commáter –tris, f., a godmother, female sponsor

commemorátio –ónis, f., commemoration, remembrance, mention

Commemorátio B.M.V. de Monte Carmélo, commemoration of Our Lady of Mount Carmel, July 16

Commemorátio ómnium Fidélium Defunctórum, the Feast of All Souls, Nov. 2

commemoratórium –ii, n., a list, record, memorandum

commémoro –áre, 1, to commemorate

comménda –ae, f., a temporal income without spiritual obligation

commendatárius –a –um, adj., commendatary

commendátio –ónis, f., recommendation

commendatítius –a –um, adj., commendatory

comméndo –áre, 1, to commend, commemorate

commensális –is, m., a table companion

commentariénsis –is, m., a court clerk

commentárium –ii, n., a record, publication

commentárius –ii, m., commentary

comméntum –i, n., fiction, invention, falsehood

commércium –ii, n., intercourse, fellowship, work, rite, transaction, dealing

cómmigro –áre, 1, to travel, go

commílito –ónis, m., a fellow soldier

comminátio –ónis, f., a threatening, threat, menacing

comminíscor –minísci –méntus sum, 4, to invent, contrive

comminíster –tri, m., a fellow minister

cómminor –ári, dep. 1, to threaten, rebuke, charge

commínuo –ere –ui –útum, 3, to break into small pieces

commisariátus –us, m., a commissioner, the office of a commissioner

commísceo –ére –míscui –míxtum or –místum, 2, to mingle, lie with

commisárius –us, m., a commissioner

commísio –ónis, f., a commission, committee

commissúra –ae, f., a patch, piece, coupling, joint

commístio –ónis, f., a mixture

commítto –ére –mísi –míssum, 3, to bring together, unite, commit, set forth, engage in

commíxtio –ónis, f., mingling, mixture, an intermingling

cómmode, adv., conveniently

cómmodo –áre, 1, to lend, oblige, adapt oneself

cómmodum –i, n., a blessing, favor, convenience

cómmodus –a –um, adj., convenient

commóneo –ére, 2, to admonish, warn, remind

commonítio –ónis, f., a warning, reminder

commorátio –ónis, f., habitation, dwelling

commórior –móri –mórtuus sum, dep. 3, to die together with

cómmoror –ári, dep. 1, to tarry, abide, remain, delay, stay, dwell

commótio –ónis, f., movement, disturbance, commotion

commóveo –ére –móvi –mótum, 2, to move, stir up, excite

communicátio –ónis, f., communication

communicátor –óris, m., a partaker

commúniceps –ipis, m., a fellow townsman

commúnico –áre, 1, to communicate, partake of

commúnio –íre, 4, to strengthen

commúnio –ónis, f., communion

commúnio láica, the lay state

commúnis –e, adj., common, ordinary

commúnitas –átis, f., commonwealth

commúniter, adv., together

commutátio –ónis, f., change

commúto –áre, 1, to change

como –ere, compsi, comptum, 3, to comb, adorn the hair, place together

compáctus –a –um, adj., compact, in a narrow compass

compágino –áre, *1*, to join together

compágo –inis, *f.*, joining together, bodily structure

compar –aris, *c.*, companion

compar –aris, *adj.*, like, equal, similar

comparátio –ónis, *f.*, preparation, comparison

compárco –ere –pársi –pársum, *3*, to scrape together, to save up

cómparo –áre, *1*, to compare, make ready, prepare, buy

compárticeps –cipis, sharing jointly

compáter –tris, *m.*, a sponsor

compátiens –éntis, *adj.*, having compassion

compátior, compáti, compássus sum, *dep. 3*, to suffer with

compedítus –i, *m.*, a captive, prisoner

compéllo –ere –púli –púlsum, *3*, to compel, oblige, subdue, overcome, restrain

compéllo –áre, *1*, to accost

compérco –ere –pérsi, *3*, to save, lay up

compério –íre –péri –pértum, *4*, to find, obtain certain knowledge

compes –edis, *f.*, a foot fetter, shackle

compésco –ere –péscui, *3*, to restrain, withhold, fasten together

compéstror –ári, *dep. 1*, to clothe in an apron

cómpetens –éntis, *adj.*, suitable, authorized

competénter –*adv.*, suitably, fitly, aptly, strivingly

competéntia –ae, *f.*, official qualification

compéto –ere –ívi *or* –ii –ítum, *3*, to be capable of

compíngo –ere –pegí –páctum, *3*, to construct, provide with, furnish with, join together

compláceo –ére –cui, *2*, to please, be acceptable to

complacítior –óris, *adj.*, more favorable

complácitus –a –um, *adj.*, well pleased, favorable, find favor with

compláno –áre, *1*, to level, plane

complánto –áre, *1*, to plant together

compléctor –plécti –pléxus sum, *dep. 3*, to surround, encircle, comprehend

complénda –ae, *f.*, the Postcommunion

cómpleo –ére –plévi –plétum, *2*, to accomplish, fill, fulfill

Compléta –ae, *f.*, the last of the canonical hours

Completórium –ii, *n.*, Compline

compléxo –áre, *1*, to embrace

cómplico –áre, *1*, to fold together

complódo –ere –plósi –plósum, *3*, to strike together

complúres, *adj.*, several

compóno –ere –pósui –pósitum, *3*, to compose, place, order, reconcile, forge

compórto –áre, *1*, to bring together, collect, lay up

compos –ótis, *adj.*, sharing in, possessed of

compositio –ónis, *f.*, arrangement, composing

compósitus –a –um, *adj.*, comely, decked out

comprehéndo –ere –prehéndi –prehénsum, *3*, to obtain, take, seize, overtake, understand, apprehend, comprehend

cómprimo –ere –préssi –préssum, *3*, to restrain, suppress, squeeze, keep down, press together

cómprobo –áre, *1*, to approve, prove, establish

compúnctio –ónis, *f.*, sorrow, compunction, remorse, sorrow for sin

compúnctus –a –um, *adj.*, goaded by the sting of conscience, remorseful

compúngo –ere –púnxi –púnctum, *3*, to feel remorse, prick, wound, puncture, grieve for

cómputo –áre, *1*, to reckon, count

compútus –i, *m.*, a reckoning, calculation

conátus –us, *m.*, an attempt

concalefáctio –ónis, *f.*, a warning

concalésco –ere –cálui, *3*, to burn, glow, glow hot

concaptívus –i, *m.*, a fellow captive

concáva –ae, *f.*, a glen

concédo –ere –céssi –céssum, *3*, to grant, concede

concelebrátio –ónis, *f.*, a celebration, concelebration, the celebration of Mass by several priests at the same time

concélebro –áre, *1*, to celebrate together, celebrate a festivity

concéntus –us, *m.*, harmony, concord, agreement, harmonized song

concéptio –ónis, *f.*, idea, conception

Concéptio Christi, the feast of the Annunciation

Concéptio Immacúlata, the Immaculate Conception of the B.V.M. Dogma defined, Dec. 8, 1854.

concéptus –us, *m.*, conception

concérto –áre, *1*, to strive eagerly

concéssio –ónis, *f.*, concession

concha –ae, *f.*, holy-water font

conchuéla –ae, *f.*, a font, a small shell

cóncido –ere –cidi, *3,* to fall down, to be disheartened

concído –ere –cídi –císum, *3,* to cut to pieces, kill

conciliábulum –i, *n.,* the market place, an unlawful council

Concília Mártyrum, *n. pl.,* a burial place for martyrs

conciliátrix –ícis, *f.,* ambassadress

concílio –áre, *1,* to obtain, procure, make friendly

concílium –ii, *n.,* a council, assembly

concínno –áre, *1,* to fit together carefully, frame, weave, contrive, forge, accomplish

cóncino –cínui –céntum, *3,* to sing, celebrate in song

cóncio –ónis, *f.,* a sermon, gathering, assembly

concionátor –óris, *m.,* a preacher

concionatórius –a –um, *adj.,* pertaining to a sermon

concípio –ere –cépi –céptum, *3,* to conceive

cóncito –áre, *1,* to arouse, excite, stir up

conciúncula –ae, *f.,* a short sermon, brief address

concláve –is, *n.,* a room, the place in which the cardinals assemble at the election of a pope

conclavísta –ae, *m.,* a cardinal in conclave

conclúdo –ere –clúsi –clúsum, *3,* to enclose, shut up

conclúsio –ónis, *f.,* ending, termination, closing, consequence, the closing words of a Collect

concólor –óris, *adj.,* of the same color

concomitántia –ae, *f.,* association, concomitance

concordántiae –árum, *f.,* a concordance

concordátio –ónis, *f.,* reconciliation, agreement

concordátum –i, *n.,* a concordate; *concordáta,* things agreed upon. A treaty between the Holy See and a secular state regulating the position of the Church in that state.

concorporális –e, *adj.,* a fellow member

cóncreo –áre, *1,* to create together

cóncrepo –ere –ui –crépitum, *3,* to sound, resound

concrésco –ere –crévi –crétum, *3,* to unite

concúlco –áre, *1,* to tread, tread underfoot, trample on

concupiscéntia –ae, *f.,* an inordinate desire, concupiscence, a yearning of the lower appetites

concupiscíbilis –e, *adj.,* valuable, desirable

concupísco –ere –cupívi –itum, *3,* to be desirous of

concurréntia –ae, *f.,* concurrence, coinciding

concúrsus –us, *m.,* concurrence, coinciding, large gathering or assembly

concútio –ere –cússi –cússum, *3,* to strike, cause to tremble

condécoro –áre, *1,* to decorate

condeléctor –ári, *dep. 1,* to be delighted with

condemnátio –ónis, *f.,* condemnation, sentence

condemnatórius –a –um, *adj.,* condemnatory

condémno –áre, *1,* to condemn

condénsa –órum, *n. pl.,* woods, leafy boughs

condénsum –i, *n.,* a thicket

condénsus –a –um, *adj.,* leafy, thickly covered

condescéndo –ere –scéndi –scénsum, *3,* to descend, condescend

condíco –ere –díxi –díctum, *3,* to appoint

condígnus –a –um, *adj.,* fit to be compared with

condiméntum –i, *n.,* seasoning, spice

cóndio –íre –ívi –ítum, *4,* to preserve, season, embalm

condiscípulus –i, *m.,* a fellow disciple

condítio –ónis, *f.,* condition, nature, a creature, a creaking

condo –ere –didi –ditum, *3,* to establish, found

condolésco –ere –dólui, *3,* to have compassion, feel pain, suffer severely

condonátus –i, *m.,* a lay brother, an oblate

condóno –áre, *1,* to pardon, condone

condúco –ere –dúxi –dúctum, *3,* to hire

conductítius –a –um, *adj.,* hired, mercenary

condúctum –i, *n.,* a dwelling place, hired house

Condúctus Paschae, a name for Low Sunday

condúlco –áre, *1,* to sweeten

confábulor –ári, *dep. 1,* to talk

confércio –íre –férsi –fértum, *4,* to cram together

conferéntia –ae, *f.,* a conference

cónfero –érre –túli, collátum, *3,* to grant, confer, accompany, gain, press down

confessárius –ii, *m.,* a confessor

conféssio –ónis, *f.,* confession, acknowledgment, profession of faith

confessionále –is, *n.,* a confessional

confessionális –e, *adj.,* pertaining to confession

conféssor –óris, *m.,* a confessor, a male saint who did not die for the Faith; a priest who has the jurisdiction to hear confessions

conféstim, *adv.,* forthwith, immediately

confício –ere –féci –féctum, *3,* to make thoroughly, complete, kill

confíctus –a –um, *adj.,* forged

confidénter, *adv.,* with confidence, confidently

confidéntia –ae, *f.,* confidence

confído –ere –físus sum, *semi-dep. 3,* to trust, hope, confide, be of good heart

configo –ere –fíxi –fíxum, *3,* to fasten, nail, fix in

configurátus –a –um, *adj.,* like, conformable, fashioned

configúro –áre, *1,* to fashion

confíngo –ere –xi –fíctum, *3,* to invent, devise

confirmándus *or* –a, *m.* and *f.,* a candidate for confirmation

confirmátio –ónis, *f.,* confirmation

confírmo –áre, *1,* to strengthen, confirm, uphold

confíteor –éri –féssus sum, *dep. 2,* to confess, acknowledge, give thanks, glory, or praise

cónflans –ántis, *adj.,* refining, purifying

conflátilis –e, *adj.,* molten

conflatórium –ii, *n.,* a furnace, crucible

conflicátio –ónis, *f.,* a struggle, conflict

conflictátio –ónis, *f.,* a dispute

conflícto –áre, *1,* to contend with, struggle with

conflíctus –us, *m.,* conflict, discussion

conflígo –ere –flíxi –flíctum, *3,* to strive, endeavor

cónflo –áre, *1,* to forge, melt, weld, refine

conflóreo –ére, *2,* to bloom or flourish together

cónfluo –ere –flúxi, *3,* to flow together, resort

confódio –ere –fódi –fóssum, *3,* to stab, pierce

confoederátio –ónis, *f.,* a union, confederation

confoédero –áre, *1,* to conform

confórmis –e, *adj.,* similar

confórmo –áre, *1,* to conform

confortátio –ónis, *f.,* comfort, consolation, solace

confórto –áre, *1,* to strengthen

confórtor –ári, *dep. 1,* to wax strong, take courage

confráctio –ónis, *f.,* breaking, breach

confractórium –ii, *n.,* the prayer at the end of the Canon in an Ambrosian Mass

confratérnitas –átis, *f.,* a sodality, confraternity, an association, generally of laymen, having some work or devotion, charity, or instruction for its object, undertaken for the glory of God

confrátres –um, *m. pl.,* guild brothers

confrátria –ae, *f.,* a sodality, confraternity

confricátio –ónis, *f.,* a rubbing together

cónfrigo –ere –fríxi –fríctum, *3,* to burn up

confríngo –ere –frégi –fráctum, *3,* to break in pieces

confúgio –ere –fúgi, *3,* to flee

confúndo –ere –fúdi –fúsum, *3,* to put to shame, confound, confuse, disturb

confúsio –ónis, *f.,* confusion, shame

confúsus –a –um, *adj.,* disordered, confused

confúto –áre, *1,* to confute, overthrow, check, silence

congaúdeo –ére –gavísus sum, *semi-dep. 2,* to rejoice with

congelátus –a –um, *adj.,* frozen

congemísco –ere, *3,* to sigh together

cóngener –éris, *adj.,* kindred, of the same kind

cóngero –ere –géssi –géstum, *3,* to keep

conglobátim, *adv.,* in a mass

conglorífico –áre, *1,* to glorify

congloríficor –ári, *dep. 1,* to be glorified with

conglútino –áre, *1,* to bind together, to cleave to

conglútinor –ári, *dep. 1,* to bind together, to cleave to

congrátulor –ári, *dep. 1,* to rejoice with

congregátio –ónis, *f.,* congregation, gathering, company, assembly, a community bound together by a common rule

cóngrego –áre, *1,* to gather together, assemble, collect

congréssio –ónis, *f.,* a meeting

cóngrua –ae, *f.,* the salary of a pastor

cóngrue, *adv.,* suitably, aptly, fitly

cóngruens –éntis, *adj.,* proper, seasonable, suitable

congruénter, *adv.,* becomingly, suitably

cóngruo –ere –ui, *3,* to correspond with, agree with, run together

cóngruus –a –um, *adj.,* becoming, fitting, agreeing

congýro –áre, *1,* to surround

conjício –ere –jéci –jéctum, *3,* to cast, hurl; to guess, conjecture, interpret, conclude

conjugális –e, *adj.,* conjugal

cónjugo –áre, *1,* to unite in matrimony

conjúnctio –ónis, *f.,* union, conjunction, joining together

conjúnctus –a –um, *adj.,* connected, joined, united

conjúngo –ere –júnxi –júnctum, *3,* to join, have affinity with

conjunx –júgis, *c.,* husband, wife, spouse

conlísio –ónis, *f.,* a striking together

connaturáliter, *adv.,* in a natural way

connécto –ere –néxui –néxum, *3,* to unite, join together, fasten

connéxio –ónis, *f.,* connection, relation

connéxus –a –um, *adj.,* joined together

conníveo –ére –nívi *or* –nixi, *2,* to wink or blink, become drowsy

connúbium –ii, *n.,* matrimony

connúmero –áre, *1,* to number among

conopaéum –i *or* conopéum –i, *n.,* a canopy

conor –ári, conátus sum, *dep. 1,* to strive endeavor

conquádro –áre, *1,* to cut square, square, harmonize

conquásso –áre, *1,* to crush, shake severely

cónqueror –quéstum sum, *dep. 3,* to complain, bewail

conquiésco –ere –quiévi –quiétum, *3,* to rest

conquíro –ere –quisívi –quisítum, *3,* to seek carefully

conquisítio –ónis, *f.,* discussion, dispute

conquísitor –óris, *m.,* a disputer

conrégno –áre, *1,* to reign with

consalúto –áre, *1,* to salute one another

consanguíneus –a –um, *adj.,* of one blood with

consanguíneus –i, *m.,* a cousin

consanguínitas –átis, *f.,* consanguinity

conscéndo –ere –scéndi –scénsum, *3,* to ascend

cónscia –ae, *f.,* a witness

consciéntia –ae, *f.,* conscience, consciousness, acknowledgment

conscíndo –ere –scídi –scíssum, *3,* to rend

cónscius –a –um, *adj.,* conscious, knowing

cónscius –i, *m.,* a witness

conscríptus –a –um, *adj.,* written

consecrátio –ónis, *f.,* consecration

consecrátor –óris, *m.,* consecrator, one who consecrates

cónsecro –áre, *1,* to consecrate, sanctify, hallow

consecútio –ónis, *f.,* attainment

consédo –ere, *3,* to sit

consénior –óris, *m.,* ancient, elder, senior

consénsus –us, *m.,* agreement, concord, harmony

consentáneus –a –um, *adj.,* fit, suitable

conséntio –íre –sénsi –sénsum, *4,* to consent

consepélio –íre –sepelívi *or* –ii –sepúltum, *4,* to bury with

consequénter, *adv.,* consequently, subsequently

cónsequor –i –secútus sum, *dep. 3,* to obtain, follow

cónsero –ere –sévi –situm, *3,* to sow, plant

conservátus –a –um, *adj.,* inviolate

consérvo –áre, *1,* to preserve, keep

consérvus –i, *m.,* a fellow servant

conséssus –us, *m.,* a seat, place, an assembly

consídero –áre, *1,* to look, regard, consider, contemplate

consído –sídere –sídi –séssum, *3,* to sit down together, hold council

consignatórium –ii, *n.,* a room in which confirmation was administered

consignátus –a –um, *adj.,* recorded

consígno –áre, *1,* to sign with

consiliárius –ii, *m.,* adviser, counselor, judge

consílior –ári, *dep. 1,* to plan, take counsel

consílium –ii, *n.,* counsel, advice, plan, assembly

consímilis –e, *adj.,* like, similar

Consisténtes, *m. pl.,* the advanced class of penitents in the early Church

consísto –ere –stiti, *3,* to stand together, stand firmly, continue

consistoriális –e, *adj.*, pertaining to a consistory

consistórium –ii, *n.*, an assemblage or consistory

consociátio –ónis, *f.*, an association

consócio –áre, *1*, to share, associate with

consolátio –ónis, *f.*, comfort, consolation

consolátor –óris, *m.*, comforter

consólido –áre, *1*, to strengthen

cónsolo –áre, *1*, to console

consólor –ári, *dep. 1*, to comfort, console, encourage

cónsonus –a –um, *adj.*, harmonious, in harmony with

consors –sórtis, *c.*, a sharer, partaker, consort

consórtium –ii, *n.*, company, companionship, consort, fellowship, partnership in

conspéctor –óris, *m.*, a beholder

conspéctus –us, *m.*, sight, presence, look, survey, view

conspérgo –ere –spérsi –spérsum, *3*, to strew, sprinkle

conspérsio –ónis, *f.*, dough, paste, sprinkling

conspício –ere –spéxi –spéctum, *3*, to see, look at, consider, perceive

conspirátio –ónis, *f.*, agreement, a common opinion

conspíro –áre, *1*, to agree, unite, conspire, to act in harmony or in conspiracy

cónspuo –ere –spui –spútum, *3*, to spit upon

constánter, *adv.*, earnestly

constántia –ae, *f.*, firmness, constancy

constellátio –ónis, *f.*, a constellation

consternátus –a –um, *adj.*, in consternation

constítuo –ere –ui –útum, *3*, to constitute, determine, set, make, appoint

constitútio –ónis, *f.*, constitution, order, foundation, making, determination

constitutívus –a –um, *adj.*, determining, constituting

constitútus –a –um, *adj.*, placed, situated

consto –áre –steti –statúrum, *1*, to exist, consist

constríngo –ere –strínxi –stríctum, *3*, to bind fast

cónstruo –ere –strúxi –strúctum, *3*, to build, frame together

constúpro –áre, *1*, to corrupt

consubstantiális –e, *adj.*, consubstantial, being of one substance with

consúdo –áre, *1*, to sweat

consuefácio –féci, *3*, to make accustomed

consuésco –ere –suévi –suétum, *3*, to be wont

consuetúdo –inis, *f.*, custom, interchange, intimacy

consuétus –a –um, *adj.*, accustomed, wonted

consul –ulis, *m.*, consul

cónsulo –ere –súlui –súltum, *3*, to consult

consúltius, *adv.*, more wisely

consúltor –óris, *m.*, a counselor, consultor

consúltum –i, *n.*, resolution

consúltus –a –um, *adj.*, wise

consummátio –ónis, *f.*, a perfecting, consummation, the end of the world

consummátor –óris, *m.*, a finisher

Consummátum est, It is consummated.

consúmmo –áre, *1*, to finish, consume

consúmo –ere –súmpsi –súmptum, *3*, to consume, bring to an end

consúmptio –ónis, *f.*, a wasting, complete destruction

cónsuo –ere –sui –sútum, *3*, to sew together

consúrgo –ere –surréxi –surréctum, *3*, to stand up, rise up, rise with

contabésco –ere –tábui, *3*, to pine or waste away

contáctus –us, *m.*, touch, contact, approach

contágio –ónis, *f.*, contagion

contagiósus –a –um, *adj.*, cantagious

contágium –ii, *n.*, touch, contagion, temptation

contaminátio –ónis, *f.*, contamination

contámino –áre, *1*, to defile, contaminate

cóntego –ere –téxi –téctum, *3*, to cover, envelop

contémno –áre, *1*, to despise

contémno –ere –témpsi –témptum, *3*, to despise, slight

contémpero –áre, *1*, to infuse, mix, conform, adapt

contemplátio –ónis, *f.*, contemplation

contemplátor –óris, *m.*, contemplator

contémplo –áre, *1*, to contemplate

contemptíbilis –e, *adj.*, contemptible

contémptio –ónis, *f.*, contempt

contémptor –óris, *m.*, despiser

contémptus –us, *m.*, contempt, scorn, disdain

conténdo –ere –téndi –téntum, *3*, to strive, strain, assert, maintain

contenébro –áre, *1*, to darken, obscure

conténtio –ónis, f., obstinacy, strife, contention

contentióse, adv., rebelliously, contentiously

contentiósus –a –um, adj., contentious

conténtus –a –um, adj., content

cónterans –tis, adj., three years of age

cóntero –ere –trívi –trítum, 3, to crush, break in pieces, grind to powder, bruise, destroy

contérritus –a –um, adj., frightened

contestátio –ónis, f., a former name for the Preface of the Mass

contéstor –ári, dep. 1, to testify, bear witness

contéxtus –a –um, adj., woven

contéxtus, m., context

conticésco –ere –tícui, 3, to be silent

contignátio –ónis, f., woodwork

continátor –óris, m., a preacher, speaker

cóntinens –éntis, f., continent, mainland

continéntia –ae, f., abstinence, restraint, self-denial

contíneo –ere –tínui –téntum, 2, to keep together, bind together, uphold, stop, possess, keep silent, contain, hold fast, confine, hold in check

contíngo (contínguo) –ere –tigi –táctum, 3, to touch, belong to, fall to, affect, defile, reach to, happen

continnátus –a –um, adj., continual

contínuo, adv., immediately, forthwith

contínuus –a –um, adj., continual, infinite

cóntio –ónis, f., a sermon, gathering

contituláris –is, m., a titular, associated titular

contórqueo –ere –tórsi –tórtum, 3, to twist, wind about, contort, turn violently

contráctus –us, m., a bargain, contract

contradíco –ere –díxi –díctum, 3, to contend with, resist, contradict, oppose, thwart

contradíctio –ónis, f., strife, contradiction

contradíctor –óris, m., an opponent, gainsayer

contráeo –íre, 4, to go against

cóntraho –ere –tráxi –tráctum, 3, to commit, draw in, contract, collect, unite

contrapúncticus –a –um, adj., pertaining to a counterpoint

contrapúnctum –i, n., a counterpoint

contraríetas –átis, f., opposite

contrárium –i, n., opposite

contrárius –a –um, adj., contrary, against

contrécto –áre, 1, to handle

contremísco –ere –trémui, 3, to tremble

cóntremo –ere –ui, 3, to tremble

contribulátus –a –um, adj., troubled

contríbulis –is, m., a countryman, tribesman, member of the same tribe

contríbulo –áre, 1, to crush, shatter

contrísto –áre, 1, to sadden, make sad

contrítio –ónis, f., grief, sorrow, contrition, detestation for past sins and determination to sin no more

contrítus –a –um, adj., contrite, sorrowful

controvérsia –ae, f., controversy

contubérnium –ii, n., intimacy, comradeship, a common dwelling

contúeor –éri –túitus sum, dep. 2, to look at attentively, consider

contúitus –us, m., mental contemplation

contumácia –ae, f., insolence

contumélia –ae, f., outrage, insult

contumélio –áre, 1, to outrage

contumeliósus –a –um, adj., contumelious

contúndo –ere –túdi –túsum, 3, to beat, bruise, subdue

conturbátio –ónis, f., trouble, vexation

contúrbo –áre, 1, to trouble, disquiet, disturb, throw into confusion

contútor –ári, dep. 1, to communicate with, keep safe

conúmero –áre, 1, to number among

conváleo –ére –válui, 2, to regain health, recover strength

convalésco –ére –válui, 2, to gain strength

convá11is –is, f., valley

convéllo –ere –vélli –vúlsum, 3, to pluck or tear up

convéniens –éntis, adj., agreeing

conveniénter, adv., duly, suitably

conveniéntia –ae, f., agreement

convénio –íre, 4, to come together, agree, assemble, be convenient

conventículum –i, n., gathering, assembly, meeting

convéntio –ónis, f., concord, agreement

Conventuális, a conventual Franciscan

conventuális –e, adj., conventual, pertaining to a convent

convéntus –us, m., an assembly, meeting, gathering, convent, religious community

convérgo –ere, 3, to incline together

conversátio –ónis, f., conversation, intercourse, conduct, manner of living

convérsio –ónis, *f.*, conversion, a moral change

convérso –áre, *1,* to turn around

convérsor –ári, *dep. 1,* to converse, dwell, live, pass one's life

convérsus –a –um, *adj.,* converse, changed, turned around

convérto –ere –vérti –vérsum, *3,* to change, convert, turn, alter, refresh

convéscor –i, *dep. 3,* to eat with

convícior, *see* convitior

convícium –ii, *n.,* insult, reproach

convínco –ere –víci –víctum, *3,* to convict

convítior –ári, *dep. 1,* to revile, reproach

convivántes –ium, *m. pl.,* banqueters

convivífico –áre, *1,* to quicken together with

convívium –ii, *n.,* banquet

convívor –ári, *dep. 1,* to feast with

cónvoco –áre, *1,* to call together

convólvo –ere –vólvi –volútum, *3,* to roll up

cooperátor –óris, *m.,* a fellow helper

coopério –íre –pérui –pértum, *4,* to clothe, cover

coópero –áre, *1,* to co-operate

coóperor –ári, *dep. 1,* to work with

coopertórium –ii, *n.,* a cover

coopértus –a –um, *adj.,* clothed, arrayed

cooptátio –ónis, *f.,* admission to an Order or society, a joining

coópto –áre, *1,* to elect, join together, make fit, form, get ready

cophínus –i, *m.,* a basket, a hod

cópia –ae, *f.,* plenty, abundance, store

copiósitas –átis, *f.,* abundance

copiósus –a –um, *adj.,* copious, plentiful, great, in great numbers

Copta –ae, *m.,* a Copt, an Egyptian Christian

Cópticus –a –um, *adj.,* pertaining to the Coptic rite

cópula –ae, *f.,* union

cópulo –áre, *1,* to join together, bless a marriage, join in marriage

cópulor –ári, *dep. 1,* to embrace, be united with

coquo –ere, coxi, coctum, *3,* to cook, bake, boil

cor, cordis, *n.,* heart

corbóna –ae, *f.,* treasury

cordíger –era –um, *adj.,* wearing a cord

Core, *indecl.,* a descendant of Levi, who rebelled against Moses.

Corínthus –i, *f.,* Corinth, the capital of Achia Proper, on the isthmus between the Peloponnesus and the mainland between the Gulf of Lepanto and the Gulf of Aegina.

córneus –a –um, *adj.,* made of horn

cornícula –ae, *f.,* a little crow

cornu –us, *n.,* a horn, a mountaintop, the side of an altar

cornucópium –ii, *n.,* a bracket for holding candles

cornútus –a –um, *adj.,* horned

corollárium –ii, *n.,* corollary

coróna –ae, *f.,* a crown, wreath, circle, a tonsure, eternal reward

coronátio –ónis, *f.,* coronation, the act of crowning

coronátor –óris, *m.,* a bestower, crowner

coronátus –a –um, *adj.,* crowned

corónis –ídis, *f.,* a cornice

coróno –áre, *1,* to crown

corporális –e, *adj.,* corporal, pertaining to the body

corporáliter, *adv.,* bodily, with one body

corpóreus –a –um, *adj.,* corporal, bodily

corpuléntia –ae, *f.,* density, corporeity

corpuléntus –a –um, *adj.,* corporeal, physical

corpus –oris, *n.,* body

Corpus Christi, a feast in honor of the Blessed Sacrament. The Thursday after Trinity Sunday.

corpúsculum –i, *n.,* a small body

corréctio –ónis, *f.,* correction, chastisement, rebuke, reproval

corréptio –ónis, *f.,* rebuke, reproach

corrígia –ae, *f.,* a latchet, a shoe lace

córrigo –ere –réxi –réctum, *3,* to establish, correct, make straight, seize, pull together

corróboro –áre, *1,* to strengthen

corrogátio –ónis, *f.,* contribution, gathering, assemblage

corrósio –ónis, *f.,* gnawing

corrúmpens –éntis, *adj.,* baleful

corrúmpo –ere –rúpi –rúptum, *3,* to corrupt, pervert

córruo –ere •–rui, *3,* to fall to the ground, sink down, be ruined

corruptélla –ae, *f.,* bribery, corruption

corruptíbilis –e, *adj.,* corruptible

corruptíbilitas –átis, *f.,* corruptibility

corrúptio –ónis, *f.,* corruption

corrúptus –a –um, *adj.,* corrupted

cortína –ae, *f.,* a curtain, caldron, kettle

corus –i, *m.,* a measure, a bushel

coruscámen –inis, n., splendor
coruscátio –ónis, f., lightning, a flash
corúsco –áre, 1, to shine, glitter
corúscus –i, m., lightning
corvus –i, m., a raven
costa –ae, f., a rib, side
cóstula –ae, f., a rib
cotta –ae, f., a surplice
cotúrnix –icis, f., a quail
coútor, coúti, coúsus sum, dep. 3, to communicate with, deal with
crápula –ae, f., drunkenness
crapulátus –a –um, adj., inebriated, surfeited
cras, adv., tomorrow
crassíties –ei, f., thickness, fatness
crassus –a –um, adj., fat, thick
crástinus –a –um, adj., relating to tomorrow
crater –eris, m., a bowl
cratícula –ae, f., a grating, gridiron
cratis –is, f., a grating, gridiron
creábilis, adj., that which can be created
creátio –ónis, f., creation, appointment
creátor –óris, m., creator. A title belonging in the strict sense to God alone, the absolute and first cause of all things.
creatúra –ae, f., creature, that which has been made out of nothing by God
crebrésco –ere, crébui, 3, to become frequent, grow strong, repeat often, increase, spread
crebro, adv., frequently, often
credéntia –ae, f., a small table for cruets, etc.
credentiárius –ii, m., the server at the credence table
credíbilis, adj., trustworthy
créditor –óris, m., creditor
créditus –a –um, adj., entrusted
credo –ere –didi –ditum, 3, to trust, believe
credúlitas –átis, f., belief, faith
crémium –ii, n., fuel, firewood, tinder, dry fuel
cremo –áre, 1, to burn
creo –áre, 1, to create
crepído –ónis, f., base, foot
crepitáculum –i, n., a clapper or rattle used in Holy Week instead of a bell
crépito –áre, 1, to crack, crackle, crash
crépitus –us, m., an explosion
crepo –áre –ui –itum, 1, to crack, burst asunder, resound

crepúsculum –i, n., twilight, the dusk of evening
cresco –ere, crevi, cretum, 3, to grow, increase, spring up
creta –ae, f., chalk
cribro –áre, 1, to sift
crimen –inis, n., sin, guilt, crime, accusation, charge
criminátor –óris, m., detractor
criminátrix –ícis, f., a slanderer, false witness, false accuser
crímino –áre, 1, to accuse
críminor –ári, dep. 1, to accuse
criminósus –a –um, adj., criminal, reproachful, slanderous, calumnious
cróceus –a –um, adj., scarlet, saffron, orange color
crócia –ae, f., a crosier, long mantle with cape and sleeves
crócio –íre, 4, to croak as a raven
crotálum –i, n., a clapper used instead of a bell in Holy Week
crotálus –i, m., a clapper used instead of a bell in Holy Week
cruciáta –ae, f., a crusade
cruciátio –ónis, f., torment, punishment
cruciátor –óris, m., crusader
cruciátus –us, m., torment, torture
crúcifer –eri, m., a cross-bearer
crucifígo –ere –fíxi –fíxum, 3, to crucify
crucifíxus –i, m., a crucifix
crúcio –áre, 1, to torment, torture, crucify (with reference to God)
crucisignátio –ónis, f., signing with the Sign of the Cross
crudélis –e, adj., cruel
crúditas –átis, f., the crudity of undigested food, an overloading of the stomach
crudus –a –um, adj., raw
cruénto –áre, 1, to lash, torment
cruéntus –a –um, adj., bleeding
cruor –óris, m., gore, blood, blood which flows from a wound
crurifrágium –ii, n., the breaking of the legs of crucified felons
crus, cruris, n., a leg
crústula –ae, f., a small cake
crux, crucis, f., a cross, an instrument of suffering, the cross of Christ
crux commíssa, a cross shaped like a letter T
crux decussáta, a cross shaped like a letter X
crux immíssa, a cross with a transverse arm

crypta –ae, *f.*, a catacomb, a crypt, vault, basement

crystállum –i, *n.*, a crystal

crystállus –i, *m.*, crystal, ice

cubiculárius –ii, *m.*, a private chamberlain

cubículum –i, *n.*, a bedroom, chamber

cubíle –is, *n.*, a bed, couch, den

cúbitum –i, *n.*, the forearm, a cubit

cúbitus –us, *m.*, a cubit

cubo –áre –ui –itum, *1,* to lie down, recline

cucúlla –ae, *f.*, a cowl or choir cloak

cucullátus –a –um, *adj.*, wearing a cowl

cucúllus –i, *m.*, a cowl

cucumerárium –ii, *n.*, a garden of cucumbers

cudo –ere, cudi, cusum, *3,* to beat, pound, stamp, coin

cuicuímodi, of what kind soever

culcíta –ae, *f.*, a bed, mattress, bolster, pillow, cushion, couch

cúlcitra –ae, *f.*, a bed, mattress, bolster, pillow, cushion, couch

cúleus –i, *m.*, a leather sack

culína –ae, *f.*, kitchen, victuals

culmen –inis, *n.*, summit, top, height

culmus –i, *m.*, a stalk

culpa –ae, *f.*, guilt, fault, error, sin, the inclination to sin

culpábilis –e, *adj.*, blameworthy

culpátus –a –um, *adj.*, blameworthy

culpo –áre, *1,* to blame, disapprove, find fault with

culte, *adv.*, elegantly

cultéllus –i, *m.*, a little knife

culter –tri, *m.*, a knife

cultor –óris, *m.*, a planter, cultivator, dresser, professor, worshiper

cultrix –icis, *f.*, a worshiper

cultúra –ae, *f.*, worship

cultus –us, *m.*, cultivation, care, adornment, worship, respect, reverence

cultus sociális, a common public service

cumulátius, *adv.*, more fully

cumulatívus –a –um, *adj.*, accruing

cumulátus –a –um, *adj.*, enlarged, increased, heaped up

cúmulo –áre, *1,* to increase, fill up, heap up

cúmulus –i, *m.*, a pile, heap, mass, addition

cunae –árum, *f.*, cradle, early childhood, a nest of young birds

cunctans –ántis, *adj.*, slow, lingering, loitering

cunctor –ári, *dep. 1,* to tarry, delay

cunctus –a –um, *adj.*, all, the whole

cúneus –i, *m.*, a wedge

cunículus –i, *m.*, a mine

cúpide, *adv.*, warmly, eagerly, vehemently, passionately

cupíditas –átis, *f.*, eager desire, greed, avarice

cupído –inis, *f.*, desire, longing

cúpidus –a –um, *adj.*, wishful, eager, desirous

cúpiens –entis, *adj.*, desirous

cupiénter, *adv.*, eagerly

cúpio –íre, *4,* to long for, desire, wish for

cupítor –óris, *m.*, one who desires

cuppa –ae, *f.*, the cup of a chalice

cura –ae, *f.*, care, solicitude, attention to

curátio –ónis, *f.*, cure, healing, attention

curátor –óris, *m.*, a curate

curátus –i, *m.*, a curate, an assistant pastor

cúria –ae, *f.*, court

Cúria Romána, the Papal Court

Cúria triumphális, the Church Triumphant

curiósus –a –um, *adj.*, attentive, diligent, careful

curo –áre, *1,* to heal, cure, take care of, pay attention to

currens –éntis, *adj.*, current

curro –ere, cucúrri, cucúrsum, *3,* to run, to run the course of life

currus –i, *m.*, a chariot

cursim, *adv.*, hastily, quickly

cúrsito –áre, *1,* to run up and down

cursor –óris, *m.*, a runner, messenger

cursus –us, *m.*, a course, voyage, a career, the Divine Office or Breviary

Cursus Mariánus, the Little Office of the Blessed Virgin

curto –áre, *1,* to lessen, abbreviate

curtus –a –um, *adj.*, shortened

curvatúra –ae, *f.*, the crook of a crosier, a curve

curvésco –ere, *3,* to bend over

curvo –áre, *1,* to bend, bow, humble

curvus –a –um, *adj.*, bent, bowed, arched, curved, crooked

cuspis –idis, *f.*, the point of a nail or a spear, a sharp point

cussínus –i, *m.*, a cushion

custódia –ae, *f.*, watch, cell, prison, care, guard, pyx

custódiens –entis, *m.*, a keeper

custódio –íre, *4,* to guard, watch, protect, preserve

custodítio –ónis, *f.,* the observance of the law

custos –ódis, *m.,* attendant, guardian, watchman, overlooker

custos mártyrum, a keeper of the relics of martyrs

cutícula –ae, *f.,* the skin

cutis –is, *f.,* the skin

cýathus –i, *m.,* a tumbler, cup

cyclas –adis, *f.,* a robe

cyclus –i, *m.,* a cycle, circle

cycnéus –a –um, *adj.,* pertaining to a swan

cycnus –i, *m.,* a swan

cymba –ae, *f.,* a small boat

cýmbalum –i, *n.,* cymbal

cýnicus –i, *m.,* a cynic

Cýnicus –a –um, *adj.,* pertaining to Cynic philosophy

cypressínus –a –um, *adj.,* pertaining to cypress

cypréssus –i, *f.,* a cypress tree

cyprus –i, *f.,* cypress, henna

Cyrenaéus –a –um, *adj.,* of Cyrene

Cyrenaícus –a –um, *adj.,* of Cyrene

Cyréne –es, *f.,* Cyrene

D

daemon –ónis, *m.,* an evil spirit, demon, devil

daemoniácus –i, *m.,* a possessed person

daemoniácus –a –um, *adj.,* demoniacal

daemónium –ii, *n.,* an evil spirit, demon, devil

Daemon Mutus, Oculi Sunday, the third Sunday in Lent

dalmática –ae, *f.,* a dalmatic, the vestment of a deacon

Damáscus –i, *m.,* Damascus, the most ancient and important city in Syria. It is mentioned in the time of Abraham. St. Paul began his ministry at Damascus, A.D. 33.

damnábilis –e, *adj.,* worthy of condemnation, damnation, eternal punishment

damnáta stirps, the human race condemned on account of Adam's fall

damnátio –ónis, *f.,* condemnation, damnation

damno –áre, *1,* to condemn

damnóse, *adv.,* ruinously

damnósus –a –um, *adj.,* harmful, mistaken

damnum –i, *n.,* punishment, injury, damage, loss, evil

dámula –ae, *f.,* a doe, gazelle

daps, dapis, *f.,* food, meal, banquet

dápsilis –e, *adj.,* plentiful

Datária –ae, *f.,* the Dataria, a bureau for benefices

Datárius –ii, *m.,* the head of a Dataria

dátio –ónis, *f.,* a giving

dator –óris, *m.,* a giver

datum –i, *n.,* a gift

dea –ae, *f.,* a goddess

dealbátus –a –um, *adj.,* bright

deálbo –áre, *1,* to make white, whitewash, purify

deambulácrum –i, *n.,* a gallery, corridor

deámbulo –áre, *1,* to walk about, walk much, circumlocute

deargénto –áre, *1,* to plate with silver

deaurátus –a –um, *adj.,* gilded

deaúro –áre, *1,* to cover with gold, gild

De Auxíliis, a theological dispute between Jesuits and Dominicans in the sixteenth–seventeenth century, concerning the *auxilia* or helps of grace

de Beáta, Office or Mass of the B.V.M.

debéllo –áre, *1,* to wage war

débeo –ére –ui –itum, *2,* to owe, ought

débilis –e, *adj.,* maimed, feeble, weak, infirm

debílitas –átis, *f.,* weakness

debilitátio –ónis, *f.,* a weakening, weakness

debílito –áre, *1,* to weaken

débitor –óris, *m.,* a debtor

débitrix –ícis, *f.,* a female debtor

débitum –i, *n.,* a debt, sin

débitus –a –um, *adj.,* due, owed

decachórdus –a –um, *adj.,* ten-stringed

decálogus –i, *m.,* the Decalogue, the Ten Commandments

decanátus –us, *m.,* a deanery, deanship

decantátio –ónis, *f.,* singing

decánto –áre, *1,* to sing, repeat often

decánus –i, *m.,* a dean, one having authority over ten

decas –adis, *f.*, a decade, a set of ten

decémber –bris, *m.*, the month of December

decénni –ae, ten years

decénnis, *adv.*, at the age of ten

decénnium –ii, *n.*, a period of ten years

decens –éntis, *adj.*, seemly, becomingly

decénter, *adv.*, fittingly

decéptio –ónis, *f.*, deception

decéptor –óris, *m.*, a deceiver, enemy

decérno –ere –crévi –crétum, *3*, to determine, intend, ordain, decree, decide

decérpo –ere –cérpsi –cérptum, *3*, to take away, pull away, pluck

decérto –áre, *1*, to strive

decéssio –ónis, *f.*, a going away

decéssor –óris, *m.*, a predecessor

décidens –éntis, fading

décido –ere –cídi, *3*, to fall down, wither, die

decído –ere –cídi, *3*, to cut off

décima –ae, *f.*, a tithe, tenth

decimátio –ónis, *f.*, tithe

décimo –áre, *1*, to levy a tithe

decípio –ere –cépi –céptum, *3*, to deceive, catch, snare, beguile

decípula –ae, *f.*, a snare, trap

declamátio –ónis, *f.*, declaration, loud speaking

declarátio –ónis, *f.*, declaration

declaratórius –a –um, *adj.*, declaratory

decláro –áre, *1*, to make clear, show, demonstrate

declíno –áre, *1*, to incline, lean to one side, turn away, step away, go aside

declívis –e, *adj.*, sloping, inclined downward

decóctus –a –um, *adj.*, ripened

de condígno, out of worthiness

de cóngruo, out of suitability

decóqueo –ere –cóxi –cóctum, *3*, to boil, roast, cook, melt down

decor –óris, *m.*, beauty, comeliness, elegance

décoro –áre, *1*, to adorn, decorate, to endow, to honor

decórtico –áre, *1*, to strip bare, tear off the bark

decórus –a –um, *adj.*, beauteous, comely, fitting, seemly

decrépitus –a –um, *adj.*, infirm

decrésco –ere –crévi –crétum, *3*, to decrease, wane, disappear

decreméntum –i, *n.*, a decree

decretália –órum, *n. pl.*, decretals

decretális –e, *adj.*, pertaining to decree

decretórius –a –um, *adj.*, imperative, decisive, peremptory

decrétum –i, *n.*, a decree

decúmbo –ere –cúbui, *3*, to lie down

decúrio –ónis, *m.*, counselor, a captain over ten men

decúrro –ere –cucúrri *or* –cúrri –cúrsum, *3*, to run through, trickle down

decúrsus –us, *m.*, a water course, a stream, a running down, a passing (of years)

decus –óris, *n.*, beauty, grace, glory, honor

decússo –áre, *1*, to cross

dédecens –éntis, *adj.*, unbecoming

dedecórus –a –um, *adj.*, shameful, vile

dédecus –oris, *n.*, shame, dishonor

dedicátio –ónis, *f.*, dedication

dédico –áre, *1*, to dedicate, consecrate

dedignátio –ónis, *f.*, scorn, indignation

dedígnor –ári, *dep. 1*, to disdain, scorn, reject as being unworthy

déditus –a –um, *adj.*, devoted

dedo, dédidi, déditum, *3*, to give up

dedúco –ere –dúxi –dúctum, *3*, to conduct, lead, bring down, lead away

dedúctor –óris, *m.*, a deserter

deféctus –us, *m.*, defect, failing, ceasing, disappearing, sin

deféndo –ere –féndi –fénsum, *3*, to defend, repel, guard

defénsio –ónis, *f.*, defense, protection

defénso –áre, *1*, to protect, defend

defénsor –óris, *m.*, a defender

défero –férre –tuli –látum, *3*, to bring, bring down, submit

defetíscor, defetísci, deféssus sum, *3*, to become weary or tired out

defício –ere –féci –féctum, *3*, to fail, faint, be wanting, pine for, waste, vanish, part from

defígo –ere –fíxi –fíxum, *3*, to fix, fasten, define

definio –íre, *4*, to solve, define, determine

definítio –ónis, *f.*, determination, measure, definition

definítor –óris, *m.*, one who defines

defíxus –a –um, *adj.*, fixed

deflagrátio –ónis, *f.*, a burning, consuming by fire

deflágro –áre, *1*, to be burnt down, be consumed by fire

deflécto –ere –fléxi –fléctum, *3*, to turn aside

défleo –ére –flévi –flétum, *2,* to weep over, bewail, lament

défluo –ere –flúxi –flúxum, *3,* to pass away, wither, fall, cease, vanish, disappear, flow from

déforis, *adv.,* from the outside, outside, from without

defórmis –e, *adj.,* deformed, misshapen

defórmo –áre, *1,* to engrave

defraúdo –áre, *1,* to cheat, defraud

defúnctio –ónis, *f.,* death

defúnctus –a –um, *adj.,* dead, deceased

defúngor –fúngi –fúnctus sum, *dep. 3,* to depart, die, finish, complete, discharge

dégener –eris, *adj.,* ignoble, unworthy

degenerátio –ónis, *f.,* degeneration

deglútio –íre, *4,* to swallow, swallow up

dego –ere, degi, *3,* to live, spend time

degradátus –a –um, *adj.,* deprived of office

degústo –áre, *1,* to taste, partake of

dehortátor –óris, *m.,* one who dissuades

déifer –era –erum, *adj.,* God-bearing

deífico –áre, *1,* to make a god

deíficus –a –um, *adj.,* rendering godlike, deific

deínceps, *adv.,* henceforth, again, any longer, any more, in order of succession

deínde, *adv.,* then, finally

deíntus, *adv.,* from within

Deípara –ae, *f.,* Mother of God

Deipnon (Greek), *n.,* a banquet, the Mass

Déitas –átis, *f.,* divinity, deity, Godhead

dejéctus –a –um, *adj.,* fallen, low-lying

dejício –ere –jéci –jéctum, *3,* to caste down, break down, hurl down

dejúro –áre, *1,* to swear solemnly

delábor –i –lápsus sum, *dep. 3,* to fall down, glide down, sink

delátor –óris, *m.,* a bearer, cross-bearer

delatúra –ae, *f.,* an accusation

delectábilis –e, *adj.,* delightful

delectaméntum –i, *n.,* delight, sweetness, a source of delight or pleasure

delectátio –ónis, *f.,* delight, pleasure

delécto –áre, *1,* to rejoice, be delighted

deléctus –us, *m.,* a choice, selection, a levy

delegátus –us, *m.,* delegate

délego –áre, *1,* to entrust, assign

déleo –ére –évi –étum, *2,* to wash out, blot out, destroy, annihilate, abolish

delibátio –ónis, *f.,* first fruit

deliberátio –ónis, *f.,* deliberation, consultation

deliberátus –a –um, *adj.,* deliberate

delíbero –áre, *1,* to consider, consult about

délibo –áre, *1,* to sacrifice, take away a little, cull, pluck, gather

delíbuo –ere –ui –utum, *3,* to destroy, wash away, blot out, anoint, besmear

delicátus –a –um, *adj.,* delightful

delícia –ae, *f.,* delight

deliciósus –a –um, *adj.,* delicious, pleasant, fond of pleasure, voluptuous

delícium –ii, *n.,* delight

delictórum reátus, sin

delíctum –i, *n.,* crime, sin, dishonor, offense, fault

déligo –ere –légi –léctum, *3,* to choose, resolve, wish

delíneo –áre, *1,* to outline, prophesy

delínquo –ere –líqui –líctum, *3,* to fail, offend, sin, do wrong

delíquium –i, *n.,* fluidity, instability

delitésco –ere –tui, *3,* to lie hidden

delúbrum –i, *n.,* a temple, shrine

delúdo –ere –lúdi –lúsum, *3,* to mock, delude, cheat

demándo –áre, *1,* to entrust, give in charge

demélior –íri, *dep. 4,* to consume, destroy, demolish, lay waste

deméntia –ae, *f.,* madness, insanity, foolishness

deménto –áre, *1,* to craze, deceive

deméreor –éri, *dep. 2,* to deserve

demérgo –ere –mérsi –mérsum, *3,* to sink, drown, submerge, plunge into, swallow

deméritum –i, *n.,* defect, demerit

demétior –íre –metitus sum, *dep. 4,* to measure, mete out

Demétrias –ádis, *f.,* Demetrias, to whom St. Jerome addressed one of his Epistles

deminorátio –ónis, *f.,* decrease, loss

demínuo –ere –ui –útum, *3,* to lessen, make less

demíror –ári, *dep. 1,* to wonder at, be amazed

demísse, *adv.,* humbly

demíssio –ónis, *f.,* lowliness

demíssus –a –um, *adj.,* lowly, humble

demítto –ere –mísi –míssum, *3,* to sink, settle, lie down, forgive sins

demo –ere, dempsi, demptum, *3,* to take away

demonstrátio –ónis, *f.*, a pointing out, description

demónstro –áre, *1*, to show, demonstrate, discover

demorátio –ónis, *f.*, lingering, abiding

demórior –móri –mórtuus sum, *dep. 3*, to die

demóror –ári, *dep. 1*, to dwell, abide, linger, delay, retard

demóveo –ére –móvi –mótum, *2*, to remove, move away

demúlceo –ére –múlsi –múlsum *or* –múlctum, *2*, to persuade, soften

demum, *adv.*, at last, at length, then at last, now at last

demúto –áre, *1*, to change

denárius –ii, *n.*, a penny (a Roman coin worth about twenty cents)

dénego –áre, *1*, to deny, refuse, reject

denotátio –ónis, *f.*, a mark of disgrace

denóto –áre, *1*, to denote, specify, mark out, point out

dens –tis, *m.*, tooth

densus –a –um, *adj.*, thick

denticulátum –i, *n.,* lace

denticulátus –a –um, *adj.*, pointed

denúbo –ere –núpsi –núptum, *3*, to marry, be married

denudátio –ónis, *f.*, the act of stripping

denúdo –áre, *1*, to lay bare, strip

denuntiátio –ónis, *f.*, denunciation, report, announcement, publication

denúntio –áre, *1*, to threaten

dénuo, *adv.*, a second time, again

deórsum, *adv.*, lower, down, beneath, downward

deósculor –ári, *dep. 1*, to kiss

depásco –ere –pávi –pástum, *3*, to feed upon, consume

depéllo –ere –púli –púlsum, *3*, to drive away, dispel

depéndeo –ére –pepéndi, *2*, to hang down, depend

depíngo –ere –pínxi –píctum, *3*, to paint, to depict

deplóro –áre, *1*, to deplore, grieve over

depóno –ere –pósui –pósitum, *3*, to take down, bring down, throw down, remove, separate, lay

depopulátio –ónis, *f.*, laying waste, plundering

depópulor –ári, *dep. 1*, to ravage

depórto –áre, *1*, to banish

depósco –ere –popósci, *3*, to demand, appoint, beseech

depositio –ónis, *f.*, deposition, burial, laying aside, putting away, putting on, day of death

Depositio S. Maríae Vírginis, a name for the Assumption of the Blessed Virgin

depositus –a –um, *adj.*, divested, laid out dead

depraédo –áre, *1*, to rob

depraédor –ári, *dep. 1*, to plunder

depravátio –ónis, *f.*, depravity

deprávo –áre, *1*, to corrupt, pervert

deprecábilis, –e, *adj.*, gracious, merciful

deprecátio –ónis, *f.*, prayer, supplication, entreaty

deprecátor –óris, *m.*, a pleader, intercessor

deprecatórius –a –um, *adj.*, pertaining to a prayer or request

déprecor –ári, *dep. 1*, to entreat, pray, supplicate

deprehéndo –ere –prehéndi –prehénsum, *3*, to perceive, find, seize, take

déprimo –ere –préssi –préssum, *3*, to press down, weigh down, afflict, oppress

deprómo –ere –prómpsi –prómptum, *3*, to bring out, produce, pour out

depudésco –ere, *3*, to become shameless

depúlsio –ónis, *f.*, a driving off, defense

depúrgo –áre, *1*, to wash

députo –áre, *1*, to depute, appoint, count, number among, class among, cut off, prune, condemn

derelíctio –ónis, *f.*, a forsaking, deserting

derelínquo –ere –líqui –líctum, *3*, to abandon, leave, forsake

derepénte, *adv.*, suddenly

derídeo –ére –rísi –rísum, *2*, to deride, laugh at, mock, scoff at

derípio –ere –rípui –réptum, *3*, to tear away, snatch away

derísus –us, *m.*, derision, scorn, mockery

derívo –áre, *1*, to convey aboard, divert

dérogo –áre, *1*, to detract from

desaévio –íre –ii –ítum, *4*, to rage violently

descéndo –ere –scéndi –scénsum, *3*, to descend, come down, go down, run down

descénsio –ónis, *f.*, descent

descénsus –us, *m.*, descent

descísco –ere –scívi –scítum, *3*, to withdraw, be true to oneself

descríbo –ere –scrípsi –scríptum, *3*, to describe, enroll, represent, delineate, copy

descríptio –ónis, *f.,* description, enrolling, a record, entry, census

désero –ere –sérui –sértum, *3,* to neglect, forsake

desérsum, *adv.,* from above

desértio –ónis, *f.,* desertion, neglect, treason

desértor –óris, *m.,* one who abandons or deserts, a rebel

desértum –i, *n.,* a desert, wilderness

desértus –a –um, *adj.,* deserted, desolate, arid

desérvio –íre, *4,* to serve

deses –ídis, *adj.,* lazy, idle, slothful

desiderábilis –e, *adj.,* desirable

desidérium –ii, *n.,* desire, lust, pining for, yearning for

desídero –áre, *1,* to desire, long for, earnestly wish for

desídia –ae, *f.,* sloth

desígno –áre, *1,* to appoint, signify

desilio –íre –sílui –súltum, *4,* to leap

désino –ere –sívi *or* –sii –sítum, *3,* to cease, leave off, close

desolátio –ónis, *f.,* desolation, ruin

desolatórius –a –um, *adj.,* destroying

desolatórius –i, *m.,* a destroyer

desolátus –a –um, *adj.,* desolate

desólo –áre, *1,* to lay waste, bring to desolation, leave alone, forsake

despéctio –ónis, *f.,* contempt, *also* an outcast

desperáte, *adv.,* desperately

desperátio –ónis, *f.,* despair, desperation

despéro –áre, *1,* to despair

despicábilis –e, *adj.,* unworthy

despício –ere –spéxi –spéctum, *3,* to look away from, neglect

despólio –áre, *1,* to strip

despóndeo –ére –spóndi –spónsum, *2,* to espouse, betroth

desponsátio –ónis, *f.,* a bethrothal

desponsátus –a –um, *adj.,* espoused

despónso –áre, *1,* to betroth

déspuo –ére –spui –spútum, *3,* to spit out

déstino –áre, *1,* to destine

destítuo –ére –stítui –stitútum, *3,* to abandon

destrúctor –óris, *m.,* a destroyer

déstruo –ere –strúxi –strúctum, *3,* to destroy

desuésco –ére –suévi –suétum, *3,* to put aside a custom

desum –ésse –fui, to fail, be wanting

desúmo –ere –súmpsi –súmptum, *3,* to select, choose

desúrsum, *adv.,* from above

détego –ere –téxi –téctum, *3,* to disclose, uncover

de témpore, of the ecclesiastical season

deténdo –ere –téndi –ténsum, *3,* to unstretch

deténtio –ónis, *f.,* abode

detérgeo –ére –térsi –térsum, *2,* to cancel, wipe away

detérior –ius, *comparative adj.,* inferior

determinátio –ónis, *f.,* determination

detérmino –áre, *1,* to determine, limit, bound

detérreo –ére –térrui –térritum, *2,* to prevent or deter by fear

detérrimus –a –um, *adj.,* worst

detéstor –ári, *dep. 1,* to curse

detíneo –ére –tínui –téntum, *2,* to withhold, detain

detórqueo –ére –tórsi –tórtum, *2,* to twist

détraho –ere –tráxi –tráctum, *3,* to slander, calumniate, apply, refer

detrécto –áre, *1,* to refuse, speak against, disparage

detriméntum –i, *n.,* a loss, detriment

detrúdo –ere –trúsi –trúsum, *3,* to thrust down, force away

Deus –i, *m.,* God, the Deity

devénio –íre –véni –véntum, *4,* to arrive at, come from

deversórium –ii, *n.,* lodging

devíncio –íre –vínxi –vínctum, *4,* to bind, fetter

devínco –ere –víci –víctum, *3,* to subdue, conquer

devíto –áre, *1,* to avoid, shun

dévius –a –um, *adj.,* devious, wandering from the way

dévoco –áre, *1,* to call down, call away

devólvo –ere –vólvi –volútum, *3,* to roll down

devorátio –ónis, *f.,* prey, devouring

devóro –áre, *1,* to devour, swallow, gulp down

devotátio –ónis, *f.,* a curse

devóte, *adv.,* devotedly, devoutly, faithfully, piously, submissively

devótio –ónis, *f.,* a vow, devotion, consecration

devótus –a –um, *adj.,* devoted, devout

devóveo –ere –vóvi –vótum, *3,* to devote

dexter –a –um *or* –tra –trum, *adj.,* right; *ad dextram,* at the right hand

déxtera –ae, *f.*, the right hand
dextéritas –átis, *f.*, skill, dexterity
dextra –ae, *f.*, the right hand
dextrále –is, *n.*, an armlet, a bracelet
dextralíolum –i, *n.*, a bracelet
diabólicus –a –um, *adj.*, diabolic, devilish, pertaining to the devil
diábolus –i, *m.*, the devil
díacon –is, *m.*, a deacon
diaconális –e, *adj.*, pertaining to a deacon
diaconándus –i, *m.*, one to be made a deacon
diaconátus –us, *m.*, diaconate, the order of deaconship
diaconía –ae, *f.*, a chapel, hospice
diacónicum –i, *n.*, a sacristy in the early churches
diaconíssa –ae, *f.*, a deaconess
diaconissátus –us, *m.*, the order of deaconess
diáconus –i, *m.*, a deacon
diadéma –atis, *n.*, a diadem, a crown
diálogus –i, *m.*, conversation, dialogue
Diána –ae, *f.*, a goddess of the Greeks and Romans
diapénte, *f.*, an interval of a fifth in music
diárium –ii, *n.*, a diary, a daily record
diatéssaron, *n.*, an interval of a fourth in music
dicanícium –ii, *n.*, a mace
dicastérium –ii, *n.*, an office
dicátus –a –um, *adj.*, hallowed, dedicated
dício –ónis, *f.*, domination
dico –áre, *1*, to devote, dedicate, consecrate
dico –ere, dixi, dictum, *3*, to say, tell, speak, relate
díctio –ónis, *f.*, language
dictor –óris, *m.*, speaker, orator
dictum –i, *n.*, word
dictus –us, *m.*, word, saying, command
Didascália Apostolórum, a treatise on the public life of the Church written in the third century
didráchma –ae, *f.*, a half shekel, a double drachma
didúco –ere –dúxi –dúctum, *3*, to divide, separate, draw apart
Dídymus –i, *m.*, a twin, the surname of St. Thomas the Apostle (John 20:24)
dies –éi, *m.* and *f.*, a day; *de die in diem,* from day to day; *in dies,* daily; *ad diem,* on the day
Dies epiphaniórum, the feast of the three appearances of our Lord, Jan. 6

Dies irae, hymn used as a Sequence in Requiem Masses, written in the thirteenth century by Thomas of Celano
Dies lúminum, a name for the Epiphany
dies natális, a birthday
Dies panis albi, a name formerly given to Maundy Thursday
diétim, *adv.*, daily, day by day
diffámo –áre, *1*, to accuse, slander, publish, spread abroad
dífferens –éntis, *adj.*, different
differéntia –ae, *f.*, difference
differéntior –ius, *adj.*, more different
díffero –érre, dístuli, dilátum, *2*, to defer, differ, cast off, put, spread, scatter
diffícile, *adv.*, with difficulty
diffícilis –e, *adj.*, difficult
difficúltas –átis, *f.*, obstinacy, difficulty
diffidéntia –ae, *f.*, unbelief, suspicion, disobedience, want of faith
diffído –ere –físus sum, *semi-dep. 3,* to mistrust
diffíndo –ere –fídi –físsum, *3*, to split, cleave, open
diffíteor –éri, *dep. 2*, to disavow, deny
díffluo –ere –flúxi –flúxum, *3*, to flow freely, fall out, dissolve, melt away
diffórmitas –átis, *f.*, disagreement, lack of conformity
diffúgio –ere –fúgi –fúgitum, *3*, to flee
diffúndo –ere –fúdi –fúsum, *3*, to pour forth, spread throughout
diffúsus –a –um, wide, extensive, spread out
dígero –ere –géssi –géstum, *3*, to digest, arrange
digéstus –a –um, *adj.*, set in order
dígitus –i, *m.*, a finger, toe
dignánter, *adv.*, worthily
dignátio –ónis, *f.*, condescension, graciousness, a sip of wine taken for courtesy
dignor –ári, *dep. 1*, to grant, vouchsafe
dignósco –ere –nóvi, *3*, to discern, distinguish
dignus –a –um, *adj.*, becoming, worthy, deserved
digrédior –i, *dep. 3*, to depart, digress
dijúdico –áre, *1*, to judge, examine, discern, discriminate, decide
dikérium (*or dikérion*), a double candlestick used by Greek bishops while blessing the people
dilácero –áre, *1*, to tear to pieces
dilánio –áre, *1*, to tear asunder, slander
dilárgio –íre, *4*, to give liberally

dilárgior –íri, *dep. 4,* to give liberally

dilátio –ónis, *f.,* delay

diláto –áre, *1,* to make broad, extend, enlarge, open wide

diléctio –ónis, *f.,* love

diléctus –a –um, *adj.,* beloved, lovely

dilículum –i, *n.,* dawn, daybreak

diligénter, *adv.,* diligently

diligéntia –ae, *f.,* diligence, accuracy, carefulness, attentiveness

diligéntius, *adv.,* more diligently, more carefully

díligo –ere –léxi –léctum, *3,* to love, prize, esteem highly

dilínio –áre, *1,* to disturb, harass, torture mentally

dilucésco –ere –lúxi, *3,* to grow light, become day

dilúcide, *adv.,* clearly

dilúcidus –a –um, *adj.,* lucid, sane

dilúculo, *adv.,* early

dilúculum –i, *n.,* dawn

díluo –ere –ui –útum, *3,* to efface, to wash

dilúvium –ii, *n.,* flood

dimáno –áre, *1,* to flow in different directions

diménsio –ónis, *f.,* reasoning, judgment

dimétior –íri –ménsus sum, *dep. 4,* to mete out, measure

dímico –áre, *1,* to fight, struggle

dimidiátus –a –um, *adj.,* half, divided in half

dimídio –áre, *1,* to divide in halves

dimídium –i, *n.,* the half, midst

dimídius –a –um, *adj.,* half, divided in half

dimínuo –ere –ui –útum, *3,* to diminish, lessen

dimissoriális –e, *adj.,* pertaining to a discharge or dismissal

dimítto –ere –mísi –míssum, *3,* to send away, dismiss, forgive, allow, permit, leave

dinúmero –áre, *1,* to number, count

dioecesánus –a –um, *adj.,* diocesan

dioecésis –is, *f.,* a diocese

dióryz –igis, *f.,* a canal, channel of a river

díplois –ídis, *f.,* a cloak, mantle, a double cloak

diplóma –atis, *n.,* a diploma, charter

dipóndium –ii, *n.,* two farthings

dipóndius –ii, *m.,* the weight of two farthings

dipsas –adis, *f.,* a kind of serpent

díptychon –i, *n.,* a diptych, a list of names of those to be commemorated in the Mass

dirécte, *adv.,* directly

diréctio –ónis, *f.,* direction, righteousness, uprightness

diréctor –óris, *m.,* a director

directórium –ii, *n.,* the Ordo

diréctum –i, *n.,* a straight line

diréctus –a –um, *adj.,* direct; in *dirécto,* the right way; in *diréctum,* without modulations, plain

dirémptio –ónis, *f.,* separation

diríbitor –óris, *m.,* a distributor

dírigo –ere –réxi –réctum, *3,* to direct, guide, straighten, set right

dírimo –ere –émi –émptum, *3,* to dissolve, discern, separate

dirípio –ere –rípui –réptum, *3,* to plunder, rob, despoil

dirúmpo –ere –rúpi –rúptum, *3,* to break asunder

díruo –ere –ui –útum, *3,* to destroy

dirus –a –um, *adj.,* fearful, dreadful, horrible

discalceátus –a –um, *adj.,* barefoot, unshod, discalced

discántus –us, *m.,* the upper voice in part singing

discédo –ere –céssi –céssum, *3,* to pass away, depart

disceptátio –ónis, *f.,* dispute

discépto –áre, *1,* to dispute, discuss, determine

discérno –ere –crévi –crétum, *3,* to distinguish, discern, separate

discérpo –ere –cérpsi –cérptum, *3,* to rend, tear

discéssio –ónis, *f.,* revolt, a going way

discéssus –us, *m.,* removal, departure

disciplína –ae, *f.,* discipline, chastisement, study, instruction, obedience to the law of God, knowledge, systematic training under authority, punishment with a view to correction

disciplína arcáni, "discipline of the secret." In the ancient Church some knowledge was kept from catechumens in order to shield teachings from misrepresentation

discipulátus –us, *m.,* discipleship

discípulus –i, *m.,* a disciple, a follower of our Lord or the Apostles

discíssus –a –um, *adj.,* rent, torn

disco –ere, dídici, *3,* to learn

díscolor –óris, *adj.*, speckled, of different colors

díscolus –a –um, *adj.*, deformed

discórdia –ae, *f.*, dissension, discord, disagreement

discórditer, *adv.*, disproportionally

discórdo –áre, *1*, to disagree

díscrepo –áre, *1*, to agree with, depart from

discrétio –ónis, *f.*, separation, discretion, power of distinguishing

discrétor –óris, *m.*, a discerner, judge

discrímen –inis, *n.*, peril, danger, hazard

discrimínále –is, *n.*, a hair pin

discrímino –áre, *1*, to braid, plait, to distinguish

discrúcio –áre, *1*, to torture

discúmbens –éntis, *m.*, a guest

discúmbo –ere –cúbui –cúbitum, *4*, to sit down, sit at table

discúrro –ere –cucúrri *or* –cúrri –cúrsum, *3*, to run to and fro

discus –i, *m.*, a dish, the Greek rite name for the paten

discússio –ónis, *f.*, dispersal

discútio –ere –cússi –cússum, *3*, to disperse, scatter

discúto –ere, *3*, to examine, discuss, inquire into

disérte, *adv.*, eloquently, distinctly, clearly, expressly

disertitúdo –inis, *f.*, eloquence

disértus –a –um, *adj.*, eloquent

dísgrego –áre, *1*, to rend asunder

disjício –ere –jéci –jéctum, *3*, to rend, scatter, disperse

disjúngo –ere –júnxi –júnctum, *3*, to put asunder

dispar –is, *adj.*, unlike, unequal, different

dísparo –áre, *1*, to part, divide, separate

dispéndo –ere –pénsus sum, *semi-dep. 3*, to dispense, weigh out

dispensátio –ónis, *f.*, dispensation, administration, management, stewardship, the relaxation of a law in a particular case

dispensátor –óris, *m.*, steward, dispenser

dispensatórius –a –um, *adj.*, dispensing, administering

dispénso –áre, *1*, to distribute, spread (of speech or writing)

dispérdo –ere –didi –ditum, *3*, to destroy, cut off

dispéreo –íre, –ii, *4*, to perish, be entirely ruined

dispérgo –ere –spérsi –spérsum, *3*, to scatter, disperse

dispérsio –ónis, *f.*, dispersal, scattering

dispértio –íre, *4*, to distribute, divide, part, separate

displíceo –ére –plícui –plícitum, *2*, to displease

dispóno –ere –pósui –pósitum, *3*, to order, dispose

dispósitio –ónis, *f.*, decree, disposition, providence

dispósitor –óris, *m.*, disposer

disputátio –ónis, *f.*, dispute, argumentation

dispúto –áre, *1*, to dispute, treat about, preach

disrúmpo –ere –rúpi –rúptum, *3*, to break asunder

dísseco –áre, *1*, to dry up

disséco –áre –sécui –séctum, *1*, to cut

disténsio –ónis, *f.*, quarrel, dissension

disséntio –íre –sénsi –sénsum, *4*, to dissent, disagree

díssero –ere –sérui –sertum, *3*, to discourse, converse, discuss, dispute, explain, expound

díssidens –éntis, *adj.*, dissenting, being at variance, inimical, discordant

dissídeo –ére –sédi –séssum, *2*, to disagree

disídium –ii, *n.*, a quarrel

dissílio –íre, *4*, to leap from one place to another

díssilo –áre, *1*, to be torn apart (of the mind)

dissimilitúdo –inis, *f.*, difference

dissímulo –áre, *1*, to conceal, dissemble, make alike

dissipátio –ónis, *f.*, desolation

díssipo –áre, *1*, to lay waste, destroy, scatter, abolish, waste

díssitus –a –um, *adj.*, widely scattered

dissolútio –ónis, *f.*, destruction, breaking down, annihilation

dissolútus –a –um, *adj.*, feeble, loose

dissólvo –ere –sólvi –solútum, *3*, to dissolve, loose, destroy, scatter

dissonántia –órum, *n. pl.*, difference, discord

dissuádeo –ére –suási –suásum, *2*, to advise against, speak against

distabésco –ere, *3*, to waste away, consume one's self

distans –ántis, *adj.*, distant, separate

distántia –ae, *f.*, distance

disténdo –ere –téndi –téntum *or* –ténsum, *3,* to stretch apart, rack, detract, perplex

disténtus –a –um, *adj.,* occupied, busy

distillátio –ónis, *f.,* bodily fluid

distíllo –áre, *1,* to drip, drop

distíncte, *adv.,* distinctly

distínctio –ónis, *f.,* distinction

distínctus –a –um, *adj.,* adorned, decorated

distíneo –ére –ui –téntum, *2,* to keep apart, separate

distínguo –ere –stínxi –stínctum, *3,* to divide, separate, discriminate, speak distinctly

disto –áre, *1,* to be apart, be distinct

distórtus –a –um, *adj.,* misshapen

distríbuo –ere –ui –útum, *3,* to distribute

distribútio –ónis, *f.,* distribution, allotment

distribútor –óris, *m.,* giver, distributor

distrícte, *adv.,* severely

distríctio –ónis, *f.,* strictness, severity

distríctus –us, *m.,* a district, division of territory

distúrbo –áre, *1,* to drive apart, thrust into confusion

ditátor –óris, *m.,* an enricher

dithalássus –a –um, *adj.,* open to two seas

dítio, –ónis, *f.,* sovereignty, power, dominion, authority

dítius, *adv.,* more abundantly

dito –áre, *1,* to endow, enrich, make wealthy

ditto –áre, *1,* to repeat, declare

diu, *adv.,* long, a long time; *quam diu,* as long as; *jam diu,* for a long time

diúrnum *or* diurnále, book of Hours

diúrnus –a –um, *adj.,* daily, per day, lasting for a day, pertaining to a day

diutúrnus –a –um, *adj.,* of long duration

divéllo –ere –vélli –vúlsum, *3,* to rend, tear asunder

divéndo –ere –véndidi –vénditum, *3,* to sell

diversífico –áre, *1,* to vary, be different

divérsitas –átis, *f.,* diversity, disagreement

diversórium –ii, *n.,* inn, lodging, stable

divérsus –a –um, *adj.,* different; *in divérsum,* back

divérto –ere –vérti, *3,* to turn aside, turn away

dives, dívitis, *m.,* rich, a rich man

divéxo –áre, *1,* to plunder, tear asunder

dívido –ere –vísi –vísum, *3,* to divide, part, put asunder

divinátio –ónis, *f.,* divination, seeking to know future or hidden things by unlawful means

divínitas –átis, *f.,* divinity, the Divine

divínitus, *adv.,* by divine help

divínus –a –um, *adj.,* divine

divisíbilis –e, *adj.,* divisible, separate

divísio –ónis, *f.,* part, portion, division

divítia –ae, *f.,* wealth; *in the plural,* riches

divórtium –ii, *n.,* divorce, division, separation

divórto, *same as* divérto

divúlgo –áre, *1,* to spread around

divus –a –um, *adj.,* divine

divus –i, *m.,* a saint

do, dare, dedi, datum, *1,* to give

dóceo –ére, dócui, doctum, *2,* to teach, instruct

docíbilis –e, *adj.,* teachable

dócilis –e, *adj.,* attentive, docile

docílitas –átis, *f.,* docility

doctor –óris, *m.,* doctor, teacher

doctorális –e, *adj.,* pertaining to the degree of doctor

Doctor Angélicus, The Angelic Doctor, St. Thomas Aquinas

Doctor Commúnis, The Universal Doctor, St. Thomas Aquinas

Doctor Ecstáticus, The Exalted Doctor, Denis the Carthusian

Doctor Eucharísticus, The Eucharistic Doctor, St. John Chrysostom

Doctor Exímius, The Excellent Doctor, Francis Suarez

Doctor Grátiae, The Doctor of Grace, St. Augustine of Hippo

Doctor Irrefragábilis, The Unanswerable Doctor, Alexander of Hales

Doctor Mariánus, Our Lady's Doctor, St. Anselm of Canterbury

Doctor Mellífluus, The Honeysweet Doctor, St. Bernard of Clairvaux

Doctor Mirábilis, The Marvelous Doctor, Roger Bacon

Doctor Seráphicus, The Seraphic Doctor, St. Bonaventure

Doctor Súbtilis, The Subtle Doctor, John Duns Scotus

Doctor Universális, The Universal Doctor, St. Albert the Great

doctrína –ae, *f.,* doctrine, instruction, teaching, learning

doctus –a –um, *adj.,* learned

documéntum –i, *n.,* document, example, proof, warning

dogma –atis, *n.*, dogma, edict, a defined doctrine, a statement on an accepted principle

dogmáticus –a –um, *adj.*, dogmatic, relating to a doctrine or dogma

dóleo –ére –ui, *2,* to grieve, suffer, be sorrowful

dolíolum –ii, *n.*, a cask, small keg

dólium –ii, *n.*, an earthenware cask

dolo –áre, *1,* to hew with an ax

dolor –óris, *m.*, dolor, sorrow, pain

dolorósus –a –um, *adj.*, sorrowful

dolóse *adv.*, deceitfully, treacherously

dolósitas –átis, *f.*, deceitfulness

dolósus –a –um, *adj.*, false, deceitful

dolus –i, *m.*, fraud, deceit, subtlety, guilt, craft, deception

doma –atis, *n.*, a roof, dwelling house

domésticus –a –um, *adj.*, domestic

doméstici –órum, *n.*, those of the household

domicelláris –is, *m.*, a candidate for a prebend

domicílium –ii, *n.*, house, home, dwelling, domicile, abode

dómina –ae, *f.*, lady, mistress

dominátio –ónis, *f.*, domination, rule, sovereignty

dominátor –óris, *m.*, ruler, lord

Domínica –ae, *f.*, Sunday

Domínica benedícta, Trinity Sunday, so called because the first words of the Introit are *Benedícta sit sancta Trínitas*

Domínica capitilávium, a name for Palm Sunday

Domínica carnis prívii, the Sunday before Lent

Domínica Competéntium, a name for Palm Sunday

Domínica daemon mutus, the third Sunday in Lent. The Gospel for this Sunday is about Jesus casting out a devil that was dumb.

Domínica de pánibus, Laetare Sunday. The Gospel tells about the multiplication of the loaves and fishes.

Domínica de Rosa, "Rose Sunday," a name for Laetare Sunday. On that Sunday the Pope blesses the Golden Rose.

Domínica Exsúrge, Exsúrge is the first word of the Introit of Sexagesima Sunday, hence a name for Sexagesima Sunday.

Domínica florum, Palm Sunday

Domínica Hosánna, Palm Sunday

Domínica in Albis, Low Sunday. In the early Church the newly baptized of Easter laid aside their white robes on this day.

Domínica indulgéntiae, another name for Palm Sunday

Domínica major, a Sunday of the first order (this classification now abolished)

Domínica mediána, a name for Laetare Sunday because it is the middle of Lent

Domínica nova, a name for Low Sunday

Domínica Pastor Bonus, the second Sunday after Easter — "Good Shepherd" Sunday. The Gospel of the Good Shepherd is read.

Domínica Quintána, a name for the first Sunday in Lent, which is the fifth Sunday before Passiontide

Domínica Ramispálma, a name for Palm Sunday

Domínica refectiónis, a name for Laetare Sunday

Domínica repus, Passion Sunday

Domínica Resurrectiónis, Easter Sunday, Resurrection Day

Domínica Resurréxi, another name for Easter Sunday. *Resurréxi* is the first word of the Introit for Easter Sunday.

Domínica Rosa, Laetare Sunday. (*See* Domínica de Rosa.)

Domínica Rosárum, a former name for the Sunday after the Ascension

Domínica Spíritus Dómini, Pentecost or Whit Sunday. *Spíritus Dómini* are the first words of the Introit.

Domínica vacans, Reminiscere Sunday, the second Sunday in Lent. Originally it had no special office.

Domínicae vagae, the 3rd, 4th, 5th, and 6th Sundays after the Epiphany. When Easter is early these Sundays are observed before Advent.

dominicále –is, *n.*, a small linen cloth in which the faithful received the consecrated bread at Mass

dominicális –e, *adj.*, pertaining to Sunday, or to the Lord

Dominicánus –a –um, *adj.*, Dominican

domínicum –i, *n.*, a church together with all its possessions

Domínicum –i, *n.*, the Holy Eucharist

domínicus –a –um, *adj.*, pertaining to the Lord, or of or belonging to a master

dóminor –ári, *dep. 1,* to rule, dominate, give dominion over, prevail over

dóminus –i, *m.*, lord, master, possessor, owner, ruler; *Dóminus,* the Lord
domnus –i, *m.*, lord, master
domo –áre –ui –itum, *1,* to conquer, **domúncula** –ae, *f.*, a little dwelling
domus –us *or* –i, *f.*, a house
donárium –ii, *n.*, a shrine
donátio –ónis, *f.*, giving, gift, donation
donátor –óris, *m.*, a giver
dono –áre, *1,* to give, grant, forgive, remit a debt, forgive a sin
donum –i, *n.*, a gift, present
dórmio –íre, *4,* to sleep, lie down to rest
dormitátio –ónis, *f.*, slumber
dormítio –ónis, *f.*, sleep, repose
Dormítio B. Maríae, the feast of the Assumption
dormíto –áre, *1,* to sleep, be lazy
dorsuále –is, *n.*, the back seat of a chair, curtain hung around the rear of an altar
dorsum –i, *n.*, the back
dos, dotis, *f.*, a gift
doto –áre, *1,* to endow
doxológia –ae, *f.*, the doxology
drachma –ae, *f.*, a drachma, small Greek coin, small coin bearing the image of the reigning king
draco –ónis, *m.*, a dragon, snake, demon
draconárius –ii, *m.*, a flag-bearer
dromedárius –ii, *m.*, a dromedary
dúbie, *adv.*, doubtfully
dubíetas –átis, *f.*, doubt
dubitánter, *adv.*, hesitantly
dúbito –áre, *1,* to doubt, hesitate, waver
dúbius –a –um, *adj.*, doubtful, doubting, uncertain
ducátus –us, *m.*, guidance, rank, leadership
ducilóquus –a –um, *adj.*, sweetly speaking

ducíssa –ae, *f.*, a duchess
duco –ere, duxi, ductum, *3,* to bring, lead, marry, hold, consider, launch out
ductílis –e, *adj.*, drawn, beaten out, made of beaten metal
ducto –áre, *1,* to lead
ductor –óris, *m.*, leader, commander
ductus –us, *m.*, the swing of a censer, leading, direction, purpose
dudum, *adv.*, even now, a little time ago
duéllum –i, *n.*, a conflict, duel, single combat
dulce, *adv.*, sweetly
dulcédo –inis, *f.*, goodness, sweetness, sweet taste
dulcésco –ere, *3,* to become sweet
dulcis –e, *adj.*, sweet, fresh, kind
dulcisónus –a –um, *adj.*, harmonious, sweet sounding
dúlciter, *adv.*, sweetly
dulcitúdo –inis, *f.*, sweetness
dulcor –óris, *m.*, sweetness
dúlia –ae, *f.*, religious veneration given to a creature
dúmmodo, *conj.*, provided that, if only
dumtáxat, *adv.*, in so far as
duplex –icis, *adj.*, twofold, double
duplicátus –a –um, *adj.*, double
duplícibus, with double garments
dúplico –áre, *1,* to repeat, double
duplo, *adv.*, doubly
duránte, *adv.*, during
durítia –ae, *f.*, hardness
duríties –ei, *f.*, hardness
duro –áre, *1,* to make hard
durus –a –um, *adj.*, hard, stiff, obstinate
dux –ucis, *m.* and *f.*, a leader, captain, guide
dyscólus –a –um, *adj.*, impudent, bold, harsh, severe

E

eádem, *adv.*, by the same road
eátenus, *adv.*, so far
ébenus –i, *m.*, ebony
ebíbo –ere –bíbi –bíbitum, *3,* to drink in, drink up, to drink up mentally
eblándior –íri, *dep. 4,* to obtain by flattery
ebóreus –a –um, *adj.*, of ivory
ebríetas –átis, *f.*, drunkenness, excess, spiritual inebriation
ebriósus –i, *m.*, a drunkard

ébrius –a –um, *adj.*, drunk, drunken
ebúllio –íre, *4,* to bubble, break forth
ebur –óris, *n.*, ivory
eburnéolus –a –um, *adj.*, of ivory
ebúrneus –a –um, *adj.*, of ivory
ecclésia –ae, *f.*, assembly, gathering, the Church
Ecclesiástes –is, *m.*, a book of the Old Testament
ecclesíóla –ae, *f.*, a little church
ecóntra, on the other hand

écstasis –is, *f.*, rapture, ecstasy, trance

ecstáticus –a –um, *adj.*, entranced, enraptured, ecstatic

ecténia –ae, *f.*, a prayer in the Greek liturgy

edíco –ere –díxi –díctum, *3*, to determine, decide

edíctum –i, *n.*, a decree

edísco –ere –dídici, *3*, to learn thoroughly, learn by heart

edíssero –ere –sérui –sértum, *3*, to explain, expound, relate, set forth

edíticius –a –um, *adj.*, put forth, proposed

edítio –ónis, *f.*, a statement, bringing forth

éditus –a –um, *adj.*, lofty

edo –ere *or* esse, edi, esum, *3*, to eat, to oppress

edo –ere, édidi, éditum, *3*, to bring forth, give birth to, bring into the world

edóceo –ére –ui –dóctum, *2*, to teach completely, instruct

édolo –áre, *1*, to plane, hew

Edom, *indecl.*, the elder Son of Isaac, sold his birthright to his twin brother for a mess of pottage. The name given to Esau and the land of his descendants.

Edomítes, the patronymic of the descendants of Edom or Esau. The Edomites were enemies of the Jews.

edórmio –íre, *4*, to sleep away, sleep one's full

educátio –ónis, *f.*, training, education, bringing up

educátor –óris, *m.*, a tutor

educátrix –ícis, *f.*, a female tutor

éduco –áre, *1*, to bring up, foster, nourish, sustain, provide for

edúco –ere –dúxi –dúctum, *3*, to take away, bring out, produce, bring forth, train, educate, lead out or forth

edúlia, *n. pl.*, food

edúlis –e, *adj.*, edible

edúlium –ii, *n.*, food

edúrus –a –um, *adj.*, very hard

effátu (*supine*), to express

effátum –i, *n.*, announcement, prediction

efféctio –ónis, *f.*, a doing

effectíve, *adv.*, efficaciously

efféctor –óris, *m.*, maker

efféctus –us, *m.*, a reward, answer, effect, work, result, accomplishment

effemínátus –a –um, *adj.*, effeminate

efferátus –a –um, *adj.*, raging, wild

éffero –férre, éxtuli, elátum, *3*, to raise up, lift up, exalt

effervésco –ere –férbui *or* –férvi, *3*, to boil up, rage

efficácia –ae, *f.*, accomplishment

efficácitas –átis, *f.*, efficiency, efficacy

efficáciter, *adv.*, effectually, effectively

efficátia –ae, *f.*, efficiency

éfficax –ácis, *adj.*, zealous, effectual, powerful

effício –ere –féci –féctum, *3*, to make, effect, become, perform

effígies –éi, *f.*, figure, image, an allusion to the Image of God in the soul restored by baptism

efflágito –áre, *1*, to entreat

efflo –áre, *1*, to give forth, breathe out or forth

efflóreo –ére –flórui, *2*, to blossom forth, flourish

éffluo –ere –flúxi, *2*, to flow forth, flow out

effódio –ere –fódi –fóssum, *3*, to break through, dig out, dig, excavate

effor –fári –fátus sum, *dep. 1*, to utter, speak out

effórmo –áre, *1*, to form, shape

effrons –tis, *adj.*, shameless, insulting, bold, brazen

effugátio –ónis, *f.*, a driving away

effúgio –ere –fúgi –fúgitum, *3*, to avoid, escape from

effúgo –áre, *1*, to drive away from

effúlgeo –ére –fúlsi –fúlsum, *2*, to shine upon

effúndo –ere –fúdi –fúsum, *3*, to pour forth, pour out, bring out, shed

effúsio –ónis, *f.*, a pouring forth

effúsus –a –um, *adj.*, excessive

effútio –íre, *4*, to babble, chatter

egens –éntis, *adj.*, needy

egénus –a –um, *adj.*, poor, needy

égeo –ére –ui, *2*, to be in want, have need of, be destitute

egéstas –átis, *f.*, need, want, poverty

égomet, *emphatic for* ego

egrédior –i –gréssus sum, *dep. 4*, to come out, march forth, go out, go forth, depart

egrégius –a –um, *adj.*, illustrious, famous, distinguished

egréssio –ónis, *f.*, departure, going forth

egréssus –us, *m.*, departure, going forth

ejéctio –ónis, *f.*, banishment, exile

ejéctus –us, *m.*, exile, banishment, a casting out

ejício –ere –jéci –jéctum, *3,* to cast out, drive out, expel, thrust out

ejulátus –us, *m.*, lamenting, bemoaning, a cry

ejúro –áre, *1,* to deny, refuse, abandon

ejúsmodi, of this sort; *et ejúsmodi,* and the like

Elamítae –árum, *m. pl.,* Elamites, the inhabitants of Elam carried to Samaria (Acts 2:9)

elánguens –éntis, becoming weak

elanguésco –ere –lángui, *3,* to grow faint, weak

elápsus –us, *m.,* a lapse

eláta –ae, *f.,* a spray

elátio –ónis, *f.,* elevation, raising up, breaker, billow, pride

elátus –a –um, *adj.,* elevated, raised, chosen

eléctio –ónis, *f.,* election, choice, selection, election to salvation

eléctrum –i, *n.,* amber

eléctus –a –um, *adj.,* chosen, elect, bright, beautiful

eleemósyna –ae, *f.,* alms

eleemosynárius –ii, *m.,* an almoner, one who gives alms

élegans –ántis, *adj.,* elegant, choice, adorned, graceful, beautiful

eléison (Greek), have mercy on us

elementáris –e, *adj.,* elementary

eleméntum –i, *n.,* element

elevátio –ónis, *f.,* lifting up, elevation

élevo –áre, *1,* to elevate, raise, lift up

Eli (Hebr.), my God

elício –ere, –lícui –lícitum, *3,* to produce, elicit, bring forth

elído –ere –lísi –lísum, *3,* to throw open, cast or dash down

éligo –ere –légi –léctum, *3,* to elect, choose, select, pick out

elimáte, *adv.,* clearly, exactly

elíngo –ere, *3,* to lick up

elógium –ii, *n.,* eulogy, an expression of praise

elóquium –i, *n.,* the language of the people, a word, speech, promise, utterance

elóquo –áre, *1,* to clarify, elucidate

éloquor –qui –cútus, *3,* speak out

elúceo –ére, *2,* to shine forth, stand out clearly, be apparent

elucésco –ere, *3,* to begin to be light

elúcido –áre, *1,* to explain

emáno –áre, *1,* to flow out

emárceo –ére, *2,* to wither, decay

embléma –átis, *n.,* an emblem

emblemáticus –a –um, *adj.,* pertaining to emblems

embólium –ii, *n.,* an episode

embolísmus –i, *m.,* an insertion

emendátio –ónis, *f.,* a correction, betterment, conversion

emendíco –áre, *1,* to beg, solicit

eméndo –áre, *1,* to amend, chastise

eméntior –íri, *dep. 4,* to pretend, falsify

eméritus –a –um, *adj.,* veteran, deserving

émico –áre –mícui –micátum, *1,* to shine forth, pour forth

émigro –áre, *1,* to wander forth, depart, remove from a place

éminens –éntis, *adj.,* excellent

eminéntia –ae, *f.,* the title of a cardinal

eminentíssimus –a –um, *adj.,* most eminent

emíneo –ére –mínui, *2,* to stand out, be above, be plain, apparent

éminus, *adv.,* at a distance

emíssio –ónis, *f.,* perfume

emítto –ere –mísi –míssum, *3,* to send out, cast out, give up, yield up, omit

emo –ere, emi, emptum, *3,* to buy

emóllio –íre, *4,* to soften

emoluméntum –i, *n.,* advantage, gain

emóneo –ére, *2,* to warn, admonish

emortuális –e, *adj.,* pertaining to death

emóveo –ére –móvi –mótum, *2,* to move out

empháticus –a –um, *adj.,* emphatic

empórium –ii, *n.,* a market

émptio –ónis, *f.,* a purchase, buying

emptor –óris, *m.,* a purchaser, a buyer

emunctórium –ii, *n.,* a snuffer for trimming lamps and candles

emundátio –ónis, *f.,* a cleansing, glory, splendor, majesty

emúndo –áre, *1,* to cleanse

enárro –áre, *1,* to relate, tell, declare, show forth, publish

enávigo –áre, *1,* to sail away, swim

Encaénia –órum, *n. pl.,* the Feast of the Dedication of the Temple

encaénio –áre, *1,* to put on something new, consecrate

enchirídion –ii, *n.,* a manual, handbook

encólpium –ii, *n.,* a medal worn around the neck

Endor, *indecl.,* a town S.E. of Nazareth. The abode of the sorceress consulted by Saul.

Enéas –ae, *m.,* the man from Lydda healed by St. Peter

energúmenus –a –um, *adj.,* possessed by the devil

enérviter, *adv.,* weakly

enimvéro, *adv.,* certainly, to be sure

enítor –i –níxus sum, *dep. 3,* to bring forth

eníxe, *adv.,* eagerly

enódo –áre, *1,* to make clear

enórmis –e, *adj.,* enormous

ensis –is, *m.,* a sword, sword blade

enúbilo –áre, *1,* to make clear

enucleáte, *adv.,* plainly

enumerátio –ónis, *f.,* enumeration

enúntio –áre, *1,* to declare, announce, disclose, tell

enútrio –íre, *4,* to nourish, sustain, preserve

Eobánus –i, *m.,* Eoban

eous –a –um, *adj.,* from the east, pertaining to the dawn, morning

eoúsque, *adv.,* to that point

epácta –ae, *f.,* an epact

epárchia –ae, *f.,* a diocese in the Greek Church

ephébeum –i, *n.,* a school, college

ephébia –ae, *f.,* a school for youth

ephébia –órum, *n.,* a youth center, a place for youth

ephébus –i, *m.,* a page, a youth between 16 and 21 years old

Ephraem, *m., indecl.,* Ephrem; *fílii Ephraem,* the sons of Ephrem or Ephremites

epiclésis –is, *f.,* an invocation. The "Supra quae" in the Mass. In the Greek Church a calling down of the Holy Spirit

epinícion –ii, *n.,* a feast celebrated after a victory.

Epiphánia –ae, *f.,* the Epiphany, known as Twelfth Day, also the feast of the Kings

Epiphánia secúnda, so called to distinguish the feast of Jan. 6 from Christmas, which was the first Epiphany

epiphónus –i, *m.,* the second of two musical notes which is smaller than the other one

episcopális –e, *adj.,* episcopal

episcopáliter, *adv.,* in episcopal fashion

episcopátus –us, *m.,* the episcopate, bishopric, an overseer, a post of authority

episcópium –ii, *m.,* a see, a bishop's house

epíscopus –i, *m.,* a bishop

epíscopus castrénsis, an army bishop

epíscopus chori, the director of a choir

epístola –ae, *f.,* an epistle, a letter

Epistolárium –ii, *n.,* the book of Epistles

epistolélla –ae, *f.,* a short epistle

epistólium –ii, *n.,* a letter

epistýlium –ii, *n.,* an architrave

epitáphium –ii, *n.,* an epitaph

epithalámium –ii, *n.,* a marriage song

epitrachélion –ii, *n.,* a stole

épulae –árum, *f.,* a feast, feasts

épulor –ári, *dep. 1,* to feast, make merry, rejoice, banquet

eques –itis, *m.,* a rider, horseman

equéster –tris –tre, *adj.,* equestrian

equídem, *adv.,* truly, indeed

equúleus –i, *m.,* a rack, an instrument of torture

erádico –áre, *1,* to root up

erádo –ere –rási –rásum, *3,* to destroy, cut off, strike

eréctio –ónis, *f.,* erection, lifting up, a permit to travel by the public post, a permit to travel

eréctus –a –um, *adj.,* attentive

ereméticus –a –um, *adj.,* pertaining to a hermit, solitary

eremíta –ae, *m.,* a hermit

éremus –i, *m.* and *f.,* a wilderness, desert, waste, solitude

ergástulum –i, *n.,* prison, house of detention for slaves, workhouse

érigo –ere –réxi –réctum, *3,* to erect, lift up, raise up, set up, place upright

erípio –ere –rípui –réptum, *3,* to deliver from, rescue, snatch away

ermellinéus –a –um, *adj.,* of ermine

érogo –áre, *1,* to distribute, disperse abroad

erro –áre, *1,* to make a mistake, err, go astray, wander, rove, wander away from God's commandments

erro –ónis, *m.,* a wanderer, night prowler, vagabond

error –óris, *m.,* error, deception

erubésco –ere –rúbui, *3,* to be ashamed, grow red with shame, blush

erúca –ae, *f.,* a palmer worm, caterpillar

erúcto –áre, *1,* to publish, utter, declare, belch forth, bring forth, overflow

erúdio –íre, *4,* to discipline, instruct, teach, educate

erudítio –ónis, *f.,* learning

erudítus –a –um, *adj.,* informed, instructed

erúmpo –ere –rúpi –rúptum, *3,* to crush, break forth, break up, erupt

éruo –ere –ui –útum, *3,* to pluck out, tear away, deliver, rescue, save

esca –ae, *f.,* food, meat, eating, a piece of meat, food for men or beasts

esculéntus –a –um, *adj.,* eatable

esséndi, esséndo, in being

esséntia –ae, *f.,* essence

essentiális –e, *adj.,* essential

esúriens –éntis, *m.* or *f.,* one hungering

esúrio –íre, *4,* to be hungry, hunger for

esus –us, *m.,* bread, food, eating

éthnici –órum, *m. pl.,* heathen, gentile

éthnicus –i, *m.,* a heathen

éthnicus –a –um, *adj.,* heathenish, pagan

etiámnum, *adv.,* still yet

etiámsi, even if, although

euchális –e, *adj.,* gracious, agreeable

eucharistía –ae, *f.,* thanksgiving; the Holy Eucharist

eucharistiále –is, *n.,* a vessel for preserving the Eucharist

eucharistiális –e, *adj.,* pertaining to the Eucharist

eucharísticus –a –um, *adj.,* pertaining to the Eucharist

eulógia –ae, *f.,* a present; term used for the Blessed Sacrament

eúnuchus –i, *m.,* a eunuch

euroaquílo –ónis, *m.,* the northeast wind

Eva –ae, *f.,* Eve

evácuo –áre, *1,* to put away, do away with, make void

evádo –ere –vási –vásum, *3,* to evade, escape

evágino –áre, *1,* to unsheathe, draw out of the scabbard

evágo –áre, *1,* to wander, stray

evanésco –ere –vánui, *3,* to vanish, fade out, become vapid, become dissipated, die

evangeliárum –ii, *n.,* the book of the Gospels

evangélicus –a –um, *adj.,* pertaining to the Gospel, evangelic

evangelísta –ae, *m.,* an evangelist, an author of the Gospel

evangelistárium –ii, *n.,* the book of the Gospels

evangélium –ii, *n.,* the Gospel, message, good tidings

evangelízo –áre, *1,* to evangelize, preach the Gospel, proclaim good tidings

evásio –ónis, *n.,* escape, deliverance

éveho –ere –véxi –véctum, *3,* to raise, carry out

evéllo –ere –vélli –vúlsum, *3,* to pluck out, tear, pull

evénio –íre –véni –véntum, *4,* to come out, come forth, happen, befall

evéntum –i, *n.,* an issue, event, outcome

evéntus, –us, *m.,* event, outcome, issue, occurrence

evérsio –ónis, *f.,* overthrow, destruction, a subverting, disruption

evérto –ere –vérti –vérsum, *3,* to overthrow, overturn, take away, make void, pervert, agitate, destroy spiritually

evidénter, *adv.,* manifestly, evidently

evidéntia –ae, *f.,* evidence

evigilátio –ónis, *f.,* an awakening

evígilo –áre, *1,* to be vigilant, awake

evínco –ere –víci –víctum, *3,* to bring about

evíscero –áre, *1,* to gnaw, waste

évoco –áre, *1,* to call forth, summon

evólvo –ere –vólvi –volútum, *3,* to develop, roll away

evúlgo –áre, *1,* to make known, publish

ex, out of, from; *ex advérso,* opposite; *ex aequo,* justly; *ex eo quod,* from the fact that; *ex fide,* in good faith; *ex improvíso,* suddenly; *ex toto,* wholly

exacerbátio –ónis, *f.,* exasperation, bitterness, provocation, irritation; the arousing of divine anger by the Jews in the desert

exacérbo –áre, *1,* to provoke, embitter

exáctio –ónis, *f.,* the levying of tribute

exáctor –óris, *m.,* tax collector, one who makes a demand, an oppressor

exáctus –a –um, *adj.,* sharpened

exácuo –ere –ui –útum, *3,* to sharpen, whet

exacútus –a –um, *adj.,* sharpened

exaedífico –áre, *1,* to build

exaéquo –áre, *1,* to equal, make equal

exaéstuo –áre, *1,* to boil, burn

exággero –áre, *1,* to grow worse, increase

exágito –áre, *1,* to attack, drive out

exaltátio –ónis, *f.,* exaltation, high praise, a raising, lifting up

exálto –áre, *1,* to extol, exalt, lift up, glorify, elevate in rank or dignity

exámen –inis, *n.,* agony, test, examination, struggle

examinátor –óris, *m.,* an examiner, arbitrator

examinátus –a –um, *adj.,* careful, exact, scrupulous

exámino –áre, *1,* to test, try, weigh, refine, purify

exántlo –áre, *1,* to exhaust, endure, bear, suffer much from toil

exapério –íre, *4,* to disclose, explain, disentangle

exárchus –i, *m.,* an exarch

exárdeo –ére –ársi –ársum, *2,* to kindle, flame, break out, break forth

exardésco –ere –ársi –ársum, *3,* to be inflamed, take fire, be kindled

exarésco –ere –árui, *3,* to become dry, wither, dry up

exármo –áre, *1,* to disarm

éxaro –áre, *1,* to write on wax

exasperátrix –ícis, *adj.,* provoking

exáspero –áre, *1,* to provoke, embitter

exaudíbilis –e, *adj.,* worthy of being heard

Exaúdi, the sixth Sunday after Easter. *Exaudi* is the initial word of the Introit for that Sunday.

exaúdio –íre, *4,* to hear favorably, hear graciously, hearken to, answer

exaudítio –ónis, *f.,* the favorable answer to a prayer

exaúditor –óris, *m.,* one who listens graciously to a prayer

excaéco –áre, *1,* to blind, make blind mentally

excalceátus –a –um, *adj.,* barefooted, discalced, unshod

excandésco –ere –cándui, *3,* to take fire, burn (with anger — to become violently angry)

excardinátio –onis, *f.,* the release of a priest from his membership in a diocese

excarnífico –áre, *1,* to tear to pieces

ex Cáthedra, from the chair; refers to the infallibility of the Pope on matters of faith or morals

excédo –ere –céssi –céssum, *3,* to go beyond, exceed, go out, go away, go from, transgress

excéllens –éntis, *adj.,* distinguished, excellent

excelléntia –ae, *f.,* excellence

excéllo –ere –céllui, *3,* to excel

excélsa, *n. pl.,* high places

excélsitas –átis, *f.,* pre-eminence

excélsum –i, *n.,* high position; *in excélsis,* in the highest; *in excélso,* on high

excélsus –a –um, *adj.,* lofty, high, glorious, august, sublime, towering aloft

Excélsus –i, *m.,* the Most High

excéptio –ónis, *f.,* exception

exceptórium –ii, *n.,* a reservoir for water

excéptus –a –um, *adj.,* only

excérebro –áre, *1,* to brain

excéssus –us, *m.,* excess, ecstasy, departure, transgression, going forth, going out

excídium –ii, *n.,* destruction

excído –ere –cídi –císum, *3,* to fall away, hew or cut down

excípio –ere –cépi –céptum, *3,* to accept, take out

excísus –us, *m.,* a slip, cut, piece

éxcitor –óris, *m.,* an awakener, one who arouses

Excitor méntium, the awakener of souls, Christ

exclámo –áre, *1,* to cry out, exclaim

exclúdo –ere –clúsi –clúsum, *3,* to drive away, keep from, exclude, reject

exclúsio –ónis, *f.,* exclusion

excogitátio –ónis, *f.,* an invention, devising

excógito –áre, *1,* to devise, invent

éxcolo –ere –cólui –cúltum, *3,* to tend, cultivate, work for

excommunicátio –ónis, *f.,* excommunication

excommúnico –áre, *1,* to excommunicate

excóquo –ere –cóxi –cóctum, *3,* to refine, boil down, destroy, burn out

excório –áre, *1,* to flay

excors –córdis, *adj.,* foolish, unlearned

excrésco –ere –crévi –crétum, *3,* to grow

excúbiae –árum, *f. pl.,* keeping watch

éxcubo –áre –ui –útum, *1,* to keep watch, be on guard

excusátio –ónis, *f.,* an excuse

excúso –áre, *1,* to excuse

excússio –ónis, *f.,* the act of shaking

excússus –a –um, *adj.,* cast out, thrown out

excútio –ere –cússi –cússum, *3,* to shake, shake off, remove, drive out

execrábilis –e, *adj.,* detestable, execrable

execraméntum –i, *n.,* an abomination

execrátio –ónis, *f.,* a curse, malediction, object of execration

éxecror –ári, *dep. 1,* to curse, execrate

éxedra –ae, *f.,* a hall, a large room

exémplar –áris, *n.,* an example, model, copy

exémplum –i, *n.,* example

exémptus –a –um, *adj.*, exempt

éxeo –íre –ívi –ítum, *4,* to go out, depart, come forth

exéquiae –árum, *f.*, funeral rites

exérceo –ére –cui –citum, *2,* to exercise, practice, meditate, pray, brood

exercítium –ii, *n.*, exercise, practice

exército –áre, *1,* to exercise, employ, use, engage, occupy, exercise diligently

exércitus –us, *m.*, host, army

exfornicátus –a –um, *adj.*, given to fornication

exhaústus –a –um, *adj.*, exhausted

exhíbeo –ére –ui –itum, *2,* to exhibit, present, return, deliver, show, display, entertain, offer, promise

exhibítio –ónis, *f.*, display, exhibition

exhílaro –áre, *1,* to make cheerful, gladden

exhonorátio –ónis, *f.*, shame

exhónoro –áre, *1,* to dishonor, disgrace

exhórreo –ére –hórrui, *2,* to shudder

exhortátio –ónis, *f.*, exhortation, an encouraging

exhórto –áre, *1,* to exhort, encourage

exhórtor –ári, *dep. 1,* to exhort, encourage

éxigo –ere –égi –áctum, *3,* to demand

exíguus –a –um, *adj.*, little

exílitas –átis, *f.*, shrillness

exílium –ii, *n.*, exile, banishment

exímius –a –um, *adj.*, wonderful, priceless, extraordinary

éximo –ere –émi –émptum, *3,* to draw out

exinánio –íre, *4,* to pour forth, empty, exhaust, raze, destroy utterly

exinanítio –ónis, *f.*, emptiness

exínde, *adv.*, henceforth, then, thenceforth, thereupon, therefrom

existéntia –ae, *f.*, existence

existimátio –ónis, *f.*, estimation, esteem

exístimo –áre, *1,* to think, reckon, take account of, consider, judge, be of opinion

exitabíliter, *adv.*, ruinously, perniciously

exitiális –e, *adj.*, destructive

exítium –ii, *n.*, destruction

éxitus –us, *m.*, death, end, result, departure, going out, going forth

éxitus viárum, highways

exomologésis –is, *f.*, confession of sins

exópto –áre, *1,* to wish eagerly, to hope

exorátio –ónis, *f.*, a petition, mercy

exorcísmus –i, *m.*, exorcism

exorcísta –ae, *m.*, an exorcist

exorcistátus –us, *m.*, the minor Order of exorcist

exorcístus –i, *m.*, exorcist

exorcízo –áre, *1,* to exorcise

exórdium –ii, *n.*, beginning, source, institution

exórior –íri –órtus sum, *dep. 3 and 4,* to spring up, rise, appear

exornátus –a –um, *adj.*, embellished

exórno –áre, *1,* to adorn, provide with

exóro –áre, *1,* to pray, plead, beseech, supplicate, implore, entreat earnestly

exósculo –áre, *1,* to kiss

exósus –a –um, *adj.*, hated

expándo –ere –pánsi –pánsum *or* –pássum, *3,* to stretch out, spread out

expavésco –ere –pávi, *3,* to be terrified, tremble

expectátio –ónis, *f.*, expectation

expécto –áre, *1,* to await, expect

expediéndus –a –um, *adj.*, settled, disentangled

expédio –íre, *4,* to deliver, detach, be expedient

expedítio –ónis, *f.*, the act of dispatching

expedítus –a –um, *adj.*, well-appointed

expéllo –ere –puli –púlsum, *3,* to expel, drive away, thrust forth

expéndo –ere –péndi –pénsum, *3,* to weigh

expergefácio –ere, *3,* to arouse, wake up

expergíscor –sci –perréctus sum, *dep. 3,* to awake

expérior –íri –pértus sum, *dep. 4,* to experience, endeavor, try, test

expers –értis, *adj.*, lacking in

expértus –a –um, *adj.*, expert, experienced, proved, tested

expértus –i, *m.*, expert, one who has experience

éxpeto –ere –ívi –ítum, *3,* to desire

expiátio –ónis, *f.*, expiation, atonement

expiatórius –a –um, *adj.*, satisfactory, expiatory

éxpio –áre, *1,* to explain, expound, to cleanse, purify, make amends for

explanátio –ónis, *f.*, explanation

expláno –áre, *1,* to explain, expound

explánto –áre, *1,* to cast out

éxpleo –ére –plévi –plétum, *2,* to fill, fulfill, finish, complete

explétio –ónis, *f.*, expiration

explícite, *adv.*, explicitly

éxplico –áre, *1,* to explain, extend, unfold

explódo *or* explaúdo –ere –plódi –plósum, *3,* to hiss

explóro –áre, *1,* to explore, investigate

expólio –íre, *4,* to redecorate, polish

expóno –ere –pósui –pósitum, *3,* to set before, make manifest, set forth, expound

expórrigo –ere –réxi –réctum, *3,* to stretch out, expand

expósco –ere –popósci, *3,* to plead, entreat earnestly, demand vehemently

expositio –ónis, *f.,* exhibition, the act of exposing

exprésse, *adv.,* expressly

éxprimo –ere –préssi –préssum, *3,* to express, represent

éxprobo –áre, *1,* to upbraid, reproach, reprove

expúgno –áre, *1,* to overthrow, fight against, afflict, oppress

éxpuo –ere –pui, *3,* to spit, spit upon

expurgátio –ónis, *f.,* justification, vindication

expurgátus –a –um, *adj.,* expurgated

expúrgo –áre, *1,* to purge, drive out, cleanse, purify

exquíro –ere –sívi –sítum, *3,* to inquire diligently, seek, seek after

exquisítor –óris, *m.,* a searcher

exquisítus –a –um, *adj.,* exquisite, painful

exsánguis –e, *adj.,* bloodless

exsaturátus –a –um, *adj.,* filled, having enough

exsáturo –áre, *1,* to satisfy

exsecrábilis –e, *adj.,* abhorrent

exsecrabílius, *adv.* (*comparative*), execrably

exsecrándus –a –um, *adj.,* detestable

exsecrátio –ónis, *f.,* abomination, curse, malediction, profanation

éxsecror –ári, *dep. 1,* to curse, execrate

exséquiae –árum, *f.,* funeral rites

éxsequor –qui –cútus sum, *dep. 3,* to follow, perform, secure

éxsero –ere –sérui –sértum, *3,* to exert, thrust forth, to give rise to

exsícco –áre, *1,* to dry up, make dry

exsílio –íre –sílui –súltum, *4,* to leap, leap out, string up

exsílium –ii, *n.,* exile, banishment

exsísto –ere –stiti –stitum, *3,* to come forth, appear

exsólvo –ere –sólvi –solútum, *3,* to pay back, restore, present

exsors –sórtis, *adj.,* deprived of

exspectátio –ónis, *f.,* expectation, hope

exspécto –áre, *1,* to expect, look for, long for, wait for, trust

exspíro –áre, *1,* to expire, die

exspólio –áre, *1,* to rob, despoil

éxspuo –ere –spui –spútum, *3,* to spit

éxstasis –is, *f.,* ecstasy, bewilderment

exstínctio –ónis, *f.,* dissolution, slaughter, annihilation

exstínctor –óris, *m.,* destroyer, annihilator

exstínguo –ere –stínxi –stínctum, *3,* to extinguish, quench, put out

exsto –áre –stiti, *1,* to stand out, stand forth, come forth, appear

éxstruo –ere –strúxi –strúctum, *3,* to build

extra, *adv.,* except, beyond, out of, without, outside of

éxtraho –ere –tráxi –tráctum, *3,* to draw out, draw or bring forth

extráneus –i, *m.,* a stranger, foreigner

extrémum –i, *n.,* end, tip, farthest part, that which is outermost

extrémus –a –um, *adj.,* extreme, last, the end

éxtrico –áre, *1,* to extricate, remove, disentangle

extrínsece, *adv.,* externally, extrinsically

extrínsecus, *adv.,* without, outwardly, on the outside

extrúdo –ere –trúsi –trúsum, *3,* to thrust out

extúrbo –áre, *1,* to drive away

exúbero –áre, *1,* to abound

exúndo –áre, *1,* to overflow, abound

éxuo –ere –ui –útum, *3,* to strip, take off, put off, deliver

exúro –ere –ússi –ústum, *3,* to consume, burn up

exúviae –árum, *f.,* remains

Ezéchiel –is, *m.,* Ezechiel, the son of Buzi, one of the four great prophets

F

faber –bri, *m.*, an artificer, carpenter

fabrefácio –ere –féci –fáctum, *3,* to make, manufacture

fábrica –ae, *f.,* a building, workshop, art, working

fabricátio –ónis, *f.,* a structure

fabricátor –óris, *m.,* a maker, framer, artificer, forger

fábrico –áre, *1,* to make, work, fashion, build, forge from hard material

fábricor –ári, *dep. 1,* to make, work, fashion, build

fabrília –ium, *n. pl.,* carpenter work

fabrílis –e, *adj.,* pertaining to a carpenter

fábula –ae, *f.,* byword, a tale

fabulátio –ónis, *f.,* a fable, idle talk

fabulátor –óris, *m.,* a storyteller, a teller of fables

fábulo –áre, *1,* to talk

fácesso –ere –céssi –ítum, *3,* to depart, go away, retire

fácies –éi, *f.,* face, appearance, countenance

fácilis –e, *adj.,* easy

facílitas –átis, *f.,* facility, ease

facíliter, *adv.,* easily

facílius, *adv.,* more easily

fácinus –oris, *n.,* a crime

fácio –ere, feci, factum, *3,* to make, cause, bring forth, bring to pass, commit, grant

fáctio –ónis, *f.,* faction

factiósus –a –um, *adj.,* quarrelsome

factítius –a –um, *adj.,* artificial

factor –óris, *m.,* a maker, doer, creator

factum –i, *n.,* deed, act, work

factúra –ae, *f.,* creation, work, deed, handiwork, performance

facúltas –átis, *f.,* ability, authority, means, resources, goods, possessions

faeculéntus –a –um, *adj.,* worthless, pertaining to age

faenerátor –óris, *m.,* a creditor, usurer, money lender

faénero –áre, *1,* to lend money at interest

faenum –i, *n.,* grass

faenus –eris, *n.,* a loan

faex, faecis, *f.,* mire, ooze, dregs, ground, sediment

fálcitas –átis, *f.,* falseness

falda –ae, *f.,* a garment of white silk worn by the Pope on solemn occasions

faldistórium –ii, *n.,* a chair with arm rests but no back, faldstool

fallácia –ae, *f.,* falsehood, deceit, deceitfulness

falláciter, *adv.,* falsely

fallax –ácis, *adj.,* deceitful, vain, unreliable, untrustworthy, not to be relied on

fallo –ere, fefélli, falsum, *3,* to make a slip, deceive, make ineffective

fálsitas –átis, *f.,* error, falsehood

falso –áre, *1,* to falsify

falsus –a –um, *adj.,* false, lying, untrue

falx, falcis, *f.,* a sickle

fama –ae, *f.,* a report, fame, good report

famélicus –a –um, *adj.,* famished, hungry

fames –is, *f.,* hunger, famine

família –ae, *f.,* family, household, a religious community

familiáris –is, *m.,* a servant in the household, an intimate acquaintance

familiáris –e, *adj.,* friendly, familiar, intimate

familiáritas –átis, *f.,* intimacy

familiáriter, *adv.,* in a familiar manner

famílicus, *see* famélicus

famósus –a –um, *adj.,* renowned, famous

fámula –ae, *f.,* a servant

famulátus –us, *m.,* service

fámulus –i, *m.,* a servant

fanále –is, *n.,* a torch, candle

fano (fanóne), *m.,* a maniple, striped amice worn by the Holy Father

farciatúra –ae, *f.,* an insertion

fárcio –íre, *4,* to fill up, fill in, repetition of words between verses

farína –ae, *f.,* meal, flour

farínula –ae, *f.,* meal, fine flour

fársia –ae, *f.,* an insertion in parts of the Mass

fas, *indecl.,* right

fáscia –ae, *f.,* a band, ribbon, bandage, sash

fascículus –i, *m.,* a sheaf, bundle, little bundle, bunch

fascinátio –ónis, *f.,* bewitching, fascination

fascinátor –óris, *m.,* charmer, enchanter

fasciola –ae, *f.,* a bandage, ribbon

fastídio –íre, *4,* to shrink from, scorn, despise, spurn

fastidiósus –a –um, *adj.*, fastidious, disdainful

fastídium –ii, *n.*, weariness, monotony, an aversion, a loathing

fastígium –ii, *n.*, height, summit, gable

fastus –us, *m.*, pride, arrogance

fáteor –éri, fessus sum, *dep. 2*, to confess, admit, avow, allow

fatigátio –ónis, *f.*, toil

fatigátus –a –um, *adj.*, weary

fatígo –áre, *1*, to tire, weary

fatísco –ere, *3*, to decrease, crack

fátue, *adv.*, foolishly

fatúitas –átis, *f.*, folly

fatum –i, *n.*, a prediction

fátuus –i, *m.*, a fool

fátuus –a –um, *adj.*, foolish

fauces –ium, *f. pl.*, throat, jaws, palate, taste

faúsitas –átis, *f.*, prosperity

fautor –óris, *m.*, patron, adviser, favorer, protector

favílla –ae, *f.*, ashes

favor –óris, *m.*, favor, care, approval

favus –i, *m.*, honey, honeycomb

fax, facis, *f.*, a torch, flame, that which inflames

febrícito –áre, *1*, to have a fever

febris –is, *f.*, fever

februárius –ii, *m.*, the month of February

fecúndo –áre, *1*, to fill, replenish

fecúndus –a –um, *adj.*, fruitful, prolific

fel, fellis, *n.*, gall

felícitas –átis, *f.*, felicity

felíciter, *adv.*, happily

felix –ícis, *adj.*, happy, blessed

fémina –ae, *f.*, a female, woman

feminália –ium, *n. pl.*, breeches

féminus –a –um, *adj.*, female

femorália –órum, *n. pl.*, breeches

fémur –óris, *n.*, thigh

fenestélla –ae, *f.*, a small window, niche

fenéstra –ae, *f.*, a window

fera –ae, *f.*, a wild beast

ferália –e, *adj.*, deadly

feráliter, *adv.*, in a savage manner

fera péssima, *f.*, a wild beast

férculum –i, *n.*, a dish, tray, food, bread, course at a banquet, a litter, a bier

ferétrum –i, *n.*, a bier

féria –ae, *f.*, day of the week

feriális –e, *adj.*, ferial, pertaining to a feria, weekday

féria major, a feria of high rank

féria quarta, Wednesday

Féria Quarta Cínerum, Ash Wednesday

féria quinta, Thursday

Féria Quinta in Coena Dómini, Maundy Thursday, the commemoration of the institution of the Blessed Eucharist

féria secúnda, Monday

féria sexta, Friday

Féria Sexta in Parascéve, Good Friday

féria tértia, Tuesday

feriátio –ónis, *f.*, feast, celebration of a feast

feriátus –a –um, *adj.*, festive

fério –íre, *4*, to strike, slay, make, make a treaty

féritas –átis, *f.*, savagery, fierceness

fermaméntus –a –um, *adj.*, fermented

ferme, *adv.*, almost

fermentáceus –i, *m.*, a person who uses leavened bread

ferménto –áre, *1*, to leaven

ferméntum –i, *n.*, leaven

fero, ferre, tuli, latum, *3*, to carry, bring

ferox –ócis, *adj.*, fierce

ferraíola –ae, *f.*, a short cape reaching halfway to the elbows

ferraméntum –i, *n.*, an iron tool

ferrátus –a –um, *adj.*, sharp

férreus –a –um, *adj.*, iron, made of iron

ferrum –i, *n.*, iron

ferrum characterátum, a form for baking hosts

ferrum oblatórium, an iron form for baking hosts

fértilis –e, *adj.*, fertile, fruitful, prolific

feruefácio –ere, *3*, to inflame, excite

férula –ae, *f.*, a wand, long staff

ferus –i, *m.*, a wild beast

ferus –a –um, *adj.*, untamed, wild

fervens –éntis, *adj.*, hot, fervent

fervénte die, in the heat of the day

fervéntius, *adv.*, more fervently

férveo –ére –bui, *2*, to glow, boil

fervor –óris, *m.*, fervor

fessus –a –um, *adj.*, weary

festa –órum, *n. pl.*, festival

festinánter, *adv.*, in haste, rapidly

festináto, *adv.*, speedily, hastily

festíno –áre, *1*, to hasten, be quick

festínus –a –um, *adj.*, hastening

festívitas –átis, *f.*, festivity, feast

festívus –a –um, *adj.*, festive, pertaining to a feast

festúca –ae, *f.*, a stalk, mote, splinter

festum –i, *n.*, a feast

Festum Dómini, a feast that commemorates some event in the life of our Lord

festum festórum, the greatest of feasts, Easter

Festum Magórum, the Epiphany

Festum Regum, the Epiphany, the feast of the Kings

Festum Stellae, the Epiphany

Festum Theopháaniae, the feast of the appearance or manifestation of our Lord, the Epiphany

festus –a –um, *adj.,* festal, sacred, hallowed, belonging to a feast

fibra –ae, *f.,* fiber, filament, voice, vocal chord

fíbula –ae, *f.,* a clasp, buckle, brooch

ficárius –a –um, *adj.,* pertaining to figs

ficétum –i, *n.,* a plantation of figs

ficte, *adj.,* falsely

fictílis –e, *adj.,* earthen, made of clay

fíctio –ónis, *f.,* guile

fictítius –a –um, *adj.,* fictitious

fictor –óris, *m.,* maker

fictus –a –um, *adj.,* deceitful, feigned

ficúlnea –ae, *f.,* a fig tree

ficus –i *or* –us, *f.,* a fig, fig tree

fidejússor –óris, *m.,* a bondsman, surety

fidélis –e, *adj.,* faithful; *fidéles,* the believers, the faithful (of the Church)

fidéliter, *adv.,* faithfully, confidently

fidénter, *adv.,* courageously, confidently

fides –ei, *f.,* faith, faithfulness, confidence, a firm belief based on the word of God, the virtue of faith, the Christian religion, the virtue of faith from baptism

fides –is, *f.,* a lute, lyre, stringed instrument

fidículus –i, *m.,* a viola, musical instrument

fído –ere, fisus sum, *3,* to trust, put confidence in

fidúcia –ae, *f.,* boldness, confidence

fiduciáliter, *adv.,* with confidence, boldly, decisively, trustingly

fiduciálius, *adv.,* more confidently

fidus –a –um, *adj.,* faithful, reliable, trustworthy

figméntum –i, *n.,* creation, formation, production, anything made, fancy, picture, image

figo –ere, fixi, fixum, *3,* to pierce, make firm

fígulus –i, *m.,* a potter, worker in clay

figúra –ae, *f.,* fashion, figure

figuráliter, *adv.,* figuratively

figurátio –ónis, *f.,* prefiguration, allegory

figurátus –a –um, *adj.,* symbolical, allegorical

figúro –áre, *1,* to symbolize, represent allegorically

fília –ae, *f.,* daughter

filiális –e, *adj.,* filial

filiátio –ónis, *f.,* sonship

fílii Adam, sons of Adam, men

filíolus –i, *m.,* a little child

Filióque, and from the Son

fílius –ii, *m.,* son, child, descendant

filum –i, *n.,* thread, cord

fímbria –ae, *f.,* hem, fringe, edge, border

fimus –i, *m.,* dung

finális –e, *adj.,* final

findo –ere, fidi, fissum, *3,* to plow

fines, –ium, *pl.,* territory

fingo –ere, finxi, fictum, *3,* to feign, pretend, imagine, mold, shape, make, give shape to anything

fínio –íre, *4,* to finish, end, make an end of

finis –is, *m.* and *f.,* end, boundary, border, limit

finítimus –a –um, *adj.,* neighboring, bordering on

fio –eri, factus sum, to become, be made, be done

firmále –is, *n.,* a brooch for a cope

firmaméntum –i, *n.,* a prop, a making fast, strength, anything that strengthens, sky, firmament

fírmitas –átis, *f.,* steadfastness

fírmiter, *adv.,* strongly, firmly, steadfastly

firmo –áre, *1,* to make strong, make firm, establish, fix

firmus –a –um, *adj.,* firm

fiscélla –ae, *f.,* a basket

fístula –ae, *f.,* a pipe, whistle, flute, reed, sweet cane

fixe, *adv.,* constantly

fixtúra –ae, *f.,* an imprint, print, opening, perforation, print of the nails

flabéllum –i, *n.,* a fan

flábilis –e, *adj.,* moving, fleeting

fláccidus –a –um, *adj.,* weak, drooping

flagellátio –ónis, *f.,* scourging

flagéllo –áre, *1,* to scourge, whip, lash, strike, beat

flagéllum –i, *n.,* whip, scourge

flagitiósus –a –um, *adj.,* disgraceful

flagítium –ii, *n.,* a shameful crime

flágito –áre, *1,* to beseech, entreat, demand earnestly

flagrans –ántis, *adj.,* zealous

flagro –áre, *1,* to burn, glow, be eager
flamen –inis, *n.,* wind, breath, a spirit
Flamen Supérnum, *n.,* divine breath, the Holy Ghost
flamma –ae, *f.,* a flame
flammans –ántis, *adj.,* flaming
flammésco –ere, *3,* to become inflamed
flámmeum –i, *n.,* a bridal veil
flámmeus –a –um, *adj.,* fiery, flaming
flámmifer –fera –ferum, *adj.,* fiery, flaming
flammo –áre, *1,* to burn with eagerness or passion
flámmula –ae, *f.,* a little flame
flatus –us, *m.,* breath, blowing
flavor –óris, *f.,* brightness
flébilis –e, *adj.,* sad, sorrowing, weeping, wretched
flecto –ere, flexi, flexum, *3,* to bend, bend low, bow
Flentes, *m. pl.,* the weepers
fleo –ere, flevi, fletum, *2,* to lament, weep
fletus –us, *m.,* weeping, bewailing
flexíbilis –e, *adj.,* flexible
flexúra –ae, *f.,* a bend, turning
flexus –a –um, *adj.,* bent
flo –are, *1,* to blow
flócculus –i, *m.,* a tassel
floccus –i, *m.,* a tassel
florens –éntis, *adj.,* in flower
flóreo –ére –ui, *2,* to flower, bloom, flourish, prosper
flóreus –a –um, *adj.,* flowery
flóridus –a –um, *adj.,* plentiful, flourishing
flos, floris, *m.,* a flower
flósculus –i, *m.,* a little flower, tuft or tassel
fluctuátio –ónis, *f.,* insecurity, tossing to and fro
flúctuo –áre, *1,* to toss about, fluctuate, be tossed about
fluctus –us, *m.,* a wave, billow, storm, affliction
fluéntum –i, *n.,* a river, stream, running water, flood
fluéntus –a –um, *adj.,* flowing
fluésco –ere, *3,* to melt, become fluid
flumen –inis, *n.,* a river, stream, flood, flowing of water
fluo –ere, fluxi, fluxum, *3,* to flow
flúvius –ii, *m.,* a river, stream, flowing water
fluxus –a –um, *adj.,* transitory
fluxus –us, *m.,* issue, flux, flowing, tide

(of time), fuel, incitement
focária –ae, *f.,* a cook
fóculus –i, *m.,* a portable stove, chafing dish
fódio –ere, fodi, fossum, *3,* to dig, pierce
foecúndo –áre, *1,* to make fruitful
foecúndus –a –um, *adj.,* abundant, fruitful
foederátus –a –um, *adj.,* united
foédero –áre, *1,* to establish by agreement
foéditas –átis, *f.,* filth
foedo –áre, *1,* to disfigure
foedus –eris, *n.,* a covenant
foedus –a –um, *adj.,* detestable, filthy, vile
foenerátor –óris, *m.,* a creditor, money lender
foéneror –ári, *dep. 1,* to lend money
foenum –i, *n., see* faenum
foenus –eris, *n., see* faenus
foetans –ántis, *f.,* a milch-ewe
foéteo –ére, *2,* to have a bad smell
foétidus –a –um, *adj.,* stinking
foeto –áre, *1,* to bring forth
foetósus –a –um, *adj.,* prolific
foetus –us, *m.,* increase, offspring, a bringing forth of fruit
fólium –ii, *n.,* foliage
fomes –itis, *m.,* nourishment, stimulant, fire, fuel, tinder, incitement
fons, fontis, *m.,* a source, fountain, fount, well, baptistry
fons baptismális, a baptismal font
fons lustrális, a holy water font
forámen –inis, *n.,* cleft, hole, the eye of a needle
foráneus –a –um, *adj.,* pertaining to the outside
foras, *adv.,* out of doors, out, forth
forceps –ipis, *m.* and *f.,* forceps, tongs
forénsis –e, *adj.,* legal, forensic
fores –um, *f. pl.* of *foris,* doors
forfex –icis, *f.,* shears
forínsecus, *adv.,* from without
foris, *adv.,* outside, outwardly, in public
foris –is, *f.,* door
forma –ae, *f.,* form, pattern, shape, formula
formábilis –e, *adj.,* that may be formed or fashioned
formále –is, *n.,* a large brooch for a bishop's cope
formáliter, *adv.,* formally
formálium –ii, *n.,* a large brooch for a bishop's cope

formátrix –ícis, *f.*, one who forms

formátus –a –um, *adj.*, formed, having formed

formélla –ae, *f.*, a cake

formíca –ae, *f.*, an ant

formído –áre, *1*, to be in awe, tremble at, be afraid

formído –inis, *f.*, terror, dread, fear

formidolósus –a –um, *adj.*, fearful

formo –áre, *1*, to form, fashion, train, guide

formósus –a –um, *adj.*, beautiful

fórmula –ae, *f.*, a set order of words

fornax –ácis, *f.*, an oven, furnace, a furnace as a symbol of trial or tribulation

fornicária –ae, *f.*, fornicatress

fornicátio –ónis, *f.*, fornication

fornicátor –óris, *m.*, fornicator

fórnico –áre, *1*, to fornicate

fórnicor –ári, *dep. 1*, to commit fornication

fórsitan, *adv.*, perhaps, perchance, peradventure

fortásse, *adv.*, perhaps

fortássis, *adv.*, perhaps

forte, *abl.* of fors, by chance

fortis –e, *adj.*, strong, valiant, mighty, steadfast, grievous

fórtiter, *adv.*, mightily, firmly, valiantly

fortitúdo –inis, *f.*, strength, power, might, fortitude

fortúito, *adv.*, by chance

fortúitu, *adv.*, by chance

fortúna –ae, *f.*, fortune

forum –i, *n.*, open space, forum, market place

forum cómpetens, the proper court

fossa –ae, *f.*, a ditch or trench

fossárius –ii, *m.*, a sexton

fossor –óris, *m.*, a sexton, grave digger

fóvea –ae, *f.*, a ditch, pit, lair, hole, pitfall, trap for men or beasts

fóveo –ére, fovi, fotum, *2*, to cherish, warm, keep warm, foment, assist

fráctio –ónis, *f.*, breaking

fractúra –ae, *f.*, a breaking, breach, crack

fraeno –áre, *1*, to restrain, bridle

frágilis –e, *adj.*, weak, poor, frail, fragile

fragílitas –átis, *f.*, frailty, weakness

fragmen –inis, *n.*, a piece

fragméntum –i, *n.*, a fragment

fragor –óris, *m.*, crash, noise, din

frámea –ae, *f.*, a sword

Franciscális –e, *adj.*, Franciscan

Francíscus –a –um, *adj.*, Franciscan

frángia –ae, *f.*, a fringe

frango –ere, fregi, fractum, *3*, to break, break off, deal

frater –tris, *m.*, brother, friar

fratérnitas –átis, *f.*, brotherhood, fraternity

fraudo –áre, *1*, to withhold, defraud, cheat, deprive

fraudulénter, *adv.*, fraudulently, falsely, deceitfully

fraus, fraudis, *f.*, error, wile, fraud, deception

frémitus –us, *m.*, anger, fury, murmuring, shouting, clashing

fremo –ere –ui –itum, *3*, to rage, roar, clamor

frendo –ere –ui, fressum *or* fresum, *3*, to gnash with the teeth

freno –áre, *1*, to bridle

frenum –i, *n.*, a bridle, curb

frequentátio –ónis, *f.*, frequentation

frequénter, *adv.*, frequently, often

frequéntia –ae, *f.*, frequency

frequénto –áre, *1*, to frequent, celebrate, have recourse to, visit frequently, collect in large numbers

fretum –i, *n.*, the sea, a raging, swelling, strait, sound

fretus –a –um, *adj.*, relying on, trusting, strengthened

frigéscso –ere, frixi, *3*, to become cold

frígidus –a –um, *adj.*, cold, causing cold, inactive, not pious

frigus –oris, *n.*, cold, frost

frisiátus –a –um, *adj.*, embroidered

frixórium –ii, *n.*, a frying pan

frondésco –ere –ui, *3*, to blossom, become leafy

frondo –ere, *3*, to be leafy, to flourish

frons, frondis, *f.*, a leaf, leafy branch, foliage

frons, frontis, *f.*, forehead

frontále –is, *n.*, the frontal of an altar

frontispícium –ii, *n.*, the front

frúctifer –fera –ferum, *adj.*, fruitful, fruit-bearing

fructificátio –ónis, *f.*, the production of fruit

fructífico –áre, *1*, to be fruitful

fructuóse, *adv.*, fruitfully, beneficially, profitably, advantageously

fructuósus –a –um, *adj.*, fruitful

fructus –us, *m.*, fruit, produce, trees, the fruit of the soil, a reward, children, posterity, the fruit of the womb

frugálitas –átis, *f.*, frugality, simplicity

frúgifer –fera –ferum, *adj.*, fruitful

fruítio –ónis, *f.*, enjoyment, use, possession

fruméntum –i, *n.*, corn, rye, wheat, barley

fruor –i, fructus sum, *dep. 3*, to enjoy

frustra, *adv.*, in vain

frustro –áre, *1*, to deceive, disappoint, trick, rob

frustror –ári, *dep. 1*, to make void, annul

frústulum –i, *n.*, a little bit

frutétum –i, *n.*, a branch, copse, thicket

frutex –icis, *m.*, a plant, shoot, shrub

frux, frugis, *f.*, fruit

fuco –áre, *1*, to paint, disguise

fucus –i, *m.*, red, purple, rouge, deceit, pretense

fuga –ae, *f.*, flight, refuge

fúgio –ere, fugi, fúgitum, *3*, to flee, flee away, flee from

fugo –áre, *1*, to put to flight

fulciméntum –i, *n.*, a prop

fúlcio –íre, fulsi, fultum, *4*, to stay, prop up, support, strengthen

fúlgeo –ére, fulsi, *2*, to shine, glow

fúlgidus –a –um, *adj.*, shining

fulgor –óris, *m.*, brightness, lightning

fulgur –úris, *n.*, lightning, a thunderbolt

fulgúro –áre, *1*, to flash forth, lighten

fullo –ónis, *m.*, a fuller

fulmen –inis, *n.*, lightning

fultus –a –um, *adj.*, charged with, supported by

fulvus –a –um, *adj.*, gold colored

fumárium –ii, *n.*, a chimney

fumigabúndus –a –um, *adj.*, smoking

fúmigo –áre, *1*, to smoke

fumo –áre, *1*, to smoke

funále –is, *n.*, a torch, candle, candlestick

funda –ae, *f.*, a sling

fundamentális –e, *adj.*, fundamental

fundaméntum –i, *n.*, a foundation

fundátio –ónis, *f.*, a foundation, establishment

fundibulárius –i, *m.*, a slinger

fundíbulum –i, *n.*, a sling

fúnditus, *adv.*, completely

fundo –áre, *1*, to found, establish

fundo –ere, fusi, fusum, *3*, to pour

fundus –i, *m.*, a base, foundation

funeráticus –a –um, *adj.*, pertaining to a funeral

fungor –i, functus sum, *dep. 3*, to perform, exercise

funículus –i, *m.*, a little cord, string, measuring line, estate, portion, lot

funis –is, *m.*, a rope, cord, band; *pl.*, fetters

funus –eris, *n.*, funeral, interment; *fúnera*, corpses, death

fur, furis, *m. and f.*, a thief

fúria –ae, *f.*, fury

furiósus –i, *m.*, a madman

furor –ári, *dep. 1*, to steal

furor –óris, *m.*, indignation, wrath, rage, fury

furtum –i, *n.*, theft

fuscínula –ae, *f.*, a fork

fuse, *adv.*, at length, in great detail

fisco –áre, *1*, to darken

fuscus –a –um, *adj.*, black

fúsius, *adv.*, more fully

fusória –ae, *f.*, a foundry

fustis –is, *m.*, a club, staff, cudgel

fusus –i, *m.*, a spindle

futúrus, *adj.*, about to be, future

G

Gábbatha –ae, *f.*, the tribunal of judgment in Jerusalem, called the "pavement" (Jn. 19:13)

Gábriel –élis, *m.*, Gabriel, one of the three Archangels mentioned in the Bible. It was he who announced to the Virgin Mary that she was to be the Mother of God.

gálbanum –i, *n.*, galbanum, an oriental gum

gálbanus –a –um, *adj.*, yellowish

gálea –ae, *f.*, a helmet

galeátus –i, *m.*, a man wearing a helmet

gáleo –ónis, *m.*, galleon

galerículum –i, *n.*, a skull cap

galérus –i, *m.*, a hat, cardinal's hat

Galilaéus –a –um, *adj.*, Galilean, pertaining to Galilee

gallicántus –us, *m.*, the crow of a cock

gallína –ae, *f.*, a hen

gallus –i, *m.*, a cock

Gamáliel –élis, *m.*, Gamaliel, a celebrated teacher among the Jews (Acts 5:34)

garális –is, *f.*, the basin used at the Lavabo at Mass

gárrule, *adv.*, garrulously

gárrulus –a –um, *adj.*, talkative, chattering, babbling

gaúdeo –ére, gavísus sum, *semi-dep. 2,* to be glad, rejoice

gaudéte, *imper. of* gaudeo. Rejoice; Gaudete Sunday, the 3rd Sunday of Advent, so called from the first word of the Introit.

gaudimónium –ii, *n.*, joy

gaudiósus –a –um, *adj.*, joyful

gaúdium –ii, *n.*, joy, gladness, delight

gaza –ae, *f.*, riches, treasure

gazophlácium –ii, *n.*, treasury, treasure, a sacristy

gelda –ae, *f.*, a guild

geldónia –ae, *f.*, a guild

gelu –us, *n.*, frost, icy cold

gemebúndus –a –um, *adj.*, groaning

geméllio –ónis, *f.*, a small cruet

geminátus –a –um, *adj.*, doubled, twofold

géminus liquor, blood and water

gémitus –us, *m.*, a groan, moan, sigh, sorrow

gemma –ae, *f.*, a jewel

gemmárius –ii, *m.*, a jeweler

gemmátus –a –um, *adj.*, adorned with gems

gémmula –ae, *f.*, a small gem

gemo –ere –ui –itum, *3,* to sigh, groan, lament

gena –ae, *f.*, a cheek

genealógia –ae, *f.*, genealogy

gener –eri, *m.*, a son-in-law, brother-in-law

generális –is, *m.*, a general

generálitas –átis, *f.*, generality

generáliter, *adv.*, in general, generally

generátim, *adv.*, in general, generally

generátio –ónis, *f.*, generation, period of time, fruit, pedigree, birth

generátor –óris, *m.*, first author

género –áre, *1,* to beget, produce, create, bring to life

generósus –a –um, *adj.*, of noble birth, noble, excellent, of superior quality

Génesis –is, *f.*, Genesis, the first book of the Old Testament

génetrix –ícis, *f.*, mother, the Mother of God

geniáliter, *adv.*, jovially, gaily

genículo –áre, *1,* to kneel, genuflect

genículor –ári, *dep. 1,* to kneel

genículum –i, *n.*, the knee

génimen –inis, *n.*, fruit, produce

genísta –ae, *f.*, broom

genitále –is, *n.*, womb

genitális –e, *adj.*, pertaining to birth

génitor –óris, *m.*, father, the Creator

génitus –a –um, *adj.*, begotten, newly born

geno –ere –ui –itum, *3,* to bear, beget

gens, gentis, *f.*, nation, family, people, the chosen people

gentes –ium, the Gentiles, the heathen, all non-Jewish peoples

génticus –a –um, *adj.*, national, belonging to a nation

gentílis –e, *adj.*, gentile, heathen

gentílitas –átis, *f.*, paganism, heathendom

gentilítius *or* gentilícius –a –um, *adj.*, pertaining to a race or family

genu –us, *n.*, a knee

Genuflecténtes, public penitents in the early Church, the kneelers

genuflécto –ere –fléxi –fléxum, *3,* to genuflect

genufléxio –ónis, *f.*, genuflection, a bending of the knee

genuflexórium –ii, *n.*, a kneeling bench

genus –eris, *n.*, nation, race, people, kind, class, descent

genus ferae, beasts

genus reptántis, reptiles

germána –ae, *f.*, sister

Germánicus –a –um, *adj.*, German

germánitas –átis, *f.*, relationship between brothers and sisters

germánus –i, *m.*, a brother

germen –inis, *n.*, a sprout, bud, sprig, fruit, produce

gérmino –áre, *1,* to bring forth, bud forth, blossom, spring up, sprout forth

gero –ere, gessi, gestum, *3,* to bear, celebrate, do, act, conduct oneself

gérula –ae, *f.*, a female carrier

gesta –órum, *n. pl.*, deeds

gestatórium –ii, *n.*, a litter

gestatórius –a –um, *adj.*, portable; *sédia gestatória*, the chair on which the Pope is carried to the church

gestátus –us, *m.*, bearing

gestículor –ári, *dep. 1,* to make gestures, gesticulate

géstio –íre, *4,* to long for, desire eagerly, *also* to exult, be joyful

gesto –áre, *1,* to carry

gigas –ántis, *m.,* hero, giant, strong man

gignó –ere, génui, génitum, *3,* to beget, bring forth

gilda –ae, *f.,* a guild, association

gipsum –i, *n.,* gypsum, plaster of Paris

glácies –ei, *f.,* ice

gládius –ii, *m.,* a sword

glans, glandis, *f.,* an acorn

glárea –ae, *f.,* gravel

glaucus –a –um, *adj.,* bluish gray

gleba –ae, *f.,* a clod, a lump of earth

glébula –ae, *f.,* a small substance, small lump

glisco –ere, *3,* to blaze up, rage, swell

glóbulus –i, *m.,* a button, bead

globus –i, *m.,* a ball

glória –ae, *f.,* glory, honor, majesty, the reward of the saints

gloriánter, *adv.,* boastingly, exultingly

gloriátio –ónis, *f.,* glory, boasting

glorificátio –ónis, *f.,* the act of glorifying

glorífico –áre, *1,* to glorify, extol

gloríola –ae, *f.,* a halo, nimbus

glórior –ári, *dep. 1,* to glory in

Gloriósae Dóminae, the "golden Bull" of Pope Benedict XIV, 1748, confirming and extending the privileges of the Children of Mary

glorióse, *adv.,* gloriously

gloriósus –a –um, *adj.,* glorious, full of glory

gluten –inis, *n.,* glue, a bond

glútinum –i, *n.,* solder, glue

glútio –íre, *4,* to swallow

gnarus –a –um, *adj.,* knowing

Gólgatha –ae, *f.,* the Hebrew name for the place where Christ was crucified

gossípium –ii, *n.,* cotton

gossýpium –ii, *n.,* cotton; *gossýpium cerátum,* a thin taper

grabátum –i, *n.,* a bed, a cot

grácilis –e, *adj.,* slender, graceful

gradále –is, *n.,* the *Graduale* (obsolete names Gradal and Grail)

grádior –i, gressus sum, *dep. 4,* to walk, follow, live, conduct oneself

graduále –is, *n.,* the Gradual, read after the Epistle at Mass; a book containing the words and music for the liturgical chants

graduális –e, *adj.,* pertaining to steps or stairs

gradus –us, *m.,* a step, degree

graece, *adv.,* in Greek

gramen –inis, *n.,* grass

grammática –ae, *f.,* grammar

grandaévus –a –um, *adj.,* of great age

grandíloquus –a –um, *adj.,* eloquent

grandis –e, *adj.,* great

grandísculus –a –um, *adj.,* a little older, somewhat grown up

gránditer, *adv.,* strongly, mightily

grando –inis, *f.,* hail, a hailstorm

gránulum –i, *n.,* a seed, small grain

granum –i, *n.,* grain

grassor –ári, *dep. 1,* to rage, be violent

grates, *f. pl.,* thanks (used only in the acc. and abl.)

grátia –ae, *f.,* grace, favor, a supernatural gift of God bestowed upon men and angels to fit them for eternal life

grátiae –árum, *f. pl.,* thanks; *gratias agere,* to give thanks

gratiárum áctio, thanksgiving

gratíficor –ári, *dep. 1,* to gratify, oblige

gratiósus –a –um, *adj.,* favored

gratúito, *adv.,* without payment

gratúitus –a –um, *adj.,* free, voluntary

gratulabúndus –a –um, *adj.,* joyful

gratulatórie, *adv.,* in a congratulatory manner

grátulor –ári, *dep. 1,* to rejoice, exult, manifest joy

gratus –a –um, *adj.,* pleasing, agreeable, gracious, thankful

gravánter, *adv.,* with difficulty

gravátus –a –um, *adj.,* heavy, loaded down

grávidor –ári, *dep. 1,* to grow heavy, become pregnant

grávidus –a –um, *adj.,* heavy, laden, filled, full

gravis –e, *adj.,* heavy, grievious

grávitas –átis, *f.,* weight

gráviter, *adv.,* seriously, gravely

gravo –áre, *1,* to grieve, burden, oppress, weigh down, be burdensome

Gregoriánus –a –um, *adj.,* Gregorian

gremiále –is, *n.,* a lap cloth for pontifical functions

grémium –ii, *n.,* a lap

gressus –us, *m.,* a step, going, stride, the whole course of one's life

grex, gregis, *m.,* a flock, herd, the flock of Christ

grossus –i, *m.,* a young fig, a green fig

grossus –a –um, *adj.,* thick, dull

gryps, gryphis, *m.,* the griffin

gubernáculum –i, *n.,* government, helm

gubernátio –ónis, *f.,* government

gubernátor –óris, *m.*, governor
gubérno –áre, *1*, to guide, direct, govern
gula –ae, *f.*, gullet, gluttony
gurges –itis, *m.*, a stream, eddy, waters, raging abyss, whirlpool
gurgústium –ii, *n.*, a cabin
gustátus –us, *m.*, taste

gusto –áre, *1*, to taste
gutta –ae, *f.*, aloes, oil of myrrh
guttur –uris, *n.*, throat, mouth, palate, taste
gymnásium –ii, *n.*, gymnasium
gypsum –i, *n.*, plaster of Paris
gyrus –i, *m.*, a circle, a compass

H

habéna –ae, *f.*, a rein, that by which anything is held
hábeo –ére –ui –ítum, *2*, to have, hold, consider
habetúdo –inis, *f.*, dullness, stolidity
hábilis –e, *adj.*, easily managed, handy, supple
habitáculum –i, *n.*, a dwelling, apartment, house
hábitans –ántis, *m.*, a dweller
habitátio –ónis, *f.*, habitation, dwelling
habitátor –óris, *m.*, a dwelling, inhabitant
hábito –áre, *1*, to dwell, abide, live
habituális –e, *adj.*, habitual
habitúdo –inis, *f.*, form, condition, appearance, state of being
hábitus –us, *m.*, a habit, garb, dress, garment, clothing, appearance, the condition of the body
hac, *adv.*, here, this way, by this side
Hacéldama (Aramaic), the field of blood, the potter's field
hac illac, here and there
háctenus, *adv.*, so far, up to this point, only this, only so much
haéccine, is this? are there?
haedínus –a –um, *adj.*, pertaining to a kid
haedúlea –ae, *f.*, a young kid
haedus –i, *m.*, a young goat, kid
haemorrhoíssus –a –um, *adj.*, having a flow of blood
haeréditas –átis, *f.*, inheritance, possession
haéreo –ére, haesi, haesum, *2*, to stick fast, cling, adhere, hang to
haeresiárcha –ae, *m.*, an arch heretic
haéresis –is, *f.*, heresy
haeréticus –i, *m.*, a heretic
haeréticus –a –um, *adj.*, heretical
haesitátio –ónis, *f.*, hesitation
haésito –áre, *1*, to hesitate, waver, doubt, be perplexed, be at a loss

hálitus –us, *m.*, breath, exhalation
halo –áre, *1*, to breathe, exhale
hama –ae, *f.*, a bucket
hámula –ae, *f.*, a small hook
hamus –i, *m.*, a hook, fishhook
hánnapus –i, *m.*, an incense boat
haréna –ae, *f.*, sand
haríolus –i, *m.*, a soothsayer
hasta –ae, *f.*, a spear
hastíle –is, *n.*, a staff, shaft, the staff of a cross used in a procession
hastílis –e, *adj.*, on a staff, supported by a shaft
haudquáquam, *adv.*, not at all, by no means
haúrio –íre, hausi, haustum, *4*, to drink up, draw out, draw water, drain off
haustus –us, *m.*, drink, a drawing of water, draught
haut, *adv.*, not at all, by no means
hebdómada –ae, *f.*, a period of seven days, a week
Hebdómada albária, the week before Low Sunday
Hebdómada authéntica, a former name for Holy Week
hebdomadárius –ii, *m.*, a choir official serving for a week
hebdomadárius –a –um, *adj.*, lasting a week
hébdomas –adis, *f.*, a period of seven days, week
Hébdomas indulgéntiae, a name for Holy Week
Hébdomas lamentatiónum, a name for Holy Week
Hébdomas luctósa, Holy Week
Hébdomas muta, Holy Week
Hébdomas nigra, Holy Week
Hébdomas última, Holy Week
hebénius –a –um, *adj.*, of ebony
hebes –étis *or* –ítis, *adj.*, stupified, dull
hébeto –áre, *1*, to blunt
Hebraéus –a –um, *adj.*, Hebrew

Hebraéus –i, *m.*, a Hebrew
hebráice, *adv.*, in Hebrew
hebráicus –a –um, *adj.*, pertaining to Hebrew
hédera –ae, *f.*, ivy
hélica –ae, *f.*, a winding
héluo –ónis, *m.*, a glutton, gormandizer
hemitónium –ii, *n.*, a half tone in music
hemorrhoíssa –ae, *f.*, one suffering from a hemorrhage
heortológia –ae, *f.*, the science of feasts
herba –ae, *f.*, grass, a blade of grass, herb, plant, blade of wheat, corn, grain
hérbidus –a –um, *adj.*, full of grass
hereditárius –a –um, *adj.*, hereditary, original
herédito –áre, *1*, to inherit, be an heir
heres –édis, *m.* and *f.*, heir
herinácius –ii, *m.*, a hedgehog, porcupine
hermitónium –ii, *n.*, a half tone
herniósus –a –um, *adj.*, ruptured
heródio –ónis, *m.* and *f.*, a heron
heróicus –a –um, *adj.*, heroic
hesitátio –ónis, *f.*, hesitation
hésito –áre, *1*, to hesitate, waver, stagger
hestérnus –a –um, *adj.*, of yesterday, pertaining to yesterday
hetaeriárcha –ae, *m.*, an official of a confraternity
Heva –ae, *f.*, Eve
Higgaíon. This word occurs three times in the Book of Psalms, and seems to have two meanings "thought or reflection," and a technical meaning pertaining to music well known by the psalmist but whose import cannot easily be determined today.
hiemális –e, *adj.*, wintry, pertaining to winter
hiemántes, *m. pl.*, a storming, raving
hiems –emis, *f.*, winter
hierárcha –ae, *m.*, a member of the hierarchy
hierárchia –ae, *f.*, the hierarchy, the governing body of the Church. It consists of the Pope, the College of Cardinals, the Sacred Congregations, the Patriarchs, Archbishops and Bishops, Apostolic Delegates, Vicars and Prefects, certain Abbots and other Prelates.
hierárchicus –a –um, *adj.*, hierarchical, pertaining to the hierarchy
Hieremías –ae, *m.*, Jeremias
Hierónymus –i, *m.*, Jerome
Hierosólyma –órum, *n.*, Jerusalem
hierothéca –ae, *f.*, a reliquary

Hierúrgia –ae, *f.*, a sacred rite; the Mass
hilarésco –ére, *3*, to become joyful
hílaris –e, *adj.*, cheerful, joyful, smiling
hiláritas –átis, *f.*, cheerfulness
hinc, *adv.*, hence, away from here, in this direction, on this side
hinc et hinc, one on each side
hínnio –íre, *4*, to neigh
hínnulus –i, *m.*, a young hart
hircus –i, *m.*, a goat
hirúdo –inis, *f.*, a leech
hirúndo –inis, *f.*, a swallow
híspidus –a –um, *adj.*, rough, coarse
história –ae, *f.*, history, narrative, narration
hódie, *adv.*, today, this day, at the present time
hodiérna die, on this day
hodiérnus –a –um, *adj.*, relating to today
hoédinus –a –um, *adj.*, pertaining to a young goat
hoedus –i, *m.*, a young goat, kid
holocaústum –i, *n.*, a burnt offering, holocaust
holocaútoma –átis, *n.*, a burnt offering, holocaust
holoséricum –i, *n.*, silk, velvet
holus –eris, *n.*, herb, vegetable
homicída –ae, *m.* and *f.*, a murderer
homicídium –ii, *n.*, murder
homiléticus –a –um, *adj.*, pertaining to preaching or homilies
homília –ae, *f.*, homily
homiliárium –ii, *n.*, the collection of homilies
homo –inis, *m.*, man, husband
homógium –ii, *n.*, homage
honéstas –átis, *f.*, honor, riches
honéste, *adv.*, honorably
honésto –áre, *1*, to make honorable, adorn with honor, dignify
honéstor –ári, *dep. 1*, to be earnest or grave
honéstus –a –um, *adj.*, honest
honor –óris, *m.*, honor, distinction, a mark of honor
honorábilis –e, *adj.*, honorable
honorárium –ii, *n.*, a stipend for a Mass
honorárius –a –um, *adj.*, of honor, honorary
honoráte, *adv.*, with honor, honorably
honorátus –a –um, *adj.*, honorable
honorificátus –a –um, *adj.*, honorable
honorifice, *adv.*, in an honorable manner, honorably
honorificéntia –ae, *f.*, honor, glory

honorífico –áre, *1,* to honor, do honor to, glorify

honoríficus –a –um, *adj.,* honorably, conferring honor

honóro –áre, *1,* to honor

honos –óris, *m.,* honor

hora –ae, *f.,* an hour

horárius –a –um, *adj.,* pertaining to hours

hordeáceus –a –um, *adj.,* of barley

Horeb (Hebr.), *indecl.,* Horeb (the same as Sinai)

horológium –ii, *n.,* a watch or clock, a sundial, a water clock

horréndus –a –um, *adj.,* dreadful, horrible, horrid, frightful

hórreo –ére –ui, *2,* to fear, shrink from, shudder at, abhor, disdain

horrésco –ere –ui, *3,* to spurn

hórreum –ei, *n.,* a granary, barn, storehouse

horríbilis –e, *adj.,* dreadful

hórridus –a –um, *adj.,* dreadful, horrible

horripilátio –ónis, *f.,* bristling of the hair

horror –óris, *m.,* horror, dread

hortaméntum –i, *n.,* exhortation

hortátio –ónis, *f.,* exhortation, encouragement

hortátor –óris, *m.,* comforter, encourager

hortatórius –a –um, *adj.,* cheering, encouraging

hortor –ári, *dep. 1,* to exhort

hortulánus –i, *m.,* a gardener

hortus –i, *m.,* a garden

hospes –itis, *m.* and *f.,* host, guest, a stranger, a guest friend

hospitále –is, *n.,* a hospital

hospitáli domo, in a hospital or guest house

hospitális –e, *adj.,* pertaining to a guest

hospitálitas –átis, *f.,* hospitality

hospítium –ii, *n.,* hospitality, hospice

hóstia –ae, *f.,* host, victim, sacrifice, offering, gift

hóstia pacífica, a peace offering

hóstia pro peccáto, a sin or debt offering

hostiária –ae, *f.,* a vessel for hosts

hósticus –a –um, *adj.,* hostile

hostílis –e, *adj.,* hostile

hostílitas –átis, *f.,* enmity, enemy

hostis –is, *m.* and *f.,* enemy, the devil

huc, *adv.,* hither; *huc et illuc,* to and fro

húccine, *adv.,* so far?

hucúsque, *adv.,* hitherto

hujúsmodi, *adj.,* of this kind

humánitas –átis, *f.,* humanity, human nature, kindness, the human nature of Christ

humánus –a –um, *adj.,* human, humane

humécto –áre, *1,* to moisten

humerále –is, *n.,* the amice, the shoulder veil used at Benediction

humérulus –i, *m.,* side

húmerus –i, *m.,* the shoulder

humicubátio –ónis, *f.,* lying on the ground

humiliátio –ónis, *f.,* humiliation

humiliátus –a –um, *adj.,* humbled

humílio –áre, *1,* to humiliate, humble, bring low, make low, level to the ground

húmilis –e, *adj.,* humble, lowly

humílitas –átis, *f.,* humility, lowness, misery, humiliation, wretchedness

humíliter, *adv.,* lowly, humbly

humor –óris, *m.,* fluid, moisture, desire

humus –i, *f.,* earth, soil, land, ground

hyacínthinus –a –um, *adj.,* violet

hybernális –e, *adj.,* wintry

hýdria –ae, *f.,* a water pot or jar

hydrópicus –a –um, *adj.,* dropsical, afflicted with dropsy

hydrópisis –is, *f.,* the dropsy

hydrops –ópis, *m.,* the dropsy

hymnárium –ii, *n.,* a collection of hymns

hýmnicus –a –um, *adj.,* pertaining to hymns

hymnódia –ae, *f.,* the singing of hymns

hymnus –i, *m.,* a hymn, a song of praise

hymnus Ambrosiánus, the *Te Deum*

hymnus angélicus, the *Gloria in Excelsis*

hyperbólice, *adv.,* with exaggeration

hyperdúlia –ae, *f.,* superior veneration

hypermétricus –a –um, *adj.,* exceeding a meter

hypócrisis –is, *f.,* imitation, hypocrisy

hypócrita –ae, *m.,* a hypocrite

hypodiáconus –i, *m.,* a subdeacon

hypógeum –i, *n.,* a basement, crypt, vault

hypostáticus –a –um, *adj.,* essential, substantial, hypostatic

hýssopus –i, *f.,* hyssop

to
dis-
de-
rove,
some,
Office
sgrace,
taunt,
oreseen,
vares
ail
in
rm
ow warm
be gray-
culate by
in
rmal incor-
a diocese
on, embodi-
ine and hu-
arnate
arnate, make
nexpectedly
m, 3, to go,
h, enter in
nsum, 3, to
e to
fire
ser
sing or censing
se
nser
frankincense
most fragrant
incensed
tive
omoter, provoker
ainty

incértus –a –um, *adj.*, uncertain, hidd

incessábilis –e, *adj.*, unceasing

incessánter, *adv.*, continually, uncea ingly

inchoátio –ónis, *f.*, beginning

ínchoo –áre, *1,* to begin, commence

íncido –ere –cídi, *3,* to fall into, ha pen upon

incído –ere –cídi, *3,* to cut into

incípio –ere –cépi –céptum, *3,* to beg

incircumcísus –a –um, *adj.*, uncircun cised

incircumscríptus –a –um, *adj.*, incon prehensible

incísus –a –um, *adj.*, cut

incitátor –óris, *m.*, an investigator

íncito –áre, *1,* to cry out loudly

inclíno –áre, *1,* to bow, bend, lean, ir cline

inclúdo –ere –clúsi –clúsum, *3,* to ir clude

inclúsa –ae, *f.*, an incluse, an anchores

inclusíve, *adv.*, inclusive

inclúsor –óris, *m.*, a smith

ínclytus –a –um, *adj.*, glorious, renowne

incoenátus –a –um, *adj.*, fasting, with out supper

íncola –ae, *m. and f.*, dweller, inhabitan

incolátus –us, *m.*, residence, sojourn stay, a dwelling in a place

incolúmnitas –átis, *f.*, safety, soundness good condition

incombústus –a –um, *adj.*, unconsumed not burnt

incommátio –ónis, *f.*, an imperfect state

incommutábilis –e, *adj.*, immutable, un changing

incommutabílitas –átis, *f.*, unchangeable ness, immutability

incommutabíliter, *adv.*, unchangeably, im mutably

incomparábilis –e, *adj.*, incomparable

incomparabíliter, *adv.*, incomparably

incompósitus –a –um, *adj.*, disordered

incomprehensíbilis –e, *adj.*, incompre hensible

inconcúbius –a –um, *adj.*, relating to the dead of night

inconcússe, *adv.*, firmly, resolutely

incongruénter, *adv.*, unsuitably

incóngruus –a –um, *adj.*, incongruous, unfitting, inconsistent

inconstántia –ae, *f.*, wandering

inconsummátus –a –um, *adj.*, unde veloped, imperfect

I

iánthinus –a –um, *adj.*, violet

ibex –icis, *m.*, wild goat

ibídem, *adv.*, in the same place, in that very place

ibis –is *or* –idis, *f.*, an ibis, an Egyptian bird

Iconoclásta –ae, *m.*, an Iconoclast, one who opposes the veneration of images of saints

Iconomáchi –órum, *m. pl.*, Iconoclasts

ictus –us, *m.*, a stream, blow, stab, stroke, thrust

idcírco, *adv.*, therefore, on that account

idem, éadem, idem, same; with *ipse*, the selfsame

idénticus –a –um, *adj.*, identical

idéntidem, *adv.*, repeatedly, again and again

identífico –áre, *1,* to be identical with

idéntitas –átis, *f.*, identity, sameness

ideo, *adv.*, therefore

idéoma –átis, *n.*, same as *idióma*

idióma –átis, *n.*, an idiom, language, peculiarity of speech

idióta –ae, *m.*, an ignorant man

idípsum, *adv.*, together, forthwith, com pletely

Idithum (Hebr.), *indecl.*, Idithun (Ethan), mentioned in the titles of three Psalms. Generally taken to signify a choir leader.

idólium –ii, *n.*, the temple of an idol

idololátra –ae, *c.*, an idolater

idololátria –ae, *f.*, idolatry

idolóthytum –i, *n.*, the food offered to idols

idólum –i, *n.*, an idol

idóneus –a –um, *adj.*, suitable, fit, ap propriate, sufficient, satisfactory

Idumaéa –ae, *f.*, Edom, the country in which the people who sprang from Esau lived. Previously this country was called Mount Seir. Only in Mark 3:8 it is called Idumaea.

Idumaéus –a –um, *adj.*, of Edom, an Edomite, an inhabitant of Idumaea. The Edomites were some of the enemies who threatened Israel.

ignárus –a –um, *adj.*, ignorant of, in experienced in, unacquainted with

ignávia –ae, *f.*, idleness, laziness, sloth, cowardice, listlessness

ignáviter, *adv.*, lazily, slothfully, with out spirit

ignávus –a –um, *adj.*, slothful, idle, in active, listless

ignésco –ere, *3,* to burn, catch fire, glow with passion

ígneus –a –um, *adj.*, fiery, burning, flaming, glowing with heat

ignis –is, *m.*, fire, conflagration, light ning, symbol of great danger; *ignes,* the desires of the flesh

ignítus –a –um, *adj.*, burning, fire-tried, refined, very pure, purified from dross

ignóbilis –e, *adj.*, base, obscure, ignoble, unknown, inglorious

ignobílitas –átis, *f.*, dishonor, obscurity

ignomínia –ae, *f.*, shame, ignominy, con fusion, disgrace, dishonor

ignominiósus –a –um, *adj.*, disgraceful, full of disgrace, ignominious

ignorábilis –e, *adj.*, unknown

ignoránter, *adv.*, through ignorance

ignorántia –ae, *f.*, ignorance, want of knowledge

ignóro –áre, *1,* to be ignorant of, not to know

ignósco –ere –nóvi –nótum, *3,* to for give, pardon, overlook, not to take notice of

ignótus –a –um, *adj.*, unknown

I.H.S., the first three letters of the Name of Jesus in Greek

ilex –icis, *f.*, holm oak

illábor –i –lápsus sum, *dep. 3,* to sink down, descend, fall, glide down, fall down or into, slip into a habit or custom

illabóro –áre, *1,* to work at, work upon

illac, *adv.*, there, at this place

illaésus –a –um, *adj.*, unharmed

illamentátus –a –um, *adj.*, unlamented

illécebra –ae, *f.*, allurement, banishment, charm, enticement

illéctus –a –um, *adj.*, unread

illéctus –us, *m.*, allurement, seduction

illibátus –a –um, *adj.*, unblemished, un diminished, unimpaired, uncurtailed

illic, *adv.*, there

illício –ere –léxi –léctum, *3,* to allure, entice, seduce, decoy, inveigle

illícite, *adv.*, illegally

illícitus –a –um, *adj.*, forbidden

íllico, *adv.,* immediately, on the spot, in that very place

illído –ere –lísi –lísum, 3, to strike, beat, knock, dash against

ílligo –áre, 1, to fetter, bind, encumber, hasten, attach to, impede, entangle

íllino –ere –lévi –litum, 3, to smear, bedaub, cover with, spread over

illuc, *adv.,* thither, to that place

illucésco –ere –lúxi, 3, to shine upon, give light, illuminate, shine forth

illúdo –ere –lúsi –lúsum, 3, to deceive, delude, mock, play, sport, laugh at, ruin, disgrace

illumináte, *adv.,* clearly, luminously

Illumináti, an heretical sect of the sixteenth and seventeenth centuries

illuminátio –ónis, *f.,* light, illumination, an enlightening

illuminatórium –ii, *n.,* a baptistry

illúmino –áre, 1, to enlighten, illuminate, cause to shine, set in a clear light, make clear, set off, adorn

illúsio –ónis, *f.,* illusion, mockery, irony

illúsor –óris, *m.,* a mocker

illustrátio –ónis, *f.,* brightness, illustration

illustrátor –óris, *m.,* an enlightener

illústris –e, *adj.,* glorious, full of light

illustríssimus –a –um, *adj.,* most illustrious

illústro –áre, 1, to enlighten, adorn, illuminate, make illustrious, make or cause to shine, glorify

ima –órum, *n.,* the lowest things, depths

imaginárius –a –um, *adj.,* decorated with pictures or images, fancied, imagined

imáginor –ári, *dep.* 1, to imagine, picture to oneself

imágo –inis, *f.,* image, picture, likeness, appearance, form

imbecílitas –átis, *f.,* weakness, feebleness, imbecility

imbecíllus –a –um, *adj.,* feeble, weak

imbéllis –e, *adj.,* cowardly

imber –ris, *m.,* rain, shower, pelting rain, water

imbíbo –ere –bíbi, 3, to drink in

ímbuo –ere –ui –útum, 3, to instruct, fill, nourish

imitátio –ónis, *f.,* example, imitation

imitátor –óris, *m.,* a follower, imitator

imitátrix –ícis, *f.,* a female follower, imitator

ímitor –ári, *dep.* 1, to imitate

immaculátus –a –um, *adj.,* immaculate,

spotless, undefiled, stainless, blameless

immánis –e, *adj.,* brutal, savage

immánitas –átis, *f.,* fierceness, cruelty

immániter, *adv.,* cruelly, frightfully, dreadfully, monstrously

immarcescíbilis –e, *adj.,* imperishable

immateriális –e, *adj.,* immaterial

immatúrus –a, –um, *adj.,* immature, unripe

immediáte, *adv.,* immediately

immediátus –a –um, *adj.,* direct, immediate

immedicábilis –e, *adj.,* incurable

ímmemor –óris, *adj.,* unmindful, forgetful

immemorábilis –e, *adj.,* immemorial

immemorátio –ónis, *f.,* forgetfulness, oblivion

imménsitas –átis, *f.,* infinity

imménsus –a –um, *adj.,* immense, infinite, unmeasurable, all pervading, omnipresent

immérgo –ere –mérsi –mérsum, 3, to dip into, immerse

immérito, *adv.,* unworthily, not deserving or meriting

immérsio –ónis, *f.,* immersion

ímminens –éntis, *adj.,* threatening, imminent

immínuo –ere –ui –útum, 3, to diminish, abate

immísceo –ére –míscui –místum *or* –míxtum, 2, to mix in, mingle with, join with

immiséricors –dis, *adj.,* merciless, unmerciful

immíssio –ónis, *f.,* infusion, setting forth, letting loose, sending in

immítia –órum, *n. pl.,* cruel sights, harsh things

immítis –e, *adj.,* harsh

immítto –ere –mísi –míssum, 3, to send, insert, put into, conduct, cast, encamp

immóbilis –e, *adj.,* immovable

immobíliter, *adv.,* steadfastly, immovably, unshakenly

immoderántia –ae, *f.,* excess

immoderáte, *adv.,* intemperately

immoderátus –a –um, *adj.,* immoderate, excessive, without measure

immodéste, *adv.,* unbecomingly

immódicus –a –um, *adj.,* immoderate, excessive

immolátio –ónis, *f.,* offering, a name for the Preface at Mass

ímmolo –áre, 1, to immolate, sacrifice,

---

imprímo –ere –préssi –préssum, 3, print, press into

ímprobe, *adv.,* wickedly, wrongly, honesty

impróbitas –átis, *f.,* importunity, pravity, wickedness

ímprobo –áre, 1, to blame, disapprove, reject, find fault with

ímprobus –a –um, *adj.,* troublesome, evil

Impropéria, the Reproaches in the ... of Good Friday

impropérium –ii, *n.,* reproach, disgrace, shame

imprópero –áre, 1, to reproach, upbraid

impróvidus –a –um, *adj.,* unforeseeing, unexpected, sudden

improvíso, *adv.,* suddenly, unawares

imprúdens –éntis, *adj.,* foolish

impúgno –áre, 1, to attack, assail

inágris –e, *adj.,* empty, void, vain

inaúris –is, *f.,* an earring

incálceo –ére –ui, 2, to be warmed

incalésco –ere –cálui, 3, to grow warm

incanésco –ere –cánui, 3, to ...

incánto –áre, 1, to charm, incant, repeating over and over again

incardinátio –ónis, *f.,* the formal incorporation of a clergyman ...

incarnátio –ónis, *f.,* incarnation, the union of the divine ... ment, the union of the divine with human nature in Jesus Christ

incarnátus –a –um, *adj.,* incarnate

incárn –áre, 1, to make incarnate, flesh, clothe with flesh

incássum, *adv.,* in vain

incastratúra –ae, *f.,* mortise

incaúte, *adv.,* unawares, unguardedly

incédo –ere –céssi –céssum, 3, to walk, go about, approach

incéndo –ere –céndi –cénsum, 3, to burn, kindle, heat, set fire to, flame

incéndium –ii, *n.,* a conflagration

incensárium –ii, *n.,* incense

incensátio –ónis, *f.,* to incense

incénso –áre, 1, to incense

incensórium –ii, *n.,* incense

incénsum –i, *n.,* incense

incénsum suavíssimum, incense

incénsus –a –um, *adj.,* ...

incentívum –i, *n.,* incentive, a provocation

incéntor –óris, *m.,* a precentor, uncertain

incértum –i, *n.,* uncertain

inconsútilis –e, *adj.*, without a seam, made in one piece

incontaminábilis –e, *adj.*, undefilable

incontaminátus –a –um, *adj.*, undefiled

incorpóreus –a –um, *adj.*, without a body, incorporeal

incórporor –ári, *dep.* 1, to be incorporated

incorruptéla –ae, *f.*, incorruption, immortality

incorruptíbilis –e, *adj.*, incorruptible

incorruptibílitas –átis, *f.*, immunity from corruption, incorruption

incorruptibíliter, *adv.*, imperishably, incorruptibly

incorrúptio –ónis, *f.*, incorruption

incorrúptus –a –um, *adj.*, incorrupted

incrassátus –a –um, *adj.*, hardened

incrásso –áre, 1, to grow fat, render gross

increátus –a –um, *adj.*, uncreated

increbrésco –ere –crébrui, 3, to become frequent, increase, prevail

incredíbilis –e, *adj.*, incredible, unbelievable

incredúlitas –átis, *f.*, incredulity, unbelief

incrédulus –a –um, *adj.*, faithless, incredulous, unbelieving

increméntum –i, *n.*, increase, growth of plants and animals

increpátio –ónis, *f.*, a rebuke, scolding, chiding

increpatórius –a –um, *adj.*, rebuking, chiding, scolding

íncrepo –áre, 1, to rebuke, reprove, blame, chide, rustle, rattle

incrésco –ere –crévi, 3, to grow in anything

íncubo –áre, 1, to lie in, lie on

incúlco –áre, 1, to trample in, mix in, impress upon, force upon

inculpábilis –e, *adj.*, blameless

inculpándus –a –um, *adj.*, not blameworthy

incúmbo –ere –cúbui –cúbitum, 3, to lie upon, recline or lean on

incunábula –órum, *n. pl.*, beginning, swaddling clothes

incunctánter, *adv.*, readily, without delay, unhesitatingly

incurábilis –e, *adj.*, incurable

incúria –ae, *f.*, neglect, indifference, carelessness

incúrro –ere –cúrri *or* –cucúrri –cúrsum, 3, to come upon, run upon

incúrsio –ónis, *f.*, attack

incúrso –áre, 1, to run against, strike against

incúrsus –us, *m.*, attack, assault

incúrvo –áre, 1, to bend, curve, bow down

incúrvor –ári, *dep.* 1, to bow down

incúrvus –a –um, *adj.*, bent, curved, crooked

incútio –ere –cússi –cússum, 3, to strike

indágo –áre, 1, to inquire into, investigate

indeclinábilis –e, *adj.*, unwavering, firm

indeféssus –a –um, *adj.*, untired, unwearied

indefíciens –éntis, *adj.*, unfailing

indeficiénter, *adv.*, unfailingly, incessantly

indefiníte, *adv.*, indefinitely

indesinénter, *adv.*, unceasingly, continually

index –icis, *m.*, a token, a sign, the list of books forbidden by the Church

indicíbilis –e, *adj.*, unable to be told in words

indícium –ii, *n.*, evidence, sign, mark, proof

índico –áre, 1, to indicate, proclaim, tell, show, reveal, make known, inform against

indíctio –ónis, *f.*, indiction

indifferénter, *adv.*, indifferently, not differently

índigens –éntis, *adj.*, needy, poor, in want; *also* a poor person

indígeo –ére –ui, 2, to stand in need of, to want, to need

indigéstus –a –um, *adj.*, undigested

indígnans –ántis, *adj.*, angry, indignant

indignátio –ónis, *f.*, indignation, anger

indígne, *adv.*, indignantly, unworthily

indígnitas –átis, *f.*, baseness, unworthiness

indígnor –ári, *dep.* 1, to be angry, indignant, offended, consider unworthy

indígnus –a –um, *adj.*, unworthy, undeserving

índigus –a –um, *adj.*, needy

indisciplinátus –a –um, *adj.*, unskillful

indissímilis –e, *adj.*, not unlike

indissolúbilis –e, *adj.*, imperishable

índitus –a –um, *adj.*, given or imposed

indivíduus –a –um, *adj.*, indivisible; *as substantive*, undivided

indivísus –a –um, *adj.*, undivided

indo –ere –didi –ditum, 3, to put in, put into, give to

índoles –is, *f.*, genius, talent
indórmio –íre, *4*, to sleep in or on anything
indubitánter, *adv.*, undubitably, without doubt
indubitátus –a –um, *adj.*, unwavering, certain
indúbito –áre, *1*, to doubt
indúciae –árum, *f. pl.*, an extension of time, a truce
indúco –ere –dúxi –dúctum, *3*, to lead, bring into
inductórius –a –um, *adj.*, misleading, seducing
indulgéntia –ae, *f.*, indulgence, pardon, forgiveness, the remission of punishment incurred
indúlgeo –ére –dúlsi –dúltum, *2*, to grant, forgive, be indulgent, indulge, give, bestow, gratify, be forbearing
indultívus –a –um, *adj.*, by indult or grant
indúltum –i, *n.*, indult, release from obligation
induméntum –i, *n.*, apparel
índuo –ere –ui –útum, *3*, to put on, clothe
indúro –áre, *1*, to dry up, harden, make hard
indúsium –ii, *n.*, a shirt
indústria –ae, *f.*, purpose, industry, diligence
indústrius –a –um, *adj.*, industrious, diligent, active, zealous
inébrio –áre, *1*, to soak, make drunk, intoxicate, inebriate, water
inédia –ae, *f.*, fasting, hunger, abstinence
ineffábilis –e, *adj.*, ineffable, unutterable
ineffabíliter, *adv.*, in an unspeakable manner, unutterably
inenarrábilis –e, *adj.*, unspeakable, indescribable
íneo –íre –ii *or* –ívi –ítum, *4*, to enter, undertake, enter upon
inéptus –a –um, *adj.*, stupid
inérmis –e, *adj.*, unarmed, defenseless
inerrabíliter, *adv.*, indescribably
iners –értis, *adj.*, simple, inactive, idle, lazy
inerudítio –ónis, *f.*, ignorance
inésse –fui, to be in or on
inevitábilis –e, *adj.*, unavoidable, inevitable
inexcusábilis –e, *adj.*, inexcusable

inexhaústus –a –um, *adj.*, inexhausted, inexhaustible
inexpectátus –a –um, *adj.*, unexpected
inexpértus –a –um, *adj.*, inexperienced, unaccustomed
inexplébilis –e, *adj.*, extraordinary, insatiable
inexplebíliter, *adv.*, insatiably
inexpugnális –e, *adj.*, invincible
inextinguíbilis –e, *adj.*, unquenchable, inextinguishable
inextricábilis –e, *adj.*, inextricable
infallíbilis –e, *adj.*, infallible
infámia –ae, *f.*, evil report
infámis –e, *adj.*, of ill repute, disreputable, infamous
infans –ántis, *m. and f.*, infant, child, babe
infántes expósiti, foundlings
infántia –ae, *f.*, childhood, infancy
infántula –ae, *f.*, a babe
infántulus –i, *m.*, infant
infatigabíliter, *adv.*, indefatigably
infatuátus –a –um, *adj.*, tasteless
infecúnditas –átis, *f.*, sterility, barrenness
infecúndus –a –um, *adj.*, sterile
infelícitas –átis, *f.*, unhappiness, wretchedness
infélix –icis, *adj.*, unhappy
infénsus –a –um, *adj.*, hostile, dangerous
ínferi –órum, *m. pl.*, the infernal regions, the lower world, hell
inférior –ius, *adj.*, lower, below
infermentátus –a –um, *adj.*, unleavened
inférnus –i, *m.*, grave, underworld, the nether world, hell
ínfero –érre –tuli, illátum, *3*, to bring, carry in, bear, place on
inferuésco –ere, *3*, to become inflamed or kindled
ínferus –a –um, *adj.*, pertaining to the grave, the underworld, hell
ínferus –i, *m.*, the underworld, hell
infestátio –ónis, *f.*, assault
infésto –áre, *1*, attack, molest, disturb
inféstus –a –um, *adj.*, hostile
infício –ere –féci –féctum, *3*, to pollute, infect, stain, dip into anything
infidélis –e, *adj.*, unfaithful, unbelieving
infidélitas –átis, *f.*, faithlessness
in fíeri, the passage from potency to act
infígo –ere –fíxi –fíxum, *3*, to fasten in, stick fast, thrust in
ínfimus –a –um, *adj.*, the lowest, the meanest, of the lower world
infinítus –a –um, *adj.*, infinite

infírmitas –átis, *f.*, infirmity, sickness, disease, weakness, pain

infírmo –áre, *1,* to weaken

infírmor –ári, *dep. 1,* to be sick, weak, diseased

infírmus –a –um, *adj.,* weak, sick, infirm

inflámmo –áre, *1,* to inflame, kindle, burn, set on fire

inflátus –a –um, *adj.,* puffed up, swollen

inflo –áre, *1,* to puff up

inflécto –ere –fléxi –fléctum, *3,* to bend

informátio –ónis, *f.,* information

informatívus –a –um, *adj.,* pertaining to information

infórmitas –átis, *f.,* lack of form, shapelessness

infórmiter, *adv.,* formlessly

infórmo –áre, *1,* to fashion

ínfremo –ere –frémui, *3,* to groan

infríngo –ere –frégi –fráctum, *3,* to infringe upon, break

infructuósus –a –um, *adj.,* barren, unfruitful

infrunítus –a –um, *adj.,* bold

ínfula –ae, *f.,* a miter, a chasuble, one of the bands hanging from a miter

infulátus –a –um, *adj.,* mitered

infúndo –ere –fúdi –fúsum, *3,* to infuse, impart, water, pour into, pour upon

infúsio –ónis, *f.,* infusion, outpouring, pouring into

infusórium –ii, *n.,* a tube, pipe

ingémino –áre, *1,* to repent

ingemísco (*or* –ésco) –ere –gémui, *3,* to wail, sigh, groan

ingénitus –a –um, *adj.,* unbegotten

ingénium –ii, *n.,* natural character

ingens –éntis, *adj.,* great, vast, huge, grown to a great size

íngero –ere –géssi –gestum, *3,* to infuse, pour into

in globo, in a collection or lump

ingravésco –ere, *3,* to become serious

ingrédior –i –gréssus sum, *semi-dep. 3,* to come in, advance, enter, walk along, conduct oneself

ingrévido –áre, *1,* to weigh down, oppress, burden

ingrévo –áre, *1,* to aggravate

ingréssus –us, *m.,* a procession, going into, entering, walk, step

íngruo –ere –ui, *3,* to assault

ínguen –inis, *n.,* the groin

inhabitábilis –e, *adj.,* not inhabited, uninhabitable

inhabitátor –óris, *m.,* a dweller, inhabitant

inhábito –áre, *1,* to dwell, abide

inhaéreo –ére –haési –haésum, *2,* to adhere to

inhiánter, *adv.,* greedily, eagerly, with open mouth

inhíbeo –ére, *2,* to prevent, check, restrain, hold back, hold in check

ínhio –áre, *1,* to long for, gape after

inhonéste, *adv.,* with dishonor

inhonorátio –ónis, *f.,* dishonor

inhonorátus –a –um, *adj.,* unrewarded, not honored

inhonóro –áre, *1,* to dishonor

inhumánitas –átis, *f.,* inhumanity

inhumánus –a –um, *adj.,* brutal, inhuman

inhumátus –a –um, *adj.,* unburied

ínibi, *adv.,* in that place, therein, in that matter

inimicítia –ae, *f.,* enmity

inimícus –i, *m.,* enemy, foe

inimícus –a –um, *adj.,* hostile

ininterpretábilis, –e, *adj.,* difficult to explain

iníque, *adv.,* wickedly, wrongly, unjustly

iníquitas –átis, *f.,* iniquity, injustice, sin

iníquus –a –um, *adj.,* unjust, wicked, godless; as *n.,* evildoer

inítio –áre, *1,* to initiate, admit to sacred rites, to baptize

inítium –ii, *n.,* the beginning, commencement

ínitus –a –um, *adj.,* entered upon, begun

injício –ere –jéci –jéctum, *3,* to lay upon, place upon, hurl into, cast into

injúngo –ere –júnxi –júnctum, *3,* to impose, enjoin

injúria –ae, *f.,* injury, wrong, injustice

injúste, *adv.,* unjustly, unrighteously

injustítia –ae, *f.,* injustice, iniquity, sin

injústus –a –um, *adj.,* unjust, godless, unrighteous

innátus –a –um, *adj.,* inborn, innate

innécto –ere, *3,* to insert

innítor –i –níxus sum, *dep. 3,* to rely on, lean upon, rest on

ínnocens –éntis, *adj.,* innocent, pure, clean, guiltless, harmless

innocénter, *adv.,* innocently

innocéntia –ae, *f.,* innocence

innócuus –a –um, *adj.,* blameless, innocent

innotésco –ere –nótui, *3,* to become known, make known

ínnovo –áre, *1,* to renew, to alter

innóxius –a –um, adj., innocent, harmless

innumerábilis –e, adj., innumerable, countless, numberless

innúmerus –a –um, adj., countless, without number

ínnuo –ere –ui, 3, to make a sign, signal to

innúptus –a –um, adj., unmarried

inobediéntia –ae, f., disobedience

inofténsus –a –um, adj., unhurt

inolésco –ere –évi –itum, 3, to grow in or on

inólitus –a –um, adj., ingrown, inveterate

inópia –ae, f., want, need, poverty

inopináte, adv., unexpectedly

inopinátus –a –um, adj., unexpected, unlooked for

inops –opis, adj., destitute, needy, afflicted, indigent, without means or resources

inordináte, adv., unequally

inordinátio –ónis, f., disorder

in plano, on the level

in próximo, at hand

inputríbilis –e, adj., incorruptible

inquiéto –áre, 1, to disturb, disquiet

inquietúdo –inis, f., restlessness, disquietude

inquiétus –a –um, adj., undefiled

inquinaméntum –i, n., a stain, a soil

inquinátio –ónis, f., a stain

inquinátus –a –um, adj., defiled

ínquino –áre, 1, to spoil, pollute, defile, contaminate

inquíro –ere –sívi –sítum, 3, to desire, search for, seek, seek after, require

inquisítio –ónis, f., search, inquiry, speculation, investigation

Inquisítio –ónis, f., Inquisition

inquisítor –óris, m., an officer of the Inquisition

inréptio –ónis, f., a creeping in

I.N.R.I., abbreviation of Iesus Nazarénus Rex Judaeórum, Jesus of Nazareth King of the Jews

insanábilis –e, adj., incurable

insánia –ae, f., insanity, madness, frenzy, folly

insánio –íre, 4, to be mad, be outrageous

insánus –i, m., a madman

insatiábilis –e, adj., ambitious, insatiable

inscítia –ae, f., ignorance

inscríbo –ere –scrípsi –scríptum, 3, to write over

inscríptio –ónis, f., an inscription, described on a pillar

inscrutábilis –e, adj., inscrutable, unsearchable

inscúlpo –ere –scúlpsi –scúlptum, 3, to carve, engrave, brand

insecútor –óris, m., persecutor, pursuer

insensátus –i, m., a fool

insensátus –a –um, adj., senseless

insensíbilis –e, adj., insensible

inseparabíliter, adv., inseparably

inseparábilis –e, adj., inseparable

insepúltus –a –um, adj., unburied

ínsero –ere –sévi –situm, 3, to implant

ínsero –ere –ui –sértum, 3, to entangle, enroll

insértus –a –um, adj., fixed, rooted

insérvio –íre, 4, to serve

insídeo –ére –sédi –séssum, 2, to rest upon

insídia –ae, f., deceit

insídiae –árum, f. pl., ambush, snare, plot, treachery

insidiátor –óris, m., traitor, spy, plotter

insídio –áre, 1, to lay snares

insídior –ári, dep. 1, to watch for, lie in wait for, lie in ambush, plot against

insígne –is, n., a distinction, distinctive badge

insígnio –íre, 4, to adorn, honor, distinguish, endow

insígnis –e, adj., noted, notable

insígniter, adv., remarkably

insignítus –a –um, adj., known, signed

insígno –áre, 1, to honor, distinguish, endow

insimulátus –a –um, adj., pretended, feigned

insínuo –áre, 1, to insinuate, convey, teach, make known

insípiens –éntis, adj., foolish, unwise

insipiéntia –ae, f., foolishness, folly

ínsitus –a –um, adj., ingrafted

insolésco –ere, 3, to become insolvent, behave extravagantly

insolúbilis –e, adj., insoluble, cannot be unlocked

insómnis –e, adj., sleepless

ínsono –áre –sónui –sónitum, 1, to sound, resound, roar

insons –óntis, adj., innocent

insperátus –a –um, adj., unhoped for, unexpected

inspérgo –ere –spérsi –spérsum, 3, to sprinkle

inspício –ere –spéxi –spéctum, *3,* to gaze upon, stir upon

inspirátio –ónis, *f.,* inspiration, breath, the power whereby God governs creation

inspíro –áre, *1,* to breathe into

instábilis –e, *adj.,* unstable, inconstant, changeable

instabíliter, *adv.,* unsteadily

instans –ántis, *adj.,* present, instant

instántia –ae, *f.,* instance

instar, *indecl., n.,* image, likeness; (*with the genitive*), like to, after the fashion of

instaurátio –ónis, *f.,* renewal

instaurátor –óris, *m.,* restorer

instaúro –áre, *1,* to comprise, renew, strengthen, begin anew, repeat

instínctus –us, *m.,* inspiration

ínstita –ae, *f.,* a winding band, bandage

instítia –ae, *f.,* goodness, according to the Law of God

ínstitor –óris, *m.,* a merchant

instítuo –ere –ui –útum, *3,* to ordain, institute, cause, procure

institútio –ónis, *f.,* institution, manner of life, a religious order

insto –áre –stiti, *1,* to insist, persist, threaten, stand, press upon, wait, follow closely, approach, be close to

instrépero –ere, *3,* to utter, make resound

instrúctio –ónis, *f.,* instruction

Instrúctio Clementína, regulations governing the forty hours' prayer, published by Pope Clement VIII in 1592

instrúctus –a –um, *adj.,* drawn up in line of battle

instruméntum –i, *n.,* an instrument

ínstruo –ere –strúxi –strúctum, *3,* to draw up, to instruct, teach

insúdo –áre, *1,* to sweat at or in

insuefáctus –a –um, *adj.,* inured to, accustomed to

insufflátio –ónis, *f.,* a breathing upon, breathing into

insúfflo –áre, *1,* to blow, blow upon, inflate, breathe upon

ínsula –ae, *f.,* an island

insulánus –i, *m.,* an islander

insúlto –áre, *1,* to scoff at, taunt, insult

insúmo –ere –súmpsi –súmptum, *3,* to consume

ínsuo –ere –sui –sútum, *3,* to sew up

ínsuper, *adv.,* in addition, moreover, furthermore, besides, yea also

insúrgo –ere –surréxi –surréctum, *3,* to rise up, revolt against

insuspicábilis –e, *adj.,* unsuspected

intáctus –a –um, *adj.,* inviolate

intaminátus –a –um, *adj.,* unspotted

ínteger –gra –grum, *adj.,* whole, entire, correct

integérrime, *adv.,* most rigidly

intégritas –átis, *f.,* integrity, wholeness, health, soundness, purity, uprightness, virginity

intellectuális –e, *adj.,* spiritual

intelléctus –us, *m.,* sense, meaning, insight, understanding

intelligéntia –ae, *f.,* knowledge, understanding, intelligence, an intelligent being

intelligibíliter, *adv.,* intellectually, intelligibly

intélligo –ere –léxi –léctum, *3,* to understand, perceive, feel, attend to, give heed to

intemerátus –a –um, *adj.,* spotless

intempésta nox, the dead of night

intempestátus –a –um, *adj.,* unseasonable, untimely

intempestívus –a –um, *adj.,* untimely, inopportune

intempéstus –a –um, *adj.,* unseasonable

inténdo –ere –téndi –ténsum *or* –tentum, *3,* to hearken, mark, be attentive, go forth, look down mercifully upon, regard, look upon, direct one's steps

intentátor –óris, *m.,* one who cannot be tempted

inténtio –ónis, *f.,* intention

inténtus –a –um, *adj.,* anxious, intent, waiting eagerly for, attentive to

intercédo –ere –céssi –céssum, *3,* to intercede, interpose on behalf of a person

intercéssio –ónis, *f.,* intercession

intercéssor –óris, *m.,* an intercessor

intercído –ere –cídi –císum, *3,* to divide, separate, cleave

intercísus –a –um, *adj.,* cut to pieces

intercúrro –ere, *3,* to intervene, run between

interdíctum –i, *n.,* interdict, prohibition

intérdiu, *adv.,* by day

intérea, *adv.,* in the meantime

intéreo –íre –ívi –ítum, *4,* to die, perish

interféctor –óris, *m.,* a slayer

interfício –ere –féci –féctum, *3,* to kill, slay, destroy, put to death

interímo –ere –émi –émptum, *3,* to slay, kill, destroy, annihilate intérior –ius, *adj.*, inward

interióra, *n. pl.*, entrails

interítio –ónis, *f.*, destruction

intéritus –us, *m.*, overthrow, destruction, death, annihilation

intérius, *adv.*, inwardly

intermínátus –a –um, *adj.*, endless, infinite

intermíssio –ónis, *f.*, ceasing

intermítto –ere –mísi –míssum, *3*, to leave, let pass

internécuo –ónis, *f.*, carnage, massacre

intérnus –a –um, *adj.*, internal

íntero –ere –trívi –tritum, *3*, to rub, crumble, break

interpellátio –ónis, *f.*, intercession

interpéllo –áre, *1*, to make intercession, intercede, interrupt

interposítio –ónis, *f.*, a bringing forward, introducing, an interval of time

intérpres –pretis, *c.*, interpreter

interpretátio –ónis, *f.*, interpretation

intérpreto –áre, *1*, to interpret

intérpretor –ári, *dep. 1*, to interpret, expound

interrásilis –e, *adj.*, intergraven, in relief

interrogátio –ónis, *f.*, question, argument, pledge

intérrogo –áre, *1*, to inquire, ask questions, request, demand, examine, test, try

interrúmpo –ere –rúpi –rúptum, *3*, to divide, break into, cleave, break asunder

intérsero –ere –sérui –sértum, *3*, to place between

intérsero –ere –sévi –situm, *3*, to sow, plant between

intersíleo –ére, *2*, to be silent in the meanwhile

interstítium –ii, *n.*, an interval of time, interruption, cessation

intertrúdo –ere, *3*, to thrust between

intervállum –i, *n.*, a space, interval

intervéntio –ónis, *f.*, intercession

intervéntor –óris, *m.*, intercessor

intervéntus –us, *m.*, intercession

íntime, *adv.*, profoundly, inwardly

íntimo –áre, *1*, to tell, intimate, make known, announce

íntimus –a –um, *adj.*, inmost, innermost

intíngo –ere –tínxi –tínctum, *3*, to steep, dip into

intolerábilis –e, *adj.*, unbearable, overwhelming

intonátio –ónis, *f.*, the act of intoning

íntono –áre –tónui –tonátum, *1*, to thunder

intortícium –ii, *n.*, a torch

intrínsecus, *adv.*, within, on the inside, internally, inwardly

intro –áre, *1*, to enter, go in, pierce

introdúco –ere –dúxi –dúctum, *3*, to bring into

intróeo –íre, *4*, to enter, go into

introgrédior –i –gréssus sum, *dep. 3*, to go, come in

intróitus –us, *m.*, entrance, entering, going in, introducing, ingress, the entrance prayer of the Mass

intromítto –ere –misi –míssum, *3*, to cast into, send into

introspício –ere –spéxi –spéctum, *3*, to look in

intúeor –éri –túitus sum, *dep. 2*, to consider, look at, gaze upon

intúitus –us, *m.*, mind

intumésco –ere –túmui, *3*, to swell

intus, *adv.*, within, inside, inwardly

inúltus –a –um, *adj.*, unpunished, unavenged

inundántia –ae, *f.*, inundation

inundátio –ónis, *f.*, flood, multitude

inúndo –áre, *1*, to overflow, flood, inundate

inúngo –ere –únxi –únctum, *3*, to anoint, smear with ointment

inútilis –e, *adj.*, useless, worthless, unprofitable

inutíliter, *adv.*, uselessly

invádo –ere –vási –vásum, *3*, to invade, swamp, enter, attack, assault

invalésco –ere –válui, *3*, to become strong, prevail

ínveho –ere –véxi –véctum, *3*, to attack, carry, bear, bear in

invénio –íre –véni –véntum, *4*, to bring about, find, discover, obtain, come upon

inventárium –ii, *n.*, an inventory, list

invéntio –ónis, *f.*, finding, discovery

invéntor –óris, *m.*, inventor

inverecúndia –ae, *f.*, impudence

invérto –ere –vérti –vérsum, *3*, to turn about, turn over

investigábilis –e, *adj.*, unsearchable, inscrutable, unfathomable, unaccountable, not to be traced

investigátio –ónis, *f.*, investigation, an inquiring into

invéstigo –áre, *1*, to search out, seek after, search into, trace

investitúra –ae, *f.*, the act of investure

inveterásco –ere –ávi, *3,* to grow old, become old

inveterátus –a –um, *adj.*, old, decrepit

invétero –áre, *1,* to grow old, become old, to be enfeebled, fail in strength

invéteror –ari, *dep. 1,* to grow old

ínvicem, *adv.*, in turn, by turns, alternately; *ad invicem,* among themselves

invíctus –a –um, *adj.*, unconquerable, invincible, unsubdued

invídeo –ére –vídi –vísum, *2,* to envy, grudge, be envious of

invídia –ae, *f.*, envy, hatred, jealousy, ill-will, odium

ínvidus –i, *m.*, an envious person

invígilo –áre, *1,* to watch over

inviolábilis –e, *adj.*, inviolable

inviolabíliter, *adv.*, inviolably

inviolátus –a –um, *adj.*, inviolable

invísco –ere, *3,* to fix deeply in the mind

invisíbilis –e, *adj.*, invisible

invisibíliter, *adv.*, invisibly

invíso –áre, *1,* to visit, go to see

invitaméntum –i, *n.*, invitation

invitátio –ónis, *f.*, invitation, an arousing, inciting to do something

invitátor –óris, *m.*, one who invites

invitatórium –ii, *n.*, invitatory

invíto –áre, *1,* to invite

invítus –a –um, *adj.*, unwilling, against one's will

ínvium –ii, *n.*, waste land, trackless land

ínvius –a –um, *adj.*, trackless, impassable, without a way

invocátio –ónis, *f.*, invocation

ínvoco –áre, *1,* to call upon, to invoke

involuméntum –i, *n.*, a covering, an envelope, swaddling clothes

invólvo –ere –vólvi –volútum, *3,* to wrap up, shut up, roll up, cover, envelop

ióta, *indecl., n.*, iota, jot

ipso facto, by that very fact

Ipsum Esse, an expression applied to God who alone is Being Itself

ira –ae, *f.*, anger, wrath of God, eternal punishment

iracúndia –ae, *f.*, anger, wrath

iráscor –i, irátus sum, *dep. 3,* to be angry, be wrathful

irátus –a –um, *adj.*, angry

iris –idis, *f.*, a rainbow

iro –áre, *1,* to be angry

irrádio –áre, *1,* to illuminate, shine, cast rays of light

irrationábilis –e, *adj.*, irrational

irrationabíliter, *adv.*, senselessly

irreparábilis –e, *adj.*, irreparable, irrevocable, cannot be restored

irrépo –ere –répsi –réptum, *3,* to creep into

irreprehensíbilis, –e, *adj.*, unspotted, blameless

irreveréntia –ae, *f.*, want of respect, irreverence

irrevocábilis –e, *adj.*, irrevocable, not to be turned back

irrídeo –ére –rísi –rísum, *2,* to laugh at, mock

irrigátio –ónis, *f.*, moistening, watering

írrigo –áre, *1,* to supply moisture, to water

irríguus –a –um, *adj.*, irrigated, watered

irrísio –ónis, *f.*, mockery, scoffing

irrísor –óris, *m.*, a derider, one who scorns

irritátio –ónis, *f.*, provocation

irritátor –óris, *m.*, a provoker

írrito –áre, *1,* to provoke, annoy, excite to anger

írritus –a –um, *adj.*, void, vain, invalid, of no effect

írrogo –áre, *1,* to impose, inflict upon

irrúgio –íre, *4,* to roar out

irrúmpo –ere –rúpi –rúptum, *3,* to extirpate

írruo –ere –ui, *3,* to rush, rush in, beset, press upon

Israel –is, *m.*, the new name given to Jacob, the nation that sprang from Jacob, and the land in which they dwelt

Israelíta –ae, *m.*, an Israelite, one belonging to the tribes of Israel

iter, itíneris, *n.*, a journey, departure, wayside, way

iterátio –ónis, *f.*, repetition, renewal

iteráto, *adv.*, again, a second time

ítero –áre, *1,* to repeat

ítidem, *adv.*, likewise, in like manner

Itinerárium –ii, *n.*, itinerary, prayers for a successful journey including the Benedictus and four Collects recited by clerics

ito –áre, *1,* to go

J

jáceo –ére –ui –itum, *2,* to lie down, sleep

jácio –ere, jeci, jactum, *3,* to cast, hurl, throw

jactans –ántis, *adj.,* boastful, vainglorious

jactánter, *adv.,* boastfully

jactántia –ae, *f.,* vainglory

jactantículus –a –um, *adj.,* somewhat boasting

jactátio –ónis, *f.,* boasting, bragging

jactátor –óris, *m.,* a boaster

jacto –áre, *1,* to cast, throw

jactúra –ae, *f.,* a loss, throwing away

jactus –us, *m.,* a cast, throw

jáculum –i, *n.,* an arrow, dart

jam, *adv.,* now, already, immediately, soon, just now; *with negatives,* no more, no longer.

jamdúdum, *adv.,* now, for a long time

jamjam, *adv.,* on the point of

jamprídem, *adv.,* now, for a long time

jámvero, *adv.,* indeed

jánitor –óris, *m.,* porter, gatekeeper

jánua –ae, *f.,* a gate, door, the outer door of a house

januárius –ii, *m.,* the month of January

jaspis –idis, *f.,* a jasper, a precious stone

jecur, jécoris *or* jecínoris, *n.,* liver

jejunátor –óris, *m.,* a faster

jejuniósus –a –um, *adj.,* fasting, hungry

jejúnium –ii, *n.,* fast, fasting, abstinence from food

jejúno –áre, *1,* to fast, abstain

jejúnus –a –um, *adj.,* fasting

Jerosólyma –ae, *f.,* Jerusalem

Jesus, *m.,* Jesus

Joann., *abbrev. for* Gospel of St. John

Joánnes –is, *m.,* John

jocor –ári, *dep. 1,* to jest or joke

jocóse, *adv.,* in jest, jokingly

jocósus –a –um, *adj.,* humorous, witty, merry, sportive

joculáris –e, *adj.,* jocular, laughable

Joseph, *indecl.,* Joseph

Joséphus –i, *m.,* Joseph

jubar –is, *n.,* radiance, a beaming light, the light of the sun, the light of glory

jube, *imper. of* júbeo, be pleased, graciously grant

júbeo –ere, jussi, jussum, *2,* to ask, order, request, grant

jubilaéum –i, *n.,* jubilee

jubilaéum majus, golden jubilee

jubilaéum minus, silver jubilee

jubilaéus –i, *m.,* jubilee

jubiláris –e, *adj.,* pertaining to a jubilee

jubilátio –ónis, *f.,* rejoicing, gladness, jubilation, a festival cry

júbilo –áre, *1,* to sing joyfully, to rejoice, exult, shout joyfully

júbilum –i, *n.,* joy, jubilee, a shout of joy

júbilus –i, *m.,* a joyful melody

jucúnde, *adv.,* merrily, pleasantly, agreeably, delightfully

jucúnditas –átis, *f.,* cheerfulness, pleasantness, pleasure

juncúndo –áre, *1,* to shout for joy

jucúndor –ári, *dep. 1,* to be glad, be joyful, have joy

jucúndus –a –um, *adj.,* pleasing, acceptable, fortunate, happy

Judaéus –i, *m.,* a Jew

Judaéus –a –um, *adj.,* Jewish

Judáicus –a –um, *adj.,* Jewish

Judaísmus –i, *m.,* Judaism

judaízo –áre, *1,* to judaize

Judas Iscariótes, Judas of Karioth who betrayed Jesus

judex –icis, *m.,* a judge

judicátio –ónis, *f.,* judgment, opinion

judicátus –us, *m.,* the office of a judge

judiciális –e, *adj.,* judicial

judícium –ii, *n.,* judgment, trial, investigation

júdico –áre, *1,* to judge, adjudge, determine, decide, esteem, value

jugális –e, *adj.,* connecting, pertaining to a yoke

júgerum –i, *n.,* an acre

jugis –e, *adj.,* continual, perpetual

júgiter, *adv.,* always, forever, ever, continually, perpetually

juglans, juglándis, *f.,* a walnut

jugo –áre, *1,* to connect, bind

júgulo –are, *1,* to slay, to cut the throat

júgulum –i, *n.,* the throat

júgulus –i, *m.,* the throat

jugum –i, *n.,* yoke, fetter, bond, slavery

július –ii, *m.,* the month of July

juméntum –i, *n.,* beast; *in the plural,* cattle

junctim, *adv.,* both together, successively

júnctio –ónis, *f.,* joining

junctúra –ae, *f.,* a joint

junctus –a –um, *adj.*, connected, joined together, united, very intimate

juncus –i, *m.*, a bulrush

jungo –ere, junxi, junctum, *3*, to join, bind, unite

júnior –óris, *adj.*, young, younger

június –ii, *m.*, the month of June

Júpiter, the chief Greek and Roman deity (Acts 14:12, 13)

juraméntum –i, *n.*, an oath

jurátus –a –um, *adj.*, bound by oath

júrgium –i, *n.*, a quarrel, wrangling

jurgo –áre, *1*, to quarrel

jurgor –ári, *dep. 1*, to quarrel

jurisdíctio –ónis, *f.*, jurisdiction

jurisprudéntia –ae, *f.*, law, jurisprudence

juro –áre, *1*, to swear, take an oath

jus, juris, *n.*, law, justice, judgment

jusjurándum, jurisjurándi, *n.*, an oath

jússio –ónis, *f.*, command

jussus –us, *m.*, a command, order (used only in the ablative)

juste, *adv.*, justly

justificátio –ónis, *f.*, justice, justification, ordinance, precept, law

justífico –áre, *1*, to do justice to, justify, make righteous, account righteous

justítia –ae, *f.*, justice, innocence, rectitude, righteousness, moral integrity

justus –a –um, *adj.*, just, right, righteous

juvámen –inis, *n.*, help

juvéncula –ae, *f.*, a maiden

juvénculus –i, *m.*, a bullock, a young steer

juvéncus –i, *m.*, a young bull

juvenésco –ere –vénui, *3*, to be young, to reach the age of youth

juvenílis –e, *adj.*, youthful, juvenile

júvenis –e, *adj.*, young, youthful; *m.*, a young man

juvénta –ae, *f.*, youth

juvéntus –útis, *f.*, youth, time of youth

juvo –áre, *1*, to aid

juxta, *adv.*, at hand, close to, near, by, according to

juxtim, *adv.*, near, close by

L

Labárum –i, *n.*, the banner of the cross, used by Constantine in his campaigns

labásco –ere, *3*, to totter, begin to fall, yield, give way

lábea –ae, *f.*, the lip

labécula –ae, *f.*, a little spot or stain

labefácio –ere –féci –fáctum, *3*, to shake, loosen, weaken

labes –is, *f.*, a stain, blemish, blot

lábia –ae, *f.*, the lip

lábilis –e, *adj.*, falling, tottering

lábium –ii, *n.*, the lip, the edge of a cup

labo –áre, *1*, to waver, totter, be unstable

labor –óris, *m.*, labor, toil, effort

labor –i, lapsus sum, *dep. 3*, to slip, glide down, fall down

laborióse, *adv.*, laboriously

laboriósus –a –um, *adj.*, toilsome, laborious

labóro –áre, *1*, to labor, toil, be tired, wearied, exhausted, bear up under

labrum –i, *n.*, the lip

labrum –i, *n.*, a vessel, basin

labrúsca –ae, *f.*, a wild grape

labúrnum –i, *n.*, the laburnum tree

lac, lactis, *n.*, milk

lacer –a –um, *adj.*, ragged, torn, maimed

lacerátio –ónis, *f.*, a tearing, mangling

lácero –áre, *1*, to rend, tear, lacerate, wound, mangle

lacésso –ere, lacessívi, lacessítum, *3*, to provoke, excite, stimulate, irritate

lacínia –ae, *f.*, a small tassel

lácrima –ae, *f.*, a tear

lacrimábilis –e, *adj.*, woeful, lamentable, deplorable, worthy of tears

lácrimo –áre, *1*, to weep, to shed tears

lácrimor –ári, *dep. 1*, to weep

lacrimósus –a –um, *adj.*, tearful, mournful, pitiable, doleful, sorrowful

lácruma –ae, *f.*, *see* lacryma

lácryma –ae, *f.*, a tear

lactens –éntis, *f.*, a suckling

lácteo –ére, *2*, to suck, be a suckling

lacticínium –ii, *n.*, food prepared from milk

lacto –áre, *1*, to allure, entice, give suck

lactúca –ae, *f.*, lettuce

lacúna –ae, *f.*, a cavern, cavity, hollow

lacus –us, *m.*, a lake, pit, pitfall, trap

laedo –ere, laesi, laesum, *3*, to injure, harm, damage, wound

laésio –ónis, *f.*, harm, wound, injury

laesúra –ae, *f.*, a lesion, an injury

laetabúndus –a –um, *adj.*, full of joy

laete, *adv.,* joyfully, gladly
laetífico –áre, *1,* to rejoice, give joy, cheer, gladden, delight
laetítia –ae, *f.,* gladness, expressed delight, happiness
laeto –áre, *1,* to cause to rejoice, make someone rejoice
laetor –ári, *dep. 1,* to rejoice, be joyful, be glad, take delight in
laetus –a –um, *adj.,* glad, joyful
laeva –ae, *f.,* the left, the left hand
laevigátus –a –um, *adj.,* smooth, polished
lagánum –i, *n.,* a cake
lagéna –ae, *f.,* a pitcher, jug
lagúncula –ae, *f.,* a bottle, small flask
laicális –e, *adj.,* lay
láicus –i, *m.,* a layman
láicus –a –um, *adj.,* lay, common, belonging to the lay state
lama (Aramaic), *adv.,* why? (Mt. 27:46; Mk. 15:34)
lambo –ere, lambi, *3,* to lick
lamentátio –ónis, *f.,* lament, lamentation, weeping, wailing
laménto –áre, *1,* to lament, weep, mourn, wail
laméntor –ári, *dep. 1,* to lament, weep, mourn, wail
laméntum –i, *n.,* wailing, lamentation
lámia –ae, *f.,* a wild beast, sea monster
lámina –ae, *f.,* a metal plate
lámpada –ae, *f.,* a lamp
lampadárium –ii, *n.,* a chandelier, a support for lamps
lampadárius –ii, *m.,* a chandelier, a support for lamps
lampas –adis, *f.,* a lamp, torch, flame
lana –ae, *f.,* wool
láncea –ae, *f.,* a lance or spear
lanceárius –ii, *m.,* a lancer
lanceátus –a –um, *adj.,* spear-shaped
lancéola –ae, *f.,* a small lance
láncino –áre, *1,* to mangle
lancis –is, *f.,* an event
láneus –a –um, *adj.,* woolen
lánguens –éntis, *adj.,* weak, faint, yearning
lángueo –ére –ui, *2,* to be faint, weak, feeble
languésco –ére, langui, *3,* to become weak, faint, languid
lánguide, *adv.,* faintly, feebly, languidly
lánguidus –a –um, *adj.,* infirm, sick, weak, faint

languor –óris, *m.,* languor, feebleness, sickness, ill health, infirmity, disease
laniátus –us, *m.,* mangling
lánio –áre, *1,* to mangle
lantérna –ae, *f.,* lantern
lantgrávius –ii, *m.,* landgrave, baron, count
lanx –cis, *f.,* a shallow pan or dish
lapidárius –ii, *m.,* a stonecutter, a mason
lapídeus –a –um, *adj.,* of stone
lapidicínus –a –um, *adj.,* pertaining to sculpture
lápido –áre, *1,* to stone
lapíllus –i, *m.,* a gem
lapis –idis, *m.,* a stone
lappa –ae, *f.,* a bur
lapsus –us, *m.,* falling, slipping, a moral fall, apostasy
láquear –is, *n.,* a rafter, panel, ceiling, a paneled ceiling
laqueátus –a –um, *adj.,* with a paneled ceiling
láqueus –i, *m.,* a snare, trap, net, halter, a noose for capturing animals
large, *adv.,* largely, abundantly, plentifully
lárgiens –éntis, *adj.,* bountiful
lárgior –íri, *dep. 4,* to bestow, grant
lárgior –óris, *m.,* one who grants
lárgitas –átis, *f.,* bounty, bountifulness, liberality
largíto –ónis, *m.,* the imperial treasury or fund for presents and distribution
largítor –oris, *m.,* one who grants
lárgius, *adv.,* more abundantly
largus –a –um, *adj.,* abundant, plentiful
láridum –i, *n.,* lard
larva –ae, *f.,* a ghost
lassitúdo –inis, *f.,* weariness, a tiresome or enervating action
lassus –a –um, *adj.,* faint, weary, tired, exhausted, languid
late, *adv.,* broadly, widely
latébra –ae, *f.,* concealment, subterfuge
latebrósus –a –um, *adj.,* secret, retired, obscure
laténter, *adv.,* secretly
láteo –ére –ui, *2,* to be hidden, concealed, to remain in private
later –eris, *m.,* a brick
laterális –e, *adj.,* lateral
latérna –ae, *f.,* a lantern
latex –icis, *m.,* water, liquid
latíbulum –i, *n.,* a hiding place, a covert
latíne, *adv.,* in Latin, the language of the Romans (Lk. 23:38; Jn. 19:20)

Latína Porta, the Latin Gate
latínus –a –um, *adj.,* Latin
látito –áre, *1,* to be concealed, lie hidden
latitúdo –inis, *f.,* breadth, length; *in latitúdine,* at liberty
latreúticus –a –um, *adj.,* pertaining to the worship of God
látria –ae, *f.,* worship, adoration
latro –ónis, *m.,* robber, thief
latro –áre, *1,* to bark
latrocínium –ii, *n.,* brigandage
latrúnculus –i, *m.,* robber, bandit, rover
latus –eris, *n.,* side, flank
latus –a –um, *adj.,* broad, wide
laudábilis –e, *adj.,* worthy of praise
laudabíliter, *adv.,* laudably, in a praiseworthy manner
laudátio –ónis, *f.,* praise, the praising of
laudátor –óris, *m.,* one who praises
Laudes –um, *f.,* the Office of Lauds
laudo –áre, *1,* to praise, glorify
laura –ae, *f.,* a kind of monastery, settlement of the Anchorites in Egypt
laúrea –ae, *f.,* laurel, triumph, victory, wreath of hay, doctor's degree
Lauréntius –ii, *m.,* Lawrence
lauréntius –a –um, *adj.,* crowned with laurel
laus, laudis, *f.,* praise
lautus –a –um, *adj.,* elegant, sumptuous, splendid
lavácrum –i, *n.,* a bath, flood, the water of baptism
lavo –áre, lavi, lautum *or* lavátum, *1,* to wash
laxo –áre, *1,* to relax, let drop
laxus –a –um, *adj.,* loose, lax, relaxed
leaéna –ae, *f.,* a lioness
lebes –étis, *m.,* a kettle, washbasin, basin, a metal vessel for holding water
lectíca –ae, *f.,* a litter
lecticárius –ii, *m.,* a coffin bearer, a litter bearer
léctio –ónis, *f.,* a lesson, reading, the Epistle at Mass
Lectionárium –ii, *n.,* a book of the lessons for the Divine Office
lectiúncula –ae, *f.,* a short lesson
lector –óris, *m.,* a reader, lector (a cleric in Minor Orders)
lectorátus –us, *m.,* the office of lector or reader
lectoríle –is, *n.,* a lecturn
lectórium –ii, *n.,* a lecturn

léctulus –i, *m.,* a small bed, a couch
lectum –i, *n.,* a bed or couch
lectus –i, *m.,* a bed
lectus –a –um, *adj.,* eminent, choice
lécythus –i, *m.,* a flask
legális –e, *adj.,* legal, according to law
legátio –ónis, *f.,* a legation, embassy
legátus –i, *m.,* a legate, ambassador, special envoy
legénda –ae, *f.,* something to be read
Legendárius –ii, *m.,* the book containing the Epistles read at Mass
légifer –i, *m.,* a lawgiver
legíle –is, *n.,* a lectern, bookstand
légio –ónis, *f.,* a legion, band
legislátio –ónis, *m.,* the making of a law
legislátor –óris, *m.,* legislator, lawgiver, lawmaker
legisperítus –i, *m.,* a lawyer
legítime, *adv.,* lawfully
Legítimum –i, *n.,* a name for the Canon of the Mass
legítimum –i, *n.,* ordinance
legítimus –a –um, *adj.,* legitimate, legal
lego –ere, legi, lectum, *3,* to read
legúmen –inis, *n.,* a vegetable, bean, pulse
lénio –íre, *4,* to relieve, mitigate
lenis –e, *adj.,* smooth, mild, easy
léniter, *adv.,* gently, softly, kindly
lentésco –ere, *3,* to relax
lentícula –ae, *f.,* a vial, small flask, little bottle
leo –ónis, *m.,* a lion
lepra –ae, *f.,* leprosy; *homo leprósus,* a leper
leprósus –a –um, *adj.,* leprous
lethális –e, *adj.,* lethal, fatal, mortal
lethárgus –i, *m.,* an unconscious person, coma
leúnculus –i, *m.,* a young lion
levámen –inis, *n.,* alleviation, consolation
levaméntum –i, *n.,* alleviation, consolation, rest, mitigation
Levi, *indecl.,* the third son of Jacob and Lia
levíathan, a serpent or a crocodile
levigátus –a –um, *adj.,* smooth, polished
lévigo –áre, *1,* to polish
levis –e, *adj.,* light
léviter, *adv.,* easily
Levítes (Levíta) –ae, *m.,* a Levite
levíticus –a –um, *adj.,* pertaining to a Levite
levo –áre, *1,* to raise, lift up

lex, legis, *f.,* law, the law of God

libámen –inis, *n.,* libation

líbanus –i, *m.,* frankincense

Líbanus –i, *m.,* Mount Libanus, on the N. border of Palestine. The *cedars of Libanus* were famous for their size.

libátio –ónis, *f.,* a partaking, libation

libatórium –ii, *n.,* a pouring vessel

libéllus –i, *m.,* a writing, bill, little book

libénter, *adv.,* gladly, willingly, freely, with pleasure

liber –a –um, *adj.,* free, abandoned, fearless

liber –bri, *m.,* a book

líbera –ae, *f.,* a free woman

liberálitas –átis, *f.,* liberality, generosity

liberátio –ónis, *f.,* freedom, a setting free

liberátor –óris, *m.,* deliverer, liberator, protector

liberátus –a –um, *adj.,* liberated, freed

líbere, *adv.,* freely, steadfastly, boldly, openly

líberi –órum, *m. pl.,* children

líbero –áre, *1,* to free, deliver, set free, liberate

libértas –átis, *f.,* liberty, freedom

libído –inis, *f.,* lust

líbitum –i, *n.,* pleasure, liking

libo –áre, *1,* to pour out, touch, taste, sacrifice

libra –ae, *f.,* a pound, balance, scales

libraméntum –i, *n.,* balancing, equilibrium

librárius –ii, *m.,* copyist

libro –áre, *1,* to weigh, balance, poise

libum –i, *n.,* an offering, cake offered to the gods

licéntia –ae, *f.,* permission

liciatórium –ii, *n.,* a beam

lícitus –a –um, *adj.,* legitimate

lícium –ii, *n.,* lace, a web

ligaméntum –i, *n.,* a bandage

ligátus –a –um, *adj.,* bound

lígito –áre, *1,* to strive, quarrel

lígneus –a –um, *adj.,* wooden

lignum –i, *n.,* wood, tree, stick, staff, the cross of Christ

ligo –áre, *1,* to bind

ligo –ónis, *m.,* a spade, hoe

lígula –ae, *f.,* a ribbon

liliátus –a –um, *adj.,* lily-white, decorated with lilies

lílium –ii, *n.,* a lily

limátus –a –um, *adj.,* polished

limax –ácis, *f.,* a snail

limen –inis, *n.,* threshold

limes –itis, *m.,* boundary, limit

limináre –is, *n.,* floor, threshold

limitróphes –is, *adj.,* neighboring

limpidíssimus –a –um, *adj.,* very smooth

limus –i, *m.,* slime, mud, mire, dirt

línea –ae, *f.,* a linen thread, line

lineaméntum –i, *n.,* feature, delineation, lineament

líneus –a –um, *adj.,* linen, of flax

lingo –ere, linxi, linctum, *3,* to lick

lingua –ae, *f.,* language, tongue, speech

linguátus –a –um, *adj.,* talkative, loquacious

linguósus –a –um, *adj.,* talkative, loquacious, evil-tongued

línio –íre –ívi –itum, *4,* to smear, bedaub, spread, anoint

linítio –ónis, *f.,* the glazing of a vestment

lino –ere, livi *or* levi, litum, *3,* to spread over

linóstimus –a –um, *adj.,* of linen

linquo –ere, liqui, *3,* to leave

linteámen –inis, *n.,* a linen cloth

lintéolum –i, *n.,* a small piece of linen

línteum –i, *n.,* a linen cloth, towel

linum –i, *n.,* flax, linen, a linen cloth

lipsanothéca –ae, *f.,* a storehouse for relics

liquefácio, *3,* to melt, dissolve

liquefactívus –a –um, *adj.,* melting

liquefáctus –a –um, *adj.,* melted

líqueo –ere, lícui *or* liqui, *3,* to be liquid, be evident

liquésco –ere, lícui, *3,* to melt, dissolve

liquo –áre, *1,* to melt, make liquid, dissolve, liquify

liquor –óris, *m.,* liquid

lis, litis, *f.,* a debate, contention

litánia –ae, *f.,* litany

litániae –árum, *f. pl.,* litany, supplication

lítera –ae, *f.,* a record

literárius –a –um, *adj.,* literary

lithóstrotos (Greek), *m.,* paved

lito –áre, *1,* to offer public sacrifice, celebrate Mass

líttera (lítera) –ae, *f.,* a letter of the alphabet

lítterae –árum, *f. pl.,* a letter, bill

litterátio –ónis, *f.,* a study of languages

litteratúra –ae, *f.,* writing, literature, culture, learning

littus (litus) –oris, *n.,* shore

litúra –ae, *f.,* a daubing or covering with paint

litúrgia –ae, *f.*, liturgy, the Mass, public worship of the Church

litúrgicus –a –um, *adj.*, pertaining to the liturgy

lívidus –a –um, *adj.*, spiteful, envious, malicious

livor –óris, *m.*, a bruise

locális –e, *adj.*, local

loco –áre, *1*, to place, hire out

lóculus –i, *m.*, a bier, coffin, casket, a purse

locúmtenens –tis, *m.*, a substitute

lócuples –étis, *adj.*, rich

locupletátio –ónis, *f.*, wealth, riches

locupléto –áre, *1*, to enrich

locus –i, *m.*, a place, room, position, station (plural *loca –órum*)

locústa –ae, *f.*, a locust

locútio –ónis, *f.*, word, phrase, expression

locútor –óris, *m.*, a speaker

lodix –ícis, *f.*, a blanket, sheet

lógice, *adv.*, logically

lógicus –a –um, *adj.*, logical

longaévus –a –um, *adj.*, aged, old

longánimis –e, *adj.*, patient, long-suffering

longanímitas –átis, *f.*, long-suffering

longanímiter, *adv.*, patiently

longe, *adv.*, afar, far off, at a distance; *a longe*, from afar; *de longínquo*, from afar

longitúdo –inis, *f.*, length

longitúrnitas –átis, *f.*, long duration

longitúrnus –a –um, *adj.*, long-enduring

lóngius, *adv.*, longer

longus –a –um, *adj.*, long

loquéla –ae, *f.*, speech, manner of speech, language

loquor, loqui, locútus sum, *dep. 3*, to converse, speak, profess, tell, utter

loraméntum –i, *n.*, a wooden frame, throng

lórica –ae, *f.*, a breastplate

loricátus –a –um, *adj.*, clothed in mail

lorum –i, *n.*, a whip, scourge, throng, leather strap

lotus –a –um, *adj.*, washed

lúbricum –i, *n.*, slipperiness

lúbricus –a –um, *adj.*, slippery, dangerous, impure

lúceo –ére, luxi, *2*, to shine, give light, glitter

lucérna –ae, *f.*, a candle, light, lamp

lucernáre –is, *n.*, an ancient name for Vespers in the Eastern Church

lucésco –ere, luxi, *3*, to begin to dawn, begin to shine

lúcide, *adv.*, clearly, plainly

lúcidus –a –um, *adj.*, bright, lightsome, full of light, clear, lucid, irreproachable

lúcifer –i, *m.*, morning star, day star, the light bringer

lúcifer –a –um, *adj.*, light-bearing

lucratívus –a –um, *adj.*, profitable, lucrative

lucrifácio, *3*, to win, gain, profit

lucror –ári, *dep. 1*, to gain, profit, convert

lucrum –i, *n.*, gain, profit, lucre, advantage

luctámen –inis, *n.*, wrestling, struggling

luctuósus –a –um, *adj.*, sorrowful

luctus –us, *m.*, grief, mourning, lamentation

lucubrátio –ónis, *f.*, laborious study

luculénte, *adv.*, admirably

luculénter, *adv.*, excellently

luculéntus –a –um, *adj.*, bright

lucus –i, *m.*, a grove

ludíbrium –i, *n.*, scorn, mockery, derision, jest, laughingstock

ludus –i, *m.*, game, sport, pastime

lues –is, *f.*, a disease

lúgeo –ére, luxi, luctum, *2*, to lament, bewail, grieve, mourn over

lumbáre –is, *n.*, a girdle

lumbus –i, *m.*, the loin

lumen –inis, *n.*, light, brightness, splendor, light of glory, a luminary

lumináre –is, *n.*, light, a source of light

luna –ae, *f.*, the moon; *dies Lunae*, Monday

lunáticus –i, *m.*, a lunatic

lúnula –ae, *f.*, a crescent-shaped container for the Blessed Sacrament

luo –ere, lui, lutúrus, *3*, to loose, atone for; *also* to wash

lupínus –a –um, *adj.*, wolfish

lupus –i, *m.*, a wolf

lustrális –e, *adj.*, blessed, holy, cleansing, purifying

lustrálus –a –um, *adj.*, blessed, holy

lustro –áre, *1*, to purify

lustrum –i, *n.*, a luster, period of five years

lusus –us, *m.*, a game, sport

luter –is, *m.*, a washbasin

lúteus –a –um, *adj.*, of clay

lutum –i, *n.*, clay, dirt, mire, mud

lux, lucis, *f.*, light, dawn, light of a

lamp, star, moon; *lucis ante términum,* before the end of daylight
luxúria –ae, *f.,* luxury, dissipation
luxúrior –ári, *dep. 1,* to live riotously
luxurióse, *adv.,* riotously, wastefully, luxuriously, extravagantly
luxus –us, *m.,* lust, debauchery

lychnúchus –i, *m.,* a frame for supporting lamps or candles, a chandelier
lychnus –i, *m.,* a lamp
lympha –ae, *f.,* water
lymphaéum –i, *n.,* a large bowl or basin of water used in the early churches
lyra –ae, *f.,* a flute, lyre

M

macerátio –ónis, *f.,* mortification
macéria –ae, *f.,* a wall, fence
mácero –áre, *1,* to mortify, afflict
machaéra –ae, *f.,* a knife, short sword
máchina –ae, *f.,* a machine, device, frame, fabric, mechanism, order, structure
machinaméntum –i, *n.,* a trick, device
máchinor –ári, *dep. 1,* to contrive, devise, plot, invent
mácies –ei, *f.,* emaciation, thinness, disease
maciléntus –a –um, *adj.,* thin, lean
macrésco –ere, mácrui, *3,* to become thin
macto –áre, *1,* to augment, enrich, sacrifice, punish, kill
mácula –ae, *f.,* stain, blemish, spot, blot
máculo –áre, *1,* to spot, accuse
maculósus –a –um, *adj.,* spotted
madefácio, *3,* to make wet, moisten
mádeo –ére, mádui, *2,* to drink too much, be drunk
madésco –ere, mádui, *3,* to become wet
Mádian (Hebr.), Madian, son of Abraham
maéreo –ére, *2,* to be sorrowful, sad, grieve, mourn
maeror –óris, *m.,* sadness, grief, mourning
maestus –a –um, *adj.,* sad, dejected, cast down, sorrowful, melancholy
Magdaléna –ae, *f.,* a woman of Magdala, called Mary
Magi –órum, *m. pl.,* the Magi
mágia –ae, *f.,* magic
mágicus –a –um, *adj.,* magical, of magic
magis, *adv.,* rather; *plus magis,* far more
magíster –tri, *m.,* a teacher, master, director
magistérium –ii, *n.,* the office of teacher
magístra –ae, *f.,* mistress, teacher
magistrátus –us, *m.,* high official, magistrate

magnália –ium, *n.,* wonders, wonderful works
magnanímitas –átis, *f.,* greatness of soul, magnanimity
magnánimus –a –um, *adj.,* high-minded, magnanimous, high-spirited, courageous
magnas –átis, *m.,* a magnate, nobleman
magnátus –i, *m.,* a great man, nobleman
magnes –étis, *m.,* a lodestone, magnet
magnífice, *adv.,* nobly, generously
magnificéntia –ae, *f.,* majesty, magnificence, splendor, glory
magnífico –áre, *1,* to magnify, exalt, glorify, praise
magníficus –a –um, *adj.,* glorious, sublime, rich
magníloquus –a –um, *adj.,* boastful, vaunting
magnipéndo –ere –péndi, *3,* to esteem highly
magnitúdo –inis, *f.,* greatness, power, majesty, size, magnitude
magnópere, *adv.,* greatly, very much, exceedingly
magnus –a –um, *adj.,* great, mighty, large
magus –i, *m.,* a wise man, learned man, wizard, magician, sorcerer
mahéleth or maeleth (Hebr.), *indecl.,* a harp or lute (Ps. 52)
maíus (majus) –i, *m.,* the month of May
majéstas –átis, *f.,* majesty, dignity, grandeur
majestáticus –a –um, *adj.,* majestic, sublime
majóres –um, *m. pl.,* elders, forefathers
majúsculus –a –um, *adj.,* rather large
malágma –átis, *n.,* a plaster, poultice
malédice, *adv.,* abusively, calumniously
maledíco –ere –díxi –díctum, *3,* to curse, speak evil, revile, reproach, abuse, slander
maledíctio –ónis, *f.,* a curse, cursing

maledíctum –i, *n.,* abusive language, railing

maledíctus –a –um, *adj.,* cursed, accursed

maledíctus –i, *m.,* a railer

malefáctor –óris, *m.,* malefactor, evildoer

malefáctum –i, *n.,* injury, ill deed

maléfice, *adv.,* maliciously, mischievously

malévolus –a –um, *adj.,* malicious, envious, spiteful, malevolent

malígnans –antis, *adj.,* wicked, malicious

malígne, *adv.,* malignantly, maliciously, enviously

malígnitas –átis, *f.,* evil, malice, malignity, ill-nature

malígno –áre, *1,* to act wickedly

malígnor –ári, *dep. 1,* to act wickedly

malígnus –a –um, *adj.,* malignant, evil, malicious

malítia –ae, *f.,* malice, evil, vice, wickedness

malitióse, *adv.,* maliciously

malle, málui, *2,* to prefer, desire, wish greatly

malleátur –óris, *m.,* a hammerer

málleus –i, *m.,* a hammer, mallet

Málleus Arianórum, the "Hammer of the Arians," title given to St. Hilary

mallúvium –ii, *n.,* a dish for washing the hands

maltha –ae, *f.,* a kind of mortar, putty

malum –i, *n.,* evil

malum –i, *n.,* an apple; *malum médicum,* a lemon; *malum púnicum,* a pomegranate

malus –a –um, *adj.,* bad, wicked

mamílla –ae, *f.,* breast

mamma –ae, *f.,* breast

mammóna –ae, *m.,* wealth, riches, cupidity, mammon (Mt. 6:24; Lk. 16:9, 11, 13)

Mammotréctus, a book containing strange words in the Bible and Breviary, composed by Fr. J. Marchesini about the year 1300.

Manásses, *genitive,* Manásse (Hebr.), the eldest son of Joseph (Ps. 59:9)

mancípium –ii, *m.,* a slave

máncipo –áre, *1,* to deliver up, transfer

mancus –a –um, *adj.,* lame, crippled, defective, incomplete

mandátum –i, *n.,* a command, order, commandment, mandate, credentials, the ritual of washing the feet on Maundy Thursday

mando –áre, *1,* to command, give charge over, order, send word, enjoin, entrust

mando –ere, mandi, mansum, *3,* to eat, chew

mandórla –ae, *f.,* a nimbus framing the figure

mandragóra –ae, *f.,* a mandrake

manducátio –ónis, *f.,* eating

mandúco –áre, *1,* to eat

mane, *adv.,* in the morning, early morning; *valde mane, sumo mane,* and *primo mane,* early in the morning

máneo –ére, mansi, mansum, *2,* to remain, tarry, abide, wait

mánica –ae, *f.,* a sleeve, manicle

manicátus –a –um, *adj.,* with sleeves

mánico –áre, *1,* to come early in the morning

manifestátio –ónis, *f.,* manifestation, showing, display, revelation

maniféste, *adv.,* plainly, openly, clearly, manifestly, evidently

manifésto –áre, *1,* to make manifest, reveal, make known

maniféstus –a –um, *adj.,* manifest, clear, open, visible, evident

maníle –is, *n.,* a basin for washing the hands

manípulus –i, *m.,* a maniple, sheaf, small bundle

manna –ae, *f.,* manna, food from heaven, the miraculous bread of the Israelites during their forty years in the desert

mano –áre, *1,* to flow, run, drip, exude, give out

mánsio –ónis, *f.,* dwelling, abode (Jn. 14:2)

mansionariátus –us, *m.,* the office of resident priest

mansionárius –ii, *m.,* a sexton, custodian, sacristan

mansiúncula –ae, *f.,* a little room, chamber, compartment, small dwelling

mansuetúdo –inis, *f.,* meekness, mildness, clemency

mansuétus –a –um, *adj.,* meek, mild, humble, gentle, soft

mansúrus –a –um, *adj.,* enduring

mantélla –ae, *f.,* a mantle, cloak

mantellétum –i, *n.,* a cape covering the surplice of a prelate

mantéllum –i (*or* mantélum), *n.,* a cloak, mantle

mantíle –is (*or* mantéle), *n.,* a napkin, towel

manto –áre, *1*, to remain, wait for

manudúctor –óris, *m.*, a choir leader in the early Church

manufácio –ere, *3*, to make by hand

manufáctus –a –um, *adj.*, made by hands

manuleátus –a –um, *adj.*, with sleeves

manus –us, *f.*, a hand

manutérgium –ii, *n.*, a napkin, towel

mappa –ae, *f.*, an altar cloth, a cloth

máppula –ae, *f.*, a napkin, a small piece of cloth, a handkerchief

Maran-átha (Aramaic), an emphatic assertion of St. Paul, meaning "the Lord cometh," or "the Lord has come" (1 Cor. 16:22)

márceo –ére, *2*, to wither, droop, be faint, grown weak, become feeble

marcésco –ere, *3*, to fade away, decay, wither

márcidus –a –um, *adj.*, withered, delicate, weak, exhausted

mare –is, *n.*, the sea

Mare Rubrum, the Red Sea, a symbol of baptism

margaríta –ae, *f.*, a pearl

margarítum –i, *n.*, a pearl

margo –ónis, *f.*, a border

María –ae, *f.*, Mary. The name is derived from the Hebrew "Miriam," "Star of the Sea."

Mariális –e, *adj.*, pertaining to Mary

Mariánus –a –um, *adj.*, of Mary

marínus –a –um, *adj.*, pertaining to the sea

maritális –e, *adj.*, marital, relating to marriage, of wedlock

maritáma –órum, *n. pl.*, seacoast

marítimus –a –um, *adj.*, maritime, by the sea

maríto –áre, *1*, to marry, give in marriage

marítus –i, *m.*, husband

marmor –óris, *n.*, marble

marmóreus –a –um, *adj.*, of marble

marsúpium –ii, *n.*, a purse, moneybag

mártius –ii, *m.*, the month of March

martyr –is, *m.*, martyr

martyrárius –ii, *m.*, a keeper of relics of martyrs

martýrium –ii, *n.*, martyrdom

martyrológium –ii, *n.*, a martyrology, a list of martyrs and saints

Martyrológium Hieronymiánum, a martyrology compiled about the year 600, bearing the name of St. Jerome

Martyrológium Románum, the Roman Martyrology

masculínus –a –um, *adj.*, masculine

másculus –a –um, *adj.*, male

massa –ae, *f.*, a lump, mass, bulk

mater –tris, *f.*, mother

materfamílias, matrisfamílias, *f.*, mistress of a home

matéria –ae, *f.*, a maternal aunt

matrícitas –átis, *f.*, mothership

matrícula –ae, *f.*, a catalogue, list

matriculária –ae, *f.*, a deaconess

matrimoniális –e, *adj.*, matrimonial, pertaining to marriage

matrimónium –ii, *n.*, marriage, matrimony

matrína –ae, *f.*, godmother, a female sponsor

matrix –ícis, *f.*, mother

matróna –ae, *f.*, matron

matrónaeum –i, *n.*, a part set off for women in the early churches

Matthaéus –i, *m.*, Matthew

Matthías –ae, *m.*, a disciple surnamed Justus, chosen by lot to succeed Judas Iscariot as an Apostle (Acts 1:23, 26)

matúre, *adv.*, early

maturésco –ere –ui, *3*, to ripen, come to maturity

matúritas –átis, *f.*, fullness, early morning, dawn

matúrus –a –um, *adj.*, developed, mature

matutínum –i, *n.*, the night watch, Matins

matutínum tenebrárum, Tenebrae service of Holy Week

matutínus –a –um, *adj.*, early, morning, pertaining to the morning

maxílla –ae, *f.*, cheek, jaw, the jawbone, the cheekbone

máxime, *adv.*, chiefly, especially

maximópere, *adv.*, exceedingly

máximus –a –um, *adj.*, very great, greatest, most grievous

mazza –ae, *f.*, a mace

mazzérius –ii, *m.*, a mace-bearer

measurábilis –e, *adj.*, measurable, easily measured

meátus –us, *m.*, a way, passage

medéla –ae, *f.*, a healing remedy, healing, cure

médeor –éri, *dep. 2*, to heal, cure

mediánte, *adv.*, by means of

mediáte, *adv.*, indirectly

mediátio –ónis, *f.*, meditation

mediátor –óris, *m.*, mediator, an inter-mediary
mediátrix –ícis, *f.*, a mediatrix, female mediator
médica –ae, *f.*, clover
medicámen –inis, *n.*, medicine
medicaméntum –i, *n.*, a drug, remedy, medicine
medicátio –ónis, *f.*, remedy, healing power
medicína –ae, *f.*, a remedy
medicinális, *adj.*, salutary, healing
médico –áre, *1*, to cure, heal
médicus –i, *m.*, a physician
medíetas –átis, *f.*, the half, medium, middle course
médio –áre, *1*, to be in the middle
meditátio –ónis, *f.*, meditation, thought, reflection, contemplation
médito –áre, *1*, to meditate
méditor –ári, *dep. 1*, to meditate, think, plan, devise
médium –ii, *n.*, middle, the midst
médius, *adv.*, in the midst
medúlla –ae, *f.*, marrow, marrow of bones, finest part
medullátus –a –um, *adj.*, full of marrow, fat
medúllitus, *adv.*, in the very marrow
meípsum, myself
mel, mellis, *n.*, honey
Melchísedech (Hebr.), Melchisedech, king and priest of Salem
melísma –átis, *f.*, a modulation in choral chant
melismáticus –a –um, *adj.*, melodious
mellífluus –a –um, *adj.*, dripping with sweetness
melos –i, *m.* or *n.*, a hymn, song, melody
melóta (melóte) –ae, *f.*, a sheepskin, sheepskin habit or coat
membrána –ae, *f.*, parchment, skin, membrane
membrátim, *adv.*, limb from limb
membrum –i, *n.*, a limb, member of the Church
meménto (*imperative*), remember, be mindful of
meminísse, *defective verb*, to be mindful of, remember
memor –óris, *adj.*, mindful of, calling to mind
memorábilis –e, *adj.*, remarkable, memorable, worthy of mention
memorátus –us, *m.*, mention

memorátus –a –um, *adj.*, mentioned, above mentioned
memória –ae, *f.*, remembrance, memory, memorial, commemoration
memoriále –is, *n.*, a memorial, remembrance, souvenir
Memoriále Rítuum Benedícti XIII, a book of ceremonies for Ash Wednesday and Holy Week: now superseded by the *Ritus Simplex*
memoriális –e, *adj.*, memorial
mémoro –áre, *1*, to recall, remember, relate
mémoror –ári, *dep. 1*, to remember
mendácium –ii, *n.*, a lie, untruth, falsehood, lying
mendax –ácis, *adj.*, false, prone to lying, deceitful, unreliable
mendax –ácis, *m.*, liar
mendicábulum –i, *n.*, a beggar, mendicant
Mendicántes –ium, *m.*, the Friar Orders, Mendicants
mendícitas –atis, *f.*, want, poverty
mendíco –áre, *1*, to beg
méndicor –ári, *dep. 1*, to beg
méndicus –i, *m.*, a beggar, mendicant
mens, mentis, *f.*, the mind, soul, spirit
mensa –ae, *f.*, a table, the upper surface of the altar
ménsio –ónis, *f.*, a measuring
mensis –is, *m.*, a month
mensor –óris, *m.*, a measurer
mensúra –ae, *f.*, measure, size
menta *or* mentha –ae, *f.*, mint
méntio –ónis, *f.*, mention
méntio –íre, *4*, to lie, tell lies
méntior –íri, *dep. 4*, to lie, tell lies
mentum –i, *n.*, throat, chin
merácus –a –um, *adj.*, pure, unmixed
mercatúra –ae, *f.*, trade
mercatúram fácere, to engage in trade
mercátus –us, *m.*, traffic
mercenárius –ii, *m.*, a paid servant, hireling
mercenárius –a –um, *adj.*, mercenary
merces –édis, *f.*, reward, ransom, hire, wages, pay, salary
mercor –ári, *dep. 1*, to buy
Mercúrius dies, Wednesday
méreo –éri –ui –itum, *2*, to merit deserve, be worthy, earn, win
méreor –éri, *dep. 2*, to merit, deserve, be worthy, earn, win
méretrix –ícis, *f.*, a harlot
mergo –ere, mersi, mersum, *3*, to sink, immerse, plunge, overwhelm

mérgulus –i, *m.*, a diving bird
meribíbula –ae, *m.*, a wine bibber
meridiánus –a –um, *adj.*, southern, pertaining to the south, noonday
merídies –ei, *m.*, noon, midday, south;
per merídiem, at noon
meridionális –e, *adj.*, south
merídior –ri, *dep. 1*, to rest at midday
mérito –áre, *1*, to deserve, merit
mérito, *adv.*, deservedly, rightly, according to desert
meritório, *adv.*, meritoriously
meritórius –a –um, *adj.*, meritorious, deserving of merit
méritum –i, *n.*, merit, desert, a good
work
merum –i, *n.*, wine
merus –a –um, *adj.*, pure, unmixed with
water
merx, mercis, *f.*, merchandise, goods,
wares
Mesopotámia –ae, *f.*, Mesopotamia
Messiánicus –a –um, *adj.*, pertaining to
the Messias
Messías –ae, *m.*, the Messias, Christ,
Anointed (Jn. 1:41; 4:25)
messis –is, *f.*, harvest, crop
messor –óris, *m.*, a reaper
mestítius –a –um, *adj.*, mixed, half-breed
meta –ae, *f.*, a goal
metállum –i, *n.*, metal, a mine
metáphora –ae, *f.*, metaphor
metaphrástes –ae, *m.*, a translator of a
book
méthodus –i, *f.*, method
métior –íri, mensus sum, *dep. 4*, to
measure, measure out, distribute by
measure
meto –ere, méssui, messum, *3*, to mow,
gather harvest
metréta –ae, *f.*, a Greek liquid measure
métricus –a –um, *adj.*, metrical
metropólicus –a –um, *adj.*, pertaining to
a metropolitan or archepiscopal see
metrópolis –is, *f.*, capital city
metropólita –ae, *m.*, an archbishop,
metropolitan bishop
metropolitánus –a –um, *adj.*, metropolitan
metropolitánus –i, *m.*, metropolitan,
archbishop
metropólitus –i, *m.*, metropolitan
metrum –i, *n.*, verse, meter
métuo –ere –ui –útum, *3*, to be afraid,
fear, dread
metus –us, *m.*, fear, dread

mica –ae, *f.*, crumb, morsel, grain
micans –ántis, *adj.*, shining, radiant,
glittering, sparkling
mico –áre, *1*, to shine, sparkle, gleam
Micrológus, a medieval explanation of
the liturgy
migma –átis, *n.*, a mixture, a mixture
of food for cattle
migrátio –ónis, *f.*, migration, departure,
removal from one place to another
migro –áre, *1*, to depart, travel, go
abroad
miles –itis, *m.*, a soldier
mílitans –ántis, *adj.*, militant
mílitans –ántis, *m.*, soldier
milítia –ae, *f.*, army, soldiers, warfare,
an office or employment at court
mílito –áre, *1*, to serve in the army,
war, hold an office at court
mílium –i, *n.*, millet
mille (*plural*, mília), one thousand
milliárium –ii, *n.*, a milestone
míllies, *adv.*, a thousand times
milvus –i, *m.*, a stork
mimus –i, *m.*, an actor, a mimic
mina –ae, *f.*, a coin
mináciter, *adv.*, by threats, threateningly
minax –ácis, *adj.*, threatening
míniae –árum, *f. pl.*, threats
mínimum –i, *n.*, a very small thing
mínimus –a –um, *adj.*, least, very small,
smallest
ministéllus –i, *m.*, a non-Catholic minister
miníster –tri, *m.*, a minister, servant,
attendant, official, altar boy
ministeriális, –e, *adj.*, pertaining to a
minister
ministérium –ii, *n.*, ministry, a sacred
vessel
minístra –ae, *f.*, servant
ministrátor –óris, *m.*, a server, one who
serves
minístro –áre, *1*, to serve, minister to,
wait on
mínor –ári, *dep. 1*, to threaten
minorátio –ónis, *f.*, decrease, diminution
Minóres, Fratres, the members of the
Order of St. Francis
Minóres, Ordines, minor orders
minorísta –ae, *m.*, one in minor orders
minóro –áre, *1*, to diminish, decrease,
shorten
mínuo –ere –ui –útum, *3*, to diminish,
abate, make less, make smaller, reduce

minúsculus –a –um, *adj.,* rather small, small

minútiae –árum, *f.,* trifles, details

minútum –i, *n.,* a minute, mite

minútum secúndum, a second of time

minútus –a –um, *adj.,* small, unimportant

mirabília –ium, *n. pl.,* wonderful works, wonders, marvelous things

mirabíliter, *adv.,* wonderfully, wondrously, singularly, marvelously

mirabílium –ii, *n.,* wonder

mirándus –a –um, *adj.,* strange, wonderful, extraordinary

mirífico –áre, *1,* to make wonderful, show forth wonderfully, exalt

miror –ári, *dep. 1,* to wonder, behold

mirus –a –um, *adj.,* wonderful, astonishing, extraordinary

Mísael (Hebr.), *indecl.,* Misael, one of the three cast into the fiery furnace

mísceo –ére –cui, mixtum, *2,* to mingle, mix

miser –a –um, *adj.,* wretched, miserable, unhappy, pitiable

miserátio –ónis, *f.,* mercy, kindness, compassion

miserátor –óris, *m.,* one who shows compassion

mísere, *adv.,* wretchedly, miserably

miséreor –éri, miséritus sum, *dep. 2,* to pity, have mercy on

miséria –ae, *f.,* misery, trouble, wretchedness

misericórdia –ae, *f.,* mercy, kindness, compassion

misericórditer, *adv.,* mercifully

miséricors –córdis, *adj.,* merciful, abounding in mercy

míseror –ári, miserátus sum, *dep. 1,* to have pity on, have compassion on

Missa –ae, *f.,* the Mass

missále –is, *n.,* the Mass book, the Missal

missális –e, *adj.,* pertaining to the Mass

míssio –ónis, *f.,* mission, a sending forth, the act of sending or of being sent

míssio canónica, an ecclesiastical appointment

missionárius –i, *m.,* a missionary

missionárius apostólicus, a missionary with faculties from the Holy See

missionárius –a –um, *adj.,* missionary, pertaining to a mission

mistum –i, *n.,* a mixture

mistúra –ae, *f.,* a mixture

mitésco –ere, *3,* to grow old, become mild, be allayed, subside

mítigo –áre, *1,* to mitigate, subdue, weaken, diminish, give rest, peace, relief, make mild

mitis –e, *adj.,* meek, mild, gentle, tender

mitra –ae, *f.,* a miter, bonnet, headdress worn by bishops and distinguished ecclesiastics

mitra auriphrygiáta, a miter made of cloth of gold, worn during Lent and Advent, and when the bishop has to sit for some time during a sacred ceremony

mitrátus –a –um, *adj.,* mitered

mitto –ere, misi, missum, *3,* to send, put, lay, rest

míxtio –ónis, *f.,* a confounding, confusing

mixtum –i, *n.,* a mixture

mixtúra –ae, *f.,* a mixture

mixtus –a –um, *adj.,* mingled, mixed

mna –ae, *f.,* a coin

Moab, *indecl.,* Moab, son of Lot

mobílitas –átis, *f.,* fickleness, inconstancy, changeability

moderáte, *adv.,* modestly, temperatively

modéstia –ae, *f.,* modesty

modéstus –a –um, *adj.,* short, brief, moderate

módicum –i, *n.,* a little while

módicum quid, a little something

módicus –a –um, *adj.,* little, small, of a moderate size, small quantity

módius –ii, *m.,* a bushel, peck, a measure of corn

modo, *adv.,* now, presently, even now, just now, provided that

modulátio –ónis, *f.,* singing, melody, the chanting or singing of a melody

modulátor –óris, *m.,* a musician

módulor –ári, *dep. 1,* to temper, regulate, mitigate

módulus –i, *m.,* melody, rhythm

modus –i, *m.,* measure, way, manner, fashion, mode, method, a mode or tone

moecha –ae, *f.,* an adulteress

moéchia –ae, *f.,* adultery

moechor –ári, *dep. 1,* to commit adultery

moechus –i, *m.,* an adulterer

moénia –ium, *n. pl.,* ramparts

moeror –óris, *m.,* sorrow, grief

moéstia –ae, *f.,* sorrow

moestitúdo –inis, *f.,* sadness

moestus –a –um, *adj.,* sorrowful, afflicted

mola –ae, *f.,* a mill, millstone

mola asinária, a millstone
moláris –is, *m.,* molar, cheek tooth
molendínum –i, *n.,* a mill
moles –is, *f.,* bulk, mass
moléstia –ae, *f.,* trouble, harm
moléstor –ári, *dep. 1,* to molest
moléstus –a –um, *adj.,* troublesome, grievous, burdensome, annoying
molímen –inis, *n.,* effort, working
mólior –íri, *dep. 4,* to plot, practice
molítio –ónis, *f.,* demolition
móllio –íre, *4,* to soften, make smooth
mollis, –e, *adj.,* soft, flexible, yielding; *as a noun,* a soft garment
mólliter, *adv.,* gently
mons, montis, *m.,* a mount, hill, mountain
monstrántia –ae, *f.,* a monstrance
monstro –áre, *1,* to show, point out
monstrum –i, *n.,* monstrosity
montána –órum, *n. pl.,* hill country
montánus –a –um, *adj.,* mountainous, belonging to a mountain
monuméntum –i, *n.,* a monument, grave, sepulcher
mora –ae, *f.,* delay, hindrance, pause, rest, space of time
morális –e, *adj.,* moral
morálitas –átis, *f.,* morality
mórbidus –a –um, *adj.,* depraved, diseased
morbus –i, *m.,* disease
mordax –ácis, *adj.,* stinging, piercing
mórdeo –ére, momórdi, morsum, *2,* to take hold upon, to bite
morígerus –a –um, *adj.,* accommodating, compliant
mórior –i, mórtuus sum, *dep. 3,* to die
moror –ári, *dep. 1,* to delay, abide
mors, mortis, *f.,* death
morsus –us, *m.,* a morsel, bite, biting, eating
mortális –e, *adj.,* mortal, subject to death
mortáliter, *adv.,* mortally
mortaríolum –i, *n.,* a little mortar (vessel)
morticínum –i, *n.,* a corpse, carcass
mórtifer –a –um, *adj.,* deadly
mortificátio –ónis, *f.,* mortification
mortífico –áre, *1,* to mortify, kill, slay
mortis ictus, the stroke of death, mortal sin
mortuális –e, *adj.,* pertaining to death, funeral Mass
mórtuus –a –um, *adj.,* dead
mórula –ae, *f.,* interval, brief delay

morus –i, *f.,* a mulberry tree
mos, moris, *m.,* custom, manner, action
motábilis –e, *adj.,* moving, changeable, fickle, capable of action
motívum –i, *n.,* motive
motéttum –i, *n.,* a short song
mótio –ónis, *f.,* motion, movement, action
motu próprio, own accord, applied to an informal decree of the Pope
motus –us, *m.,* motion, moving, tumult, tempest
móveo –ére, movi, motum, *2,* to move, stir, effect, influence, quake
Móyses –is, *m.,* Moses (genitive and dative, *Moysi;* accusative, *Moysen*)
mozétta (mozzétta) –ae, *f.,* a short cape worn over the rochet
mucro –ónis, *m.,* a point, sharp edge, sharp point of anything
múgio –íre –ívi *or* –ii –ítum, *4,* to rumble, groan
mula –ae, *f.,* a mule
múlceo –ére, mulsi, mulctum, *2,* to milk out
muliebris –e, *adj.,* feminine
múlier –eris, *f.,* woman, wife
muliércula –ae, *f.,* a disgraceful woman
mulíeris –e, *adj.,* womanly
mulsum –i, *n.,* sweet wine
multifáriam, *adv.,* at sundry times, on many sides, in many places
multifórmis –e, *adj.,* manifold
multifórmiter, *adv.,* in divers ways
multígenus –a –um, *adj.,* of many things, prolific, numerous
multilóquium –ii, *n.,* much speaking
multímodus –a –um, *adj.,* manifold, various
múltiplex –icis, *adj.,* manifold, many, many times more, far more
multiplícitas –átis, *f.,* multiplicity, manifoldness
multiplicátio –ónis, *f.,* multiplicity
multiplíciter, *adv.,* in many ways, in various ways, greatly
multíplico –áre, *1,* to multiply, enrich
multisónus –a –um, *adj.,* loud
multitúdo –inis, *f.,* multitude, large number
multívolus –a –um, *adj.,* having many desires
multo, *adv.,* many
multum, *adv.,* much, long, to a great degree or extent
multus –a –um, *adj.,* many

mulus –i, *m.*, a mule
mundánus –a –um, *adj.*, mundane, pertaining to the world
mundátio –ónis, *f.*, cleansing, purification
múndicors –dis, *adj.*, clean of heart
munditia –ae, *f.*, cleanliness
mundo –áre, *1*, to cleanse, make clean, to purify from sin
mundus –i, *m.*, the world
mundus –a –um, *adj.*, clean, pure, elegant
múnero –áre, *1*, to bestow a gift upon, to honor or reward with a gift
múneror –ari, *dep. 1*, to present
múnia –ium, *n. pl.*, gifts, services
muníficens –éntis, *adj.*, munificent
munímen –inis, *n.*, protection, rampart
múnio –íre, *4*, to defend, make strong, strengthen, preserve, fortify
munísculum –i, *n.*, a snare
munítio –ónis, *f.*, a fort
munitiúncula –ae, *f.*, a small fortress
munítus –a –um, *adj.*, secure, fortified, defended
munus –eris, *n.*, a gift, bounty, offering
munúsculum –i, *n.*, a little gift
murénula –ae, *f.*, a necklace
murmur –uris, *n.*, a murmuring
murmurátio –ónis, *f.*, a murmur
múrmuro –áre, *1*, to murmur
murus –i, *m.*, a wall
musca –ae, *f.*, a fly
muscárium –ii, *n.*, a fan
música –ae, *f.*, instrumental music
músicus –a –um, *adj.*, pertaining to music

músicus –i, *m.*, a musician
musívum –i, *n.*, mosaic
musívus –a –um, *adj.*, artistic
mussitátor –óris, *m.*, a murmurer
mustum –i, *n.*, new wine
mutabílitas –átis, *f.*, change
mutátio –ónis, *f.*, a change
mutatórium –ii, *n.*, change, a sacristy
mutatórius –a –um, *adj.*, pertaining to a change
muto –áre, *1*, to change, to move
mútuo –, *adv.*, mutually, to one another
mútuor –ári, *dep. 1*, to borrow
mutus –a –um, *adj.*, dumb, unable to speak
mútuus –a –um, *adj.*, mutual
mýrica –ae, *f.*, a tamarisk shrub, tamaric
myrrha –ae, *f.*, myrrh
myrrhátus –a –um, *adj.*, mingled with myrrh
myrtétum –i, *n.*, a bush of myrtle trees
myrum –i, *n.*, an ointment
mysteriále –is, *n.*, a vessel in which the Blessed Sacrament was kept
mystérion, *n.*, a mystery
mystérium –ii, *n.*, a mystery, secret, secret knowledge, that which transcends human intelligence
mystérius –a –um, *adj.*, having to do with a mystery
mystétum –i, *n.*, a grove of myrtle trees
mýstice, *adv.*, mystically
mýsticus –a –um, *adj.*, of deep meaning, mystical

N

Nain, a city in Galilee where Jesus restored a widow's son to life
nancíscor –i, nanctus sum *or* nactus sum, *dep. 3*, to obtain, get, reach, meet with
narcíssus –i, *m.*, a daffodil, narcissus
nardus –i, *f.*, *and* nardum –i, *n.*, a spike, spikenard
nares –ium, *f. pl.*, nose, nostrils
narrátor –óris, *m.*, narrator, relater
narro –áre, *1*, to say, speak, relate, tell, record
narthex –icis, *f.*, the interior vestibule of a church
nascor –i, natus sum, *dep. 3*, to be born
nassa –ae, *f.*, a trap, snare, net

natalícius –a –um, *adj.*, pertaining to a birthday
natális –e, *adj.*, natal, pertaining to birth
natális –is, *m.*, birthday, the anniversary of a saint
Natális cálicis, the "Feast of the Chalice," an early name for Maundy Thursday
Natális Eucharístiae, Maundy Thursday
natalítia –órum, *n. pl.*, birthday festival, the feast of a saint
natalítium –ii, *n.*, a feast, birthday
natalítius –a –um, *adj.*, pertaining to a birthday
natatória –ae, *f.*, a pool

Nathan (Hebr.), *indecl.*, Nathan, one of David's prophets (Ps. 51)

Nathániel –is, *m.*, Nathaniel, a native of Cana in Galilee; supposed to be the same as Bartholomew (Jn. 1:45–49)

nátio –ónis, *f.*, nation, people; *in the plural*, heathen, gentiles

natívitas –átis, *f.*, nativity, birth, birthday

natúra –ae, *f.*, nature

naturális –e, *adj.*, natural, illegitimate

naturáliter, *adv.*, according to nature

natus –a –um, *adj.*, born

natus –us, *m.*, birth

natus –i, *m.*, sons; *in the plural*, offspring, children, race, posterity

naúclerus –i, *m.*, the captain of a ship

naufrágium –ii, *n.*, a shipwreck

naúfragus –a –um, *adj.*, shipwrecked

naúfrago –áre, *1*, to suffer shipwreck

naúsea –ae, *f.*, nausea, squeamishness

naúseo –áre, *1*, to vomit

nauta –ae, *m.*, a sailor

naúticus –a –um, *adj.*, nautical, pertaining to a ship

naútici –órum, *m. pl.*, sailors

navicélla –ae, *f.*, an incense boat

navícula –ae, *f.*, an incense boat, little ship

naviculárius –a –um, *adj.*, relating to small boats

navígium –ii, *n.*, a ship

navis –is, *f.*, a ship, vessel, the nave of a church

navo –áre, *1*, to do something zealously, actively, assiduously, diligently

Názara –ae, *f.*, Nazareth, a city in Zebulum, in Lower Galilee

Nazarénus –a –um, *adj.*, of Nazareth, Nazarene (Mt. 2:23; Acts 24:5)

Nazarethánus –a –um, *adj.*, of Nazareth

nébula –ae, *f.*, a cloud, mist, fog, anything soft and transparent

necessário, *adv.*, necessarily

necessárius –a –um, *adj.*, needful, necessary

necésse, *adj.* (with *habere* and *esse*), necessary, needful, need

necéssitas –átis, *f.*, want, need, poverty

necessitúdo –inis, *f.*, necessity, inevitableness

neco –áre, *1*, to kill, slay

necrológium –ii, *n.*, a list of deceased persons

nectar –áris, *n.*, nectar

necto –ere, néxui *or* nexi, nexum, *3*, to weave, twine

nedum, *adv.*, to say nothing of, much less, still less

nefárie, *adv.*, impiously

nefárius –a –um, *adj.*, impiously

nefas, *n.* (*indecl.*), a wrong, crime, sin

negátio –ónis, *f.*, denial

négito –áre, *1*, to deny frequently

néglego –ere –léxi –léctum, *3*, to neglect, despise

négligens –éntis, *adj.*, negligent, careless

negligénter, *adv.*, negligently

negligéntia –ae, *f.*, negligence

nego –áre, *1*, to deny, say no, refuse

negotiátor –óris, *m.*, merchant, businessman

negótio –ónis, *f.*, merchandise, traffic

negótium –ii, *n.*, business, affair, matter, occupation

nemo –inis, *n.* and *f.*, no one, nobody, no man

nemorális –e, *adj.*, sylvan, pertaining to woods or groves

nemorénsis –e, *adj.*, of a wood or grove

nempe, *conj.*, truly, to be sure, namely

nemus –óris, *n.*, forest, wood, grove, a place of solitude

neo –ere, nevi, netum, *2*, to spin

neoménia –ae, *f.*, new moon

neóphyta –ae, *f.*, a female convert

neóphytus –i, *m.*, a convert, novice

neoprésbyter –eri, *m.*, a recently ordained priest

nepa –ae, *f.*, a scorpion, crab

nepos –ótis, *m.* and *f.*, nephew, niece, grandchild, posterity

neptis –is, *f.*, a granddaughter

nequam, *adj.* (*indecl.*), wicked, evil, worthless, iniquitous

nequándo, *conj.*, lest, lest at any time

nequáquam, *adv.*, no, not, by no means, in nowise

néqueo –íre –ívi *or* –ii –ítum, *4*, to be unable

néquior –ius, *adj.*, more wicked

nequíssimus –i, *m.*, most wicked one

nequítia –ae, *f.*, malice, evil, wickedness, iniquity

nervíceus –a –um, *adj.*, made of nerves or sinews

nervus –i, *m.*, a nerve, sinew, tendon, string of a musical instrument

nescéntia –ae, *f.*, ignorance

néscio –íre –ivi –ítum, *4*, not to know, be ignorant of

neumatízo –áre, *1*, to chant a protracted modulation over a syllable neuter –tra –trum, *adj.*, neither

nex, necis, *f.*, a violent death

nexus –us, *m.*, a bond

nictus –us, *m.*, the winking of an eye

nidífico –áre, *1*, to build a nest

nidus –i, *m.*, a nest, brood

Niger, surname of Simeon, one of the teachers at Antioch when St. Paul and Barnabas returned there after carrying the contributions of the brethren to the poor saints at Jerusalem (Acts 13:1)

niger –gra –grum, *adj.*, black

nigrans –ántis, *adj.*, black

nigríta –ae, *m.* and *f.*, a Negro

nigríticus –a –um, *adj.*, relating to Negroes

nihil, *n.* (*indecl.*), nothing, not at all

nihíldum, *conj.*, nothing as yet

nihilóminus, *adv.*, yet, nevertheless, notwithstanding

níhilum –i, *n.*, nothing

nil, *n.* (*indecl.*), nothing

Nil Sine Númine, nothing without God

nimbátus –a –um, *adj.*, in a cloud or mist

nimbus –i, *m.*, a cloud, storm, shower of rain, a halo or auriole — a symbolic oval of light placed over the head of saints in Christian art to symbolize their special honor in heaven

nímie, *adv.*, very, very much, extremely

nimíetas –átis, *f.*, superfluity, excess

nimírum, *adv.*, truly, certainly, undoubtedly, doubtless

nimis, *adv.*, exceedingly, greatly, beyond measure, overmuch, too much

nímius –a –um, *adj.*, excessive, too great, too much

ningo –ere, ninxi, *3*, to snow

nínguo –ere, ninxi, *3*, to snow

nisi, *conj.*, unless, except, if not, but, in case that

nisus –us, *m.*, strength, striving, effort, labor, endeavor

nitens síderis, the sun, daystar, Christ (fig.)

níteo –ére –ui, *2*, to glitter, shine, glisten, be bright

nitésco –ere, *3*, to begin to shine

nítidus –a –um, *adj.*, smooth

nitor –óris, *m.*, splendor, brilliance, brightness, shining light

nitor, niti, nisus *or* nixus sum, *dep. 3*, to endeavor, strive, lean upon, rest

nitrum –i, *n.*, nitre, natural soda

níveus –a –um, *adj.*, snow-white

nix, nivis, *f.*, snow

nixor –ári, *dep. 1*, to lean upon, rest upon, strive, strain

Noah, son of Lamech, and father of Shem, Ham, and Japheth

nóbilis –e, *adj.*, noble, high-born, of noble birth, of distinguished ancestry

nobílitas –átis, *f.*, nobility, noble birth, excellence, worth

nobíliter, *adv.*, nobly, excellently

nobílito –áre, *1*, to make known, make illustrious

nóceo –ére, nócui –itum, *2*, to hurt, harm, injure

nocívus –a –um, *adj.*, harmful, hurtful, injurious

noctu, *adv.*, by night

nóctua –ae, *f.*, owl

Nocturnále –is, *n.*, a book containing the choral melodies for chanting Matins

nocturnális –e, *adj.*, pertaining to night

noctúrnus –a –um, *adj.*, of the night, nocturnal, nightly, by night, pertaining to the night

nócuus –a –um, *adj.*, injurious, hurtful

nodósitas –átis, *f.*, intricacy, knottiness

nodósus –a –um, *adj.*, injurious, hurtful

nodus –i, *m.*, a knot, the bond or tie of the tongue

nolle, nólui, to be unwilling, not to wish, refuse

nomen –inis, *n.*, a name

nominátim, *adv.*, by name

nominátio –ónis, *f.*, a naming

nominátus –a –um, *adj.*, renowned, famed

nómino –áre, *1*, to name, give a name to

Nona –ae, *f.*, the canonical hour of None

nondum, *adv.*, not yet

nonna –ae, *f.*, a nun

nonne, *introduces a question to which an affirmative reply is expected*

nonníhil, *n.*, not nothing (something)

nonnúllus –a –um, *adj.*, some

nonnúmquam, *adv.*, sometimes

nonnus –i, *m.*, a monk

nonúsus –i, *m.*, disuse

norma –ae, *f.*, a rule, standard, gauge, way of life

nosco –ere, novi, notum, *3*, to know how, be acquainted with

nosocómium –ii, *n.*, hospital, infirmary

nosse, short for *novisse*

nota –ae, *f.*, a note, sign, notice, mark

notábilis –e, *adj.*, notable, remarkable

nota fácere, to show

notámen –inis, *n.,* a token, sign

notárius –ii, *m.,* a scribe

notátio –ónis, *f.,* a mental impression

nótio –ónis, *f.,* notion

notítia –ae, *f.,* knowledge, news, fame, patron, fosterer

noto –áre, *1,* to mark, prepare, denote

notórius –a –um, *adj.,* notorious

notus –i, *m.,* friend, acquaintance

notus –a –um, *adj.,* known

novácula –ae, *f.,* a sharp knife, razor

novále –is, *n.,* new land, fallow land

nove, *adv.,* recently, lately, newly, in an unusual manner

novélla –órum, *n. pl.,* young shoots

novéllus –a –um, *adj.,* young, new

novémber –bris, *m.,* the month of November

novéna –ae, *f.,* a period of nine days, novena, devotion lasting nine days

novendiális –e, *adj.,* lasting nine days

novensílis –e, *adj.,* new

novénus –a –um, *adj.,* nine, nine each

novilúnium –ii, *n.,* new moon

novíssima –órum, *n. pl.,* last state

novíssime, *adv.,* at last, latest, last of all

novíssimus –a –um, *adj.,* last, latest

nóvitas –átis, *f.,* new condition, new work, freshness, newness, conversion, new life

nóviter, *adv.,* newly

novítius –i, *m.,* novice

novus –a –um, *adj.,* fresh, young

nox, noctis, *f.,* night

nox, *adv.,* sometimes used for *vigilia*

noxa –ae, *f.,* injury, offense, crime, earthly honors

noxiális –e, *adj.,* evil, harmful, baneful

nóxie, *adv.,* injuriously

nóxius –a –um, *adj.,* evil, sinful, guilty, harmful, hurtful

nox saéculi, spiritual darkness, sin

nubes –is, *f.,* a cloud

núbilum –i, *n.,* a cloudy sky; *in the plural,* clouds

nubo –ere, nupsi, nuptum, *3,* to marry

núcleus –i, *m.,* kernel

nudátus –a –um, *adj.,* bare

núdipes –pedis, *adj.,* barefooted

núditas –átis, *f.,* nakedness, nudity, bareness, want

nudiustértius, *adv.,* the day before yesterday

nudus –a –um, *adj.,* naked, bare, nude

nugae –árum, *f. pl.,* trifles, nonsense

nugátor –óris, *m.,* a jester, a foolish man

nugax –ácis, *adj.,* frivolous, trifling

núgitas –átis, *f.,* vanity, frivolity, trifling

nullátenus, *adv.,* not at all

núllibi, *adv.,* in no part, nowhere

nullus –a –um, *adj.,* none, not any

nullúsdam, none as yet

num, *interrogative adverb, used when a negative reply is expected*

numélla –ae, *f.,* a torture rack

numen –inis, *n.,* divine power, the divine will, divinity

numerátor –óris, *m.,* a counter, numberer

número –áre, *1,* to number, count, reckon, enumerate

numerósitas –átis, *f.,* number, numbers, a great number, multitude

númerus –i, *m.,* a number

numísma, –átis, *n.,* a piece of money, coin, medal

nummulárius –i, *m.,* money changer, banker

númmulus –i, *m.,* a small coin

nummus –i, *m.,* a coin

numquam, *adv.,* never

numquid, *interrogative adverb, used when a negative reply is expected*

nunc, *adv.,* now, at present, at this moment

nunc . . . nunc, at one time . . . at another

núncius –ii, *m.,* a messenger

nuncupátio –ónis, *f.,* a public offering, the pronouncing of a vow

nuncupatíve, *adv.,* nominally, in name

núncupo –áre, *1,* to call, name

núndinae –árum, *f. pl.,* market place

nundítio –ónis, *f.,* a spiritual cleansing

nunquam, *adv.,* never

núntia –ae, *f.,* a herald

nuntiátio –ónis, *f.,* declaration, announcement

núntio –áre, *1,* to announce, proclaim, declare, tell

núntium –ii, *n.,* message, news

núntius –ii, *m.,* a messenger, herald, ambassador of the Holy See, Angel Gabriel

nuper, *adv.,* recently, newly

nupta –ae, *f.,* a bride, spouse, wife

núptiae –árum, *f. pl.,* marriage, marriage feast

nuptiális –e, *adj.,* nuptial, wedding, pertaining to a wedding

nuptus –i, *m.,* a husband

nuptus –us, *m.*, marriage, wedlock
nurus –us, *f.*, a young married woman, a daughter-in-law
nusquam, *adv.*, on no occasion, nowhere, never, at no time
nutans –ántis, *adj.*, feeble, inconstant
nuto –áre, *1*, to wander, fail, waver, totter, be unstable, unresolved, unsettled
nutrícius –ii, *m.*, a guardian, foster father
nutriméntum –i, *n.*, food

nutrítor –óris, *m.*, a patron, fosterer
nutritórius –a –um, *adj.*, pertaining to bringing up
nutrix –ícis, *f.*, nurse
nutus –us, *m.*, a nod, command, beck, invitation
nux, nucis, *f.*, a nut
nycticórax –ácis, *m.*, a night hawk (Ps. 101:7; Lev. 11:16; Deut. 14:15)
nyphaéum –i, *n.*, a basin used for ablutions in the early churches

O

ob, on account of, in consideration of, for, because of
obaeráti –órum, *m. pl.*, debtors
obaerátus –a –um, *adj.*, in debt
obarmátus –a –um, *adj.*, armed
obármo –are, *1*, to arm
obaúdio –íre, *4*, to obey, cause to be heard
obcaecátio –ónis, *f.*, blindness
obcaecátus –a –um, *adj.*, blinded
obcrésco –ere, *3*, to increase, grow larger
obdórmio –íre, *4*, to sleep, fall asleep
obdúco –ere –duxi –ductum, *3*, to produce
obdúctio –ónis, *f.*, doubt, cloudiness, covering
obdúlco –áre, *1*, to sweeten
obdúlésco –ere, *3*, to become sweet
obdurátio –ónis, *f.*, stubbornness
obdúro –áre, *1*, to harden, make insensible
Obed, son of Boaz by Ruth, and father of Jesse
obediénter, *adv.*, obediently
obediéntia –ae, *f.*, obedience, compliance, submission to one in authority, one of the chief counsels made into a vow
obédio –íre, *4, with the dative,* to obey, submit to, yield obedience to
obedítio –ónis, *f.*, obedience
óbeo –íre, *4*, to die
obérro –áre, *1*, to wander about
obésse –fui, to impede, injure, be prejudicial
obésus –a –um, *adj.*, fat, stout
obex –icis, *m.* and *f.*, obstacle, hindrance
óbfero –férre –tuli –látum, *3*, to put to

obfúsco –áre, *1*, to make dark, darken, blacken, obscure
óbitus –us, *m.*, death
objéctio –ónis, *f.*, contempt, abjection, humble condition
objécto –áre, *1*, to put in the way, set against
objéctum –i, *n.*, object
objéctus –us, *m.*, an obstacle
objício –ere –jéci –jéctum, *3*, to drive away, charge against
objurgátio –ónis, *f.*, injury, blaming, reproving
objurgátor –óris, *m.*, a blamer, reprover, scolder, chider
obláta –órum, *n. pl.*, bread and wine offered at Mass
oblátio –ónis, *f.*, offering, oblation, the act of offering, religious sacrifice
oblatória –ae, *f.*, a cruet
oblátus –a –um, *adj.*, offered
oblectaméntum –i, *n.*, pleasure, amusement, allurement
oblectátio –ónis, *f.*, pleasure
obligátio –ónis, *f.*, obligation, binding
óbligo –áre, *1*, to entangle
oblíquum –i, *n.*, that which is different; *in oblíquo,* indirectly
oblítero –áre, *1*, to blot out
oblívio –ónis, *f.*, oblivion, forgetfulness, a state of being forgotten
obliviósus –a –um, *adj.*, forgetful
oblivíscor –i –lítus sum, *dep. 3*, to forget
oblívium –ii, *n.*, forgetfulness
oblóngus –a –um, *adj.*, long
oblóquor –i –locútus sum, *dep. 3*, to revile, speak against someone, slander, detract

obmúrmuro –áre, *1,* to murmur against
obmutésco –ere –mútui, *3,* to be dumb, mute, speechless, silent
obníxe, *adv.,* earnestly, with all one's might
obnóxius –a –um, *adj.,* subject to, obedient
obnúbilo –áre, *1,* to darken, obscure, overcloud
obnúbo –ere –núpsi –núptum, *3,* to cover
óbolus (*or* óbulus) –i, *m.,* a small coin Obolus S. Petri, Peter's pence
obórior, oboríri –órtus sum, *dep. 4,* to arise, appear
obrépo –ere –répsi –réptum, *3,* to take by surprise, to creep upon, crawl to, steal upon
obrigésco –ere –rígui, *3,* to become stiff
obrízus –a –um, *adj.,* fine, refined, finest (referring to gold)
óbruo –ere –rui –rúptum, *3,* to overwhelm, bury, cover over
obscoénus –a –um, *adj.,* foul
obscúre, *adv.,* obscurely, secretly, covertly
obscúritas –átis, *f.,* spiritual darkness
obscúro –áre, *1,* to darken, made dark, obscure, darken spiritually
obscúrus –a –um, *adj.,* obscure; *in obscurum,* into the darkness
obsecrátio –ónis, *f.,* prayer, supplication, entreaty, a public prayer
óbsecro –áre, *1,* to beseech, implore, entreat
obsecúndo –áre, *1,* to comply with, fall in with, be subservient to
óbsequens –éntis, *adj.,* dutiful, obedient, yielding
obséquiae –árum, *f. pl.,* funeral services
obséquium –ii, *n.,* homage, service, worship, deference, respect
óbsequor –i –secútus sum, *dep. 3,* to obey, pay homage to
óbsero –áre, *1,* to bolt, bar, fasten
óbsero –ere –sévi –situm, *3,* to sow, plant
observántia –ae, *f.,* observance, practice, abstinence, observance of religious duties
observátio –ónis, *f.,* observance
obsérvo –áre, *1,* to observe, watch, regard, mark, note
obses –idis, *c.,* hostage
obsídeo –ere –sédi –séssum, *2,* to beset, enclose, remain anywhere

obsídio –ónis, *f.,* siege
obsígno –áre, *1,* to seal
obsísto –ere –stiti, *3,* to resist, oppose, withstand
obsolésco –ere –évi, *3,* to grow old, wear out
obsolétus –a –um, *adj.,* obsolete, worn out, cast off
obsónium –ii, *n.,* relish, sweetmeats
obstáculum –i, *n.,* hindrance
obsto –ere –stiti, *3,* to stop, check
obstríngo –ere –strínxi –stríctum, *3,* to be indebted to
óbstruo –ere –strúxi –strúctum, *3,* to close, stop up
obstrúsus –a –um, *adj.,* concealed, covered
obstupefácio –ere, *3,* to astonish, astound, amaze
obstupésco –ere –stípui *or* –stúpui, *3,* to be astonished, amazed, astounded, frightened
obtéctus –a –um, *adj.,* covered over
obtémpero –áre, *1,* to obey, comply with, submit to, attend to
obténdo –ere –téndi –téntum, *3,* to spread before, stretch before, cover, hide
obténebror –ári, *dep. 1,* to be obscured
obténtus –us, *m.,* pleading, excuse
óbtero –ere –trívi –trítum, *3,* to trample, crush
obtéstor –ári, *dep. 1,* to entreat, implore, call to witness, adjure
obtíneo –ére –tínui –téntum, *2,* to obtain, secure, lay hold of, prevail
obtíngo –ere –tigi, *3,* to fall to the lot of
obtrectátio –ónis, *f.,* detraction, envious disparagement
obtrécto –áre, *1,* to disparage, decry
obtúndo –ere –tudi –túsum, *3,* to weary, weaken, dull, make blunt
obturátio –ónis, *f.,* a stopping up (of the ears)
obtúro –áre, *1,* to close, stop up
obtúsus –a –um, *adj.,* blunt
obumbrátio –ónis, *f.,* shadow, overshadowing, darkening
obúmbro –áre, *1,* to overshadow
obvénio –íre, *4,* to meet
óbviam, *adv.,* on the way
óbvio –áre, *1,* to meet, go forth to meet
óbvius –a –um, *adj.,* in the way, meeting
obvólvo –ere –volvi –vólutum, *3,* to wrap up, cover all around

occásio –ónis, f., occasion
occásus –us, m., the setting of the sun
óccidens –entis, m., the west, evening
occídens –éntis, adj., deathly
occidentális –e, adj., western
óccido –ere –sídi –cásum, 3, to set, go down (of the sun), fall, perish, die
occído –ere –cídi –císum, 3, to put to death, kill, slay, knock down, beat to the ground, kill spiritually
occipítium –ii, n., the occiput, back of the head
occísio –ónis, f., slaughter
occísor –óris, m., killer, murderer
occúbitus –us, m., setting, the setting of the sun, prostration
ócculo –áre, 1, to tread, trample upon
ócculo –ere –cúlui –cúltum, 3, to conceal, hide
occúlte, adv., privately, secretly, in secret
occúltis –e, adj., secret, hidden
occúlto –áre, 1, to hide, conceal
occúltum –i, n., hidden thing, secret sin
occúltus –a –um, adj., hidden, secret, concealed, private
occúmbo –ere –cúbui –cúbitum, 3. to fall, fall down
occupátio –ónis, f., occupation
occupátus –a –um, adj., busy, engaged, occupied
óccupo –áre, 1, to cumber, occupy, seize
occúrrens –éntis, adj., current, of the day
occurréntia –ae, f., the meeting of two feasts on the one day
occúrro –ere –curri –cúrsum, 3, to go to meet, meet, come to, occur
occúrso –áre, 1, to meet, go to meet
occúrsus –us, m., meeting, course, occurrence, a falling in with
océllus –i, m., a little eye
ócius, adv., more quickly, speedily, rapidly
ócrea –ae, f., a metal greave
octáva –ae, f., an octave, a period of eight days, the eighth day after a feast
Octáva infántium, Low Sunday
Octáva mediána, Passion Sunday
Octavárium –ii, n., a book containing readings for an octave
octávus –a –um, adj., eighth
octóber –bris, m., the month of October
octóber –bris –bre, adj., belonging to the month of October

octogenárius –ii, m., octogenarian
oculáris –e, adj., ocular
oculátus –a –um, adj., sharp-eyed
odíbilis –e, adj., hateful
odísse, 4, defec., perfect with present meaning, to hate, detest
ódium –ii, n., hatred
Ódium Theológicum, theological hatred, a hatred due to differences in religious beliefs
odor, odóris, m., smell, odor
odoraméntum –i, n., odor
odorátus –us, m., smell, smelling, odor
odóro –áre, 1, to smell
odóror –ári, dep. 1, to smell
oeconómia –ae, f., economy, the temporalities of an institution
oecónomus –i, m., a manager of an institution
oecuménicus –a –um, adj., ecumenical
oenópola –ae, m., a dealer in wines
offendículum –i, n., a stumbling block
offéndo –ere –féndi –fénsum, 3, to offend, err, stumble, knock against, strike
offénsio –ónis, f., an offense
ófferens principális, the principal celebrant
óffero –érre, obtúli, oblátum, 3, to offer, permit, allow, present, bring, consecrate to God
offertória –ae, f., a cruet
offertórium –ii, n., offertory
offertórium –ii, n., a linen cloth with which the subdeacon held the paten
officiális –is, m., an official
officiális –e, adj., official, a diocesan curial officer
offícians –tis, m., the celebrant
officiátor –óris, m., the celebrant
officiatúra –ae, f., a term of office
officína –ae, f., a workshop
offício –ere –féci –féctum, 3, to impede hinder
offícium –ii, n., office, service, duty
Offícium Divínum, the Divine Office, the official service of prayer
Offícium Parvum B.M.V., the Little Office of the B.V.M.
Offícium Sanctae Maríae in Sábbato, the Office of the B.V.M. for Saturday
Offícium Tenebrárium, Matins and Lauds of the three last days of Holy Week, formerly anticipated in the evening
offúndo –ere –fúdi –fúsum, 3, to pour out

offúsus –a –um, *adj.*, concealing, spread around

Og, *indecl.*, Og, King of Basan (Ps. 136:20)

ólea –ae, *f.*, an olive tree

oleárius –a –um, *adj.*, of oil

oleáster –tri, *m.*, a wild olive tree

olens –éntis, *adj.*, sweet-smelling

ólera –ae, *f.*, an herb

óleum –i, *n.*, oil

Oleum catechumenórum, holy oil

Oleum infirmórum, oil for anointing the sick

olfactoriólum –i, *n.*, a smelling flask

olfáctus, *m.*, sense of smell

olfácio –ere –féci –fáctum, *3,* to smell

olíbanum –i, *n.*, frankincense

olim, *adv.*, formerly, once, once upon a time, at times, long ago, for a long while

olíva –ae, *f.*, an olive tree

olivétum –i, *n.*, an olive grove

Olivétum –i, *n.*, Mount Olivet, the Mount of Olives, a range of hills in the east of Jerusalem. Also called the Mount of Corruption (2 Kings 23:13; Acts 1:12; Mt. 21:1; 24:3; 26:30).

Olivétus –i, *m.*, Olivet

olívum –i, *n.*, olive oil, oil for anointing

olla –ae, *f.*, a pot, caldron

olor –óris, *m.*, a swan

olus –eris, *n.*, herb, any kind of garden herb

omítto –ere, *3,* to omit, leave undone

omnícreans –ántis, *adj.*, all-creating

omnímodus –a –um, *adj.*, complete, entire

omníno, *adv.*, altogether, entirely, totally, wholly by no means

omnípotens –éntis, *adj.*, almighty, all-powerful, omnipotent, holding all things, all-swaying

omnipoténtia –ae, *f.*, might

omophórion (Greek), *n.*, the pallium of a bishop

onáger (onágrus) –i, *m.*, a wild ass

onerátus –a –um, *adj.*, burdened

ónerus –a –um, *adj.*, burdensome

onomásticus –a –um, *adj.*, pertaining to names

ontológia –ae, *f.*, ontology

onus –eris, *n.*, burden, load, cargo

onustátus –a –um, *adj.*, burdened, laden

onústus –a –um, *adj.*, laden

onychínus –a –um, *adj.*, of onyx

opácus –a –um, *adj.*, dark, obscure

operárius –ii, *m.*, a laborer, worker, workman

operátio –ónis, *f.*, operation, work, toil, labor, business, trade

operátor –óris, *m.*, a worker, framer, maker, creator

operatótius –a –um, *adj.*, conducive to action

operculátus –a –um, *adj.*, with a lid or cover

opérculum –i, *n.*, a lid, cover

operiméntum –i, *n.*, a covering

opério –íre, *4,* to clothe, cover over, cover

óperor –ári, *dep. 1,* to work, labor, be occupied with, produce, cause

operósus –a –um, *adj.*, hard, laborious

opertórium –ii, *n.*, cover, vesture, mantle

opes, opum, *f.*, riches

ópifex –icis, *c.*, a worker

opifícium –ii, *n.*, aid

opímus –a –um, *adj.*, rich, fruitful, fat

opínio –ónis, *f.*, rumor, fame

opínor –ári, *dep. 1,* to think

opitulátio –ónis, *f.*, help, assistance

opítulo –áre, *1,* to help, aid, assist

opítulor –ári, *dep. 1,* to help, aid, assist

opórtet, opórtuit, *impers.*, it is (was) necessary, needful, fit, proper, it behooves

óppeto –ere –ívi *or* –ii –ítum, *3,* to meet, meet with, encounter

oppidánus –i, *m.*, a citizen, townsman

oppídulum –ii, *n.*, a little town, village

óppidum –i, *n.*, a town

oppígnoro –áre, *1,* to pledge

oppílo –áre, *1,* to close up, shut up, stop

óppleo –ére –plévi –plétum, *2,* to fill, fill up

opportúne, *adv.*, conveniently, in season

opportúnitas –átis, *f.*, want, need, due time, a suitable time

opportúnus –a –um, *adj.*, fit, right, seasonable, opportune

oppósitum –i, *n.*, opposite

ópprimo –ere –préssi –préssum, *3,* to oppress, overwhelm, press down, press together, crush

oppróbrium –ii, *n.*, reproach, taunt, an object of scorn, derision, mockery, a disgrace

ops, opis, *f.*, help, aid, assistance, solace

optábilis –e, *adj.*, desired, desirable, to be wished for

optátio –ónis, *f.*, a wish

óptimas –átis, *m.*, chief, most important man, aristocrat

óptime, *adv.*, very well

óptimus –a –um, *adj.*, best, perfect

óptio –ónis, *f.*, choice

opto –áre, *1*, to wish, desire

opus –eris, *n.*, deed, work

opúsculum –i, *n.*, a little work

Opus Dei, the work of God, the Divine Office

ora –ae, *f.*, border, edge, rim, the extremity of a thing

oráculum –i, *n.*, revelation, oracle, utterance, chapel, oratory

orárium –ii, *n.*, a stole

orátio –ónis, *f.*, prayer, supplication, beseeching, oration, discourse

oratiónale –is, *n.*, a book containing the Collects said at Mass

orátio reális, effective or real prayer

oratiúncula –ae, *f.*, a short prayer

orátor –óris, *m.*, a speaker

oratórium –ii, *n.*, oratory

orátus –us, *m.*, a request, an entreaty

orbátus –a –um, *adj.*, bereaved

orbis –is, *m.*, world, earth, circle, ring

orbis terrárum, the earth

orchéstra –ae, *f.*, an orchestra

orcus –i, *m.*, the infernal regions

Ordinále –is, *n.*, a former name for the ritual

ordinándus –i, *m.*, a candidate for Holy Orders

Ordinárium –ii, *n.*, a book containing a ritual

Ordinárium Divíni Offícii, the Ordinary of the Divine Office, containing the parts that do not change

ordinárius –i, *m.*, one who has the jurisdiction of an office, an ecclesiastic with ordinary (not delegated) jurisdiction

ordinárius –a –um, *adj.*, ordinary, regular

ordinátio –ónis, *f.*, ordination, ordinance, decree, the creation of sacred ministers in the Church

ordinátor –óris, *m.*, one who ordains, an orderer, arranger, regulator

ordinátus –a –um, *adj.*, orderly

órdino –áre, *1*, to arrange, order, ordain, establish, appoint

órdior –íri, orsus sum, *4*, to commence, begin

ordo –inis, *m.*, order, rite, manner, the order, authority, ascendancy

Oreb (Hebr.), *indecl.*, Oreb, a prince of Midian defeated by Gibeon, and slain by the Ephramites at the Jordan (Ps. 82:12)

organísmus –i, *m.*, organism

organíso –áre, *1*, to play the organ

organísta –ae, *m.*, an organist

órgano –áre, *1*, to sing harmonized chant

órganum –i, *n.*, an organ, organ of the body

óriens –éntis, *m.*, the orient, east, dawn, rising sun; Óriens, a scriptural title of the Messias

orientális –e, *adj.*, oriental, east

originális –e, *adj.*, original

orígo –inis, *f.*, origin, beginning

órior –íri, ortus sum, *dep. 4*, to arise, come forth, appear

ornaméntum –i, *n.*, ornament

ornátus –us, *m.*, adornment, furniture

ornátus –a –um, *adj.*, adorned

orno –áre, *1*, to adorn, garnish, trim, decorate

oro –áre, *1*, to pray, supplicate, pray to, offer petition to

orphanotróphium –ii, *n.*, an orphanage

órphanus –i, *m.*, orphan

orthodóxus –a –um, *adj.*, orthodox

orto mane, *adv.*, early morning

ortus –us, *m.*, the east, the rising of the sun

ortygométra –ae, *f.*, a quail

oryx –gis, *m.*, a wild goat

os, oris, *n.*, mouth, face, countenance

os, ossis, *n.*, bone; ossa, *pl.*; *fig.*, the inmost part, the soul

óscito –áre, *1*, to gape

osculatórium –ii, *n.*, a crucifix with which the kiss of peace was given at Mass

ósculor –ári, *dep. 1*, to kiss, caress

ósculum –i, *n.*, a kiss

osor –óris, *m.*, one who hates

osténdo –ere –téndi –ténsum *or* –tentum, *3*, to show, display, expose

osténsio –ónis, *f.*, a showing, display, evidence

ostentátio –ónis, *f.*, a showing, displaying, revealing

osténtum –i, *n.*, prodigy

ostiária –ae, *f.*, portress

ostiariátus –us, *m.*, the minor order of porter

ostiárius –ii, *m.*, a porter

ostiárius –a –um, *adj.*, pertaining to a gate or door

ostiátim, *adv.,* from door to door

ostíolum –i, *n.,* a small door

óstium –ii, *n.,* a door, gate, an entrance to anything

óstrea –ae, *f.,* an oyster

otiósus –a –um, *adj.,* idle, at leisure, with no occupation

ótium –ii, *n.,* sloth

ovíle –is, *n.,* sheepfold

ovínus –a –um, *adj.,* pertaining to sheep

ovis –is, *f.,* sheep

ovo –áre, *1,* to rejoice

ovum –i, *n.,* an egg

P

pábulum –i, *n.,* food, fodder, nourishment

pacális –e, *adj.,* relating to peace, peaceful

pacátrix –icis, *f.,* a peacemaker

pacátus –a –um, *adj.,* peaceful, pacified, quiet

pácifer –a –um, *adj.,* peace-bringing

pacificále –is, *n.,* a metal disk with the image of the crucifix, passed to the priests and people, for giving the Pax at Mass

pacificátio –ónis, *f.,* pacification, an establishing of peace

pacificátor –óris, *m.,* a peacemaker

pacífice, *adv.,* peacefully, amicably, without anger

pacífico –áre, *1,* to pacify, grant peace

pacíficor –ári, *dep. 1,* to make peace

pacíficum –i, *n.,* a peace offering

pacíficus –a –um, *adj.,* peaceful, peaceable, disposed to peace

pacíscor –i, pactus sum, *dep. 3,* to make a bargain or covenant

paco –áre, *1,* to pacify, make peace

pacta –ae, *f.,* a betrothed spouse

páctio –ónis, *f.,* a bargain, contract, agreement

pactum –i, *n.,* a covenant, contract, agreement

pactus –a –um, *adj.,* agreed upon, settled, appointed, promised

paean –is, *m.,* a hymn, paean, a song of triumph

paedagógus –i, *m.,* an instructor

paedor –óris, *m.,* filth, dirt

paene, *adv.,* almost, well-nigh

paénula –ae, *f.,* the chasuble, a cloak

pagánus –i, *m.,* a pagan

pagélla –ae, *f.,* an altar card, a card

pagína –ae, *f.,* a leaf of paper, page

pagus –i, *m.,* a village

palaéstra –ae, *f.,* a gymnasium, school

palam, *adv.,* openly, publicly, without concealment, apparently, evidently

palátha –ae, *f.,* a dried fig

palatínus –i, *m.,* a palace official

palátium –ii, *n.,* a palace, the imperial court

palátum –i, *n.,* palate, taste

pálea –ae, *f.,* straw, chaff

paliúrius –i, *m.,* a thorny shrub

palla –ae, *f.,* a maniple, an altar cloth, the pall

pallens –éntis, *adj.,* pale in color

pálleo –ére –ui, *2,* to fade, be pale, grow pale

pallésco –ere, pállui, *3,* to grow pale, turn pale, lose color

pállidus –a –um, *adj.,* pale, pallid, wan

pállio –áre, *1,* to soften, relieve, cover, cloak

pallíolum –i, *n.,* a small cloak

pállium –ii, *n.,* a cloth, garment, mantle, cloak, cover for the altar cloth, pallium — band of white worn on the shoulders, with two strings of the same material, and four purple crosses worked on it, sent by the Pope to primates, archbishops, and sometimes bishops, as a token that they possess the fullness of the episcopal office

pallor –óris, *m.,* paleness, pallor, a pale color

palma –ae, *f.,* victory, hymn of victory

Palmárum áltera (dies), a name for the feast of the Ascension

palmatória –ae, *f.,* a hand candlestick

palmes –itis, *m.,* a branch, shoot of a vine, vine sprout

palmus –i, *m.,* palm of the hand, a span; *Domínica in ramis palmárum,* Palm Sunday

palor –ári, *dep. 1,* to wander about, stray about

palpébra –ae, *f.,* an eyelid

pálpita –áre, *1,* to blink, tremble

palpo –áre, *1,* to handle, feel
palus –údis, *f.,* a swamp
palus –i, *m.,* a post, stake
palúster –tris –tre, *adj.,* marshy
Pamphýlia –ae, *f.,* Pamphylia, a province in the south of Asia Minor. Perge is the only one of its cities mentioned in the New Testament (Acts 13:13).
pampínus –i, *m.* and *f.,* a vine leaf
panárium –ii, *n.,* a bread basket
pando –ere, pandi, passum *or* pansum, *3,* to open, lay bare, stretch out, expand, announce, tell, publish, lay open in speech
pandus –a –um, *adj.,* bent, curved, crooked
pango –ere, panxi, panctum, *3,* to make, compose, sing
pango –ere, pegi *or* pepígi, pactum, *3,* to make, compose, sing
panhágia –ae, *f.,* "all holy"; the pectoral cross worn by Greek bishops
panífica –ae, *f.,* a cook, baker
panis –is, *m.,* bread, a loaf, food in general
Panis angélicus, a Scriptural allusion to the manna of old, which was a type of the Manna of the New Law
Panis coélicus, *see Panis angélicus*
paniséllus –i, *m.,* a linen cloth formerly attached to the knob of a crosier
pannículus –i, *m.,* a small piece of cloth
pannus –i, *m.,* cloth
panthéra –ae, *f.,* a panther
Papa –ae, *m.,* the Pope
papális –e, *adj.,* papal
papátus –us, *m.,* the papacy
Paphus –u, *f.,* Paphos, a city in the west of Cyprus (Acts 13:6)
papílio –ónis, *m.,* a tent, pavilion, butterfly
papílla –ae, *f.,* nipple, breast
pápula –ae, *f.,* a blister
papýrio –ónis, *f.,* a place filled with reeds, a papyrus marsh
papýrum –i, *n.,* papýrus, –i, *m.,* papyrus — the reed from which papyrus was made
par, paris (*used with dat.*), *adj.,* like, equal
parábilis –e, *adj.,* procurable
parábola –ae, *f.,* a parable, figure, similitude, illustration, fictitious narrative to illustrate a truth of comparison
parabolánus –i, *m.,* a person who visited the sick in the Eastern churches

parabólicus –a –um, *adj.,* parabolic
Parácletus *or* Paráclitus –i, *m.,* the Holy Ghost, the Paraclete (advocate)
paradígma –atis, *n.,* a model, example
Paradísus –i, *m.,* Paradise (Lk 23:43; 2 Cor. 12:4)
paradísus –i, *m.,* the vestibule of a church
parágraphus –i, *f.,* a paragraph
paralýticus –i, *m.,* one stricken with palsy
paralýticus –a –um, *adj.,* paralyzed, palsied
paramánus –us, *f.,* a cuff, upturned edge of a sleeve
paraméntum –i, *n.,* a sacred vestment, ornament
paramonárius –ii, *m.,* a sacristan, sexton, prebendary
paranýmpha –ae, *f.,* a bridesmaid
paranýmphus –i, *m.,* a groomsman
paraphonísta –ae, *m.,* a leader of a section of a choir
Parascéve –es, *f.,* the day of preparation, Parasceve, Good Friday
parátio –ónis, *f.,* a striving after, preparation
paratúra –ae, *f.,* furniture, furnishings, appurtenances
parátus –a –um, *adj.,* ready, prepared
parce, *adv.,* sparingly, moderately
parcimónia –ae, *f.,* self-denial
párcitas –átis, *f.,* frugality, temperance, moderation, sparingness
parco –ere, pepérci, parsum, *3,* to spare, keep, preserve
parcus –a –um, *adj.,* sparing, stingy
parcus –i, *m.,* a park, enclosure
pardus –i, *m.,* a leopard
parecclésia –ae, *f.,* an oratory, chapel
parens –éntis, *m.* and *f.,* a parent
parentális –e, *adj.,* pertaining to parents
páreo –ére –ui, *2,* to appear, become visible
páries –étis, *m.,* a wall, wall of a house
párilis –e, *adj.,* similar, like, equal
pário –ere, pepéri, partum, *3,* to bear, bring forth, be delivered of a child
páriter, *adv.,* at the same time, with one accord, together, equally, similarly
paro –áre, *1,* to prepare, provide, make ready, furnish, establish, make firm
paróchia –ae, *f.,* a parish
Parochiále –is, *n.,* a book of instructions for pastoral duties

parochiális –e, *adj.*, pertaining to a parish

parochiánus, *m.*, a parishioner

párochus –i, *m.*, a parish priest

paroécia –ae, *f.*, a parish

paroeciális –e, *adj.*, parochial, pertaining to a parish

parópsis –idis, *f.*, a dish

parra –ae, *f.*, a bird of ill omen, the owl, the woodpecker

parricída –ae, *m.* and *f.*, a parricide, murderer

parrúcca –ae, *f.*, a wig

pars, partis, *f.*, part, portion, lot, share, allotted possession

partes, *f.*, quarters

párticeps –ipis, *m.* and *f.*, a partaker, sharer, sharing, participating in

partícipans –ántis, *m.*, a taking part

participátio –ónis, *f.*, participation, partaking, sharing

particípium –ii, *n.*, participle

partícula –ae, *f.*, a part, particle, small piece, a small host

partim, *adv.*, partly, in part

pártior –íri, *dep. 4,* to divide, part, distribute

partítio –ónis, *f.*, division

partúrio –íre, *4,* to travail, meditate, intend, desire to bring forth

parturítio –ónis, *f.*, travail, a bringing forth

partus –us, *m.*, bringing forth, birth, childbirth

parum, *adv.*, little, less, too little, not enough

parúra –ae, *f.*, an ornament, embroidered work

parvipéndo –ere –pepéndi –pénsum, *3,* to esteem lightly

párvitas –átis, *f.*, a small quantity

párvulus –a –um, *adj.*, little, small, youthful, young

párvulus –i, *m.*, a little child

parvus –a –um, *adj.*, small, little

Pascha –átis, *n.*, Pasch, Passover, Easter

Pascha –ae, *f.*, Pasch, Passover, Easter

Pascha annotínum, *n.*, the anniversary of a baptism

Pascha clausum, *n.*, Low Sunday

Pascha competéntium, Palm Sunday

Pascha flóridum, Palm Sunday

Paschále Praecónium, an ancient song of praise chanted on Holy Saturday

paschális –e, *adj.*, paschal, pertaining to the Pasch

Pascha médium, the Wednesday after Easter

Pascha rosárum, Pentecost Sunday

pasco –ere, pavi, pastum, *3,* to feed, nourish, shepherd

pascor –i, *dep. 1,* to eat, feed oneself

páscua –ae, *f.*, pasture, food

páscua –órum, *n. pl.*, pasture, grazing places

pascuális –e, *adj.*, of the pasture

páscuum –i, *n.*, pasture

páscuus –a –um, *adj.*, grazing, relating to a pasture

passer –is, *m.*, a sparrow

passíbilis –e, *adj.*, susceptible to pain, capable of suffering

passim, *adv.*, here and there, far and wide, up and down

pássio –ónis, *f.*, suffering, passion, the suffering of Christ or the martyrs

Passionále –is, *n.*, a book containing the Acts of Martyrs

Passionárium –ii, *n.*, a book of the lessons for the second nocturn of the Divine Office

passus –us, *m.*, a step, pace

pastophórium –ii, *n.*, a chamber adjoining the temple, sacristy, room for keeping the sacred vessels

pastor –óris, *m.*, a shepherd, pastor

pastorále –is, *n.*, a book containing instructions for pastors, a staff or crosier

pastorális –e, *adj.*, pastoral

pastorális báculus, a crosier

pastorálitas –átis, *f.*, the office of pastor

pastus –us, *m.*, food, sustenance, pasture

patefácio –ere, *3,* to open, lay open, make open

patélla –ae, *f.*, a dish, plate

paténa –ae, *f.*, the paten

patens –téntis, *adj.*, open, wide, manifest

páteo –ere –ui, *2,* to be extended or open, to lie open, stand open

pater –tris, *m.*, father

patéra –ae, *f.*, a shallow bowl

paterfamílias, patrisfamílias, *m.*, the master of a house, householder

Patérna cláritas, Christ

patérne, *adv.*, paternally

patérnitas –átis, *f.*, paternity

patérnus –a –um, *adj.*, paternal, fatherly, belonging to a father

patésco –ere –ui, *3,* to lie open or extended

patíbulum –i, *n.*, yoke, gibbet, ignominy

pátiens –éntis, *adj.*, patient, long-suffering

patiéntia –ae, *f.*, patience

patína –ae, *f.*, a dish

pátior –i, passus sum, *dep. 3*, to endure, suffer, bear with, undergo

patrátus –a –um, *adj.*, accomplished, performed

pátria –ae, *f.*, country, fatherland

patriárcha –ae, *m.*, a patriarch

patriarchális –e, *adj.*, patriarchal

patriarchátus –us, *m.*, a district under the jurisdiction of a patriarch

patrícius –ii, *m.*, a patrician, a distinguished citizen

patrimónium –ii, *n.*, a patrimony

patrínus –i, *m.*, a godfather, sponsor

Patrítius *or* Patrícius –ii, *m.*, Patrick

pátrius –a –um, *adj.*, pertaining to a father

patro –áre, *1*, to perform, achieve, accomplish

patrocínium –ii, *n.*, protection, patronage

patrocínor –ári, *dep. 1*, to defend, protect

patróna –ae, *f.*, patroness, protectress

patrónus –i, *m.*, a patron

patruélis –is, *m.*, a cousin

pátruus –i, *m.*, an uncle

pátulus –a –um, *adj.*, extended, open

paúcitas –átis, *f.*, fewness, scarcity, smallness of number

paucus –a –um, *adj.*, few, little

paulátim, *adv.*, gradually, little by little

paulísper, *adv.*, a little, a little while

paulo minis, *adv.*, almost, nearly

paúlulum, *adv.*, a very little, a short time

paúlulus –a –um, *adj.*, very little

Paulus –i, *m.*, Paul

pauper –eris, *adj.*, poor, needy, helpless, destitute, indigent, impoverished

paupérculus –a –um, *adj.*, poor

paupéries –éi, *f.*, poverty

paúpertas –átis, *f.*, poverty, misery, wretchedness, abandonment

pausa –ae, *f.*, a pause, stop, cessation, end, rest

pausátio –ónis, *f.*, repose, pausing, rest, halting

páveo –ére, pavi, *2*, to fear, tremble with fear

pavésco –ere, pavi, *3*, to fear

pávidus –a –um, *adj.*, terrified, fearful, trembling

paviméntum –i, *n.*, floor, pavement, ground, earth, dust

pávio –íre, *4*, to beat down

pávito –áre, *1*, to fear, tremble, quake with fear

pavor –óris, *m.*, fear, terror, dread

pax, pacis, *f.*, peace, blessing, prosperity

paxíllus –i, *m.*, a stick, peg, pin

peccátor –óris, *m.*, sinner, transgressor

peccátrix –ícis, *adj.*, sinful

peccátrix –ícis, *f.*, a sinner

peccátum –i, *n.*, sin

pecco –áre, *1*, to sin, commit a sin

pecten –inis, *n.*, a comb

pectorále –is, *n.*, a brooch for fastening a cope

pectorális –e, *adj.*, pertaining to the chest

pectus –oris, *n.*, breast, heart, soul, mind, the seat of the affections

peculiáris –e, *adj.*, peculiar, unique

pecúlium –ii, *n.*, property

pecúnia –ae, *f.*, money

pecuniárius –a –um, *adj.*, relating to money

pecuniósus –a –um, *adj.*, rich, wealthy

pecus –óris, *n.*, sheep, cattle

pecus –udis, *f.*, a single head of cattle

pedáneus –a –um, *adj.*, pertaining to the feet

pedes –itis, *m.*, a foot soldier

pedéster –tris –tre, *adj.*, on foot

pedes viátor, a pilgrim

pédica –ae, *f.*, a snare, trap, fetter

pediséquus –i, *m.*, a follower, attendant

pedum –i, *n.*, a shepherd's crook, crosier

pélagus –i, *n.*, the sea

pellax –ácis, *adj.*, deceitful, seductive

pellicánus –i, *m.*, a pelican

pellícea –ae, *f.*, a cassock

pellíceus *or* pellícius –a –um, *adj.*, of leather, made of skins

pellício –ere –léxi –léctum, *3*, to seduce, entice, decoy

pellícula –ae, *f.*, a little skin

pellis –is, *f.*, hide, skin, tent, tent cloth

pello –ere, pepúli, pulsum, *3*, to cast out, banish, drive away

pellúvium –ii, *n.*, a basin for washing the feet

pelta –ae, *f.*, a shield

pelvícula –ae, *f.*, a small basin or dish

pelvis –is, *f.*, a basin, dish

péndeo –ére, pepéndi, *2*, to hang, be hanged or suspended, depend

péndo –ere, pepéndi pensum, *3*, to cause to hang down, weigh, estimate

péndulus –a –um, *adj.*, hanging

pene *or* **paene**, *adv.*, almost, well-nigh

penes, *adv.*, with, before, in possession of

penetrábilis –e, *adj.*, sharp, piercing

penetrália –ium, *n. pl.*, inmost recesses, inner chambers, inmost self, spirit, the life of the soul

pénetro –áre, *1*, to penetrate, enter into

pénite, *adv.*, inwardly, internally

pénitus –a –um, *adj.*, inward

pénitus, *adv.*, wholly

penna –ae, *f.*, a feather

pennátus –a –um, *adj.*, winged, feathered

pensátor –óris, *m.*, a careful weigher

pénsio –ónis, *f.*, payment, pension

pénsito –áre, *1*, to pay, weigh, consider, ponder

penso –áre, *1*, to weigh, counterbalance, compensate, make good, repay

pensor –óris, *m.*, one who weighs or considers

pensus –a –um, *adj.*, valued, prized, esteemed, weighty

pentacontárchus –i, *m.*, a commander of fifty men

Péntateuch, *indecl.*, the first five books of the Old Testament, attributed to Moses

pentecostális –e, *adj.*, Pentecostal

Pentecóste –es, *f.*, Pentecost, or Whit Sunday, the day on which the Church commemorates the descent of the Holy Ghost upon the Apostles. Fifty days after Easter.

Pentecóstes Domínica, Pentecost

Pentecóstes média (dies), the Wednesday in Ember Week after Pentecost

penúria –ae, *f.*, want, penury, need of anything

pera –ae, *f.*, a wallet, bag

perágens –éntis, *m.*, one who goes through to the end

perágo –ere –égi –áctum, *3*, to accomplish, finish, attain to, celebrate, transfix, pierce through

perágro –áre, *1*, to visit, travel, pass through

peramánter, *adv.*, very lovingly

perámbulo –áre, *1*, to walk about, go about, pass through, traverse

percéllo –ere –cúli –cúlsum, *3*, to repel, shatter, ruin, strike down, overturn, daunt

percéptio –ónis, *f.*, a partaking, perception, collecting, reception

percéptor –óris, *m.*, a receiver, imbiber

percípio –ere –cépi –céptum, *3*, to take,

partake, seize, attain, receive, be given, give ear to, hear, hearken, perceive

pércitus –a –um, *adj.*, aroused, driven

pércolo –ere –cólui –cúltum, *3*, to reverence, honor, adorn, decorate

percóntans –ántis, *adj.*, inquiring

percóntor –ári, *dep. 1*, to inquire

percrebrésco –ere –crébui, *3*, to spread abroad, be well known

percrésco –ere –crévi –crétum, *3*, to increase greatly

percúlsus –a –um, *adj.*, struck, smitten

percúpidus –a –um, *adj.*, very desirous

percúrro –ere –cucúrri *or* –cúrri –cúrsum, *3*, to run through, hasten to, persevere to the end

percúrsio –ónis, *f.*, a rapid reflection or consideration

percússio –ónis, *f.*, a striking, beating, beating time, rhythm

percússor –óris, *m.*, a striker, headsman, executioner

percússus –a –um, *adj.*, blighted

percútio –ere –cússi –cússum, *3*, to strike down, smite, kill, wound, pierce through, transfix

perdítio –ónis, *f.*, perdition, ruin

pérditus –a –um, *adj.*, destroyed, lost

perdo –ere –didi –ditum, *3*, to lose, ruin, destroy

pérdolens –éntis, *adj.*, sorrowing, most sorrowful

perdúco –ere, *3*, to bring to, lead to, lead through, guide, conduct

perdúro –áre, *1*, to endure, last a long time

perédo –ere, *3*, to eat up, consume

péregre, *adv.*, in a strange country, abroad, to foreign parts

peregrínans –ántis, *m.*, a traveler, pilgrim

peregrinátio –ónis, *f.*, travel, pilgrimage

peregrínor –ári, *dep. 1*, to travel, go through life as a pilgrim

peregrínus –i, *m.*, a stranger, wanderer, pilgrim, traveler

perémptor –óris, *m.*, destroyer, slayer

perénnis, –e, *adj.*, everlasting, lasting, eternal, perennial, perpetual

perénnitas –átis, *f.*, eternity

péreo –ére –ii –itum, *2*, to perish, be lost, pass away, vanish, disappear

perfécte, *adv.*, perfectly

perféctio –ónis, *f.*, perfection

perféctor –óris, *m.*, perfecter

perféctus –a –um, *adj.*, perfect, complete, righteous

pérfero –férre –tuli –látum, 3, to bring, bear, carry, carry through

perfício –ere –féci –féctum, 3, to finish, make perfect, perform, accomplish, work, effect, make, do, establish, complete, consummate

pérfíde, adv., treacherously

perfídia –ae, f., faithlessness

perfidiósus –a –um, adj., faithless, treacherous

pérfidus –a –um, adj., faithless, treacherous

pérfluo –ere –flúxi –flúctum, 3, to flow, stream through

perfódio –ere –fódi –fóssum, 3, to break open, dig through

perforátus –a –um, adj., pierced

pérforo –áre, 1, to pierce

perfricátio –ónis, f., rubbing

perfríngo –ere –frégi –fráctum, 3, to finish, break through, shatter

pérfruor –frui –frúctus sum, dep. 3 (with abl.), to enjoy thoroughly

pérfuga –ae, m., a deserter, fugitive

perfúgio –ere –fúgi –fúgitum, 3, to flee, take refuge

perfúgium –i, n., refuge

perfúnctio –ónis, f., performance

perfúndo –ere –fúdi –fúsum, 3, to overwhelm, pour fourth, pour over, fill with apprehension

pergaméntum –i, n., parchment

pérgamum –i, n., a pulpit

pergo –ere, perréxi, perréctum, 3, to go forward, proceed, continue

pérgula –ae, f., a beam for tapers or candles above an altar

perhíbeo –ére –ui –itum, 2, to bear witness, report, propose, bring forward

períbolus –i, m., a circuit

períclitor –ári, dep. 1, to be in danger

periculósus –a –um, adj., dangerous

perículum –i, n., danger

perillústris –e, adj., shining

périmo –ere –émi –émptum or –émtum, 3, to destroy, slay, ruin, annihilate

perínde, adv., in like manner

periódicus –a –um, adj., at regular intervals, periodical

períodus –i, f., a period, legend, story

perípsema –atis, n., refuse, offscouring

perirátus –a –um, adj., angry, very angry

periscélis –idis, f., a garter

peristérium –ii, n., a dove-shaped vessel

peristróma –atis, n., tapestry

períte, adv., cleverly, skillfully

perítia –ae, f., skill

peritúrus –a –um, adj., perishable

perítus –a –um, adj., skilled

perizóma –atis, n., an apron

perjúro –áre, 1, to swear falsely

perlábor –lábi –lápsus sum, dep. 3, to glide along, glide through

pérlego –ere –légi –léctum, 3, to examine accurately

perliminária –órum, n. pl., lintels

perlíno –ere –lívi or –lévi –lítum, 3, to besmear, anoint

perlúcidus –a –um, adj., transparent

perlústro –áre, 1, to traverse, pass over

permáneo –ére –mánsi –mánsum, 2, to remain, continue, endure, abide

permánsio –ónis, f., a remaining, an abiding in a place

permissíve, adv., permissively

permítto –ere –mísi –míssum, 3, to permit, suffer, allow, give leave, cede

permíxtus –a –um, adj., mingled

permóveo –ére –móvi –mótum, 3, to agitate, arouse

permúltus –a –um, adj., very many, very much

permúndo –áre, 1, to cleanse

permutátio –ónis, f., exchange

permúto –áre, 1, to change completely

pernícies –éi, f., disaster, destruction

pernócto –áre, 1, to spend the night

perósus –a –um, adj., hating

perpéllo –ere –púli –púlsum, 3, to drive, urge, compel, constrain, prevail upon

perpéndo –ere –péndi –pénsum, 3, to weigh, consider, investigate, examine

perpénsus –a –um, adj., carefully examined

pérperam, adv., perversely, wrongly, falsely

pérperus –a –um, adj., perverse

perpes –etis, adj., perpetual, continuous, never-ending

perpéssio –ónis, f., suffering, endurance

perpétior, perpéti, perpássus sum, dep. 3, to endure, undergo, suffer

pérpetim, adv., continually, unceasingly

pérpetro –áre, 1, to do, perform, accomplish

perpetúitas –átis, f., eternity, perpetuity, continuance

perpétuo –áre, 1, to continue, make perpetual

perpétuo, adv., permanently, perpetually, forever

perpétuus –a –um, *adj.,* everlasting, perpetual, continuous, unfailing

perplúres –ium, *adj.,* very many

perpúlcher –chra –chrum, *adj.,* very beautiful

perquíro –ere –sívi –sítum, *3,* to seek, make inquiry

perrúmpo –ere –rúpi –rúptum, *3,* to break through, subdue, overpower

perscríbo –ere –scrípsi –scríptum, *3,* to write down, relate in writing, notify

perscrutátio –ónis, *f.,* scrutiny

persecútio –ónis, *f.,* persecution

persecútor –óris, *m.,* a persecutor

persecútus –a –um, *adj.,* having persecuted

pérsequor –qui –secútus sum, *3,* to pursue, follow perseveringly, persecute, persecute for religious belief

perseverábilis –e, *adj.,* enduring, persevering

perseverántia –ae, *f.,* perseverance

persévero –áre, *1,* to persevere, continue, persist, remain constant, continue in a state of grace

persísto –ere, *3,* to resist

persitátio –ónis, *f.,* a gift, payment

persólvo –ere –sólvi –solútum, *3,* to discharge a duty, perform, explain, recite, offer

persóna –ae, *f.,* a person

personáliter, *adv.,* in person, personally

personátus –a –um, *adj.,* masked, disguised

pérsono –áre –sónui –sónitum, *1,* to shout, proclaim, sound, resound, cause to resound

perspício –ere –spéxi –spéctum, *3,* to have regard to, look into

perspicúitas –átis, *f.,* clearness

perspícuus –a –um, *adj.,* evident, visible

persuádeo –ére –suási –suásum, *2,* to persuade

persuasíbilis –e, *adj.,* convincing, persuasive, eloquent

persuásio –ónis, *f.,* doctrine

perstríngo –ere –strínxi –stríctum, *3,* to lay hold upon

pertaésus –a –um, *adj.,* thoroughly weary

perténto –áre, *1,* to put to the test

perterrefáctus –a –um, *adj.,* exceedingly terrified

pertérreo –ére, *2,* to terrify

pertérritus –a –um, *adj.,* terrified

pertimésco –ere –tímui, *3,* to fear greatly

pertinácia –ae, *f.,* obstinacy

pertináciter, *adv.,* obstinately

pértinax –ácis, *adj.,* obstinate

pertíneo –ére –tínui, *2,* to reach to, extend to, pertain to

pertíngo –ere, *3,* to extend to, come to

pertrácto –áre, *1,* to celebrate, busy oneself with

pertránseo –íre –ívi *or* –ii –itum, *4,* to pierce, pass through, traverse, pass by, go away

perturbátio –ónis, *f.,* disturbance, confusion, perturbation, disorder, trouble

pertúrbo –áre, *1,* to disturb, perturb

pertúsus –a –um, *adj.,* with holes

perúngo –ere –únxi –únctum, *3,* to anoint

perúrgeo –ére –úrsi, *2,* to urge forward

perúro –ere –óssi –óstum, *3,* to parch, burn up, burn through

perútilis –e, *adj.,* very useful

pervádo –ere –vási –vásum, *3,* to go through, come through

pérvago –áre, *1,* to wander through

pérvagor –ári, *dep. 1,* to wander, rove about

pervénio –íre –véni, –véntum, *4,* to come to, attain to, arrive, come

pervéntio –ónis, *f.,* arrival, coming

pervéntor –óris, *m.,* one who arrives

pervérse, *adv.,* perversely

pervérsitas –átis, *f.,* perverse inclination

pervérsus –a –um, *adj.,* wrong, perverse

pervérto –ere –vérti –vérsum, *3,* to turn around, turn about

pervestútus –a –um, *adj.,* very old

pervicácia –ae, *f.,* stubbornness

pervígil –ilis, *adj.,* ever watchful, very watchful

pervigílium –ii, *n.,* the watch, vigil of a feast

pervígilo –áre, *1,* to watch

pervínco –ere –víci –víctum, *3,* to overcome

pérvius –a –um, *adj.,* passable, accessible, having a road through

pervúlgo –áre, *1,* to make publicly known

pes, pedis, *m.,* a foot

péssimo –áre, *1,* to oppress, inflict harm on

péssimus –a –um, *adj.,* worst, wicked, evil, very evil, very grevious

péssulus –i, *m.,* a bolt for a door

péstifer –a –um, *adj.,* pestilential

péstilens –éntis, *adj.,* pestilential

pestiléntia –ae, *f.,* pestilence, plague

pestis –is, *f.,* plague
petála –ae, *f.,* the antipendium
petens –éntis, *m.,* a petitioner
petítio –ónis, *f.,* a petition, request, desire, prayer
peto –ere –ívi *or* –ii –ítum, *3,* to beseech, entreat, ask, request, seek, beg for
petra –ae, *f.,* a rock, a symbol of something solid
Petra Ecclésiae, St. Peter
Petrus –i, *m.,* Peter
pétulans –ántis, *adj.,* wanton, lustful, freakish, capricious
petulánter, *adv.,* boldly, wantonly
phalánga –ae, *f.,* a band
phálero –áre, *1,* to adorn
phantásia –ae, *f.,* a delusion, fancy, an illusion
phantásma –atis, *n.,* a phantom, apparition, appearance, vision, an illusion or delusion
phantásticus –a –um, *adj.,* imaginary, fantastic
pharétra –ae, *f.,* a quiver
Pharisaéus –i, *m.,* a Pharisee. The Pharisees were the largest of the Jewish sects, noted for their conceit and long prayers.
pharisáicus –a –um, *adj.,* pertaining to the Pharisees, hypocritical
phármacum –i, *n.,* a remedy, a medicine
pharocántharus –i, *m.,* a large chandelier
pharus –i, *f.,* a candlestick, large chandelier
phase –es, *f.,* rite, phase
Phase, *indecl.,* the Passover
phíala –ae, *f.,* a phial, small flask
Philíppus –i, *m.,* Philip
philosophía –ae, *f.,* philosophy
philosóphicus –a –um, *adj.,* philosophical
philósophus –i, *m.,* a philosopher
philósophor –ári, *dep. 1,* to philosophize
phrenésis –is, *f.,* madness, delirium
phrenéticus –a –um, *adj.,* frantic
phthísicus –a –um, *adj.,* consumptive
phylactérium –ii, *n.,* phylactery — the frontlet worn by devout Jews
physharmónium –ii, *n.,* a reed organ, parlor organ
phýsicus –a –um, *adj.,* physical
piaculáris –e, *adj.,* cleansing, expiatory
piáculum –i, *n.,* sin, crime, evil deed
pictor –óris, *m.,* a painter
pictúra –ae, *f.,* a picture
pie, *adv.,* piously, mercifully

píetas –átis, *f.,* piety, love of devotion, goodness, kindness, godliness, pity, mercy, compassion, love and duty toward God
piger –gra –grum, *adj.,* lazy, slothful, disinclined, unwilling
pignus –oris *or* –eris, *n.,* a pledge
pigrédo –ínis, *f.,* laziness, slothfulness
pígritor –ári, *dep. 1,* to be slow
pígro –áre, *1,* to be slothful
pila –ae, *f.,* mortar
Pilátus –i, *m.,* Pilate
pileátus –a –um, *adj.,* wearing a felt cap
piléolus –i, *m.,* a small skullcap
pilósus –a –um, *adj.,* hairy
pilus –i, *m.,* hair, a hair
pincéra –ae, *m.,* a cupbearer, butler
pingo –ere, pinxi, pictum, *3,* to paint, adorn, embellish
pinguédo –ínis, *f.,* richness, fatness
pinguésco –ere, *3,* to grow fat, become fertile
pínguia –órum, *n. pl.,* fat meats
pinguis –e, *adj.,* fat, strong, mighty
pinna –ae, *f.,* a pinnacle, edge, point, feather, wing
pinnáculum –i, *n.,* a pinnacle
pípio –áre, *1,* to chirp
pirum –i, *n.,* a pair
pirus –i, *f.,* a pear tree
piscátor –óris, *m.,* a fisherman, angler
piscículus –i, *m.,* a little fish
piscína –ae, *f.,* a pool, pond, the sacrarium, a baptismal font
piscis –is, *m.,* fish
piscor –ári, *dep. 1,* to fish
písticus –a –um, *adj.,* true, genuine, pure, of the best quality
pistor –óris, *m.,* a baker
pius –a –um, *adj.,* holy, pious, just, merciful, loving, devoted, virtuous
pix, picis, *f.,* pitch
placábilis –e, *adj.,* appeased
placátio –ónis, *f.,* appeasing, soothing, ransom, propitiation
placénta –ae, *f.,* a cake
pláceo –ére –ui –itum, *2,* to please, be well pleasing to
placet, *impers.,* it is pleasing, it pleases
plácide, *adv.,* peacefully
plácidus –a –um, *adj.,* favorable, quiet, still, placid
plácitum –i, *n.,* pleasure, resolution, purpose, decision, pledge, agreement
plácitus –a –um, *adj.,* acceptable

placo –áre, *1,* to pacify, appease, placate, make atonement

plaga –ae, *f.,* a plague, scourge, blow, affliction, chastisement

plagátus –a –um, *adj.,* sore, wounded

plagiárius –ii, *m.,* a kidnaper, robber of souls

plago –áre, *1,* to wound

plágula –ae, *f.,* an embroidered ornament on vestments, a curtain

planatárium –ii, *n.,* a branch, shoot

planctum –i, *n.,* lamentation

planctus –us, *m.,* mourning, lamentation

plane, *adv.,* plainly, surely, simply

planéta –ae, *f.,* a chasuble

plango –ere, planxi, planctum, *3,* to lament, bewail

planíties –éi, *f.,* plain

plano –áre, *1,* to make plain

planta –ae, *f.,* the sole of the foot, twig, shoot

plantárium –ii, *n.,* a nursery of trees, ground, source

plantátio –ónis, *f.,* a planting, setting a plant

plantátio rosae, a rose plant

planto –áre, *1,* to plant, create, set in place

planum –i, *n.,* plain

planus –a –um, *adj.,* plain, level, flat

plasma –atis, *n.,* creation, anything formed

plasmátor –óris, *m.,* a maker, shaper, one that makes anything

plasmo –áre, *1,* to shape, mold, fashion, form, make

plastes –ae *or* –is, *m.,* maker, shaper

platánus –i, *f.,* plane tree

platéa –ae, *f.,* a street, highway

plaudo –ere, plausi, plausum, *3,* to clap, strike, applaud

plaustrum –i, *n.,* a cart, wagon

plausus –us, *m.,* applause

plebéius –a –um, *adj.,* plebian, pertaining to the people

plebs –is, *f.,* people, the chosen people; *plural,* congregations

plecta –ae, *f.,* a border, ledge

plecto –ere, plexi *or* pléxui, plexum. *3,* to plait, braid, weave

plenárie, *adv.,* plentifully

Plenárium –ii, *n.,* a book containing the Epistles, Gospels, etc., read at Mass

plenárius –a –um, *adj.,* plenary, full, plentiful

plenilúnium –ii, *n.,* a full moon

pléniter, *adv.,* completely, fully

plenitúdo –inis, *f.,* plenitude, fullness

plénius, *adv.,* more fully

plenus –a –um, *adj.,* full, filled, plentiful, complete, entire

pleríque, *adj.,* very many

plicátus –a –um, *adj.,* folded

plico –áre, *1,* to fold

plinthus –i, *m.* or *f.,* a plinth

plorátus –us, *m.,* lamentation, weeping, wailing

ploro –áre, *1,* to lament, weep, bewail, mourn

plumárius –ii, *m.,* an embroiderer

plumbáta –ae, *f.,* a leaden ball

plumbátum –i, *n.,* a whip weighted with lead

plumbum –i, *n.,* lead

plumésco –ere, *3,* to grow feathers (Job 39:26)

pluráliter, *adv.,* in the plural

plúreus –i, *m.,* a desk

plúries, *adv.,* often, frequently

plúrimus –a –um, *adj.,* very great, very many; *quam plúrimi,* as many as possible

plus, pluris, *adj.,* more

plúvia –ae, *f.,* rain

pluviále –is, *n.,* a cope

pluvialísta –ae, *m.,* a pluvialist

plúvius –a –um, *adj.,* rainy

pneuma –tis, *n.,* spirit, breath

poculéntum –i, *n.,* a drink

póculum –i, *n.,* a goblet, a drinking cup

podátus –i, *m.,* two musical notes, the second being higher than the first

pódium –ii, *n.,* a platform, stage

poena –ae, *f.,* pain, fine, punishment, expiation

poenális –e, *adj.,* penal, punishing, culpable, sinful, worthy of punishment, laborious

poenáliter, *adv.,* in a manner deserving of punishment

poénitens –éntis, *adj.,* penitent

poeniténtia –ae, *f.,* repentance, penance, penitence

poenitentiális –e, *adj.,* pertaining to penance

Poenitentiária –ae, *f.,* an ecclesiastical tribunal in Rome

poenitentiárius –ii, *m.,* a priest authorized to absolve from reserved sins

poeníteo –ére –ui, *2,* to punish, repent, regret, be sorry, displease poénitet, *impers.*, it repents one, one relents, one is displeased

poésis –is *or* –eos, *f.*, poetry

poéta –ae, *m.*, a poet

polénta –ae, *f.*, barley, a dish made of barley

pólio –íre, *4*, to polish, make smooth

políticus –a –um, *adj.*, political

pólitus –a –um, *adj.*, polished, polite

pólleo –ére, *2*, to be strong, able, powerful, mighty

pollíceor, pollicéri, pollícitus sum, *dep. 2*, to promise, offer, proffer

pollicitátio –ónis, *f.*, promise, offer

pollínctor –óris, *m.*, one who prepares corpses for burial

pólluo –ere –ui –útum, *3*, to defile, profane, pollute, befoul, to render unclean ceremonially

pollútio –ónis, *f.*, defilement

polónia –ae, *f.*, defilement

polus –i, *m.*, the sky, heaven, a pole of the earth

polycandélium –ii, *n.*, a frame for holding candles

polyglóttus –a –um, *adj.*, polyglot

polymitátius –ii, *m.*, an embroiderer, weaver

polymítus –a –um, *adj.*, of diverse colors, of many colors

polytheísmus, *m.*, the worship of several gods, polytheism

polyphónicus –a –um, *adj.*, polyphonic

polýphonus –a –um, *adj.*, polyphone

pomárium –ii, *n.*, an orchard

poméllum –i, *n.*, a knob, the node of a chalice

pómifer –a –um, *adj.*, fruit-bearing

pompa –ae, *f.*, pomp, a procession, parade

pompátice, *adv.*, with pomp

pomum –i, *n.*, an apple

pomus –i, *f.*, a fruit tree

ponderátor –óris, *m.*, a weigher

póndero –áre, *1*, to weigh

pondus –eris, *n.*, a load, weight, burden

pone, *adv.*, behind, at the back of

ponens, ponéntis, *m.*, one who submits a case to a Roman or diocesan tribunal

pono –ere, pósui, pósitum, *3*, to place, put, set aside, lay down, lay aside, appoint, take account

pons, pontis, *m.*, a bridge

póntifex –icis, *m.*, pontiff, high priest, bishop

pontificále, *n.*, pontifical, the book of rites performed by a bishop

pontificális –e, *adj.*, pertaining to a bishop, pontifical

pontificátus –us, *m.*, the reign of a pontiff, pontificate

pontifícium –ii, *n.*, pontifical power, papacy

pontíficus –a –um, *adj.*, papal, pontifical

pontus –i, *m.*, the deep, the sea

popína –ae, *f.*, food, fare

populáres –ium, *m. pl.*, the people

populáris –e, *adj.*, friendly, all-embracing

pópulus –i, *m.*, people, the populace, the chosen people

porcínus –a –um, *adj.*, pertaining to swine

porcus –i, *m.*, a pig, swine

porósus –a –um, *adj.*, porous

porphýrio –ónis, *m.*, a water fowl

porréctus –a –um, *adj.*, stretched out

pórrigo –ere –réxi –réctum, *3*, to stretch forth, stretch out, extend, hold out, reach out, spread out before

porta –ae, *f.*, a door

portábilis –e, *adj.*, portable

porténdo –ere –téndi –téntum, *3*, to portent

porténtum –i, *n.*, wonder, portent

portícula –ae, *f.*, a small door

pórticus –i, *m.*, a porch, vestibule

pórtio –ónis, *f.*, a portion, lot

portionárius –ii, *m.*, a prebendary

pórtitor –óris, *m.*, a carrier, bearer

portiúncula –ae, *f.*, a portion, a small piece

Portiúncula –ae, *f.*, the Portiuncula Indulgence, originally granted for visiting the church of Our Lady of Angels, near Assisi

porto –áre, *1*, to carry, bear, bring, uphold, sustain

portus –us, *m.*, a harbor, haven, port

posco –ere, popósci, *3*, to ask, demand, ask earnestly

posítio –ónis, *f.*, a position, the act of placing

posítor –óris, *m.*, a founder

posséssio –ónis, *f.*, possession, property, substance

posséssor –óris, *m.*, a possessor

possíbilis –e, *adj.*, possible

possibílitas –átis, *f.*, possibility, power

possídeo –ére –sédi –séssum, *2*, to possess, acquire, occupy, get possession of

possum, posse, pótui, to be able, have power

postcommúnio –ónis, *f.,* the Postcommunion at Mass

póstea, *adv.,* afterward, hereafter

posteáquam, *adv.,* after

postergále –is, *n.,* the back of a seat

pósteri –órum, *m. pl.,* posterity, descendants

postérior –ius, *adj.,* later, posterior, behind

pósterus –a –um, *adj.,* following, subsequent, coming after, next

posthábeo –ére, *2,* to esteem less

postícum –i, *n.,* a back door

postílla –ae, *f.,* a popular commentary on scriptural readings at Mass

postis –is, *m.,* a doorpost, a side post

postlimínium –ii, *n.,* a return home

póstmodum, *adv.,* after, afterward

postpóno –ere –pósui –pósitum, *3,* to put after

postquam, *adv.,* after, as soon as, when

postrémo *adv.,* lastly, finally

postrémus, *adj.,* latest, last

postrídie, *adv.,* the day after

póstulans –ántis, *m.* and *f.,* one who petitions

postulátio –ónis, *f.,* entreaty, prayer, hope

postulátor –óris, *m.,* one who demands or requests

póstulo –áre, *1,* to ask, request, entreat, demand

potábilis –e, *adj.,* fit to drink

potens –éntis, *adj.,* powerful, mighty, strong

potentátus –us, *m.,* might, power, strength

poténter, *adv.,* powerfully, efficaciously

poténtia –ae, *f.,* power, strength, might, rule, potency, ability

potentiáliter, *adv.,* in might, in power

potéstas –átis, *f.,* power, authority, strength, might, jurisdiction

pótio –ónis, *f.,* a drinking, a potion

pótior –ius, *adj.,* better, preferable, greater

pótior –íri, potítus sum, *dep. 4,* to obtain, get possession of, become partaker of, be master of

potíssimum, *adv.,* chiefly, especially, most preferable

pótius, *adv.,* rather, more abundantly

poto –áre, *1,* to drink, make a drink, give a drink

potus –us, *m.,* a drink

práctica –ae, *f.,* practice

prácticus –a –um, *adj.,* practical

praeámbulus –a –um, *adj.,* going before

praebénda –ae, *f.,* a benefice, prebend

praebendárius –ii, *m.,* a beneficiary, prebendary

praebendátus –i, *m.,* a choral prebendary

práebeo –ére –bui –bitum, *2,* to grant, furnish, offer, hold out, exhibit

praecáveo –ére –cávi –caútum, *2,* to be careful, be on guard, take precaution

praecedéntia –ae, *f.,* precedence

praecédo –ere –céssi –céssum, *3,* to precede, go before, prepare

praecéllo –ere, *3,* to excel, surpass, exceed

praecélsus –a –um, *adj.,* very high, very lofty

praecéntor –óris, *m.,* a capitular dignity, leader in chant

praeceps –ípitis, *n.,* a steep place, precipice

praecéptor –óris, *m.,* a master, instructor, teacher

praecéptrix –icis, *f.,* a female teacher

praecéptum –i, *n.,* a command, precept, law, ordinance

praecéssor –óris, *m.,* a leader, superior

praecído –ere –cídi –císum, *3,* to cut, cut off, cut down, cut in front, cut to pieces

praecinctórium –ii, *n.,* an ornamental maniple worn by the Pope

praecíngo –ere –cínxi –cínctum, *3,* to gird, surround with a girdle

práecino –ere –cécini *or* –cínui –céntum, *3,* to sing before, play before

praecípio –ere –cépi –céptum, *3,* to command, instruct, teach, advise, warn, charge, prescribe, preach, anticipate, know beforehand

praecipitátio –ónis, *f.,* ruin, destruction

praecipítium –ii, *n.,* precipice

praecípito –áre, *1,* to cast headlong

praecípue, *adv.,* especially, principally

praecípuus –a –um, *adj.,* special

praecísio –ónis, *f.,* destruction, cutting down, cutting off, cutting away

praecisíve, *adv.,* precisely

praeclára –órum, *n. pl.,* valuables

praecláre, *adv.,* excellently

praecláritas –átis, *f.,* distinction, renown

praeclárus –a –um, *adj.,* excellent, glorious, splendid, brilliant, very bright, illustrious

praeclúdo –ere –clúsi –clúsum, *3,* to close, shut up, close in front

praeco –ónis, *m.*, a herald, crier, publisher, one who praises

praecógnitus –a –um, *adj.*, known beforehand

praecognósco –ere –nóvi –nitum, *3,* to learn beforehand

praécolo –ere –cólui –cúltum, *3,* to cultivate before, revere, honor highly

praeconátio –ónis, *f.*, the singing of the Gospel, a proclamation

praeconisátio –ónis, *f.*, the ratification of a bishop's appointment

praecónium –ii, *n.*, praise, commendation, making known, publishing

praeconsecrátus –a –um, *adj.*, previously consecrated

praecóquus –a –um, *adj.*, premature

praecórdia –órum, *n. pl.*, hearts, inmost heart

praecox –ócis, *adj.*, premature

praecúrro –ere –cúrri *or* –cucúrri –cúrsum, *3,* to run before, take precedence over

praecúrsio –ónis, *f.*, a going before

praecúrsor –óris, *m.*, a precursor, one who goes or runs before

praecútio –ere –cússi –cússum, *3,* to brandish, shake before

praeda –ae, *f.*, booty, plunder, prey

praedátio –ónis, *f.*, robbery, taking the spoils, plundering

praedátor –óris, *m.*, a robber, plunderer, a greedy person, a hunter

praedecéssor –óris, *m.*, predecessor

praedélla –ae, *f.*, the platform of an altar

praedestinátio –ónis, *f.*, predestination, a determining beforehand

praedestinátus –a –um, *adj.*, predestined

praedéstino –áre, *1,* to ordain, appoint, ordain beforehand

praedicábilis –e, *adj.*, praiseworthy

praedicaméntum –i, *n.*, that which is predicted

praédicans –ántis, *m.*, a preacher

praedicátio –ónis, *f.*, preaching, making known publicly, praise, commendation

praedicátor –óris, *m.*, preacher

praédico –ere, *3,* to foretell, predict, prophesy

praédico –áre, *1,* to preach

praedíctio –ónis, *f.*, predicting, prophesying

praedíctus –a –um, *adj.*, aforesaid

praéditus –a –um, *adj.*, endowed, provided with, furnished

praédium –ii, *n.*, estate, farm, plot of land

praedo –ónis, *m.*, a robber, plunderer

praedóceo –ére –dócui –dóctum, *2,* to teach beforehand, instruct before

praedor –ári, *dep. 1,* to rob, plunder, despoil

praedúlcis –e, *adj.*, very sweet

praeéligo –ere –légi –léctum, *3,* to forechoose

praeeminéntia –ae, *f.*, distinction, superior eminence

praeémino –ere, *3,* to excel, be remarkable

praéeo –íre –ívi *or* –ii –ítum, *4,* to go before, precede

praeésse –fui, to rule

praefátio –ónis, *f.*, preface, formula, a form of words

praefátus –a –um, *adj.*, aforesaid, abovementioned

praeféctus –i, *m.*, a prefect, overseer, governor, head, president

praéfero –érre –tuli –látum, *3,* to bear, carry in front, manifest, display, show, give preference to, carry by

praéferox –ócis, *adj.*, very cruel

praefício –ere –féci –féctum, *3,* to set over, place in command

praefídens –éntis, *adj.*, overconfident, very confident

praefidénter, *adv.*, too confidently

praefigúro –áre, *1,* to prefigure

praefínio –íre, *4,* to appoint

praefinítio –ónis, *f.*, purpose

praefóco –áre, *1,* to choke, strangle, drown, suffocate

praefúlgeo –ére –fúlsi, *2,* to shine forth

praegnans –ántis, *adj.*, pregnant, be with child

praegrándis –e, *adj.*, very great, intense, exceeding

praégravo –áre, *1,* to oppress, weigh down, weigh upon, press heavily upon

praegrédior –i –gréssus sum, *dep. 3,* to go before, precede

praegréssio –ónis, *f.*, precedence, a going before

praegustátor –óris, *m.*, a taster, foretaster

praegústo –áre, *1,* to taste beforehand

praeintonátio –ónis, *f.*, intoning beforehand, the intoning of an antiphon

praejudícium –ii, *n.*, a previous judgment, preliminary examination

praejúdico –áre, *1,* to decide beforehand

praelátio –ónis, f., dignity, preferment, guidance, bearing forward

praelatítius –a –um, adj., pertaining to a prelate

praelatúra –ae, f., prelateship, governing position

praelátus –i, m., a prelate, superior

praélego –ere –légi –léctum, 3, to sail past, coast above

praeliátor –óris, m., a warrior

praelibátio –ónis, f., oblation

praéligo –ere –légi –léctum, 3, to bind beforehand, bind in front

praélio –áre, 1, to fight

praélium –ii, n., battle, war

praéloquor –qui –locútus sum, dep. 3, to announce beforehand

praelúceo –ére –lúxi, 2, to surpass, outshine, shine before

praelúdium –ii, n., a prelude, an eve, a vigil

praematúrus –a –um, adj., eager, too early, premature

praemeditátio –ónis, f., considering beforehand, premeditation

praemédito –áre, 1, to meditate before

praeméditor –ári, dep. 1, to meditate before

praemítto –ere –mísi –míssum, 3, to send before

praémium –ii, n., reward, prize, recompense

praemóneo –ére, 2, to advise beforehand

praemónstro –áre, 1, to indicate, point out

praenóbilis –e, adj., distinguished

praenósco –ere –nóvi –nótum, 3, to know beforehand

praenóto –áre, 1, to mark, indicate

praenuntiátor –óris, m., a foreteller

praenúntio –áre, 1, to show before, announce, report, tell beforehand

praenúntius –ii, m., a forerunner

praeóccupo –áre, 1, to take by surprise, overtake, come before

praeordinátus –a –um, adj., preordained

praeparátio –ónis, f., preparation, a getting or making ready

práeparo –áre, 1, to prepare, make ready, provide

praepédio –íre, 4, to shackle, fetter, obstruct, hinder, impede

praepedítio –ónis, f., a hindrance, impediment

praepéndeo –ére –pepéndi, 2, to hang before, hang in front

praepínguis –e, adj., very rich

praepóno –ere –pósui –pósitum, 3, to prefer

praepositúra –ae, f., archdeaconry, prelacy, priory, provostship

praepósitus –i, m., dean, prior, provost, head, overseer, governor, an ecclesiastical superior

praepósterus –a –um, adj., absurd, inverted

praépotens –éntis, adj., mighty

praepróperus –a –um, adj., overhasty

praerípio –ere –rípui –réptum, 3, to carry off

praerogatíva –ae, f., prerogative, privilege, special right

praeságio –íre, 4, to presage, forebode, foretell

praeságus –a –um, adj., predicting

praesanctificátus –a –um, adj., previously sanctified

praesciéntia –ae, f., foreknowledge

praescíndo –ere –scídi –scissum, 3, to prescind

praéscio –íre –scívi –scítum, 4, to foresee, foreknow

praescísco –ere –scívi, 3, to learn, find out beforehand

praéscius –a –um, adj., foreboding

praescríptum –i, n., a precept, order

praescríptus –a –um, adj., preached, commanded

praeséfero –férre –túli –látum, 3, to display

praesens –éntis, adj., present, present time

praesentátio –ónis, f., offering, presentation

Praesentátio Dómini, Candlemas day

praeséntia –ae, f., presence

praeséntio –íre –sénsi –sénsum, 4, to feel beforehand, have a presentiment

praesénto –áre, 1, to present

praesépe –is, n., a manger

praesépium –ii, n., a crib, stall, manger

praesértim, adv., especially, chiefly

praesérvo –áre, 1, to preserve

praeses –idis, m., president, chairman

praesidátus –us, m., governorship

praesídeo –ére –sédi –séssum, 3, to preside over, guard, govern, direct, give audience to

praesídium –ii, n., protection, defense, guard, aid

praesignífico –áre, 1, to signify, announce beforehand

praesígnis –e, *adj.*, distinguished
praesígno –áre, *1*, to represent, fore-shadow, prefigure
praésono –áre –sónui, *1*, to resound, sound forth
praestábilis –e, *adj.*, powerful, remarkable, pre-eminent
praestans –ántis, *adj.*, gracious, eminent, distinguished, excellent
praestántia –ae, *f.*, excellence, superiority
praestigiátor –óris, *m.*, a deceiver
praestítuo –ere –stítui –stitútum, *3*, to prescribe, appoint beforehand
praesto, *adv.*, here, at hand
praesto –áre –stiti –stitum, *1*, to give, furnish, grant, provide, guarantee, excel, stand before, accomplish, surpass, bestow, serve, do good
praestólor –ári, *dep. 1*, to expect, wait for, perform
praestríngo –ere –strínxi –stríctum, *3*, to bind up
praéstruo –ere –strúxi –strúctum, *3*, to build in front, make ready for anything
praesul –is, *c.*, a patron; *m.*, bishop, prelate
praesúlto –áre, *1*, to leap, spring before
praesum –ésse –fui, *3*, to rule, govern, be placed over, preside over
praesúmo –ere –súmpsi –súmptum, *3*, to take before, presume, take for granted
praesúmptio –ónis, *f.*, boldness, presumption, arrogance
praesúmptus –a –um, *adj.*, taken for granted
praesuppóno –ere –pósui –pósitum, *3*, to presuppose
praeténdo –ere –téndi –téntum, *3*, to extend, stretch out before, present to, place before, pretend
praeténto –áre, *1*, to feel, try beforehand, try, test
praeter, *adv.*, besides, except, but, save, more than
praetérea, *adv.*, besides, and, further, henceforth, hereafter
praetéreo –íre –ii –itum, *4*, to pass by, pass away, come to an end, cease to be
praetergrédior –i –gréssus sum, *dep. 3*, to go beyond, transgress, walk past, pass by
praetérita –órum, *n.*, the past, bygone things
praeterítio –ónis, *f.*, a passing, passing away
praetoríolum –i, *n.*, a cabin

praetórium –ii, *n.*, palace, governor's hall, praetorium, courtroom, judgment hall, official residence of the governor (Mk. 15:16)
praetórius –a –um, *adj.*, pretorian
praeváleo –ére –ui, *2*, to master, prevail against, to be very strong or powerful
praeválidus –a –um, *adj.*, very strong, very powerful, too productive
praevaricátio –ónis, *f.*, prevarication, transgression, violation of duty
praevaricátor –óris, *m.*, transgressor, sinner, especially an apostate
praevárico –áre, *1*, to commit sin
praeváricor –ári, *dep. 1*, to transgress, break the law, rebel, be guilty of collusion
praevéniens –éntis, *adj.*, preceding
praevénio –íre –véni –véntum, *4*, to prevent, anticipate, come before, come ahead, precede, look forward to
praevérto –ere –vérti –vérsum, *3*, to go before, anticipate, surpass
praevídeo –ére –vídi –vísum, *2*, to foresee, know beforehand
praévius –a –um, *adj.*, preceding
praévius –i, *m.*, a forerunner
prándeo –ére, prandi, pransum, *2*, to eat
prándium –ii, *n.*, dinner, breakfast, luncheon, a midday meal
pratum –i, *n.*, a meadow
právitas –átis, *f.*, wickedness, guilt, evil
pravus –a –um, *adj.*, evil, perverse, crooked, deformed
praxis –is, *m.*, exercise, practice
prebénda –ae, *f.*, a benefice
precátio –ónis, *f.*, prayer, entreating
precátor –óris, *m.*, one who prays
precátus –us, *m.*, a prayer
precor –ári, *dep. 1*, to pray, beseech, entreat, beg, invoke
predélla –ae, *f.*, the platform immediately in front of the altar
predicátor –óris, *m.*, preacher
prehéndo –ere –di –sum, *3*, to seize, lay hold of, catch
prehénso –áre, *1*, to seize, lay hold of
premo –ere, pressi, pressum, *3*, to oppose, press, press upon
prendo –ere, *see* prehéndo
prenso –áre, *1*, to grasp mentally
présbyter –eri, *m.*, a priest
presbyterális –e, *adj.*, priestly
presbyterátus –us, *m.*, priesthood
presbytérium –ii, *n.*, presbytery
presentátio –ónis, *f.*, presentation

presso –áre, *1*, to distress, press
pressúra –ae, *f.*, distress, oppression, anguish, affliction, persecution
pretiósus –a –um, *adj.*, precious, of great price
prétium –ii, *n.*, money, price, ransom money, value, worth
prex, precis, *f.*, prayer, request
pridem, *adv.*, long ago, long since
prídie, *adv.*, yesterday, on the day before
prima –ae, *m.*, primate
Prima –ae, *f.*, the hour of Prime
primaévus –a –um, *adj.*, youthful
primário, *adv.*, primarily
primárius –a –um, *adj.*, first, principal
primas –átis, *m.*, a primate, chief, one of the first
primatiális –e, *adj.*, primatial, pertaining to a primate
primátus –us, *m.*, primacy
primicérius –ii, *n.*, a dean of an official class
primissárius –i, *m.*, a prebendary obliged to say an early Mass
primítiae –árum, *f. pl.*, first, first-born
primitívus –a –um, *adj.*, first-born, first
prímitus, *adv.*, first, for the first time
primo, *adv.*, first, first of all, in the first place
primo die, the day on which God began the creation of the world
primogénitum –i, *n.*, first birthright
primogenitúra –ae, *f.*, primogeniture
primogénitus –a –um, *adj.*, first-born
primórdium –ii, *n.*, the origin, the first beginning
primum, *adv.*, at first, first, in the first place
primus –i, *m.*, chief man
primus –a –um, *adj.*, first, foremost
princeps –ipis, *m.*, chief, ruler, prince, leader
principális –e, *adj.*, first, original, free, perfect
principálitas –átis, *f.*, principality
principáliter, *adv.*, from the beginning, in the first place
principátus –us, *m.*, public office, dominion
principíssa –ae, *f.*, princess
princípium –ii, *n.*, beginning, source, foundation, principality, sovereignty
príncipor –ári, *dep. 1*, to rule
prior –ius, *adj.*, first, former, previous
priorátus –us, *m.*, a priory, priorship
prioríssa –ae, *f.*, a prioress

priscus –a –um, *adj.*, original, ancient, antique, venerable
prístinus –a –um, *adj.*, former, previous, earlier, original, pristine
prius, *adv.*, before, previously
priúsquam, *adv.*, before, before that
privátim, *adv.*, privately
privátio –ónis, *f.*, a freeing from
privatívus –a –um, *adj.*, lacking, deprived of
privátus –a –um, *adj.*, private
privilegiárius –a –um, *adj.*, enjoying a privilege
privilégium –i, *n.*, privilege, private law, a law relating to one person only, a right specially granted
privo –áre, *1*, to withhold, deprive, free from
probábilis –e, *adj.*, probable, credible, not impossible
probabílius, *adv.*, more probably
probáticus –a –um, *adj.*, pertaining to sheep
probátio –ónis, *f.*, test, trial, probation
probátor –óris, *m.*, an examiner
probe, *adv.*, rightly, fitly, properly, excellently
probo –áre, *1*, to try, test, prove, examine, learn, find out, know
probrum –i, *n.*, disgrace, shame, reproach, a shameful act
probrus –a –um, *adj.*, shameful
probus –a –um, *adj.*, happy, good, fine, excellent
procédo –ere –céssi –céssum, *3*, to come forth, go forth, proceed from
procélla –ae, *f.*, storm, tempest, gale
procer –eris, *m.*, a prince, noble
procére, *adv.*, outstretched
procéssio –ónis, *f.*, procession, source, origin
processionále –is, *n.*, a book of ritual for processions
processionális –e, *adj.*, processional
processionáliter, *adv.*, in procession
procéssus –us, *m.*, a process
prócido –ere –cídi, *3*, to fall down, fall forward, fall flat, prostrate
procínctus –us, *m.*, preparation for departure
proclámo –áre, *1*, to proclaim
procónsul –ulis, *m.*, proconsul
proconsuláris –e, *adj.*, proconsular
prócreo –áre, *1*, to beget
procul, *adv.*, afar off, far, far away, at a distance from

procúlco –áre, *1*, to tread, trample upon

proculdúbio, *adv.*, without doubt

procúmbo –ere –cúbui –cúbitum, *3*, to lean or bend forward, sink down, fall

procurátio –ónis, *f.*, administration, management, a taking care of, procuring, obtaining

procurátor –óris, *m.*, a steward, agent, manager

procúro –áre, *1*, to administer, govern, take care of, tend, look after, bring back, cause to be done

procúrro –ere –cúrri *or* –cucúrri –cúrsum, *3*, to rush forward, run forward

procus –i, *m.*, a suitor, wooer

pródeo –íre, *4*, to come forth, come out, go forth

prodésse, prófui, *3*, to avail, benefit

prodigiósus –a –um, *adj.*, miraculous, marvelous

prodígium –ii, *n.*, wonder, prodigy, marvel, miracle

pródigo –ere –égi –áctum, *3*, to drive forth

pródigus –a –um, *adj.*, prodigal, profuse, extravagant

prodítio –ónis, *f.*, a betraying, betrayal, treason, treachery

próditor –óris, *m.*, betrayer, traitor

prodo –ere –didi –ditum, *3*, to betray, bring forth, become profitable

prodóceo –ére –ui –tum, *2*, to teach, inculcate

prodúco –ere –dúxi –dúctum, *3*, to produce, make grow, shoot forth, bring, bring forth

productílis –e, *adj.*, drawn out, beaten

proeliáris –e, *adj.*, relating to battle

proélium –ii, *n.*, battle, war

profanátio –ónis, *f.*, profanation or defilement of something sacred

profáno –áre, *1*, to defile, profane, desecrate

profánus –a –um, *adj.*, profane

profáror –i, *dep. 1*, to speak in behalf of

proféctio –ónis, *f.*, journey, departure

profécto, *adv.*, really, certainly, truly, without doubt, in fact, in truth

proféctum, *adv.*, truly

proféctus –us, *m.*, source

prófero –érre –tuli –látum, *3*, to display, lay before, bring forth, bring out, produce, offer, obtain, speak, utter

proféssio –ónis, *f.*, profession, declaration, acknowledgment

proféssor –óris, *m.*, professor

proféssus –a –um, *adj.*, professed; *ex profésso*, openly

profício –ere –féci –féctum, *3*, to help, assist, advance, increase, prevail, effect, make progress, contribute, go forth

profícuus –a –um, *adj.*, profitable

profiscíscor –císci –féctus sum, *dep. 3*, to set out, depart, travel, take a journey, go toward, arise from, spring from

profíteor –éri –féssus sum, *dep. 2*, to admit, profess, acknowledge

proflígo –áre, *1*, to abolish, overthrow, scatter

proflo –áre, *1*, to blow forth, breathe forth

prófluens –éntis, *adj.*, flowing, river, running water

prófluo –ere –flúxi –flúxum, *3*, to flow forth

proflúvium –ii, *n.*, flowing flood

profúgio –ere –fúgi –fúgitum, *3*, to flee away

prófugus –a –um, *adj.*, fugitive

profúndo –ere –fúdi –fúsum, *3*, to pour forth, pour out, cause to flow, rush forth

profúndum –i, *n.*, depth, profoundness

profúndus –a –um, *adj.*, deep, profound

profúsio –ónis, *f.*, profusion, pouring out

profutúrus –a –um, *adj.*, profitable

progenerátor –óris, *m.*, ancestor, progenitor

progénies –éi, *f.*, offspring, progeny, generation, race, descent, descendants, a body of men living at one period

progénitor –óris, *m.*, ancestor, founder of a family

progrédior –i –gréssus sum, *dep. 3*, to advance, go further

progréssus –us, *m.*, a course, advance

pro hac vice, for this once

prohíbeo –ére –ui –itum, *2*, to forbid, restrain, hinder, hold in check

prohibítio –ónis, *f.*, prohibition

proínde, *adv.*, hence, accordingly, just as, in like manner, in the same manner

projício –ere –jéci –jéctum, *3*, to cast away, cast down, cast upon, throw into

prolábor –i –lápsus sum, *dep. 3*, to fall away, lapse

prolátio –ónis, *f.*, pronouncement

proles –is, *f.*, offspring

pro líbito, at pleasure

prolíxe, *adv.*, freely, abundantly

prolíxitas –átis, *f.*, fullness

prolíxium, *adv.*, the longer

prolíxus –a –um, *adj.,* long drawn out

prolongátus –a –um, *adj.,* long

prolóngo –áre, *1,* to prolong, lengthen

próloquor –qui –locútus sum, *dep. 3,* to declare, speak out

prolúdo –ere –lúsi –lúsum, *3,* to practice beforehand

próluo –ere –ui –útum, *3,* to wash out, wash off

prolúsio –ónis, *f.,* a prelude

prólyta –ae, *m.,* a student of law

prolytátus –us, *m.,* the prolytate

prománo –áre, *1,* to derive from

proméreo –ére –ui –itum, *2,* to merit, obtain

proméreor –éri –eritus sum, *dep. 2,* to merit, deserve

promíco –áre, *1,* to shine forth

promíssio –ónis, *f.,* a promise, a person promised

promíssor –óris, *m.,* a promiser

promíssum –i, *n.,* a promise

promíssus –a –um, *adj.,* promised

promítto –ere –mísi –míssum, *3,* to promise, assure

promo –ere, prompsi, promptum, *3,* to utter, bring forth, send forth

promóneo –ére –ui –itum, *2,* to warn

promótio –ónis, *f.,* promotion, encourager

promótus –a –um, *adj.,* raised, promoted

prompte, *adv.,* promptly

prómptius, *adv.,* more quickly, more promptly

promptuárium –ii, *n.,* a garner, storehouse

promptus –a –um, *adj.,* prompt, willing, quick, visible

promptus –us, *m.,* visibility, readiness; *in promptu esse,* to be prepared

promúlgo –áre, *1,* to publish, make known

pronáus *or* pronáos, *m.,* the vestibule of a church

pronuntiátio –ónis, *f.,* a publication, judgment

pronúntio –áre, *1,* to declare, speak, pronounce

pronus –a –um, *adj.,* prone, flat, inclined, bent forward

propagátio –ónis, *f.,* spreading, extension, propagation

propagátor –óris, *m.,* propagator

propágo –áre, *1,* to spread, extend, enlarge, propagate

propágo –ínis, *f.,* a branch, shoot, generation

própalo –áre, *1,* to make manifest, make known, divulge

prope, *adv.,* near, nigh, at hand

propéllo –ere –púli –púlsum, *3,* to drive out, drive before, drive away

propémodum, *adv.,* almost

propéndeo –ére –péndi –pénsum, *2,* to hang down

propénsius, *adv.,* mercifully, speedily

propénsus –a –um, *adj.,* disposed to

própero –áre, *1,* to hasten, hurry

prophéta –ae, *m.,* a prophet

prophétes –is, *m.,* a prophet

prophétia –ae, *f.,* prophecy

prophéticus –a –um, *adj.,* prophetic

prophétis –idis, *f.,* a prophetess

prophetíssa –ae, *f.,* a prophetess

prophetízo –áre, *1,* to prophesy

prophéto –áre, *1,* to prophesy, foretell, predict

própino –áre, *1,* to offer a drink to, set before, drink to, pledge

propínquitas –átis, *f.,* relationship, nearness

propínquo –áre, *1,* to approach, attain

propínquus –a –um, *adj.,* near, approaching, neighboring, near of kin

própior –ius, *adj.,* nearer

propitiábilis –e, *adj.,* propitious, forgiving, forgivable, capable of atoning for

propitiátio –ónis, *f.,* clemency, mercy, forgiveness, propitiation

propitiatórium –ii, *n.,* mercy seat, propitiatory, the "throne of mercy" in the temple

propitiátus, *adv.,* mercifully

propítio –áre, *1,* to be merciful, be favorable

propítior –ári, *dep. 1,* to be merciful

propítius, *adv.,* kindly, favorably

propítius –a –um, *adj.,* merciful, propitious, forgiving, favorable, favorably inclined

propóno –ere –pósui –pósitum, *3,* to set before, resolve, determine, prefer, offer, place before, display, propose, expose

propositio –ónis, *f.,* proposition, setting forth

propósitum –i, *n.,* design, purpose, plan, resolution, proposition

propósitus –a –um, *adj.,* proposed, intended

próprie, *adv.,* properly, peculiarly

propríetas –átis, *f.,* distinction, property, peculiarity

Próprium (Officium), the part of the

Missal or Breviary that has Offices for special days

Próprium De Témpore, the Proper of the Season, the third division of the Breviary

Próprium Sanctórum, the Proper of the Saints, the fourth division of the Breviary

próprius –a –um, *adj.,* belonging to one, particular, personal, own

propter, *adv.,* because of, by reason of, on account of, for the sake of

proptérea, *adv.,* therefore, on that account, for that cause

propugnáculum –i, *n.,* a bulwark, rampart

propugnátor –óris, *m.,* defender

propúlso –áre, *1,* to repel

prorípio –ere –rípui –réptum, *3,* to escape, rush forth

prórogo –áre, *1,* to defer, put off

prorsus, *adv.,* wholly, turned toward or forward

prorúmpo –ere –rúpi –rúptum, *3,* to thrust forth, send forth, cause to break forth

prosa –ae, *f.,* a Sequence at Mass

proscríbo –ere –scrípsi –scríptum, *3,* to publish, make known publicly

prosélytus –i, *m.,* a proselyte

prósequor –qui –secútus sum, *dep. 3,* to look down upon, follow, accompany

prosílio –íre –ui, *4,* to spring, leap forth

prospécto –áre, *1,* to look forward, look forth upon

prospéctor –óris, *m.,* a guardian, provider

prosper –a –um, *adj.,* prosperous, favorable

próspera –órum, *n. pl.,* prosperity

próspere, *adv.,* prosperously, agreeable to one's wishes

prospérgo –ere –spérsi –spársum, *3,* to sprinkle

prospéritas –átis, *f.,* prosperity

próspero –áre, *1,* to succeed, prosper

prósperor –ári, *dep. 1,* to succeed, prosper

prospício –ere –spéxi –spéctum, *3,* to look, foresee, look into the distance

prostérno –ere –strávi –strátum, *3,* to spread over, overthrow, cast to the ground, prostrate, fall down

prostítuo –ere –ui –útum, *3,* to prostitute

prostitútio –ónis, *f.,* fornication

prosto –áre –stiti, *1,* to stand before, stand forward

prostrátus –a –um, *adj.,* humble, prostrate, lying on the ground

prosum, prodésse –fui, to be profitable, advantageous, useful, to profit

protéctio –ónis, *f.,* protection, covering

protéctor –óris, *m.,* protector

protéctrix –ícis, *f.,* protectress

prótego –ere –téxi –téctum, *3,* to protect, defend, help, cover, shelter

proténdo –ere –téndi –téntum *or* –tensum, *3,* to hold up, stretch forward

prótenus, *adv.,* constantly, immediately, straightway, forward, further on

prótero –ere –trívi –trítum, *3,* to trample under foot, tread down

protérvus –a –um, *adj.,* stubborn

prótinus, *adv.,* constantly, immediately, straightway, forward, further on

protocóllum –i, *n.,* a record of a transaction

protomártyr –is, *m.,* a protomartyr

protonotariátus –ii, *m.,* the dignity of protonotary

Protonotárius –ii, *or* Prothonotárius –ii, *m.,* a notary of the first class

prótraho –ere –tráxi –tráctum, *3,* to draw out, remain, extend

protúrbo –áre, *1,* to disturb

prout, *conj.,* according to

provéctio –ónis, *f.,* progress, advancement

provéctus –a –um, *adj.,* advanced in age

próveho –ere –véxi –véctum, *3,* to lead on, carry forward

provénio –íre, *4,* to come for, be granted, result

provéntus –us, *m.,* result, issue, revenue, crop

provérbium –ii, *n.,* a proverb

providéntia –ae, *f.,* providence, the providence of God

provídeo –ére –vídi –vísum, *2,* to see, behold, set, provide for, make preparation for

província –ae, *f.,* province

provinciális –e, *adj.,* provincial

provísio –ónis, *f.,* foresight, provision

províso, *adv.,* with forethought

províso –ere, *3,* to store, stock, look out for

provísor –óris, *m.,* provider

provísus –a –um, *adj.,* provided

provísus –us, *m.,* a looking before, provision, precaution

próvoco –áre, *1,* to provoke, rouse, stir up

provolútus –a –um, adj., lying prostrate

próximus –a –um, adj., near, neighboring; in próximo, near at hand, very near, next, nearest

próximus –i, m., a neighbor

prudens –éntis, adj., wise, prudent, foreseeing

prudénter, adv., prudently, wisely

prudéntia –ae, f., prudence, wisdom, understanding

pruína –ae, f., hoarfrost

pruna –ae, f., live coal

prúriens –éntis, adj., itching

psallo –ere, psalli, 3, to chant, chant the Psalms, sing, give praise, to sing to the accompaniment of a stringed instrument

Psalmi poenitentiáles, the Penitential Psalms: 8, 31, 37, 50, 101, 129, and 142

psalmísta –ae, m., a psalmist

psalmódia –ae, f., psalmody, the chanting of psalms

psalmum –i, n., a psalm

psalmus –i, m., a psalm

Psalmus Anthanasiánus, the Athanasian Creed

psalteriális –e, adj., pertaining to the psalms

psaltérium –ii, n., a psaltery; the 150 psalms of David

Psaltérium –ii, n., the Psalter, the part of the Divine Office immediately following the Ordinarium, and containing the Invitatory, hymn, antiphons, psalms, etc., for each day of the week, and for the Hours of that particular day

pseudo-Christus –i, m., a false Christ

pseudo-póntifex –icis, m., an antipope

pseudo-prophéta –ae, m., a false prophet

ptisána –ae, f., barley

Ptolemaéus –i, m., Ptolemee or Ptolemais, a seaport in Asher between Carmel and Tyre, now Akka (Acts 22:7)

pubes –is, f., offspring, youth

publicánus –i, m., a publican, a tax gatherer, a sinner

públice, adv., publicly

público –áre, 1, to make public, publish

públicus –a –um, adj., public

púdeo –ére –ui –itum, 2, to be ashamed

pudicítia –ae, f., purity, chastity

púdicus –a –um, adj., chaste

pudor –óris, m., purity, modesty, shame

puélla –ae, f., a girl

puéllus –i, m., a child, boy

puer –i, m., a boy

puérilis –e, adj., childish

puerínus –i, m., a diminutive of puer

puerítia –ae, f., childhood, boyhood, girlhood

puérpera –ae, f., mother, child-bearer

puérperus –a –um, adj., child-bearing

pugilláres –ium, m., a writing tablet

pugíllus –i, m., handful

púgio –ónis, f., a sword, dagger

pugna –ae, f., a fight, battle

pugnátor –óris, m., fighter, combatant, warrior

pugno –áre, 1, to fight, to do battle

pugnus –i, m., a fist

pulcher –chra –chrum, adj., beautiful, fair

pulchritúdo –inis, f., beauty, splendor, majesty

púllulo –áre, 1, to sprout, shoot up

pullus –i, m., a chicken, young fowl, colt, young animal

pulmentárium –ii, n., meat, food, anything to eat

pulméntum –i, n., savory meat, pottage

púlpitum –i, n., a lectern, pulpit, bookstand

pulsátor –óris, m., one who knocks or strikes

pulso –áre, 1, to knock, strike, beat upon

pulsus –us, m., a stroke, beating, pushing, blow

pulvíllum –i, n., a small cushion

pulvínar –áris, n., a pillow

pulvínum –i, n., a small cushion

pulvínus –i, m., a cushion

pulvus –eris, m., dust, ashes

púnctio –ónis, f., pricking

punctum –i, n., a period, moment, a very small space

pungo –ere, púpugi, punctum, 3, to pierce, puncture, stab

puníceus –a –um, adj., reddish color, of pumice stone

púnio –íre, 4, to punish

pupílla –ae, f., the pupil of the eye, a little girl

pupíllus –i, m., an orphan

pupíllus –a –um, adj., very small

puppis –is, f., stern of a ship, a ship

pure, adv., purely, altogether

purgaméntum –i, n., refuse

purgátio –ónis, f., purification, purgation, expiation

purgatórium –ii, n., purgatory

purgatórius –a –um, *adj.,* purifying, cleansing

purgátus –a –um, *adj.,* cleansed, purged, freed from

purgo –áre, *1,* to purify, cleanse

purificátio –ónis, *f.,* purification, cleansing

purificatórium –ii, *n.,* a purifier, the purificator

puríficо –áre, *1,* to cleanse, purify

púritas –átis, *f.,* purity, cleanness

púriter, *adv.,* purely, cleanly

púrpura –ae, *f.,* purple, purple cloth

purpurária –ae, *f.,* a seller of purple (Acts 16:14)

purpurátus –a –um, *adj.,* clad in purple

purpúreus –a –um, *adj.,* purple

purus –a –um, *adj.,* pure, clean, undefiled

pusillánimis –e, *adj.,* timid, fainthearted

pusillanímitas –átis, *f.,* faintheartedness, timidity, cowardice

pusíllitas –átis, *f.,* insignificance, smallness

pusíllum –i, *n.,* a little

pusíllus –a –um, *adj.,* little, small

puta, for example

putátio –ónis, *f.,* pruning

putatíve, *adv.,* supposedly

putatívus –a –um, *adj.,* reputed

púteus –i, *m.,* a pit, well, trench, grave

puto –áre, *1,* to think

putrédo –inis, *f.,* rottenness, corruption, putridness

putrefáctus –a –um, *adj.,* rotten

putrésco –ere –ui, *3,* to become rotten or putrified

pútridus –a –um, *adj.,* corrupt, putrid

putris –e, *adj.,* rotten, mortifying

pygárgus –i, *m.,* a fish hawk

pyra –ae, *f.,* a large fire, a pyre

pýramis –idis, *f.,* a pyramid

pyrus –i, *f.,* a pear tree

pytho –ónis, *c.,* a soothsayer

pythónicus –a –um, *adj.,* pertaining to divination

pythoníssa –ae, *f.,* a witch

pyxis –idis, *f.,* a ciborium, pyx, vessel of gold or silver in which the Host is preserved or carried

pyxómelum –i, *n.,* a pyx, ciborium

Q

qua . . . qua, partly

quacúmque, *adv.,* whatsoever, wherever, in every manner

quadragéna –ae, *f.,* a period of forty days

quadragenárius –a –um, *adj.,* of forty days

Quadragésima –ae, *f.,* Lent, a fast of forty days

quadragesimális –e, *adj.,* pertaining to Lent, Lenten, of forty days

Quadragésimo Anno, the Encyclical of Pope Pius XI "forty years" after the "Rerum Novarum" of Pope Leo XIII, on the Reconstruction of the Social Order, May 15, 1931

Quadragínta Horárum Orátio, the forty hours' adoration

quadrans –ántis, *m.,* a fourth part, a farthing

quadrátus –a –um, *adj.,* square, squaring, squareness

quadro –áre, *1,* to correspond with, agree, fit exactly

quádrupes –edis, *m.* and *f.,* a four-footed animal

quádruplum –i, *n.,* fourfold

quadrus –a –um, *adj.,* square

quaérito –áre, *1,* to collect, beg, solicit arms

quaero –ere –sívi *or* –sii –sítum, *3,* to require, reason, seek, ask for, desire

quaerulósus –a –um, *adj.,* complaining, querulous

quaesco –ere –ívi *or* –ii –ítum, *3,* to beseech

quaesítor –óris, *m.,* an investigator

quaesítus –a –um, *adj.,* select, uncommon, extraordinary

quaeso –ere –ívi *or* –ii –ítum, *3,* to beg, pray, entreat, beseech

quaéstio –ónis, *f.,* inquiry, question, asking a preacher of indulgences for giving alms

quaestuárius –i, *m.,* a collector of alms

quaestuátio –ónis, *f.,* begging, collecting alms

quaéstuo –áre, *1,* to collect, beg, solicit alms

quaestuósus –a –um, *adj.,* profitable

quaestus –us, *m.,* gain, profit, advantage

qualis –e, *adj.*, what manner? what kind? what sort? as, such as

qualiscúmque, of whatever kind, of whatever sort, any whatever

quálitas –átis, *f.*, quality

quáliter, *adv.*, in what manner, how, as, just as

quam, *adv.*, than, rather than, how much, how great

quámdiu, *adv.*, while, as long as, until, how long

quámobrem, *adv.*, wherefore, for which reason, why

quamplúrimi –ae –a, *adj.*, as many as possible

quamprímum, *adv.*, as soon as possible

quamquam, *adv.*, although, though, and yet, nevertheless

quamvis, *adv.*, even, as you will

quando, *adv.*, when? at what time? how long?

quandóque, *adv.*, at one time or another

quandóquidem, *adv.*, seeing that, because, since

quantíllus –a –um, *adj.*, how little! how small!

quántitas –átis, *f.*, quantity

quanto, *adv.*, by how much, the more

quantócius, *adv.*, sooner, more quickly, as soon as possible

quantópere, *adv.*, how much, to what extent, with what care

quantum, *adv.*, as much as

quantumcúmque, *adv.*, however much

quantúmvis, *adv.*, as great as you please, how great, how much soever

quantus –a –um, *adj.*, what, how great, how much, as great as, as much as

quantúslibet –álibet –úmlibet, *adj.*, however great

quápropter, *adv.*, wherefore, on which account

quaqua, *adv.*, wherever, whithersoever

quaquavérsum, *adv.*, every way, to all sides

quare, *adv.*, why? wherefore? for what cause? by which means? whereby

quartus –a –um, *adj.*, fourth

quasi, *adv.*, as if, as it were, like, about, just as if, a sort of

Quasimódo géniti, Low Sunday, the first Sunday after Easter

quassátio –ónis, *f.*, a scourge, plague, shaking

quasso –áre, *1*, to shake

quátenus, *adv.*, so that, in so far as, how far

quatérnio –ónis, *f.*, a company of four, a body of four soldiers (Acts 12:4)

quátio –ere, quassi, quassum, *3*, to beat, strike, shake

quátuor témpora, *n.*, the Ember Days

quemádmodum, *adv.*, just as, how? how greatly? in what manner?

queo –íre –ívi *or* –ii –ítum, *4*, to be able, can

quercus –i, *f.*, an oak tree

queréla –ae, *f.*, blame, complaint

querimónia –ae, *f.*, complaint

questus –us, *m.*, complaint

quicúmque, quaecúmque, quodcúmque, whoever, whatever, whichever

quid, *adv.*, what? *ut quid*, to what purpose? why?

quidam, quaedam, quoddam, certain

quídditas –átis, *f.*, essence

quidem, *adv.*, indeed, to be sure, at least

quídlibet, anyone, anything whatsoever

quidnam, what then?

quídpiam, anything

quiéo –íre, *4*, to be able

quies –étis, *f.*, rest, quiet, repose from labors, cares, etc.

quiéscens –éntis, *adj.*, pertaining to rest

quiésco –ere –évi –étum, *3*, to cease, rest, be still, be at peace, become quiet

quiétus –a –um, *adj.*, peaceful, quiet, restful

quílibet, quaélibet, quódlibet, any

quilísma –atis, *n.*, a serrated note in music

quin, *adv.*, that not

quínimo *or* quínimmo, yea rather

Quinquagésima –ae, *f.*, Quinquagesima Sunday, the Sunday before Ash Wednesday

Quinquagésima paschális, the paschal season

quíntilis, –is, *m.*, the fifth month, counting from March as the first — i.e., the month of July

quippe, *adv.*, for, certainly, indeed, to be sure, by all means

quíppiam, anyone

quisnam, quidnam, what then? who then?

quíspiam, quaépiam, quódpiam, any, anyone, someone, something

quisquam, quaequam, quidquam, any person, anyone, anything

quisque, often used for *quisquis* or *quicúnque,* whosoever

quisque, quaeque, quidque, any, which, whoever, whatever

quivis, quaevis, quidvis, whosoever you will, whatever you will

quo, *adv.,* where, whither, so that, in order that, to the end that

quoadúsque, *adv.,* until, until that

quocírca, *adv.,* on that account, therefore

quocúmque, *adv.,* to whatever place, whithersoever

quodámmodo, *adv.,* as it were, in a certain way, in a certain measure

quodcúmque, *adv.,* whatsoever

quólibet, *adv.,* whithersoever you please

quóminus, *adv.,* so as not

quómodo, *adv.,* how, as, in what manner, in what way

quomodocúmque, *adv.,* in any way, in any way whatsoever, howsoever

quondam, *adv.,* once, formerly, at a certain time

quóniam, *conj.,* for, because, since, that, seeing that, whereas, inasmuch as

quoquo, *conj.,* also

quot, how many?

quotánnis, *adj.,* yearly

quotidiánus –a –um, *adj.,* daily

quotídie, *adv.,* every day, daily

quóties, *adv.,* how often?

quotquot, *adv.,* as many as

quoúsque, *adv.,* how long?

quuam, *adv.,* since, when, as often as

R

rabbi, *m.* (Hebr.), *indecl.,* master, teacher, rabbi

rabbóni, *m.* (Hebr.), *indecl.,* master, teacher, rabbi (Jn. 20:16)

rábide, *adv.,* madly, savagely, fiercely

rábidus –a –um, *adj.,* mad

rábies –éi, *f.,* madness, fury, rage, fierceness

raca, *m., indecl.,* a silly person, a worthless fellow, a fool

racémus –i, *m.,* a cluster

radiátus –a –um, *adj.,* provided with rays

radicátus –a –um, *adj.,* rooted

radícitus, *adv.,* by the roots

rádico –áre, *1,* to take root

rádius –ii, *m.,* a ray, beam of light

radix –ícis, *f.,* root

rado –ere, rasi, rasum, *3,* to scrape away, shave, erase, scratch

raméntum –i, *n.,* a thin stick, a reed

ramus –i, *m.,* a branch, bough, twig

rana –ae, *f.,* frog

rapax –ácis, *adj.,* ravening; *as a noun, m.,* an extortioner

rápiens –éntis, *adj.,* ravening

rapína –ae, *f.,* robbery, plundering, pillage

rápio –ere –ui, raptum, *3,* to catch, seize, carry off, take away, take by force, to catch a glimpse of

rapto –áre, *1,* to drag away

raptor –óris, *m.,* a robber, plunderer, extortioner

raptus –a –um, *adj.,* caught, carried up

rarus –a –um, *adj.,* rare, strange

rastrum –i, *n.,* a rake

ratio –ónis, *f.,* reckoning, retribution, reasoning, way, account, record, rule, plan, reason, order

ratiocínium –i, *n.,* reasoning

rationábilis –e, *adj.,* rational, reasonable, endowed with reason

rationabíliter, *adv.,* reasonably

rationále –is, *n.,* a morse, a formale, one of the medieval episcopal insignia

rationális –e, *adj.,* rational

ratus –a –um, *adj.,* valid, settled, ratified, fixed, reckoned, calculated

raúcitas –átis, *f.,* harshness, hoarseness

raucus –a –um, *adj.,* hoarse

reaedífico –áre, *1,* to rebuild

reális –e, *adj.,* real

reáliter, *adv.,* really

reampléctor –i –pléxus sum, *dep. 3,* to embrace again

reápse, *adv.,* in truth, indeed

reátus –us, *m.,* guilt, fault, crime, the condition of an accused person

rebaptízo –áre, *1,* to rebaptize

rebéllio –ónis, *f.,* rebellion

rebéllo –áre, *1,* to renew a war, rebel

recálcitro –áre, *1,* to kick, kick back

recapitulátio –ónis, *f.,* repetition

recédo –ere –céssi –céssum, *3,* to fall away, stray, depart, leave, forsake, recede, retire, turn back, turn aside

recens –éntis, *adj.,* recent, fresh, young

recénseo –ére –ui –cénsitum *or* –censum, 2, to recall, review, examine, celebrate

recénsio –ónis, *f.*, a reviewing, mustering

recénter, *adv.*, recently, newly

receptáculum –i, *n.*, a vessel, receptacle

receptíbilis –e, *adj.*, acceptable

recéptio –ónis, *f.*, a receiving

recépto –áre, *1*, to draw back, receive back, retire

recéptor –óris, *m.*, a receiver

receptórium –ii, *n.*, a parlor, sacristy

recéssus –us, *m.*, retirement, withdrawal, a going back, secret design, secret, mystery

recído –ere –cídi, *3*, to fall back

recípio –ere –cépi –céptum, *3*, to receive, take, recover

recitátio –ónis, *f.*, recitation

recitátor –óris, *m.*, a reciter, one who reads aloud

récito –áre, *1*, to recite

reclámo –áre, *1*, to cry out against, contradict loudly

reclinatórium –ii, *n.*, the back of a couch

reclíno –áre, *1*, to lay back, bend back, recline, cause to lean back

reclúsa –ae, *f.*, an anchoress, a female recluse

reclusérium –ii, *n.*, a cell

reclúsus –i, *m.*, an anchorite

recognítio –ónis, *f.*, recognition, reflection, recollection, examination, revision of a book

recógnito –áre, *1*, to reflect, consider, think again, weigh, ponder

récolo –ere –cólui –cúltum, *3*, to recollect, contemplate, reflect upon, renew, repair, cultivate again

reconciliátio –ónis, *f.*, reconciliation

reconciliátor –óris, *m.*, intermediary

reconciliátus –a –um, *adj.*, reconciled

reconcílio –áre, *1*, to reconcile, absolve from sin, reconcile to the Church

recónditus –a –um, *adj.*, concealed, hidden

recóndo –ere –didi –ditum, *3*, to lay up, lay aside, hide

recordátio –ónis, *f.*, record, receiving, remembrance, memory

recordátus –a –um, *adj.*, mindful

recórdo –áre, *1*, to record, remember

recórdor –ári, *dep. 1*, to remember, recollect, be mindful of, recall, call to mind

récreo –áre, *1*, to treat, refresh

récrepo –áre, *1*, to echo

recrudésco –ere –crúdui, *3*, to refuse, decline

recte, *adv.*, well, rightly

rectitúdo –inis, *f.*, righteousness, rectitude

rector –óris, *m.*, a ruler, rector

rectus –a –um, *adj.*, right, correct, straight, upright, just, steadfast, stable, steady, clean, pure

recúbitus –us, *m.*, a seat at table

récubo –áre, *1*, to recline

recúmbo –ere –cúbui, *3*, to lean, sit down, recline at table, eat with, dine with, sup

recúpero –áre, *1*, to recover

recúrro –ere –cúrri –cúrsum, *3*, to occur, run back, hasten back, come back, return to

recúso –áre, *1*, to refuse, decline

recútio –ere –cússi –cússum, *3*, to strike back, cause to rebound

redámo –áre, *1*, to return love for love, love again

redárguo –ere –gui –gútum, *3*, to confute, disprove, refute, contradict, admonish, urge to penance

redargútio –ónis, *f.*, retort, rejoinder, reply to accusations, refutation, reproof

reddítio –ónis, *f.*, return, restoration

reddo –ere –didi –ditum, *3*, to restore, pay, render, return, give back, reward, give forth, render what is due

redémptio –ónis, *f.*, redemption, deliverance, ransoming, release from sin and its penalties

redémpto –áre, *1*, to redeem, ransom

redémptor –óris, *m.*, redeemer, rescuer, savior

rédeo –íre –ívi *or* –ii –ítum, *4*, to return, go back, come back

redíco –ere, *3*, to respond

rédigo –ere –égi –áctum, *3*, to bring down, reject, despise, treat contemptuously, abhor

redímo –ere –émi –émptum, *3*, to redeem, ransom, set free, deliver

redíntegro –áre, *1*, to restore, raise up

réditus –us, *m.*, return, revenue, a coming back, going back

redóno –áre, *1*, to give back

redúco –ere –dúxi –dúctum, *3*, to bring back

redúctio –ónis, *f.*, a bringing back

redúndo –áre, *1*, to overflow

redux –úcis, *adj.*, returned

reféctio –ónis, *f.*, refreshment, refectory, repairing, restoring
reféllo –ere –félli, *3*, to disprove, refute
réfero –érre, rétuli *or* réttuli –látum, *3*, to yield, refer, relate, tell, bring back, bear back
refértus –a –um, *adj.*, crowded
refício –ere –féci –féctum, *3*, to repair, refresh, mend, restore, make over
refígo –ere –fíxi –fíctum, *3*, to tear, loose, unfasten, pluck apart
reflécto –ere –fléxi –fléxum, *3*, to turn back, divert
refléxus –a –um, *adj.*, crooked
reflóreo –ére –ui, *2*, to bloom, bloom again, flower, be refreshed or revived
reflorésco –ere –ui, *3*, to flourish, bloom again, be refreshed or revived
réfluus –a –um, *adj.*, flowing back
refocíllo –áre, *1*, to relieve
refódio –ere –fódi –fóssum, *3*, to dig out, dig up
reformátio –ónis, *f.*, reformation
refórmo –áre, *1*, to renew, reform, remake
refórmido –áre, *1*, to dread
refóveo –ére –fóvi –fótum, *2*, to revive, refresh, cherish, supply
refractárius –a –um, *adj.*, stubborn, contentious, refractory
refraéno –áre, *1*, to bridle, check, restrain, curb, hold back
refrágor –ári, *dep. 1*, to oppose
refréno –áre, *1*, to bridle, check, restrain, hold back, curb
refrigérium –ii, *n.*, refreshment, recreation, cooling, consolation
refrígero –áre, *1*, to cook, refresh
refrigésco –ere –fríxi, *3*, to grow cold
refríngo –ere –frégi –fráctum, *3*, to break up, break open
réfuga –ae, *m.*, a forsaker, fugitive, deserter
refúgio –ere –fúgi –fúgitum, *3*, to flee away, escape, take to flight
refúgium –ii, *n.*, refuge
refúlgeo –ére –fúlsi, *2*, to shine brightly, glitter, illuminate
refúndo –ere –fúdi –fúsum, *3*, to restore, pour back, pour out
refúto –áre, *1*, to resist, oppose, refute, repress
regália –ium, *n. pl.*, rights and privileges
regális –e, *adj.*, royal
regáliter, *adv.*, royally, regally

regenerátio –ónis, *f.*, regeneration, renewal, rebirth
regenerátor –óris, *m.*, regenerator
regénero –áre, *1*, to bring forth again, to regenerate spiritually
regens –tis, *m.*, a director
régero –ere –géssi –géstum, *3*, to bring back, carry back, return, retort
regéstum –i, *n.*, a record, register
régimen –inis, *n.*, direction, guidance, government
regína –ae, *f.*, queen
régio –ónis, *f.*, region, country, territory, land, section
regionárius –ii, *m.*, a deacon of a region
regístrum –i, *n.*, a register, a bookmark
régius –a –um, *adj.*, royal, pertaining to a king
regnátor –óris, *m.*, a ruler, governor
regno –áre, *1*, to reign, rule, direct
regnum –i, *n.*, kingdom, the papal tiara
rego –ere, rexi, rectum, *3*, to rule, govern, guide, direct
regrédior –i –gréssus sum, *dep. 3*, to return, go back
régula –ae, *f.*, a rule, standard
reguláris –e, *adj.*, regular, pertaining to a rule
reguláris –is, *m.*, an adder, basilisk, an inferior ruler, a nobleman
reinvénio –íre, *4*, to find again
rejício –ere –jéci –jéctum, *3*, to cast away, reject
reláte, *adv.*, in relation to
relatíve, *adv.*, relatively
relátor –óris, *m.*, a reporter
relátus –us, *m.*, recital, narrative
reláxio –ónis, *f.*, relaxation
reláxo –áre, *1*, to forgive, loose
relegátio –ónis, *f.*, banishment
relégo –áre, *1*, to banish, remove
rélego –ere –légi –léctum, *3*, to collect, traverse again
relígio –ónis, *f.*, religion, devotion, reverence, worshiping, conscientiousness, a religious order
religiósitas –átis, *f.*, religiousness
religiósus –a –um, *adj.*, religious, pious, conscientious, God-fearing
réligo –áre, *1*, to fasten, bind
relínquo –ere –líqui –líctum, *3*, to forsake, leave behind, abandon, relinquish
relíquia –ae, *f.*, a relic; *relíquiae*, remains, relics, the remainder, the rest
reliquiárum –ii, *n.*, a reliquary, container of relics

réliquus –a –um, *adj.,* remaining; *et réliqua,* and so forth

reluctátio –ónis, *f.,* assistance

relúctor –ári, *dep. 1,* to contend, strive, struggle against

remáneo –ére –mánsi –mánsum, *2,* to remain, be left, abide

remédium –ii, *n.,* remedy, cure

rememorátio –ónis, *f.,* remembrance, memory

remémoror –ári, *dep. 1,* to remember, be remembered

rémeo –áre, *1,* to go back, come back, return

remérgo –ere, *3,* to immerse again

remétior –íri –ménsus sum, *dep. 4,* to measure again, be measured back

remígro –áre, *1,* to wander back, come back, return

reminíscor –i, *dep. 3,* to remember, call to mind, recollect, be mindful of

remíssio –ónis, *f.,* remission, forgiveness, absolution, pardon

remíssus –a –um, *adj.,* remiss, negligent, tolerable, slothful

remítto –ere –mísi –míssum, *3,* to remit, forgive, pardon, relax

remonstrántia –ae, *f.,* a monstrance, ostensorium

remótus –a –um, *adj.,* far off, distant, remote

remóveo –ére –móvi –mótum, *2,* to take away, remove, set aside, put away

remunerátio –ónis, *f.,* reward

remunerátor –óris, *m.,* rewarder

renáscor –násci –nátus sum, *3,* to be regenerated, be born again, be born again spiritually by Baptism

renáto –áre, *1,* to swim back

renes –um *or* –ium, *m. pl.,* kidneys, loins, interior

renídeo –ére, *2,* to shine

renovátio –ónis, *f.,* renovation

renóvo –áre, *1,* to renew, build anew, restore

renuntiátio –ónis, *f.,* renunciation (as a virtue)

renúntio –áre, *1,* to renounce, appoint, relate, report

rénuo –ere –úi, *3,* to refuse, deny by a motion of the head

reor, reri, ratus sum, *dep. 2,* to suppose, think, esteem

repágula –ae, *f.,* an enclosure, a fence

repágulum –i, *n.,* restraint, barrier

reparátio –ónis, *f.,* reparation, healing, regeneration

reparátrix –icis, *f.,* restorer

réparo –áre, *1,* to restore, repair

repéllo –ere –púli –púlsum, *3,* to overcome, cast off, repel, reject, thrust away, drive back, drive away

repéndo –ere –péndi –pénsum, *3,* to repay, return, reward, requite

repénte, *adv.,* suddenly

repentínus –a –um, *adj.,* sudden

repério –íre –péri –pértum, *4,* to reveal, discover, find, obtain

répeto –ere –ívi *or* –ii –ítum, *3,* to repeat, exact of, demand, ask back

répleo –ére –plévi –plétum, *2,* to fill, satisfy, refill, complete, replete, replenish

replétus –a –um, *adj.,* filled

repo –ere –si –tum, *3,* to crawl, creep

repóno –ere –pósui –pósitum, *3,* to keep, preserve, place, set back

repórto –áre, *1,* to bring back, receive

reportórium –ii, *n.,* an inventory

repósco –ere, *3,* to claim, ask back again, demand back

reposítio –ónis, *f.,* the act of replacing

repositórium –ii, *n.,* a repository

repósitus –a –um, *adj.,* laid up

repraesénto –áre, *1,* to show, lead, represent, make manifest

reprehéndo –ere –héndi –hénsum, *3,* to censure

reprehensíbilis –e, *adj.,* deserving of rebuke

reprehénsio –ónis, *f.,* censure

réprimo –ere –préssi –préssum, *3,* to repress, curb

reprobátio –ónis, *f.,* condemnation, rejection

réprobo –áre, *1,* to reject, refuse, disapprove

réprobus –a –um, *adj.,* reprehensible

réprobus –i, *m.,* a castaway

repromíssio –ónis, *f.,* promise

repromítto –ere –mísi –míssum, *3,* to promise to return

reptíle –is, *m.,* a reptile, a creeping thing

repto –áre, *1,* to crawl, creep

repúdium –ii, *n.,* a divorce

repúgno –áre, *1,* to resist, fight against, disagree with

réputo –áre, *1,* to esteem, repute, account, reckon

Réquiem, Mass for the dead; so called from first word of Introit

réquies –étis *or* –éi, *f.,* rest, repose, resting place

requiésco –ere –évi –étum, *3,* to be at rest

requiétio –ónis, *f.,* rest, repose

requiétus –a –um, *adj.,* rested, refreshed

requíro –ere –sívi –sítum, *3,* to need, require, care for, seek, seek after, long for, long earnestly for

requítio –ónis, *f.,* rest

res, rei, *f.,* thing, object, matter, circumstance

rescindíbilis –e, *adj.,* revocable

rescíndo –ere –scídi –scíssum, *3,* to annul, repeal

rescíndo –ere –scívi *or* –scii –scítum, *3,* to find out

rescríbo –ere –scrípsi –scríptum, *3,* to write back, write again

rescríptum –i, *n.,* copy of a writing, a written answer

réseco –áre –sécui –séctum, *1,* to cut out, root out

reserátus –a –um, *adj.,* open

résero –áre, *1,* to reveal, make clear, open

resérvo –áre, *1,* to save, preserve, keep back

res familiáris, inheritance

residéntia –ae, *f.,* residence

resídeo –ére –sédi –séssum, *2,* to remain, reside, sit up

resíduum –i, *n.,* remainder

resíduus –a –um, *adj.,* remaining, left behind

resígno –áre, *1,* to open, unseal

resína –ae, *f.,* balm

resipísco –ere –sípui *or* –sipívi, *3,* to repent, come to one's right mind

resísto –ere –stiti, *3,* to withstand, oppose, resist

resolútio –ónis, *f.,* dissolution

resolútus –a –um, *adj.,* careless, relaxed

resólvo –ere –sólvi –solútum, *3,* to loosen, unbind, loose

résono –áre, *1,* to resound, re-echo, express, convey

respéctio –ónis, *f.,* esteem, regard, visitation, judgment

respectívus –a –um, *adj.,* respective

respéctus –us, *m.,* respect, care, regard, consideration

respérgo –ere –spérsi –spérsum, *3,* to scatter, sprinkle, stain, shed

respício –ere –spéxi –spéctum, *3,* to look, behold, consider, look back, look upon, regard, respect, observe

respiraméntum –i, *n.,* relief, a breathing space

respíro –áre, *1,* to breathe, find relief, sigh with love or longing

respléndeo –ére –ui, *2,* to shine, show forth, be bright

respóndeo –ére –spóndi –spónsum, *2,* to reply, answer, respond

responsális –e, *adj.,* pertaining to a response

respónsio –ónis, *f.,* reply, answer, response

Responsoriále –is, *n.,* a book containing the responses of the Office

Responsórium Graduále, a book containing the parts chanted at Mass

responsórium –i, *n.,* a response, answer, reply, the Gradual of the Mass

responsúra –ae, *f.,* response

respública, reipúblicae, *f.,* republic, commonwealth

réspuo –ere –ui, *3,* to reject, despise, spit upon

restaúro –áre, *1,* to restore

restícula –ae, *f.,* a line, cord

restínguo –ere –stínxi –stínctum, *3,* to extinguish, quench

restítuo –ere –ui –útum, *3,* to restore

restitútio –ónis, *f.,* restitution, restoration

restitútor –óris, *m.,* a restorer

restríctio –ónis, *f.,* restraint, restriction

resúlto –áre, *1,* to resound, rebound, spring or leap back

resúmo –ere –súmpsi –súmptum, *3,* to take back, take again, recover, restore one's courage

resúrgens –éntis, *m.* or *f.,* the risen one

resúrgo –ere –surréxi –surréctum, *3,* to rise again, rise, rise from the dead

resurréctio –ónis, *f.,* resurrection

resúscito –áre, *1,* to rise up again, restore, revive, stir up, resuscitate

retárdo –áre, *1,* to check, stop, retard, keep back

rete –is, *n.,* a net

retéxo –ere –téxui –téctum, *3,* to weave again, repeat

retiáculum –i, *n.,* a network, snare

retíceo –ére –ui, *2,* to be silent about

retículum –i, *n.,* a network, lace

retíneo –ére –tínui –téntum, *2,* to restrain, hold back

retórqueo –ére –tórsi –tórtum, *2,* to turn back, cast back

rétraho –ere –tráxi –tráctum, *3,* to withdraw, restrain

retríbuo –ere –ui –útum, *3,* to bring, repay, render, reward, requite

retribútio –ónis, *f.,* retribution, recompense, reward, benefit, repayment

retro, *adv.,* back, behind, backward, again, after

retroáctus –a –um, *adj.,* past

retrofrontále –is, *n.,* a reredos or retable

retrográdior –i –gréssus sum, *dep. 3,* to go backward

retrógradus –a –um, *adj.,* going backward

retrórsum, *adv.,* back, backward

retrotábula –ae, *f.,* a retable

retúndo –ere –túdi –túsum, *3,* to blunt

reus –i, *m.,* guilty one, criminal, culprit, accused

revelátio –ónis, *f.,* revelation

revélo –áre, *1,* to make known, reveal, disclose, uncover, show

revéra, *adv.,* truly, indeed, in truth

revérbero –áre, *1,* to turn back, to reproach

reveréndus –a –um, *adj.,* reverend, to be revered

reverénter, *adv.,* reverently

reveréntia –ae, *f.,* reverence

reverentiális –e, *adj.,* reverent

revéreor –éri, *dep. 2,* to be ashamed

revértor –i –vérsus sum, *dep. 4,* to bind, bind fast, tie back

revínco –ere –víci –víctum, *3,* to subdue again

revirésco –ere –vírui, *3,* to become green again

revivísco –ere –víxi, *3,* to revive, come to life again

revívo –ere –víxi –víctum, *3,* to revive

révoco –áre, *1,* to recall, call back, call away

revólvo –ere –vólvi –vólutum, *3,* to roll back

rex, regis, *m.,* king

rhamnus –i, *m.,* a bramble, thorny shrub

rhetórica –ae, *f.,* rhetoric

rhetóricus –i, *m.,* a rhetorician

rhomphaéa –ae, *f.,* a sword, a long javelin

rhythmus –i, *m.,* rhythm

rídeo –ére, rísi, rísum, *2,* to laugh, laugh at, smile

rigens –éntis, *adj.,* unbending

rigésco –ere, rígui, *3,* to grow stiff, become numb

rígidus –a –um, *adj.,* rigid, stiff, unbending

rigo –áre, *1,* to water, wash, sprinkle, moisten, wet, irrigate

rigor –óris, *m.,* rigor, stiffness

ripa –ae, *f.,* bank

risus –us, *m.,* laughter

rite, *adv.,* rightly, fitly, properly, with suitable ceremony

rituális –e, *adj.,* pertaining to rites

rituálitas –átis, *f.,* the correct ritual

ritus –us, *m.,* rite, ceremony

rívulus –i, *m.,* rivulet, brook, stream

rivus –i, *m.,* river, brook, stream

rixa –ae, *f.,* quarrel, strife, dispute

rixor –ari, *dep. 1,* to quarrel

robor (robur) –oris, *n.,* strength, oak

roborátor –óris, *m.,* one who strengthens

roborátus –a –um, *adj.,* strengthened

róboro –áre, *1,* to strengthen, make strong, prevail

robúste, *adv.,* stoutly, strongly, firmly

robústus –a –um, *adj.,* strong, mighty, powerful, hard, firm

róccua –i, *m.,* an alb

rochétta –ae, *f.,* a rochet, surplice with narrow sleeves

rochéttum –i, *n.,* a rochet, surplice with narrow sleeves

rodo –ere, rosi, rosum, *3,* to gnaw

rogátio –ónis, *f.,* a request, petition, rogation

rogátus –us, *m.,* a request

rógito –áre, *1,* to ask eagerly, inquire frequently

rogo –áre, *1,* to ask, pray, entreat, beseech

rogus –i, *m.,* a funeral pyre, bonfire

róridus –a –um, *adj.,* covered with dew

roro –áre, *1,* to bedew, cause dew to drop

ros, roris, *m.,* dew

rosa –ae, *f.,* a rose

rosáceus –a –um, *adj.,* rose-colored, pink

rosárium –ii, *n.,* a rosary

róseus –a –um, *adj.,* roseate

rostrum –i, *n.,* prow, beak

rota –ae, *f.,* a wheel (whirlwind)

rota –ae, *f.,* a tribunal of the Roman Curia where cases relating to marriage, ordination, and religious professions are heard in the second or third instances

roto –áre, *1,* to revolve, turn, cause (something) to turn around

rúbeo –ére –ui –utum, *2,* to blush, redden
ruber –bra –brum, *adj.,* red
rubésco –ere –ui, *3,* to become red
rubéta –órum, *n. pl.,* thorns
rúbeus –a –um, *adj.,* red
rubicúndus –a –um, *adj.,* ruddy, red
rubígo –inis, *f.,* rust, mildew
rubínus –a –um, *adj.,* of ruby color
rubor –óris, *m.,* shame
rúbrica –ae, *f.,* rubric
rubricátus –a –um, *adj.,* dyed red, reddened
rubricísta –ae, *m.,* a writer on rubrics
rubrus –a –um, *adj.,* red
rubus –i, *m.,* bush, bramble
rudiméntum –i, *n.,* rudiment
rudis –e, *adj.,* rough, ignorant, unused, undressed (of cloth)
rudus –a –um, *adj.,* brutish
rufus –a –um, *adj.,* red, ruddy
ruga –ae, *f.,* a wrinkle
rúgio –íre –ívi –ítum, *4,* to roar, to roar as a lion
rugítus –us, *m.,* roaring
rugo –áre, *1,* to fold

ruína –ae, *f.,* ruin, destruction, invasion, breach
rúmino –áre, *1,* to eat, feed upon
rumor –óris, *m.,* fame
rumpo –ere, rupi, ruptum, *3,* to break, break asunder, interrupt
runcína –ae, *f.,* a carpenter's plane
ruo –ere, rui, rutum, *3,* to rush, hasten, fail, be ruined, fall down
rupes –is, *f.,* a rock, sharp cliff, stony hill
rúptio –ónis, *f.,* a breaking open, an injuring
ruptor –óris, *m.,* a violator
rurícola –ae, *c.,* a peasant
rursum, *adv.,* anew, again
rursus, *adv.,* anew, again
rus, ruris, *n.,* the country
rusticátio –ónis, *f.,* agriculture, husbandry
rústice, *adv.,* awkwardly, like a rustic
rústicus –i, *m.,* rustic, farmer
ruta –ae, *f.,* rue
rútilo –áre, *1,* to glow, glitter like gold, shine with a reddish glow
rutíllus –a –um, *adj.,* yellow, auburn, golden

S

Saba, *indecl.,* Saba, the chief city of Arabia Felix, famous for its frankincense and myrrh
sabactháni (Aram.), Thou hast forsaken me (Mt. 27:46; Mk. 15:34)
Sábaoth (Hebr.), hosts, armies, an appellation of the Lord as Ruler over all (Rom. 9:29)
sabbáticus –a –um, *adj.,* pertaining to the Sabbath
sabbatínus –a –um, *adj.,* pertaining to the Sabbath
sabbatísmus –i, *m.,* a day of rest, the Sabbath rest, keeping the Sabbath
sabbatízo –áre, *1,* to rest on the Sabbath
Sábbata –órum, *n. pl.,* Sabbath; *una sabbatórum,* the first day of the week
Sábbatum –i, *n.,* Sabbath, Saturday, the seventh day of the week. The Jewish day of rest. Under Christian law the day of rest was changed to Sunday in honor of the Resurrection (Mk. 15:42).
sabulósus –a –um, *adj.,* sandy, gravelly
sábulum –i, *n.,* sand, gravel

saccárius –a –um, *adj.,* pertaining to sacks
saccellárius –ii, *m.,* a chaplain
saccéllus –i, *m.,* a small sack
saccínus –a –um, *adj.,* made of sackcloth
sacculárius –ii, *m.,* an almoner
sácculus –i, *m.,* a purse, a small pouch, a sack
saccus –i, *m.,* sackcloth, garb for times of penance, cassock worn by some confraternities
sacellánus –i, *m.,* a sacristan, chaplain
sacellárius –ii, *m.,* a chaplain
sacéllum –i, *n.,* a chapel
sacer –cra –crum, *adj.,* sacred, holy, consecrated
sacérdos –ótis, *m.,* a priest
sacerdotále –is, *n.,* a ritual
sacerdotális –e, *adj.,* sacerdotal, priestly, relating to a priest or priesthood
sacerdótium –ii, *n.,* the priesthood
Sacramentále –is, *n.,* a book of instructions for the administration of the sacraments
sacramentális –e, *adj.,* sacramental

sacramentáliter, *adv.,* sacramentally

sacramentárium –ii, *n.,* a sacramentary, a book containing the prayers of the Mass for the different feasts

Sacramentárium Gelasiánum, a missal ascribed to Pope Gelasius

Sacramentárium Gregoriánum, a missal ascribed to Pope St. Gregory

Sacramentárium Leoniánum, a missal ascribed to Pope Leo I

sacraméntum –i, *n.,* symbol, dignity, rite, dispensation, secret, mystery, a sacrament, sacramental grace, the Eucharist

sacrárium –ii, *n.,* sacristy, shrine, chapel

sacratórium –ii, *n.,* a sacristy

sacrátus –a –um, *adj.,* sacred, holy, hallowed, consecrated

sacrificátio –ónis, *f.,* an actual sacrificing

sacrificátor –óris, *m.,* a sacrificer

sacrifícium –ii, *n.,* sacrifice, offering, oblation

sacrífico –áre, *1,* to sacrifice, offer up, make an offering of

sacrísta –ae, *m.,* a sacristan

sacristánus –i, *m.,* a sacristan

sacristía –ae, *f.,* a vestry, sacristy

sacro –áre, *1,* to consecrate

sacrosánctus –a –um, *adj.,* most sacred, most holy, inviolable

sacrum –i, *n.,* a holy thing, grace, the sacrifice of the Mass

Sacrum septenárium, the sevenfold gifts

Sadducaéi –órum, *m. pl.,* the Sadducees, a sect of Jews denying the resurrection and the existence of angels and spirits

Sadoc, son of Azor and father of Achim (Mt. 1:14)

saéculum –i, *n.,* time, period, age, eternity, forever, an indefinite period of time, the world, worldliness

saeculária –órum, *n. pl.,* a feast, celebration

saeculáris –e, *adj.,* worldly, belonging to an age, pertaining to an age

saecularisátio –ónis, *f.,* a release from a vow

saéculum –i, *n.,* time, period; *in saécula saeculórum,* world without end; *a saéculo,* from the beginning

saepe, *adv.,* often, oftentimes, frequently

saepenúmero, *adv.,* many times, often

saépio –íre, saepsi, saeptum, *4,* to enclose, hedge in

saéviens –éntis, *adj.,* fierce

saévio –íre, *4,* to rage, be fierce, be furious

saevítia –ae, *f.,* fury, ferocity, cruelty, fierceness, harshness, severity

saevus –a –um, *adj.,* cruel, fierce, wild, raging, violent

saga –ae, *f.,* a witch

sagácitas –átis, *f.,* sagacity, keenness, shrewdness, mental acuteness

sagáciter, *adv.,* keenly, sharply, acutely, sagaciously

sagax –ácis, *adj.,* having keen sense

sagéna –ae, *f.,* a net, drag net

sagína –ae, *f.,* food, fodder, nourishment, fattening

saginátus –a –um, *adj.,* fatted

sagíno –áre, *1,* to feed, fatten, to cram

ságio –íre, *4,* to feel keenly, to perceive quickly

sagítta –ae, *f.,* an arrow

sagítto –áre, *1,* to shoot with arrows

sagma –atis, *n.,* a saddle

sagum –i, *n.,* a military cloak

sal –is, *m. and f.,* salt

salárium –ii, *n.,* salary

salárius –a –um, *adj.,* relating to salt

Salem (Hebr.), Salem *or* Jerusalem

salínae –árum, *f. pl.,* salt pits, salt works

sálio –íre, *4,* to salt

sálio –íre, sálui, saltum, *4,* to spring, leap, bound, jump

saliúnca –ae, *f.,* a shrub, the wild nard

salíva –ae, *f.,* spittle

salix –icis, *f.,* a willow

Sálomon –ónis, *m.,* King Solomon

salsiúsculus –a –um, *adj.,* rather salty

salsúgo –inis, *f.,* saltiness, a salty waste or desert

saltátio –ónis, *f.,* dance, dancing

saltátrix –ícis, *f.,* a dancing girl

saltem, *adv.,* at least, at all events

salto –áre, *1,* to dance

saltus –us, *m.,* a forest, waste land, marsh, glade, pass, pasture, a bound, a leap

salúber –bris –bre, *adj.,* strong, useful, good, wholesome

salúbris –e, *adj.,* good, strong, useful, wholesome

salúbritas –átis, *f.,* health

salúbriter, *adv.,* healthfully, wholesomely, serviceably, advantageously

sálus –útis, *f.,* salvation, deliverance, health, greeting, safety, help

salutáre –is, *n.,* a savior, the Savior, salvation

salutáris –e, *adj.,* salutary, saving, wholesome, helping, beneficial, pertaining to salvation

salutátio –ónis, *f.*, salutation, greeting

salutatórium –ii, *n.*, a reception room for the bishop in the early churches

salútifer –a –um, *adj.*, saving, salutary, health-giving

salúto –áre, *1*, to salute, greet, keep, save, preserve

salutórius –a –um, *adj.*, theatrical

salvátio –ónis, *f.*, salvation, the act of saving

salvátor –óris, *m.*, savior

salve! (imperative of *salveo*), hail!

sálveo –ére, *2*, to be well

salvífico –áre, *1*, to save

salvo –áre, *1*, to save, keep, preserve, rescue, deliver

salvus –a –um, *adj.*, safe, whole, saved, sound, well

samárdocus –i, *m.*, a juggler

Samárita –ae, *m.*, a Samaritan

sambúca –ae, *f.*, a sackbut, a kind of musical instrument, a species of harp, a crosier, a kind of pastoral staff

sambúcus –i, *f.*, an elder tree

Sámuel –élis, *m.*, Samuel, a Levite, son of Elkanah and Hannah, the first of the prophets after Moses

sáncio –íre, sanxi, sanctum, *1*, to make sacred, inviolable, appoint, ordain, sanction

sancta –ae, *f.*, a saint

sanctificátio –ónis, *f.*, blessing, sanctuary, sanctification, holiness, holy place, shrine

sanctificátor –óris, *m.*, sanctifier, one who sanctifies

sanctifícium –ii, *n.*, a sanctuary, temple, shrine

sanctífico –áre, *1*, to sanctify, make holy, make inviolable

sanctimónia –ae, *f.*, holiness, piety

sanctimoniális –e, *adj.*, pious, holy

sanctimoniális –is, *f.*, a nun

sánctio –ónis, *f.*, rule, sanction

Sanctíssimum –i, *n.*, the Blessed Sacrament

sanctitúdo –inis, *f.*, holiness, sanctity

Sanctoróle –is, *n.*, the part of the Breviary with the offices for feasts of saints

sanctuárium –ii, *n.*, sanctuary, shrine, holy place

sanctum –i, *n.*, a sanctuary, holy place

sanctus –a –um, *adj.*, holy, saintly, godly, the Sanctus

sanctus –i, *m.*, a canonized saint

sandálium –ii, *n.*, a sandal, slipper

sane, *adv.*, soberly, sensibly, rationably

sanguíneus –a –um, *adj.*, of blood

sanguis –inis, *m.*, blood

sanguisúga –ae, *f.*, a leech

sánitas –átis, *f.*, health, soundness, sanity

sano –áre, *1*, to heal, cure, restore to health

sanus –a –um, *adj.*, healthy, whole

sápidus –a –um, *adj.*, relishing, savory

sápiens –éntis, *adj.*, wise

sapiénter, *adv.*, wisely

sapiéntia –ae, *f.*, wisdom

Sapiéntia –ae, *f.*, the Book of Wisdom

sapientális –e, *adj.*, pertaining to wisdom

sápio –ere –ii, *3*, to understand, be wise, taste, savor of; *idípsum sápere,* to be of one mind

sapor –óris, *m.*, taste, a delicacy

sapphirínus –a –um, *adj.*, pertaining to a sapphire

sapphírus –i, *f.*, a sapphire

sárcina –ae, *f.*, burden, pack

sárcio –íre, sarsi, sartum, *4*, to restore, repair

sarcóphagum –i, *n.*, a sarcophagus

sárculum –i, *n.*, a spade, hoe

sárdius –ii, *n.*, a sarx, carnelian

sardo –inis, *m.*, a carnelian

sardónychus –a –um, *adj.*, pertaining to a carnelian or sardonyx

sárdonyx –chis, *m.* or *f.*, a carnelian

sartatécta –órum, *n. pl.*, repairs

sartus –a –um, *adj.*, repaired

satágito –áre, *1*, to be very busy

sátago –ere, *3*, to be very busy, be in trouble

Satan, *indecl.*, Satan, the devil (Mt. 4:10; Acts 26:18)

Sátanas –ae (*voc.*, Satana), Satan, the devil

satánicus –a –um, *adj.*, pertaining to the devil, devilish, satanic

satélles –itis, *c.*, guard, servant, companion

satellítium –ii, *n.*, support

sátio –áre, *1*, to satisfy, nourish, satiate, fill, feed

sátio –ónis, *f.*, a sowing

satis, *adv.*, enough, greatly, exceedingly, sufficiently

satisfácio –ere –féci –fáctum, *3*, to satisfy, give satisfaction

satisfáctio –ónis, *f.*, satisfaction, amends, reparation

satisfáctio pro poena, remission by satisfaction

satispássio –ónis, *f.,* punishment to be undergone

sator –óris, *m.,* a sower, source, begetter

satum –i, *n.,* a dry measure, standing corn; *plural,* crops

satur –úra –úrum, *adj.,* full, sated

saturátio –ónis, *f.,* a satisfying, filling, repletion, fullness

satúritas –átis, *f.,* satisfaction, abundance, fullness, satiety

satúro –áre, *1,* to fill, satisfy, sate

satus –i, *m.,* a sowing, a measure

satus –us, *m.,* a sowing, a measure

saúcio –áre, *1,* to wound, hurt, injure

saúcius –a –um, *adj.,* wounded, injured, hurt

Saul, *indecl.* 1. First king of Israel. 2. The original name of Paul, a native of Tarsas, first a persecutor of the Church, afterward the great Apostle St. Paul.

sáxeus –a –um, *adj.,* stony

saxum –i, *n.,* a rock, stone, large rough stone

scabéllum –i, *n.,* a footstool, small stool, low seat, altar step

scala –ae, *f.,* a ladder

scaláris, –e, *adj.,* pertaining to steps or ladders

scalprum –i, *n.,* a chisel

scamnum –i, *n.,* a bench, seat

scandalízo –áre, *1,* to scandalize, give scandal, cause to stumble

scándalum –i, *n.,* scandal, stumbling block, trap, obstacle

scando –ere, scandi, scansum, *3,* to climb, climb up, climb a tree

scapha –ae, *f.,* a boat, skiff

scápulae –árum, *f. pl.,* shoulders, wings, the back, the shoulder blades

scapuláre –is, *n.,* a scapular, covering for the shoulders

scáteo –ére, *2,* to gush, gush forth, abound, flow forth, bubble

scatúrio –íre, *4,* to gush forth

scelerátus –a –um, *adj.,* wicked

sceléstus –a –um, *adj.,* wicked, shameless

scelus –eris, *n.,* a crime, wickedness

scenofactórius –a –um, *adj.,* pertaining to tentmaking (Acts 18:3)

scenopégia –órum, *n. pl.,* the Feast of the Tabernacles

scéptriger –a –um, *adj.,* scepter bearing

sceptrum –i, *n.,* a scepter

Sceva –ae, *m.,* a Jewish priest at Ephesus, father of seven sons who attempted to cast out a devil in the name of Jesus, but were wounded by it and had to flee (Acts 19:14)

scheda –ae, *f.,* a sheet of paper

schédula –ae, *f.,* a small sheet of paper

schema –atis, *n.,* a form, outline, speech

schinus –i, *f.,* the mastic tree

schisma –atis, *n.,* a schism, division, the term applied to a formal separation from the unity of the Church

schismáticus –a –um, *adj.,* schismatic, pertaining to schism

schistus –i, *m.,* a kind of stone

schola –ae, *f.,* a school, class, lecture, debate

scholáris –e, *adj.,* pertaining to a school

sciens –éntis, *adj.,* expert, knowing something

sciénter, *adv.,* wisely

sciéntia –ae, *f.,* knowledge

scílicet, *adv.,* actually, of course, naturally

scindo –ere, scidi, scissum, *3,* to cut, rend, tear asunder, divide, separate, part; *scíndere médium,* to cut into two pieces

scíniphes –ium, *m. pl.,* stinging insects, gnats

scintílla –ae, *f.,* a spark

scintíllo –áre, *1,* to sparkle, glitter

scio, scire, scivi, scitum, *4,* to know, know how, understand, know a person

scírpeus –a –um, *adj.,* made of rushes

scirpus –i, *m.,* a bulrush

scíscitor –ári, *dep. 1,* to inquire, inquire into

scisco –ere, scivi, scitum, *3,* to investigate, inquire, find out

scissúra –ae, *f.,* a splitting, rending, division, parting

scissus –a –um, *adj.,* torn, rent, broken

scitum –i, *n.,* statute, decree, ordinance

scopa –ae, *f.,* a thin twig, broom

scopo –áre, *1,* to sweep

scópulus –i, *m.,* a rock, cliff, crag

scopus, *m.,* aim, object

scória –ae, *f.,* dross

scórpio –ónis, *m.,* a scorpion, whip leaded with metal

scórpius –ii, *m.,* a scorpion

scortor –ári, *dep. 1,* to commit uncleanness

scortum –i, *n.,* immorality, uncleanness

scotísta –ae, *m.,* Scotist, one who follows the doctrine of Duns Scotus

scriba –ae, *m.*, a scribe, writer, member of a Jewish sect

scribo –ere, scripsi, scriptum, *3*, to write, write down, record

scrínium –ii, *n.*, a chest, closet, archives

scríptio –ónis, *f.*, writing, the art of writing

scriptor, –óris, *m.*, a writer, narrator, composer

scriptum –i, *n.*, publication, writing

Scriptúra –ae, *f.*, Holy Scripture

scrita –órum, *n. pl.*, trifles

scrutátio –ónis, *f.*, discerning

scrutátor –óris, *m.*, a searcher

scrutinárium –ii, *n.*, an investigation, inquiry, search

scruto –áre, *1*, to search, examine, scrutinize, investigate

scrutor –ári, *dep. 1*, to search, examine, scrutinize, investigate

scúlptile –is, *n.*, idol, graven thing

scúlptilis –e, *adj.*, carved

sculptúra –ae, *f.*, graven work, graving

sculptus –a –um, *adj.*, graven

scurrílitas –átis, *f.*, scurrility

scutárius –ii, *m.*, a shield-bearer

scutra –ae, *f.*, a shovel

scutulátus –a –um, *adj.*, checkered

scútulum –i, *n.*, escutcheon

scutum –i, *n.*, shield, buckler

scyphus –i, *m.*, a cup, goblet

sebáceus –a –um, *adj.*, of tallow

secédo –ere –céssi –céssum, *3*, to retire, depart, withdraw, go away

secérno –ere, *3*, to separate, set apart, hide

secéssus –us, *m.*, retreat, place of retirement

seclúdo –ere –clúsi –clúsum, *3*, to exclude, shut off, shut away

seco –áre, sécui, sectum, *1*, to cut, cut off, cut in pieces

secólligo –ere, *3*, to become part of

secréta –ae, *f.*, the Secret of the Mass

secretális –e, *adj.*, hidden, secret

secretária –ae, *f.*, a secretary's office

secretárium –ii, *n.*, a secret place, private chapel, place of retirement

secréto, *adv.*, in secret

Secrétum Missae, the Canon of the Mass

secrétus –a –um, *adj.*, secret, separate, apart

secta –ae, *f.*, sect, a mode of life

sectátor –óris, *m.*, a follower, pursuer, a member of a sect

sector –ári, *dep. 1*, to follow eagerly or continually

sectúra –ae, *f.*, a cutting

secúmfero –érre, *3*, to take along

secundicérius –ii, *n.*, the subdean of a college

secúndo, *adv.*, a second time

secúndo –áre, *1 (no perfect or supine)*, to make favorable, direct favorably

secúndum, *adv.* and *prep.*, according to, in accordance with

secúndus –a –um, *adj.*, second, next, following in order, favorable

secúre, *adv.*, securely, safely, composedly

secúris –is, *f.*, an ax

secúritas –átis, *f.*, security, safety, freedom from care

secus, *adv.*, otherwise, not so

sedátus –a –um, *adj.*, quiet, tranquil, composed

sédeo –ére, sedi, sessum, *2*, to sit

sedes –is, *f.*, seat, throne, place, habitation

sedes confessionális, *f.*, a confessional

sedíle –is, *n.*, seat, station

sedítio –ónis, *f.*, sedition

seditiósus –a –um, *adj.*, seditious

seditiósus –i, *m.*, a conspirator

sedo –áre, *1*, to soothe, calm, appease, allay

sedúco –ere –dúxi –dúctum, *3*, to lead astray, deceive, seduce

sedúctilis –e, *adj.*, easy to be seduced

sedúctor –óris, *m.*, deceiver

seductórius –a –um, *adj.*, seductive

sédule, *adv.*, diligently, zealously, designedly

sedúlitas –átis, *f.*, watchfulness

sédulo, *adv.*, industriously, purposely, busily, zealously

sédulus –a –um, *adj.*, earnest, diligent, careful

seges –étis, *f.*, corn, harvest, crop, produce

segméntum –i, *n.*, a piece, segment, shaving

segnis –e, *adj.*, slow, sluggish, slothful

segnítia –ae, *f.*, slowness, tardiness, sluggishness

segníties –éi, *f.*, slothfulness, slowness, tardiness

Segóvia –ae, *f.*, Segovia

segregátio –ónis, *f.*, a separation

ségrego –áre, *1*, to separate, set aside

Sehon (Hebr.), *indecl.*, Sehon, King of the Amorrhites

seípse, he, himself
seípsum, himself
seismógraphon –i, n., seismograph
sejúngo –ere –júnxi –júnctum, 3, to sever, disjoin, separate from
seléctio –ónis, f., selection
Selúcia –ae, f., Selucia, a city of Syria five miles north of the mouth of the Orontes (Acts 14:4)
séligo –ere –légi –léctum, 3, to choose, select
sella –ae, f., a chair, stool
Selmon (Hebr.), indecl., Selmon, a wooded mountain in Samaria
Sem, indecl., son of Noah
semántron, n., a sounding board
semel, adv., once, a single time
semen –inis, n., a seed, offspring, descendant
seméntis –is, f., sowing, seeds
seménto –áre, 1, to bear seed
seméstris –e, adj., of six months
semetípsum, himself, and other third person forms in self (emphatic)
semiánimis –e, adj., half-dead
semicínctium –ii, n., a narrow girdle
semi-dúplex –icis, adj., semidouble
semifáctus –a –um, adj., half-finished
semijejúnium –ii, n., a half-fast
semimórtuus –a –um, adj., half-dead
seminariáta –ae, m., a student of a seminary
seminarísticum –i, n., a tax for the maintenance of a seminary
seminárium –ii, n., a seminary, a school for training clergy
seminátor –óris, m., a sower
seminivérbius –ii, m., a talker, word sower
sémino –áre, 1, to sow, produce, beget
semi-púnctum –i, n., an inflection in chanting a Collect
semisaúcius –a –um, adj., half-wounded
sémita –ae, f., a path, way, narrow path
sémitum, gen. pl., seed
semiústus –a –um, adj., half-burnt
semivívus –a –um, adj., half-dead, half-alive
semóveo –ére –móvi –mótum, 2, to renounce, separate
semper, adv., always, ever, at all times
sempitérnum sacerdótium, an everlasting priesthood
sempitérnus –a –um, adj., everlasting, eternal
senátor –óris, m., a senator

senatórium –ii, n., a section reserved
senatórius –a –um, adj., senatorial
senátus –us, m., senate
senécta –ae, f., old age
senéctus –útis, f., old age
séneo –ére, 2, to be old
senésco –ere –ui, 3, to grow old, become aged, grow old in strength, become weak, waste away
senex –is, adj., old, ancient, advanced in years; noun, m., old man
Senex cum puélla, Joseph and Mary
senílis –e, adj., aged, senile, pertaining to an old man
sénior –óris, m., elder
sénium –ii, n., old age
sensa –órum, n. pl., thoughts, notions
sensátus –a –um, adj., wise
sensíbilis, adj., perceptible, apprehensible
sensibíliter, adv., sensibly, in such a way as to effect the senses
sensífico –áre, 1, to endow with sensation
sensus –us, m., mind, feeling, sense, perception, understanding, purpose
senténtia –ae, f., opinion, thought, sentiment, meaning, purpose
sentína –ae, f., the hold of a ship
séntio –íre, sensi, sensum, 4, to feel, experience, perceive, think, judge, learn, notice, observe, remark
seórsum, adv., aside, apart, especially, particularly
separátim, adv., separately, apart
separátio –ónis, f., separation, severance
séparo –áre, 1, to separate, sunder
sepélio –íre –ívi or –ii, sepultum, 4, to bury
sepes –is, f., fence, hedge
sepiméntum –i, n., a chancel, enclosure
sépio –íre, sepsi, septum, 4, to guard, fence in
sepóno –ere –pósui –pósitum, 3, to put aside, put apart, put by
septémber –bris, m., the month of September
septémber –bris –bre, adj., belonging to September
Septem Psalmi Paenitentiáles, the seven Penitential Psalms
septentrionális –e, adj., north
Septimána major, Holy Week
septimanárius –ii, m., a choir official serving for a week
Septimána sancta, Holy Week
Septuagésima –ae, f., Septuagesima, the

seventieth day. The third Sunday before Lent.

Séptuagint –a, –ae, *f.*, the chief Greek translation of the Old Testament

sepúlchrum –i, *n.*, sepulcher, grave, tomb

sepulcrétum –i, *n.*, a cemetery, crypt, burial vault

sepúlcrum –i, *n.*, sepulcher

sepultúra –ae, *f.*, burial, burial place

sepúltus –a –um, *adj.*, buried

sequála –ae, *f.*, a follower

sequéntia –ae, *f.*, sequence, continuance, a continuation of the Gradual

Sequentiále –is, *n.*, a book containing the Sequences

sequentiális –e, *adj.*, pertaining to the Sequences

sequéstro –áre, *1,* to deposit for safe-keeping, separate, move, put aside

sequor, sequi, secútus sum, *dep. 3,* to follow, strive after, seek to attain

séquior –ius, *adj.*, worse, lesser

sera –ae, *f.*, a bolt, bar

seráphicus –a –um, *adj.*, seraphic

séraphim (Hebr.), *indecl.*, the seraphim, the highest choir of angels

seréne, *adv.*, calmly

sereníssimus –a –um, *adj.*, most serene, sovereign

serénitas –átis, *f.*, clearness, sereneness, fair weather

serénus –a –um, *adj.*, bright, serene, clear, fair

séria –ae, *f.*, a large earthenware jar

seríceus –a –um, *adj.*, silken

séricum –i, *n.*, silk

séricus –a –um, *adj.*, silken

séries –éi, *f.*, succession, row

sério, *adv.*, seriously

sérius, *adv.*, more seriously

sermo –ónis, *m.*, speech, discourse, words, sermon, saying, homily

sermocinátio –ónis, *f.*, discussion

sermocinátor –óris, *m.*, a preacher

sermócino –áre, *1,* to preach a sermon

sermócinor –ári, *dep. 1,* to converse, talk

Sermólogus –i, *m.*, a book containing the discourses of the Fathers of the Church

sero, *adv.*, in the evening, late

sero –ere, sevi, satum, *3,* to sow

serótinus –a –um, *adj.*, late

serpens –éntis, *m.* and *f.*, a serpent, a creeping thing

serpentínus –a –um, *adj.*, serpentlike

serra –ae, *f.*, a saw

serrans –ántis, *adj.*, like a saw

serrátus –a –um, *adj.*, saw-toothed

serta –ae, *f.*, a wreath, a garland of flowers

serus –a –um, *adj.*, late; *sera nocte*, late at night

Servátor –óris, *m.*, Savior

Servi ímpii, impious servants, *i.e.*, the Jews

servílis –e, *adj.*, servile

sérvio –íre –ívi –ítum, *4,* to serve, be in bondage, wait upon, do service to

servítium –ii, *n.*, servitude, serving, service

sérvitus –útis, *f.*, service, servitude

servo –áre, *1,* to watch, observe, reserve, deliver, keep, preserve

sérvulus –i, *m.*, a servant boy, young slave

servus –i, *m.*, servant, slave, bondman

séssio –ónis, *f.*, a sitting down, sitting, the act of sitting

sessor –óris, *m.*, a rider

Seth, *indecl.*, the son of Adam and Eve, born after the death of Abel

sevére, *adv.*, seriously, gravely, severely, austerely

sevérus –a –um, *adj.*, severe, sharp

sévoco –áre, *1,* to call away

Sexagésima –ae, *f.*, Sexagesima, the sixtieth (day), the Sunday after Septuagesima Sunday. The second Sunday before Lent.

sexta –ae, *f.*, sext, the canonical hour to be recited at the sixth hour of the day

sextílis –is, *m.*, the month of August

sexus –us, *m.*, sex

síbilo –áre, *1,* to hiss

síbilus –i, *m.*, hissing

sibimetípsi, to itself, himself, or herself

sicárius –ii, *m.*, an assassin

sicca –ae, *f.*, the dry land as opposed to the sea

síccitas –átis, *f.*, drought, dryness

sicco –áre, *1,* to dry up, make dry

siccum –i, *n.*, desert, dry land

siccus –a –um, *adj.*, dry

sicéra –ae, *f.*, strong drink, cider

siclus –i, *m.*, a sickle, shekel

sícubi, *adv.*, if anywhere

sidéreum –i, *n.*, a star, heavenly body

sidéreus –a –um, *adj.*, starry

sido –ere, sidi *or* sedi, sessum, *3,* to settle, sit down

Sidon –ónis, *f.*, Sidon, a city in Phoenicia, now called Saida (Acts 12:20)

Sidóni –órum, *m. pl.*, Sidonians, the inhabitants of Sidon
Sidónius –a –um, *adj.*, of Sidon
sidus –eris, *n.*, a star
sigillatívus –a –um, *adj.*, pertaining to a seal
sigillátus –a –um, *adj.*, ornamented with small figures
sigíllum –i, *n.*, a seal, signet
signáculum –i, *n.*, a sign, mark, little seal
signánter, *adv.*, carefully, significantly
signátor –óris, *m.*, a witness
Signatúra –ae, *f.*, the Segnatura, a papal tribunal
sígnifer –i, *m.*, a leader, standard bearer
significánter, *adv.*, plainly, clearly, distinctly
significátio –ónis, *f.*, warning, sign, standard, banner
signífico –áre, *1*, to warn, give a sign
signo –áre, *1*, to mark, sign, seal, signify, imprint; to make the Sign of the Cross
signum –i, *n.*, sign, token, signet, miracle, banner, signal with a bell
Sihon, an Amorite king
siléntio, *adv.*, secretly
siléntium –ii, *n.*, silence
síleo –ére –ui, *2*, to be silent, hold one's peace
silex –icis, *m.*, flint, rock, any hard stone
silíqua –ae, *f.*, husk, pod
Silo (Hebr.), *indecl.*, a city in Ephraim
Síloam, *indecl.*, a pool at the king's gardens south of Jerusalem
silva –ae, *f.*, wood, grove, forest
silvésco –ere, *3*, to grow wild
silvéster –tris –tre, *adj.*, woodland
silvéstris –e, *adj.*, wild, belonging to the woods
Simeónis Festum, the feast of Candlemas
símila –ae, *f.*, fine flour
similagíneus –a –um, *adj.*, of fine flour
similágo –inis, *f.*, fine meal or flour
símilis –e, *adj.*, similar, like
simíliter, *adv.*, likewise, in like manner
similitúdo –inis, *f.*, similitude, likeness, parable, resemblance
símilo –áre, *1*, to compare, liken, make like
simónia –ae, *f.*, simony
simoníace, *adv.*, simoniacally
simoníacus –a –um, *adj.*, simoniacal
simplex –icis, *adj.*, pure, honest, frank, simple, upright, unmixed
simplícitas –átis, *f.*, simplicity

simplíciter, *adv.*, simply, uprightly, purely
simplificátus –a –um, *adj.*, simplified
simplífico –áre, *1*, to simplify
símplius –a –um, *adj.*, simple
simul, *adv.*, at the same time, at once, together
simulácrum –i, *n.*, idol, image, likeness
simulátio –ónis, *f.*, pretense, dissimulation
símulo –áre, *1*, to make like
simúltas –átis, *f.*, enmity, jealousy, dissension, animosity
Sina or **Sinas** (*indecl.*), a mountain between the gulfs of Suez and Akaba. The wilderness of Sina is particularly the plain of Sebayeh, at the south of Gebel Mousa
Sinaíta –ae, *m.*, a dweller on Mount Sinai
sínapi, *indecl.*, *n.*, mustard, mustard seed
sincére, *adj.*, sincerely
sincériter, *adv.*, sincerely
sincérus –a –um, *adj.*, sincere, genuine
sindon –ónis, *f.*, fine linen, muslin, linen cloth
singillátim, *adv.*, singly, one by one
singuláre, *adv.*, one by one, separately
singuláre sacrifícium, the sole and peculiar sacrifice
singuláris –e, *adj.*, remarkable, unique, excellent, solitary, single, singular, individual, eminent, not common with others
singuláritas –átis, *f.*, oneness
singuláriter, *adv.*, alone, singularly, in singleness of mind or purpose
singulátim, *adv.*, one by one
síngulus –a –um, *adj.*, each, each one, each separatively, every one; *per síngula*, particularly
singúltus –us, *m.*, weeping, sobbing
siníster –tra –trum, *adj.*, left, left hand
sinístra –ae, *f.*, the left hand
sino –ere, sivi, situm, *3*, to allow, permit, let be, let alone
sinópis –idis, *f.*, a red ocher, vermillion color
sinus –us, *m.*, breast, bosom
Sion, *indecl.*, the city of Zion or Jerusalem. Sion is one of the hills on which Jerusalem was built.
síquidem, *conj.*, if, indeed, for, because of, since
sisto –ere, stiti *or* steti, statum, *3*, to stand, become, be, exist, cause to stand
sistrum –i, *n.*, a cornet

sitárcia –ae, *f.*, a bag for carrying food

sitárcium –ii, *n.*, a bag for carrying food, vessel

sítiens –éntis, *adj.*, thirsty

Sitiéntes, the Saturday before Passion Sunday

sitiénter, *adv.*, thirstily, eagerly, greedily

sítio –íre –ívi –ítum, *4*, to thirst, be thirsty

sitis –is, *f.*, thirst, drought

sítula –ae, *f.*, a small pail

situs –us, *m.*, a place, site, situation

smarágdina –ae, *f.*, emerald

smarágdinus –a –um, *adj.*, pertaining to an emerald

smarágdus –i, *m.* and *f.*, an emerald

smegma *or* smigma –atis, *n.*, a washing ball, soap

sóboles –is, *f.*, offspring

sóbrie, *adv.*, soberly, prudently, carefully

sobríetas –átis, *f.*, sobriety

sóbrius –a –um, *adj.*, sober, temperate, prudent, thoughtful, recollected

socer –i, *m.*, father-in-law

sócia –ae, *f.*, a female companion

sociábilis –e, *adj.*, sociable

sociális –e, *adj.*, social, sociable

socíetas –átis, *f.*, society, union, fellowship, company, association

sócio –áre, *1*, to share in, combine, unite, associate

sócius –a –um, *adj.*, allied, together

sócius –ii, *m.*, a companion, partaker, comrade, ally

socórdia –ae, *f.*, indolence, folly, stupidity

socors –córdis, *adj.*, silly, weak-minded

socrus –is, *f.*, mother-in-law

sodális –is, *c.*, companion, comrade, associate, member of a sodality

sodálitas –átis, *f.*, a sodality or confraternity, guild, intimate association

sodalítium –ii, *n.*, a sodality, confraternity

sodalítius –a –um, *adj.*, pertaining to a sodality

Sódoma –ae, *f.*, Sodom, a city on the shore of the Salt Sea, destroyed with Gomorrah. The dwelling place of Lot.

Sódami –órum, *m.*, the people of Sodom

sol –is, *m.*, the sun

solácium –ii, *n.*, consolation, comfort, support, solace

soláris –e, *adj.*, solar, pertaining to the sun

solárium –ii, *n.*, the top of a house

solátium –ii, *n.*, comfort, solace, consolation, support

sólea –ae, *f.*, the entrance to the sanctuary

solémne –is, *n.*, solemnity, solemn festival

solémnis –e, *adj.*, solemn, festive

solémnitas –átis, *f.*, solemnity, festival, feast day

solémniter, *adv.*, solemnly

sóleo –ére, sólitus sum, *semi-dep. 2*, to be accustomed, be wont

solers –értis, *adj.*, skillful, watchful, adroit, clever

solérter, *adv.*, skillfully, cleverly, adroitly

sólide, *adv.*, firmly, solidly, densely

solidaméntum –i, *n.*, a solid foundation, that which makes firm

solíditas –átis, *f.*, solidity, steadfastness

sólido –áre, *1*, to establish, found, strengthen, comfort, make firm

sólidus –a –um, *adj.*, solid, firm, dense

solilóquium –ii, *n.*, a soliloquy

solitárius –a –um, *adj.*, lonely, solitary, alone, by itself

solitárius –ii, *m.*, a solitary, anchorite

solitúdo –inis, *f.*, solitude

sólitus –a –um, *adj.*, usual, customary

sólium –ii, *n.*, throne, seat, chair of state

sollémnia –órum, *n. pl.*, sacred festivals, sacred observances

sollémnis –e, *adj.*, solemn

sollémnitas –átis, *f.*, a festival, solemnity

sollémniter, *adv.*, solemnly

sollícitúdo –inis, *f.*, solicitude, care, carefulness, anxiety

sollícitus –a –um, *adj.*, solicitous, careful, anxious

solor –ári, *dep. 1*, to console

solum –i, *n.*, the ground, earth

solum, *adv.*, only, alone

solúmmodo, *adv.*, only, alone

solus –a –um, *adj.*, only, alone

solútio –ónis, *f.*, freedom, dissolution, loosening

solvo –ere, solvi, solútum, *3*, to undo, set free, loose, release

somiátor –óris, *m.*, a dreamer

sómnio –áre, *1*, to dream

sómnium –ii, *n.*, a dream

somnoléntia –ae, *f.*, drowsiness, sleepiness

somnoléntus –a –um, *adj.*, sleepy, drowsy

somnus –i, *m.*, sleep

sonans –ántis, *adj.*, sounding

sónitus –us, *m.*, noise, sound, crash, din

sono –áre, sónui, sónitum, *1,* to roar, sound, make a noise, make a tumult, resound

sonórus –a –um, *adj.,* sounding, sonorous

sons, sontis, *adj.,* guilty

sonus –i, *m.,* noise, sound

sópio –íre –ívi *or* –ii, –ítum, *4,* to lull to sleep

sopor –óris, *m.,* sleep, a heavy sleep, lethargy

sopóro –áre, *1,* to put to sleep

sopóror –ári, *dep. 1,* to go to sleep

sórbeo –ére –ui, *2,* to suck up, swallow

sorbitiúncula –ae, *f.,* a dish, a mess, small draught

sórdeo –ére –ui, *2,* to be dirty, be filthy

sórdes –is, *f.,* dirt, filth, defilement

sórdide, *adv.,* sordidly

sórdido –áre, *1,* to dirty, defile, soil, pollute, stain morally

sórdidus –a –um, *adj.,* unclean

soror –óris, *f.,* sister

sors, sortis, *f.,* chance, lot, part, fate, destiny, share, portion, dowry, divine ordinance

sórtior –ári, *dep. 1,* to cast lots, decide by lots

sortítio –ónis, *f.,* lot

sospes –itis, *adj.,* safe, unhurt, uninjured

sóspitas –átis, *f.,* preservation from harm, welfare

spado –ónis, *m.,* eunuch

spargo –ere, sparsi, sparsum, *3,* to strew, fling, scatter, sprinkle, sow

sparsim, *adv.,* scattered here and there

spatiósus –a –um, *adj.,* spacious, widespread, broad, long, large

spátium –ii, *n.,* space, extent, distance, size, division of time

spátula –ae, *f.,* a branch, the twig of a palm tree, scraper

speciális –e, *adj.,* special, one's own, particular, individual

speciáliter, *adv.,* specially

speciátim, *adv.,* especially

spécies –éi, *f.,* loveliness, beauty, appearance, view, species, kind, beauty of form, comeliness

spécimen –inis, *n.,* mark, sign, token, sample

speciósitas –átis, *f.,* beauty, handsomeness

speciósus –a –um, *adj.,* fair, beautiful, comely, handsome

spectáculum –i, *n.,* spectacle, show, sight

spectátor –óris, *m.,* an observer, spectator, watcher, one who looks on

spectátrix –ícis, *f.,* a female watcher, observer, onlooker, spectator

specto –áre, *1,* to behold, look at carefully, observe, contemplate

speculatívus –a –um, *adj.,* speculative

speculátor –óris, *m.,* observer, eyewitness

spéculor –ári, *dep. 1,* to watch, observe, spy, look about

spéculum –i, *n.,* mirror, glass

specus –us, *m.* and *n.,* a cave, hollow of a rock

spelúnca –ae, *f.,* cave, den

spero –áre, *1,* to hope, trust, expect

sperno –ere, sprevi, spretum, *3,* to scorn, despise, spurn, reject

spes –éi, *f.,* hope, hope of salvation, a theological virtue

sphaera –ae, *f.,* a circle, sphere

sphaérula –ae, *f.,* a spherical bowl

spica –ae, *f.,* an ear of grain

spicátus –a –um, *adj.,* with thorns, spiked

spiculátor –óris, *m.,* an executioner

spículum –i, *n.,* an arrow, dart, ray

spina –ae, *f.,* a thorn

spinétum –i, *n.,* a thorn bush

spíneus –a –um, *adj.,* of thorns

spínula –ae, *f.,* a pin, thorn, small thorn

spiráculum –i, *n.,* breath

spirámen –inis, *n.,* breathing, inspiration

spirans –ántis, *m.,* that which breathes

spirátio –ónis, *f.,* breath, spiration

spiratívus –a –um, *adj.,* breathing

spirituália –ium, *n. pl.,* spirits

spirituális –e, *adj.,* spiritual

spirituáliter, *adv.,* spiritually, in a spiritual sense

spíritus –us, *m.,* spirit, breath, ghost, wind, life, soul

Spíritus Sanctus, the Holy Spirit, the Third Person of the Blessed Trinity

spiro –áre, *1,* to breathe, blow gently

spléndeo –ére, *2,* to shine, shine forth

splendésco –ere –ui, *3,* to shine

spléndide, *adv.,* sumptuously

splendor –óris, *m.,* splendor, brightness, light of morning in contrast to the midday heat

spólia –órum, *n. pl.,* spoils

spóndeo –ére, spopóndi, sponsum, *2,* to promise solemnly

spóngia –ae, *f.,* a sponge

spons, spontis, *f.,* will, free will

sponsa –ae, *f.,* a bride
sponsor –óris, *m.,* sponsor, surety, the godparent at baptism or confirmation
sponsus –i, *m.,* spouse, bridegroom
spontánee, *adv.,* willingly, freely
spontáneus –a –um, *adj.,* voluntary, spontaneously
sponte, *adv.,* voluntarily, willingly; *sua sponte,* of his own volition
sporta –ae, *f.,* a basket, hamper
spórtula –ae, *f.,* a little basket
spuma –ae, *f.,* foam
spumo –áre, *1,* to foam, froth
spumósus –a –um, *adj.,* foaming, full of foam
spurcítia –ae, *f.,* filthiness
spúrius –a –um, *adj.,* illegitimate, base-born
sputo –áre, *1,* to spit
sputum –i, *n.,* spittle
squálidus –a –um, *adj.,* rough, bad-looking, stiff, unpolished
squalor –óris, *m.,* neglect, roughness
squama –ae, *f.,* scale
squamátus –a –um, *adj.,* with scales
squilla –ae, *f.,* a small hand bell
stabílio –íre, *4,* to make firm, fix, establish
stábilis –e, *adj.,* steadfast, firm, stable
stabílitas –átis, *f.,* stability, firmness, solid foundation
stabulárius –ii, *m.,* host, innkeeper
stábulum –i, *n.,* an inn, shelter for cattle
stacta –ae, *f.,* myrrh, oil of myrrh
stacte –es, *f.,* myrrh, oil of myrrh
stádium, –ii, *n.,* a furlong, race, race course
stagno –áre, *1,* to overflow, inundate
stagnum –i, *n.,* a lake, pool
stallum –i, *n.,* a choir stall, stall
stannum –i, *n.,* tin
stantáreum –ei, *n.,* a large chandelier
stater –eris, *m.,* a Jewish coin, a skekel
statéra –ae, *f.,* scales, a balance, the value of a thing
statim, *adv.,* immediately, presently
státio –ónis, *f.,* station, anchorage
stationális –e, *adj.,* pertaining to a station
státua –ae, *f.,* statue, image
statuárius –ii, *m.,* sculptor
státuo –ere –ui –útum, *3,* to set, place, establish, appoint, resolve, cause to stand
statúra –ae, *f.,* form, height, size

status –us, *m.,* position, state, condition, standing position
statútus –a –um, *adj.,* appointed
stearína –ae, *f.,* stearin (used in making candles)
stella –ae, *f.,* a star
stellans –ántis, *adj.,* starry
stellátus –a –um, *adj.,* starry
stéllifer –a –um, *adj.,* starry
stemma –ae, *f.,* a genealogical tree
stercus –oris, *n.,* dung, dunghill
stérilis –e, *adj.,* barren, unfruitful, sterile
sterílitas –átis, *f.,* barrenness, sterility, unfruitfulness
sterno –ere, stravi, stratum, *3,* to furnish, spread, saddle, strew
sterquilínium –ii, *n.,* dunghill, dung pit
sterto –ere, *3,* to snore
stíbinus –a –um, *adj.,* pertaining to stibium or antimony
stíbium –ii, *n.,* antimony, a stibic stone
stigma –atis, *n.,* stigma, mark, a reproduction of the Savior's wounds
stilla –ae, *f.,* a drop, drip, tiny portion of time
stillo –áre, *1,* to drip
stillicídium –ii, *n.,* a raindrop
stilus –i, *m.,* that which is written, a writing
stímulo –áre, *1,* to prick, goad, stimulate
stímulus –i, *m.,* the lower end of a crosier, a sting, spur, goad, prod
stipéndia –órum, *n. pl.,* wages
stipéndium –ii, *n.,* recompense, wage, stipend
stipes –itis, *m.,* a stem, trunk of tree
stipo –áre, *1,* to pack, surround, compass about
stípula –ae, *f.,* stubble, straw
stírpitus, *adv.,* utterly, by the roots
stirps –is, *f.,* stock, branch, kindred; *stirps damnáta,* the human race condemned on account of Adam's fall.
stiva –ae, *f.,* a plow handle
sto –are, steti, statum, *1,* to stand, remain standing
stola –ae, *f.,* a robe, garment, a stole, any long garment, a long narrow vestment worn around the neck indicative of priestly power
stomachánter, *adv.,* irritably
stómachus –i, *m.,* stomach
storax –ácis, *f.,* storax, a gum
strages –is, *f.,* slaughter, massacre
stragulátus –a –um, *adj.,* made of tapestry, pertaining to a covering

strágulum –i, n., a covering, rug, carpet
stragus –a –um, adj., pertaining to a cover, serving as a cover
stramen –inis, n., straw, litter
straméntum –i, n., straw
strángulo –áre, 1, to strangle
strator –óris, m., one who throws down or breaks
stratórium –ii, n., bedding, a couch
stratum –i, n., a bed, couch
strénue, adv., actively, resolutely, briskly, promptly
strénuus –a –um, adj., steadfast, vigorous, brisk, active, strenuous
strépitus –us, m., a din, loud noise, creaking, rumbling
strepo –ere –ui, 3, to make a loud noise, rattle, clash, clatter, rumble
striátus –a –um, adj., striped
stricte, adv., severely
strictim, adv., briefly
strictus –a –um, adj., close, tight, severe, strict, drawn tight
strídeo –ére, stridi, 2, to gnash
stridor –óris, m., gnashing of teeth, creaking, grating, grinding, hissing
stringo –ere, strinxi, strictum, 3, to hold tight
stropha –ae, f., a line of poetry, a strophe
stróphicus –i, m., a group of musical notes all of the same pitch
stróphium –ii, n., a girdle, garment
structílis –e, adj., related to building
structor –óris, m., a builder
structúra –ae, f., a building
strues –is, f., a pile, heap
struo –ere, struxi, structum, 3, to arrange, devise, pile up
stúdeo –ére –ui, 2, to strive, be zealous, study
studióse, adv., eagerly, diligently, zealously
stúdium –ii, n., deed, practice, doing, striving, zeal, diligence
stultilóquium –ii, n., foolish talking
stultítia –ae, f., foolishness, folly, stupidity
stultus –a –um, adj., silly, stupid
stultus –i, m., fool
stupefácio –ere –féci –fáctum, 3, to numb, stupefy
stupefáctus –a –um, adj., amazed
stúpeo –ére –ui, 2, to be struck, astonished, amazed, stunned
stupor –óris, m., astonishment

stuppa –ae, f., cotton, tow
stuprum –i, n., violation, lewdness, ravishing
stylus –i, m., a pen
Styx, Stygis, f., hell, the river Styx
suádeo –ére, suasi, suasum, 2, to exhort, persuade, advise
suasor –óris, m., an adviser
suasus –us, m., persuasion
suave, adv., sweetly, pleasantly
suaveoléntia –ae, f., fragrance, a sweet odor
suavídicus –a –um, adj., sweet, soft
suavis –e, adj., kind, good, sweet, gracious, pleasant, suave, agreeable
suávitas –átis, f., sweetness, goodness, pleasantness, suavity
suáviter, adv., sweetly, agreeably, pleasantly, delightfully
subárrho –áre, 1, to pledge, give earnest money, espouse
subaúdio –ire, 4, to hear, heed
subcinctórium –ii, n., an ornamental maniple worn by the pope
subcinerícius –a –um, adj., baked in ashes
subcíngulum –i, n., an ornamental maniple attached to the singulum worn by the pope
subconféssio –ónis, f., the tomb of a martyr beneath a high altar
súbcrepo –áre, 1, to crackle beneath
subdecánus –i, m., a subdean
subdiácon –onis, m., a subdeacon
subdiaconális –e, adj., pertaining to a deacon
subdiaconátus –us, m., subdeaconship
subdiáconus –i, m., subdeacon
sub dio (divo), adv., in the open air
súbditus –i, m., subject, servant, layman
súbdiu, adv., in the open air
subdo –ere –didi –ditum, 3, to subject, subdue, to put, place, lay
subdóceo –ére, 2, to assist in teaching, teach as an assistant to someone
súbdolus –a –um, adj., sly, cunning, deceitful, crafty
súbeo –íre –ívi or –ii –ítum, 4, to go up
subésse –fui, to be under
subínde, adv., immediately
subíndico –áre, 1, to indicate, point out
subínfero –férre –tuli –illátum, 3, to add
subintélligo –ere –léxi –léctum, 3, to understand
subíntro –áre, 1, to enter into, enter stealthily, insinuate itself

subintrodúco –ere, *3,* to introduce secretly

subintróeo –íre –ívi *or* –ii, –ítum, *4,* to enter stealthily

subitátio –ónis, *f.,* suddenness

súbito, *adv.,* suddenly

súbito –áre, *1,* to apply, supply

súbitus –a –um, *adj.,* sudden, unexpected

subjáceo –ére –ui, *2,* to lie under, be subject to

subjectíbilis –e, *adj.,* obedient, subject

subjéctio –ónis, *f.,* subjection, yielding

subjectívus –a –um, *adj.,* subordinate

subjéctum –i, *n.,* subject, proposition

subjício –ere –jéci –jéctum, *3,* to set, place under, subject, subdue, throw from under

subjugális –is, *c.,* used to the yoke, an ass

súbjugo –áre, *1,* to subject

subjúngo –ere –júnxi –júnctum, *3,* to add, add to, unite to, say again

sublátio –ónis, *f.,* lifting up, elevation

sublevátio –ónis, *f.,* a raising up

súblevo –áre, *1,* to exalt, lift up, raise up, support

sublímia –ium, *n. pl.,* lofty things

sublímis –e, *adj.,* lofty, sublime, on high, high, exalted

sublímitas –átis, *f.,* height, high station, excellency

sublímiter, *adv.,* aloft, on high

sublímo –áre, *1,* to exalt

sublúceo –ére –lúxi, *2,* to gleam forth, glimmer

súbluo –ere –lui –lútum, *3,* to flow beneath, wash from below

submérgo –ere –mérsi –mérsum, *3,* to sink, be drowned

subministrátio –ónis, *f.,* supply, aid, ministration, service

subminístro –áre, *1,* to minister

submitrále –is, *n.,* a skullcap worn beneath a miter

submítto –ere –mísi –míssum, *3,* to let down

submóveo –ére –móvi –mótum, *2,* to move away from, put away from

submúrmuro –áre, *1,* to murmur a little

súbniger –gra –grum, *adj.,* somewhat black

subobscúre, *adv.,* somewhat obscurely

subobscúrus –a –um, *adj.,* somewhat obscure or dark

súboles –is, *m.* or *f.,* offshoot, offspring, progeny

subórno –áre, *1,* to instigate secretly

subrelínquo –ere, *3,* to leave

subrépo –ere –répsi –réptum, *3,* to creep in, crawl, approach imperceptively

subréptio –ónis, *f.,* deceit

subrídeo –ére –rísi –rísum, *3,* to smile

subrúbeus –a –um, *adj.,* somewhat reddish

súbruo –ere –rui –rútum, *3,* to destroy, overthrow

subrútilo –áre, *1,* to glimmer forth

subsannátio –ónis, *f.,* derision, scorn, mockery, an object of scorn, a sneer

subsannátor –óris, *m.,* a mocker, scoffer

subsánno –áre, *1,* to deride, mock, laugh at

subsédeo –ére –sédi –séssum, *2,* to rest against, rest under

subséllium –ii, *n.,* a seat, pew, bench

súbsequor –qui –secútus sum, *dep. 3,* to follow after

subsidárius –a –um, *adj.,* subsidiary

subsídium –ii, *n.,* help, aid

súbsido –ere –sédi *or* –sídi –séssum, *3,* to sit down, settle down, sink down

subsidiárius –a –um, *adj.,* subsidiary

subsídium –ii, *n.,* help, aid, relief

subsílio –íre –sílui *or* –ii –súltum, *4,* to leap up, skip

subsísto –ere –stiti, *3,* to stand, withstand, be, exist, last, endure, remain

substántia –ae, *f.,* substance, nature, essence, being, existence

substantiális –e, *adj.,* substantial

substantiáliter, *adv.,* actually, in substance

substérno –ere –strávi –strátum, *3,* to spread out, strew

substómachor –ári, *dep. 1,* to be somewhat vexed

substráti –órum, *m. pl.,* prostrate, the kneelers

substratórium –ii, *n.,* an altar cloth

subsútum –i, *n.,* the lining of a garment

subtána *or* subtánna –ae, *f.,* a soutane

súbtego –ere, *3,* to spread underneath

subter, *adv.,* beneath, under, below, underneath

subterfúgio –ere –fúgi, *3,* to shun, evade, spare

subterfúgium –ii, *n.,* deceit, subterfuge

subterpósitus –a –um, *adj.,* placed under

subtéxo –ere –téxui –téxtum, *3,* to add, join to

súbtile –is, *n.,* the tunicle of a subdeacon

súbtraho –ere –tráxi –tráctum, *3,* to take away, to remove from under

subtus, *adv.,* under, beneath, below

suburbánum –i, *n.,* suburb

súbveho –ere –véxi –véctum, *3,* to bring up from below

subvénio –íre, *4,* to come in, come up to, relieve, assist, come to the aid of

subvérsio –ónis, *f.,* ruin, destruction

subvérsor –óris, *m.,* destroyer, overthrower

subvérto –ere –vérti –vérsum, *3,* to upset, pervert, destroy, overthrow

succéndo –ere –céndi –cénsum, *3,* to heat, burn, kindle, set on fire

succénseo –censére –cénsui –cénsum, *2,* to be enraged, inflamed with anger

succéntor –óris, *m.,* a subchanter

succéssio –ónis, *f.,* succession

succéssor –óris, *m.,* successor

succéssus –us, *m.,* succession, an advance, progress, a succession of time

succído –ere –cídi –císum, *3,* to cut off, cut down

súccinum –i, *n.,* amber

succlámo –áre, *1,* to cry again, shout at

succrésco –ere –crévi –crétum, *3,* to grow, increase

succúrro –ere –cúrri –cúrsum, *3,* to aid, succor, hasten to the aid of

succúrsus –us, *m.,* help

succus –i, *m.,* sap, juice

succúto –ere, *3,* to shake lightly, pluck softly

sucósus –a –um, *adj.,* juicy, succulent

sudaríolum –i, *n.,* a handkerchief, maniple

sudárium –ii, *n.,* a handkerchief, napkin, maniple

sudor –óris, *m.,* sweat, perspiration

sudes –is, *f.,* a stake, stick

sufferéntia –ae, *f.,* patience, toleration, endurance

súffero –érre, *3,* to suffer, bear

sufficiénter, *adv.,* enough, sufficiently

sufficiéntia –ae, *f.,* sufficiency, contentment

suffício –ere –féci –féctum, *3,* to be enough, suffice, cause to grow up

suffitórium –ii, *n.,* a censer

sufflatórium –ii, *n.,* bellows

súffoco –áre, *1,* to choke, throttle, strangle

suffódio –ere –fódi –fóssum, *3,* to dig underneath, undermine, dig up

suffragáneus –i, *m.,* a suffragan — a bishop subject to an archbishop

súffragans –ántis, *adj.,* helping, favorable

suffragátio –ónis, *f.,* prayer

suffrágium –ii, *n.,* suffrage, vote, support, approval, intercession, mediation

suffrágor –ári, *dep. 1,* to aid, approve

suffúlcio –íre –fúlsi –fúltum, *4,* to support beneath

suffusórium –ii, *n.,* a spout, pitcher

súggero –ere –géssi –géstum, *3,* to bring to mind, add, annex, subjoin

suggéstum –i, *n.,* a platform, stage, gallery

suggéstus –us, *m.,* a platform, stage, gallery

sugo –ere, suxi, suctum, *3,* to suck

sulcus –i, *m.,* a furrow

sulphur –uris, *n.,* brimstone, sulphur

summa –ae, *f.,* the highest, the highest place, the main thing, the important matter

summárium –ii, *n.,* a summary

summátim, *adv.,* in short, briefly

summe, *adv.,* highly, gently

súmmitas –átis, *f.,* top, summit, point, tip

summítto –ere –mísi –míssum, *3,* to let down

summópere, *adv.,* exceedingly, ardently, highly

summum –i, *n.,* top, summit, end, brim

summus –a –um, *adj.,* highest, chief

Summus magíster, the pope as teacher of the Church

sumo –ere, sumpsi, sumptum, *3,* to take, take up, lay hold of, assume

súmptio –ónis, *f.,* reception, receiving, taking up, assumption

sumptus –us, *m.,* cost, charges

sumptuóse, *adv.,* sumptuously, expensively

supéllex, supelléctilis, *f.,* furniture

super, *adv.,* on, above, open, over, toward, concerning, on top of

superabundánter, *adv.,* more abundantly

superabundántia –ae, *f.,* great abundance

superabúndo –áre, *1,* to abound

superadúltus –a –um, *adj.,* grown up

superaedífico –áre, *1,* to build up

superámbulo –áre, *1,* to walk upon

superátor –óris, *m.,* one who overcomes, a conqueror

supérbe, *adv.,* proudly, haughtily

supérbia –ae, *f.,* pride, haughtiness, insolence

supérbio –íre, _1,_ to be proud, haughty, insolent

supérbus –a –um, _adj.,_ arrogant, proud, haughty, insolent

supercádo –ere –cecídi, _3,_ to fall upon, fall over

supercaeléstis –e, _adj.,_ more than heavenly, supercelestial, _i.e.,_ above the heavens

supercértor –ári, _dep. 1,_ to contend

supercílium –ii, _n.,_ arrogance, pride, the eyebrow

supercúrro –ere –cucúrri –cúrsum, _3,_ to surpass, run beyond

superéffluens –éntis, _adj.,_ overflowing

superéffluo –ere –flúxi, _3,_ to run over, overflow

superéminens –éntis, _adj.,_ surpassing, unsurpassable

superemíneo –ére, _2,_ to overtop, excel

superérogo –áre, _1,_ to ask over and above, spread over and above

superexálto –áre, _1,_ to exalt greatly, exalt above all others

superexténdo –ere –téndi –ténsum _or_ –téntum, _3,_ to cover, stretch over

superextóllo –ere, _3,_ to exalt above

supérfero –férro –tuli –látum, _3,_ to carry over, excel, bear over

superfícies –éi, _f.,_ surface, face, top, external appearance

superflúitas –átis, _f.,_ excess, superfluity

supérfluo, _adv.,_ needlessly

supérfluus –a –um, _adj.,_ superfluous, overflowing

superfrontále –is, _n.,_ a reredos

superfúndo –ere –fúdi –fúsum, _3,_ to pour over, pour upon

supergáudeo –ére, _2,_ to rejoice over

supergloriósus –a –um, _adj.,_ exceedingly glorious

supergrédior –i –gressus sum, _dep. 3,_ to surpass, overreach, go over, exceed, overstep

superhumerále –is, _n.,_ the humeral, the amice

superímpleo –ére –plévi –plétum, _2,_ to fill to overflowing

superimpóno –ere –pósui –pósitum, _3,_ to place over, place upon, lay over

superínduo –ere –ui –útum, _3,_ to put on over

superioríssa –ae, _f.,_ a superioress

superlaudábilis –e, _adj.,_ to be praised exceedingly

superlimináre –is, _n.,_ the lintel of a door

superliminária –ium, _n. pl.,_ upper doorposts

superlúcro –áre, _1,_ to gain more, gain over and above

supernaturális –e, _adj.,_ supernatural

supérne, _adv.,_ upward, from above

supernumerárius –a –um, _adj.,_ supernumerary

supérnus –a –um, _adj.,_ celestial, heavenly, above

súpero –áre, _1,_ to overcome, conquer

superpellíceum –i, _n.,_ a surplice

superplénus –a –um, _adj.,_ brimful

supérnae –árum, _f. pl.,_ heaven

superpóno –ere –pósui –pósitum, _3,_ to lay over, put over, set over

superscríbo –ere –scrípsi –scríptum, _3,_ to write over or upon

superscríptio –ónis, _f.,_ superscription

supersédeo –ére –sédi –séssum, _3,_ to omit, leave off, refrain, sit upon or above

supersémino –áre, _1,_ to oversow, sow above other seeds

supérspero –áre, _1,_ to trust in greatly, hope greatly

supérstes –itis, _m.,_ a survivor

superstítio –ónis, _f.,_ superstition, fear, fanaticism

superstitiósus –a –um, _adj.,_ superstitious

supersubstantiális –e, _adj.,_ necessary for sustenance

supérsum –esse –fui, to be over and above, remain, be left, be superfluous

súperus –a –um, _adj.,_ upper, higher, divine, supreme, supernal

súperus –i, _m.,_ angel

supervacáneus –a –um, _adj.,_ superfluous

supervácue, _adv.,_ without cause, wantonly, uselessly, superfluously

supervénio –íre –véni –véntum, _4,_ to come in, come upon, come over, come up, overtake

superventúrus –a –um, _adj.,_ approaching, coming

supervéstio –íre, _4,_ to clothe, put clothes on

supínus –a –um, _adj.,_ bent or inclined backward, lying on the back

suppedále –is, _n.,_ a platform

suppedáneum –i, _n.,_ the platform or upper step of an altar

suppédito –áre, _1,_ to give abundantly

suppéto –ere –ii _or_ –ívi –ítum, _3,_ to be

present, suffice, be enough, demand secretly or stealthily

supplantátio –ónis, *f.*, treachery, the act of tripping

supplánto –áre, *1*, to overthrow, supplant, trip by the heels

suppleméntum –i, *n.*, supply, supplement, fulfilling

súppleo –ére –plévi –plétum, *2*, to use, supply, complete, make full

supplex –icis, *adj.*, suppliant, low, humbly entreating

supplicátio –ónis, *f.*, prayer, supplication, a procession

suppliciter, *adv.*, humbly, suppliantly

supplícium –ii, *n.*, punishment, penalty

súpplico –áre, *1*, to entreat

suppóno –ere –pósui –pósitum, *3*, to put under, hold over

suppórto –áre, *1*, to bear, support, bear with, convey, carry

supprésse, *adv.*, in a subdued voice

súpputo –áre, *1*, to count, compute

supradíctus –a –um, *adj.*, aforesaid

supránus –a –um, *adj.*, high, soprano

suprémus –a –um, *adj.*, last

súrculus –i, *m.*, a twig, sprout, young shoot, branch

súrditas –átis, *f.*, deafness

surdus –a –um, *adj.*, deaf

surgo –ere, surréxi, surréctum, *3*, to rise up, arise, awake, stand by

surréctio –ónis, *f.*, a rising again spiritually

surrípio –ere –rípui –réptum, *3*, to take by stealth, steal away

súrrogo –áre, *1*, to grant

sursum, *adv.*, above, upward

sursum corda, lift up your hearts

sus, suis, *m.* or *f.*, a pig, hog

suscéptio –ónis, *f.*, protection, receiving, defense

suscéptor –óris, *m.*, receiver, taker up, protector, helper, defender

suscípio –ere –cépi –céptum, *3*, to receive, uphold, undertake, guard, protect, support

súscito –áre, *1*, to rouse, awaken, raise up

suspéndium –ii, *n.*, suspense of judgment

suspéndo –ere –péndi –pénsum, *3*, to hang up, suspend, hang oneself

suspénse, *adv.*, lightly

suspénsio –ónis, *f.*, suspending, a withholding, an interruption

suspénsus –a –um, *adj.*, suspended, hanging, wavering, uncertain, in doubt

suspício –ere –spéxi –spéctum, *3*, to look up, regard, contemplate

suspíciosus –a –um, *adj.*, in a suspicious manner

súspicor –ári, *dep. 1*, to suspect, dread, look enviously at, to form an opinion

suspírium –ii, *n.*, a sigh, desire

suspíro –áre, *1*, to sigh, sigh for, long for

sustenátor –óris, *m.*, a supporter

sustentáculum –i, *n.*, a support, prop, nourishment, sustenance

sustentátio –ónis, *f.*, forbearance, delay, deferring

susténto –áre, *1*, to support, maintain

sustinéntia –ae, *f.*, endurance

sustíneo –ére –ui –téntum, *2*, to endure, sustain, undergo, wait upon, wait for, tarry, rely, abide, bear with

sustóllo –ere, *3*, to raise, elevate, lift up

susúrro –áre, *1*, to whisper, murmur, mutter

susúrrus –i, *m.*, a whisperer, murmurer, a muttering, whispering, murmuring, humming

susúrrus –a –um, *adj.*, whispering, murmuring

sycomórus –i, *f.*, a sycamore tree

sycophánta –ae, *m.*, a flatterer, sycophant

sycophántia –ae, *f.*, craft, deception

sýllaba –ae, *f.*, a syllable

sýlloge –es, *f.*, a list, roll

sýmbolum –i, *n.*, a creed, a symbol, the Creed, the profession of faith

sýmbolus –i, *m.*, the Creed, the profession of faith

sympathía –ae, *f.*, sympathy

symphónia –ae, *f.*, music, symphony, concert, band, orchestra

symphoniácus –a –um, *adj.*, harmonized, relating to a choir of mixed voices

symphoniácus –i, *m.*, a musician

synagóga –ae, *f.*, a synagogue, assembly, congregation

synáxis –is, *f.*, Mass, Holy Communion, a gathering

sýncope –es, *f.*, a faint, swoon

synedrísta –ae, *f.*, the sanhedrin

synníchium –ii, *n.*, a cone-shaped umbrella

synódicus –a –um, *adj.*, synodal

sýnodus –i, *m.*, a synod, council

synónymus –a –um, *adj.*, synonymous

Sýntyche –es, *f.*, St. Syntyche, mentioned in St. Paul's Epistle to the Philippians

Sýria –ae, *f.,* Syria, a country in Asia Minor

syrtis –is, *f.,* a sandbank

systéma –átis, *n.,* a system

T

tabélla –ae, *f.,* a table, a small flat board or tablet

tabélla secretárum, an altar card

tabernáculum –i, *n.,* a tent or tabernacle, pavilion, hut, the Jewish tabernacle

tabes –is, *f.,* a melting or wasting away, pestilence

tabésco –ere –ui, *3,* to melt, waste away, pine away, languish, faint, be gradually consumed

tábidus –a –um, *adj.,* a decaying, melting, wasting away, pining away, consuming, dissolving

tabífico –áre, *1,* to consume

Tábitha –ae, *f.,* a female in Joppa restored to life by the prayer of St. Peter (Acts 9:36, 40)

tabitúdo –inis, *f.,* a wasting away

tábula –ae, *f.,* a tablet or table, a writing table, a board, a wooden instrument used instead of a bell on Holy Thursday and Good Friday

tabulárium –ii, *n.,* archives, a registry office

tabulátio –ónis, *f.,* boarding, flooring

tabulátum –i, *n.,* a board, the floor of a building, platform

tabum –i, *n.,* pestilence, plague, clotted blood, moisture

táceo –ére –ui –itum, *2,* to be silent, dumb, not to speak, hold one's peace, pass over in silence

tácite, *adv.,* silently

tacitúrnitas –átis, *f.,* silence

tácitus –a –um, *adj.,* silent

tactus –us, *m.,* touch, touching, blemish

taeda (teda) –ae, *f.,* a torch, a pine tree, a board of pine

taédere, taedet, taéduit, *3, impers.,* it disgusts, wearies one

taédium –ii, *n.,* weariness, heaviness, care, loathing

taláris –e, *adj.,* reaching to the ankles or heels

taléntum –i, *n.,* talent

tálio –ónis, *f.,* retaliation

talis –e, *adj.,* such, such kind, of such a kind

táliter, *adv.,* thus, so, in such wise, in such manner

talus –i, *m.,* an ankle

támdiu, *adv.,* so long, so very long

tamen, *adv.,* nevertheless, yet

tamquam (tanquam), *adv.,* just as, as it were, like, as if, as though

tandem, *adv.,* at length, finally

tango –ere, tetígi, tactum, *3,* to touch, touch upon, reach, seize, strike, push, undertake, comprehend

Tanis –eos (*acc.,* Tanim; *abl.,* Tani), Tanis or Zoan, a city of ancient Egypt

tantísper, *adv.,* meanwhile

tanto . . . quanto, so much . . . as

tántulus –a –um, *adj.,* so little, so small

tantum, *adv.,* so much, so great, only

tantúmden, *adv.,* as much, just as much

tantúmmodo, *adv.,* only

tantus –a –um, *adj.,* such, so much, so great, of such size

tapes –étis, *n.,* a carpet

tapéte –is, *n.,* carpet, tapestry, drapery

tapétum –i, *n.,* carpet, tapestry

tarde, *adv.,* slowly

tárditas –átis, *f.,* slowness, tardiness

tardo –áre, *1,* to tarry, delay, loiter, be slow

tardus –a –um, *adj.,* slow, tardy

taríncha –ae, *f.,* a long needle, a spit

tártarus –i, *m.,* the infernal regions, hell (*plural,* tártara –órum)

taúrea –ae, *f.,* a whip made of the hide of a bull

taurus –i, *m.,* an ox, bull, bullock

taxa –ae, *f.,* a fee or tax

taxátio –ónis, *f.,* taxation, assessment

taxus –i, *f.,* a yew tree

tectum –i, *n.,* a roof, housetop, abode, dwelling

tectus –a –um, *adj.,* covered

tegmen *or* tégimen –inis, *n.,* a shelter, covert, refuge, protection, covering

tego –ere, texi, tectum, *3,* to cover

tégula –ae, *f.,* a tile

tégulum –i, *n.,* a covering

teguméntum –i, *n.,* a covering

tegúrium –ii, *n.,* the canopy above an altar

tela –ae, *f.*, cloth, web, warp, that which is woven

teláre –is, *n.*, a wooden frame covered with cloth

telárium –ii, *n.*, a wooden frame covered with cloth

telégraphum –i, *n.*, an instrument for sending telegraph messages

tellus –úris, *f.*, earth, land, district, country

telónium –ii, *n.*, a toll booth, place of toll, custom house

telum –i, *n.*, a dart

temerárius –a –um, *adj.*, rash

témere, *adv.*, by chance

teméritas –átis, *f.*, rashness, recklessness, chance, accident

temetípsum, thyself

temno –ere, tempsi, *3,* to despise, contemn, view with contempt

temperaménter, *adv.*, moderately, temperately

temperaméntum –i, *n.*, tempered mortar

temperatúra –ae, *f.*, tempering

tempéries –ei, *f.*, tempering, refreshment, a proper mixture, organization

témpero –áre, *1,* to be temperate, mingle, govern, rule, control, regulate, observe proper limits, set bounds, learn to avoid

tempéstas –átis, *f.*, storm, tempest

templum –i, *n.*, temple, church

temporális –e, *adj.*, temporal, temporary, lasting for a time

temporáliter, *adv.*, temporally, lasting for a time

temporáneus –a –um, *adj.*, early, timely

tempto –áre, *1,* to tempt, try

tempus –oris, *n.*, time, season; *ad tempus,* for a while; *quanto témpore,* as long as; *tempus acceptábile,* a time of grace

temuléntus –a –um, *adj.*, drunk

tenácitas –átis, *f.*, a firm holding, tenacity

tenax –ácis, *adj.*, steadfast, firm, holding fast, gripping, tenacious

tendícula –ae, *f.*, a snare, a trap

tendo –ere, teténdi, tentum *or* tensum, *3,* to extend, stretch, direct one's course of life

ténebrae –árum, *f. pl.*, darkness, shadows, affliction, the Office of Matins and Lauds on the three last days of Holy Week

tenebrésco –ere, *3,* to become dark

tenebricósus –a –um, *adj.*, dark

tenebrósus –a –um, *adj.*, dark

téneo –ére –ui, tentum, *2,* to have, hold, keep, possess, seize, take, obtain, hold fast, regard, consider

tener –a –um, *adj.*, tender

teneritúdo –inis, *f.*, tenderness, softness

tenor –óris, *m.*, tension, a stretching, the dominant — the note on which the body of a verse is chanted

tentaméntum –i, *n.*, trial

tentátio –ónis, *f.*, temptation, trial, test

tentátor –óris, *m.*, tempter, the devil

tentátrix –icis, *f.*, temptress

tento –áre, *1,* to try, prove, tempt, to handle

tentoríolum –i, *n.*, a small tent, the canopy over a tabernacle

tentórium –ii, *n.*, a tent

ténuis –e, *adj.*, small, weak, little, slight, thin, tender, frail

ténuo –áre, *1,* to lessen, diminish, make thin

tepefáctus –a –um, *adj.*, warm

tépeo –ére, *2,* to be tepid, lukewarm

tepésco –ere –ui, *3,* to become tepid

tépide, *adv.*, feebly, faintly

tergemínus –a –um, *adj.*, threefold

tergo –ere, tersi, tersum, *3,* to wipe

tergum –i, *n,* the back

tergus –oris, *n.*, the back

terminátio –ónis, *f.*, the modulation at the end of a psalm

término –áre, *1,* to limit

términus –i, *m.*, end, border, boundary, limit, terminus, term

tero –ere, trivi, tritum, *3,* to smooth, rub down, wear down, bruise, afflict

terra –ae, *f.*, land, earth, ground

terraemótus –us, *m.*, earthquake

terrénus –a –um, *adj.*, earthly, transitory as opposed to eternal

térreo –ére –ui– itum, *2,* to frighten, terrify, affright

terréster –tris –tre, *adj.*, earthly

terréstris –e, *adj.*, pertaining to the earth, terrestrial

térreus –a –um, *adj.*, earthly

terríbilis –e, *adj.*, terrible, fearful, dreadful, frightful

terribíliter, *adv.*, fearfully

terrífico –áre, *1,* to frighten, terrify, scare

terrígena –ae, *c.*, a mortal

territórium –ii, *n.*, district, territory, country

terror –óris, *m.*, terror, fright, fear, dread, panic

tersus –a –um, *adj.*, clean, neat, free from mistakes

tértia –ae, *f.*, Terce or Tierce, the canonical hour of the Divine Office to be recited at the third hour of the day

Tertiánus –a –um, *adj.*, of a Third Order

Tertiárus –a –um, *adj.*, of a Third Order

tértio, *adv.*, third time

tértium *adv.*, for the third time

téssera –ae, *f.*, token, distinguishing mark

testa –ae, *f.*, clay, potsherd, pitcher, jug, urn

testáceus –a –um, *adj.*, of tile or brick

testaméntum –i, *n.*, covenant, testament, will, written witness, the Bible, the Old and New Testaments

testamónium –ii, *n.*, testimony

testátor –óris, *m.*, testator, one who makes a will

testificátio –ónis, *f.*, witness, testimony

testífico –áre, *1,* to witness

testíficor –ári, *dep. 1,* to testify, bear witness, charge

testimónium –ii, *n.*, witness, evidence, testimony, laws, commandments

testis –is, *m.*, a witness, one who gives evidence

testor –ári, *dep. 1,* to bear witness, testify

testúdo –inis, *f.*, a tortoise

téstula –ae, *f.*, potsherd

teter –tra –trum, *adj.*, foul, filthy, hideous, offensive

tetrárcha –ae, *m.*, a tetrarch or governor, the chief or ruler of a fourth part

tetrávela –órum, *n. pl.*, the four curtains formerly surrounding the altar

tétricus –a –um, *adj.*, harsh, severe, gloomy, forbidding

texens –éntis, *m.*, a weaver

texo –ere –ui, textum, *3,* to weave

textor –óris, *m.*, a weaver

textrínus –a –um, *adj.*, pertaining to weaving, weaving

textum –i, *n.*, woven goods

textum dentículatum, lace

textus –us, *m.*, context

Thabor (Hebr.), *indecl.*, Mount Thabor, a mountain five miles east of Nazareth

Thaddéus –i, *m.*, one of the 12 Apostles

thálamus –i, *m.*, bedroom, bridal chamber, couch or platform

thallus –i, *m.*, a bough or stem

Tharsis –is, *f.*, Tartessus or Tarshish, an ancient city in Spain

thaumatúrgus –i, *m.*, a miracle worker, St. Gregory Thaumaturgus

theátricus –a –um, *adj.*, theatrical, pertaining to the theater

theátrum –i, *n.*, theater, show

theca –ae, *f.*, covering, case, sheath

thema –atis, *n.*, theme, topic, subject of discourse

theológia –ae, *f.*, theology

theológicus –a –um, *adj.*, theological

theólogus –i, *m.*, theologian

theoréticus –a –um, *adj.*, theoretical

théraphim, *n. pl., indecl.*, idols

therístrum –i, *n.*, a veil

thermae –árum, *f. pl.*, baths, hot springs

thesaurízo –áre, *1,* to lay up treasure

thesaúrus –i, *m.*, treasure, treasury, storehouse

thesis –is, *f.*, a proposition, thesis

Thessalónica –ae, *f.*, a city of Macedonia, on the shore of the Aegean Sea. Now called Salonika.

Thessalonicénses –ium, *m. pl.*, Thessalonians

Theudas –ae, *m.*, a Jewish imposter

thorax –ácis, *m.*, the breast, chest, breastplate

threnus –i, *m.*, wailing, lamentation

thronus –i, *m.*, throne, a throne for a bishop, a small canopy for exposition of the Blessed Sacrament

thorus –i, *m.*, bed, marriage couch

thuríbulum –i, *n.*, a censer, the vessel in which incense is burned during sacred ceremonies

thuriferárius –ii, *m.*, a thurifer or censer bearer

thurificátio –ónis, *f.*, incensing, the offering of incense

thurífico –áre, *1,* to incense

thus, thuris, *n.*, incense, frankincense

thyára –ae, *f.*, the tiara

thymíama –atis, *n.*, frankincense

thymiamatérium –ii, *n.*, a censer

thymiatérium –ii, *n.*, a vessel for holding incense

thyrsus –i, *m.*, the stem of a plant

tiára –ae, *f.*, the papal tiara, a crown, cap, tiara, turban

tíbia –ae, *f.*, shinbone, leg, pipe, flute

tíbicen –inis, *m.*, minstrel, piper, flute player, trumpeter

tignum –i, *n.*, a beam

tigris –is, *m.*, a tiger

timéndus –a –um, *adj.*, fearful, to be feared

tímide, *adv.*, timidly, fearfully

tímidus –a –um, *adj.,* fearful, timid, fainthearted

timor –óris, *m.,* fear, terror, dread, apprehension, an object of fear

timorátus –a –um, *adj.,* fearful, devout

tinctúra –ae, *f.,* dye, dyeing

tinctus –a –um, *adj.,* dyed

tínea *or* tínia –ae, *f.,* a moth

tingo –ere, tinxi, tinctum, *3,* to dye, color, wet, moisten; also used in the sense "to baptize"

tínnio –íre –ívi –ítum, *4,* to tinkle, ring, jingle

tínnitus –us, *m.,* a ringing, tinkling

tintinnábulum –i, *n.,* a small hand bell

tiro –ónis, *m.,* a beginner, recruit, novice

tirocínium –ii, *n.,* noviceship, novitiate, apprenticeship, training

títio –ónis, *m.,* a firebrand

títubo –áre, *1,* to stagger, waver, totter

tituláris –e, *adj.,* titular

títulus –i, *m.,* title, inscription, heading, pledge, label

tobálea –ae, *f.,* a cloth, altar cloth

tolerábilis –e, *adj.,* light, bearable

tólero –áre, *1,* to bear

tollo –ere, sústuli, sublátum, *3,* to lift up, raise, elevate, hold in suspense, remove, take away

tomus –i, *m.,* a volume

tondens –éntis, *m.,* a shearer

tóndeo –ére, totóndi, tonsum, *2,* to shear, cut, shave

tonítrus –i, *m.,* thunder

tonítruum –i, *n.,* thunder

tono –áre, *1,* to sound, resound, thunder

tonsúra –ae, *f.,* tonsure — a crown made by shaving the upper part of the head

tonsurátus –i, *m.,* one tonsured or shaven

tonus –i, *m.,* a tone

topárchia –ae, *f.,* a province or district

topázion –i, *n.,* topaz

topázus –i, *n.* or *f.,* a precious stone, topaz

tórcular –áris, *n.,* a wine press

tórculus –i, *m.,* a group of three notes in which the middle one is higher than the others

torméntum –i, *n.,* torment, rack

tornátilis –e, *adj.,* turned, revolving

tornatúra –ae, *f.,* turning

tórpeo –ére –ui, *2,* to be listless, torpid, sluggish, inactive, numb

torpísco –ere, tórpui, *3,* to grow stiff, grow numb, halt

torpor –óris, *m.,* torpor, dullness, stupefaction, inactivity, sloth

tórqueo –ére, torsi, tortum, *2,* to torture, torment, twist

torquis –is, *m.* and *f.,* collar, chain, necklace, wreath, ring

torrens –éntis, *m.,* torrent, stream, brook

tórreo –ére –ui, tostum, *2,* to burn, roast, parch, dry

torta –ae, *f.,* roll

tortor –óris, *m.,* tormentor, torturer

tórtula –ae, *f.,* a small cake

tortuóse *adv.,* crookedly

tórulus –i, *m.,* the red cord on cassocks, etc.

torus –i, *m.,* bed

totális –e, *adj.,* total, entire

totáliter *adv.,* wholly, totally, entirely

totídem *adj., indecl.,* so many, just as many

tóties quóties as often as

totus –a –um, *adj.,* all, the whole, entire; *per totum,* throughout

trábea –ae, *f.,* a robe

trabs –is, *f.,* a beam of wood

tractábilis –e, *adj.,* manageable, that can be handled, palpable

tractátus –us, *m.,* tract, treatise, discourse, sermon, homily

tracto –áre, *1,* to treat, celebrate, behave toward, handle, haul

tractus –us, *m.,* a tract, the Tract of the Mass

tradítio –ónis, *f.,* tradition

tráditor –óris, *m.,* traitor, betrayer

trado –ere –didi –ditum, *3,* to deliver up, surrender, give up, hand over, betray

tradúco –ere –dúxi –dúctum, *3,* to lead, lead over, bring over

tradux –úcis, *m.,* tradition, transmission

traha –ae, *f.,* a drag or sledge

traho –ere, traxi, tractum, *3,* to drag, draw, catch

trames –itis, *m.,* crossroad, road, course, path, byway

tranquílitas –átis, *f.,* tranquillity, calmness

tranquíllius *adv.,* peacefully

tranquíllo –áre, *1,* to make calm, pacify

tranquíllus –a –um, *adj.,* tranquil, undisturbed

transcendentális –e, *adj.,* transcendental

transcénsus –us, *m.,* a ford, crossing of a stream

transénna –ae, *f.,* an altar rail

tránseo –íre –ívi *or* –ii –ítum, *4,* to pass

through, across to, go over to, depart hence, pass by or away

tránsfero –érre –tuli –látum, *3,* to move, remove, transfer, transform, translate

transfígo –ere –fíxi –fíxum, *3,* to pierce through, transfix

transfigurátio –ónis, *f.,* transfiguration

transfigúro –áre, *1,* to transfigure

transfíxio –ónis, *f.,* the act of piercing

transformatívus –a –um, *adj.,* transforming

transfóssus –a –um, *adj.,* pierced

transfréto –áre, *1,* to pass over, cross the sea

transglútio –áre, *1,* to swallow

transgrédior –i –gréssus sum, *semi-dep. 3,* to go over, pass over, transgress

transgréssor –óris, *m.,* transgressor

tránsiens –éntis, *adj.,* transient

tránsigo –ere –égi –áctum, *3,* to get along, drive through, transact, accomplish, stab, pierce

transílio –íre –ui *or* –ii *or* –ívi, *4,* to leap over, skip over

transítio –ónis, *f.,* a transferring, translation

tránsmeo –áre, *1,* to go across, come across

transmigrátio –ónis, *f.,* transmigration, carrying away, removal, transportation

transmígro –áre, *1,* to flee, migrate, remove from one place to another

transmítto –ere, *3,* to send across, send over, transfer from one place to another

transmutátio –ónis, *f.,* change

transmúto –áre, *1,* to change, turn

transplánto –áre, *1,* to plant

transvádo –ere, *3,* to ford, pass over

tránsveho –ere –véxi –véctum, *3,* to carry over, convey, transport

transvérbero –áre, *1,* to pierce, transfix, perforate

transvérsim, *adv.,* across, obliquely

transvérto –ere –vérti –vérsum, *3,* to overturn

tremefácio –ere, *3,* to cause to tremble

tremefáctus –a –um, *adj.,* terrified

treméndus –a –um, *adj.,* tremendous, aweful, fearful, terrible, dread

tremo –ere –ui, *3,* to tremble, quake

tremor –óris, *m.,* fear, trembling, an object that causes fear

trepidátio –ónis, *f.,* agitation, anxiety, alarm, disquiet, trepidation

trépido –áre, *1,* to tremble, be agitated, be busy, swarm about

triángulum –i, *n.,* a triangle

trias –ádis, *f.,* a triad, a group of three, the Blessed Trinity

tríbula –ae, *f.,* a threshing sledge

tríbulans –ántis, *m.,* an oppressor

tribulátio –ónis, *f.,* tribulation, trouble, distress, anguish, affliction

tríbulo –áre, *1,* to afflict, oppress, harass

tríbulor –ári, *dep. 1,* to be in trouble

tríbulum –i, *n.,* a threshing machine

tríbulus –i, *m.,* a thorn, briar, thistle

tribúna –ae, *f.,* a tribune or gallery

tribúnal –is, *n.,* tribunal, place of judgment, court of justice

tribúnus –i, *m.,* tribune, captain over a thousand men

tríbuo –ere –ui –útum, *3,* to give, bestow, grant

tribus –us, *f.,* a tribe, a division of people

tribútum –i, *n.,* a tribute

tricéreus –ei, *m.,* the three-branched candle formerly used for the *Lumen Christi* on Holy Saturday

triclínium –ii, *n.,* stewardship

trico –áre, *1,* to delay, tarry, dally

tricor –ári, *dep. 1,* to trifle

tridens –éntis, *adj.,* having three teeth or prongs

tridentális –e, *adj.,* trident, fork-shaped

triduánus –a –um, *adj.,* of three days

tríduum –i, *n.,* a space of three days, a three days' devotion

trifórium –ii, *n.,* an arched gallery

Trínitas –átis, *f.,* the Blessed Trinity

trinus –a –um, *adj.,* three, triune

tripes –edus, *m.,* a tripod

triplex –icis, *adj.,* threefold

tripúdio –áre, *1,* to dance

tripúdium –ii, *n.,* joy, delight, festivities connected with great feasts of the middle ages

trirégnum –i, *n.,* the papal tiara

trirémis –is, *f.,* galley with three banks of oars

triságion *or* triságiun –ii, *n.,* the word *sanctus* repeated three times

triste, *adv.,* sorrowfully

trístega –órum, *n. pl.,* the third story of a building

tristis –e, *adj.,* sad, sorrowful, dejected, cast down

tristítia –ae, *f.,* sadness, sorrow

tristor –ári, *dep. 1,* to be sad

trístropha –ae, *f.*, a group of three notes in the same pitch

tríticeus –a –um, *adj.*, wheated, of wheat

tríticum –i, *n.*, wheat

tritúra –ae, *f.*, threshing, the season for threshing

tritúro –áre, *1*, to thresh

triumphális –e, *adj.*, triumphant

triumpháliter, *adv.*, solemnly, with the insertion of antiphons after each verse of the Magnificat or Benedictus

triumphátor –óris, *m.*, conqueror

triumphatórus –a –um, *adj.*, triumphant

triúmpho –áre, *1*, to triumph

triúmphus –i, *m.*, triumph

tróchlea –ae, *f.*, a pulley

tropárium –ii, *n.*, a book containing the chants formerly used in the Kyrie, the Gloria, etc.

trophéum or **tropaéum** –i, *n.*, trophy, spoils, triumph, monument of victory

troponárius –a –um, *adj.*, pertaining to tropes

tropus –i, *m.*, a trope, figure of speech

trucído –áre, *1*, to cut to pieces, slaughter, slay, massacre

trudo –ere, trusi, trusum, *3*, to push, thrust, press, shove

truélla –ae, *f.*, a trowel

trunco –áre, *1*, to mutilate, maim, cut off

truncus –i, *m.*, a trunk, stump

trux –cis, *adj.*, rough, savage, grim, ferocious

tuba –ae, *f.*, a trumpet

túeor –éri, túitus or tutus sum, *dep. 2*, to guard, protect, defend, uphold

tugúrium –ii, *n.*, a hut, cabin

tuítio –ónis, *f.*, defense, protection, preserving

tulo –ere, tuli or tétuli, *3*, to bring, bear

tumba –ae, *f.*, a tomb, catafalque

tumefácio –ere –féci –fáctum, *3*, to puff up with pride

túmeo –ére, *2*, to swell, be swollen, be puffed up

tumetípse, you yourself

túmide, *adv.*, pompously, bombastically

túmidus –a –um, *adj.*, tumid, swollen

tumor –óris, *m.*, tumor, pride, bombast

túmulo –áre, *1*, to bury

tumultárie, *adv.*, suddenly, in a disorderly manner

tumúlto –áre, *1*, to make a tumult

tumúltuor –ári, *dep. 1*, to make a tumult, be in confusion

tumúltus –i, *m.*, a tumult, noise, confusion, bustle

túmulus –i, *m.*, a grave

tundo –ere, tutúndi, tusum or tunsum, *3*, to beat, strike

túnica –ae, *f.*, coat, shirt, tunic, dalmatic

tunicélla –ae, *f.*, the dalmatic worn by a subdeacon

túnsio –ónis, *f.*, beating, striking

turba –ae, *f.*, crowd, multitude

turbátio –ónis, *f.*, fear, confusion

turbátus –a –um, *adj.*, disturbed, disordered, perturbed

turben –inis, *n.*, a whirlwind

túrbidus –a –um, *adj.*, disordered, confused

turbo –áre, *1*, to disturb, trouble, dismay, throw into confusion

turbo –inis, *m.*, a whirlwind, gale, storm

turbuléntus –a –um, *adj.*, troublesome

túrgeo –ére, *2*, to swell up, be swollen

túrgidus –a –um, *adj.*, turgid, swollen

turma –ae, *f.*, a troup, throng

turnus –i, *m.*, a turn

turpis –e, *adj.*, foul, filthy, base, shameful, unsightly

túrpiter, *adv.*, in an unsightly manner

turpitúdo –inis, *f.*, disgrace, obscenity

turpo –áre, *1*, to befoul, defile, make ugly

turrícula –ae, *f.*, a small tower, turret

turris –is, *f.*, a tower, turret, tabernacle

turtur –uris, *m.*, a turtle dove

tussis –is, *f.*, a cough

tutaméntum –i, *n.*, safety, defense, protection

tutéla –ae, *f.*, a guard, protection, safety, charge

tuto, *adv.*, safely

tuto –áre, *1*, to defend

tutor –óris, *m.*, tutor

tutus –a –um, *adj.*, safe

tympanístria –ae, *f.*, the accompaniment of a timbrel, a timbrel player, a female drummer

týmpanum –i, *n.*, a drum, timbrel, small hand drum, tambourine

typhus –i, *m.*, pride, vanity

týpice, *adv.*, prefiguratively

týpicus –a –um, *adj.*, typical

týpicus –i, *m.*, figure, emblem

typográphicus –a –um, *adj.*, pertaining to print

typus –i, *m.*, figure, type, figures of things or persons which were about to take place in the New Testament

tyránnis –idis, *f.*, tyranny

tyránnus –i, *m.*, tyrant, ruler, the devil
tyrocínium –ii, *n.*, apprenticeship, noviciate

Tyrus –i, *f.*, Tyre, a city in Phoenicia

U

uber –eris, *adj.*, fruitful, copious, abundant, plentiful, rich, abounding in anything
uber –eris, *n.*, breast
ubértim, *adv.*, abundantly, copiously
ubértas –átis, *f.*, fullness, fruitfulness, abundance, plenty, fertility
ubérto –áre, *1,* to make fruitful
ubicúmque, *adv.*, wherever, wheresoever
ubilíbet, *adv.*, anywhere you please, everywhere
ubínam, *adv.*, where
ubíque, *adv.*, wherever, everywhere, in all places
udo –ónis, *f.*, a stocking worn by a bishop during pontifical High Mass
udus –a –um, *adj.*, wet, moist, tearful
ulcerátus –a –um, *adj.*, covered with sores
ulcíscor –i, ultus sum, *dep. 3,* to avenge one's self on, punish, take vengeance on
ulcus –eris, *n.*, sore, ulcer, boil
ullus –a –um, *adj.*, any
ulna –ae, *f.*, arm, elbow
ultérior –óris, *adj.*, further, beyond
últimus –a –um, *adj.*, farthest, last
últio –ónis, *f.*, revenge, vengeance, punishment
ultor –óris, *m.*, avenger, punisher
ultra, *adv.*, further, beyond, longer, on the farther side of, any more, besides
ultro, *adv.*, spontaneously, of itself, voluntarily, of one's own accord
ululátus –us, *m.*, wailing, shrieking, shouting, howling
úlulo –áre, *1,* to shriek, howl, wail
umbélla –ae, *f.*, a small canopy shaped like an umbrella used in processions of the Blessed Sacrament
umbra –ae, *f.*, shade, shadow
umbráculum –i, *n.*, a covering for the tabernacle, a shade, covert, shady place
umbráticus –a –um, *adj.*, pertaining to the shade
umbro –áre, to shade, overshadow
umbrósus –a –um, *adj.*, shady
umquam, *adv.*, ever, at any time
una, *adv.*, together, at the same place or time

unánimis –e, *adj.*, of one mind, heart or will, like-minded
unanímiter, *adv.*, with one accord, unanimously
unánimus –a –um, *adj.*, with one voice, of one mind
úncia –ae, *f.*, an ounce, an inch
uncínus –i, *m.*, a hook or barb
únctio –ónis, *f.*, anointing, unction
unctus –a –um, *adj.*, anointed, smeared
unda –ae, *f.*, a wave, water, stream, surge, storm
unde, *adv.*, whence, wherefore, thence, whereupon
undequáquam, *adv.*, from everywhere
undíque, *adv.*, on every side, on all sides, from everywhere
undulátus –a –um, *adj.*, wavy
ungo –ere, unxi, unctum, *3,* to anoint
unguentária –ae, *f.*, a maker of ointments, confectionery
unguéntum –i, *n.*, ointment, fragrant oil
unguis –is, *m.*, claw, nail
úngula –ae, f., hoof, claw, talon, a claw-shaped torturing hook
ungulátus –a –um, *adj.*, having hoofs, having claws
únguo –ere, *3,* to anoint
única –ae, *f.*, darling, only one
unicórnis –is, *m.*, unicorn
unicórnis –e, *adj.*, having only one horn
unicórnuus –i, *m.*, the unicorn
únicus –a –um, *adj.*, alone, lonely, only, single, sole
unigéna –ae, *m.*, only-begotten
unigénitus –a –um, *adj.*, only-begotten
únio –ónis, *f.*, union
únio –íre, *4,* to unite
únitas –átis, *f.*, unity
únitus –a –um, *adj.*, united, joined
universális –e, *adj.*, universal
universáliter, *adv.*, universally, all together
univérsitas –átis, *f.*, completeness, wholeness, university, company, community, society, the whole world, the entire number of things, the whole, the universe

univérsum –i, *n.,* the universe, the whole world

univérsus –a –um, *adj.,* all, entire, whole

unquam, *adv.,* ever, at any time

unus –a –um, *adj.,* one, only one, single

unus post unum, one by one

unusquísque, unaquaéque, unumquídque *or* unumquódque, *adj.,* every, every one

urbánitas –átis, *f.,* good breeding

urbs, urbis, *f.,* city, town, the City of Rome

úrceus –i, *m.,* earthenware jug, pitcher, vessel

urédo –inis, *f.,* rust, a blight on plants

urens –éntis, *adj.,* scorching, burning

úrgeo –ére, ursi, *2,* to press hard, be urgent, shut

urna –ae, *f.,* a pot, pitcher for drawing water

uro –ere, ussi, ustum, *3,* to burn, dry up, parch

ursa –ae, *f.,* a female bear

ursus –i, *m.,* a bear

úsio –ónis, *f.,* use, using

úsito –áre, *1,* to use

usque, *adv.,* as far as, all the way, to, up to, constantly, continuously

usque ad, *adv.,* as far as, even, until

usquédum, *adv.,* until

usquequáque, *adv.,* everywhere, utterly, altogether, exceedingly

usquéquo, *adv.,* how long? wherefore?

ústulo –áre, *1,* to singe, burn a little

usúra –ae, *f.,* usury

usúrpo –áre, *1,* to usurp, assert one's right to, make use of, bring into use

usus –us, *m.,* use, want, need

utcúmque, *adv.,* however, after a sort

utensília –órum, *n. pl.,* utensils, furnishings

uter –tris, *m.,* wine skin, bottle, vessel, the skin of an animal used as a container

utercúmque, *adj.,* whichever of two

uterínus –a –um, *adj.,* of the same mother

utérlibet, *adj.,* either one you please

utérque, utráque, utrúmque, *adj.,* both, each of two

úterum –i, *n.,* the womb

úterus –i, *m.,* the womb

útilis –e, *adj.,* useful, profitable, beneficial, serviceable

utílitas –átis, *f.,* profit, benefit, advantage, utility, usefulness

utíliter, *adv.,* usefully, profitably, advantageously, serviceably

útinam, *adv.,* would that!

utíque, *adv.,* indeed, doubtless, surely, certainly, verily

utor, uti, usus sum, *dep. 3,* to use, make use of, employ, enjoy

útpote, *adv.,* inasmuch as, since

utrímque *or* utrínque, *adv.,* on both sides, in both cases

utrobíque, *adv.,* in both places, on both sides, both . . . and

utróque, *adv,* to both, to both sides, in both directions

utrum, *adv.,* whether

uva –ae, *f.,* a grape, a bunch of grapes

uvens –éntis, *adj.,* moist, wet

úvidus –a –um, *adj.,* moist, damp, wet

uvor –óris, *m.,* moistness, dampness

uxor –óris, *f.,* wife

uxórius –a –um, *adj.,* pertaining to a wife

V

vacans –ántis, *adv.,* empty, vacant

vacátio –ónis, *f.,* exemption from anything, freedom from anything

vacca –ae, *f.,* a cow

vacca fosta, *f.,* a milch cow

vacíllo –áre, *1,* to doubt

vaco –áre, *1,* to leave off, desist, to be without, free from, have time, keep one's self from something

vacúitas –átis, *f.,* vanity, vacuity, emptiness

vácuo –áre, *1,* to make empty, to empty, to void

vácuus –a –um, *adj.,* void; *in vácuum,* in vain

vado –ere, *3,* to go, walk, hasten, rush

vadósus –a –um, *adj,* shallow

vafer –fra –frum, *adj.,* sly, crafty, artful, subtle

vágina –ae, *f.,* sheath

vágio –íre, *4,* to whimper like a child, wail, cry.

vago –áre, *1,* to wander about, rove, ramble
vagor –ári, *dep. 1,* to wander, prowl, ramble
vagus –a –um, *adj.,* wandering, harborless, roaming, unsettled
vagus –i, *m.,* wanderer, vagrant; *in Canon Law,* one without a domicile
vah, *interj.,* aha! ah!
valde, *adv.,* greatly, exceedingly, very, very much
valefácio –ere, *3,* to bid farewell to, abandon
valens –éntis, *adj.,* strong, powerful
valénter, *adv.,* strongly, with a strong voice
váleo –ére –ui –itum, *2,* to be well, healthy, strong, able
valésco –ere –ui, *3,* to grow strong
valetudinárium –ii, *n.,* a sanatorium, hospital
valetúdo –inis, *f.,* health, strength, state of health
válide, *adv.,* strongly, mightily, powerfully
valíditas –átis, *f.,* validity
válidus –a –um, *adj.,* mighty, strong, powerful, boisterous, influential, efficacious
valles *or* **vallis** –is, *f.,* valley
vallo –áre, *1,* to enclose, fortify
vallum –i, *n.,* a trench
valor –óris, *m.,* value
valva –ae, *f.,* the blade of a door
valvae –árum, *f. pl.,* doors
vanilóquium –ii, *n.,* useless talk
vaníloquus –i, *m.,* a prattling person, a vain talker
vanitántes –um, *c. pl.,* vain people
vánitas –átis, *f.,* vanity, vain things, emptiness
vanitúdo –inis, *f.,* idle talk, lying talk
vanus –a –um, *adj.,* vain, idle, profitless, null, empty, void
vapor –óris, *m.,* vapor
vaporáliter, *adv.,* like vapor
váporo –áre, *1,* to incense, perfume
vápulo –áre, *1,* to cry out, be beaten, flogged, whipped
várie, *adv.,* variously, in various ways
varíetas –átis, *f.,* variety
vário –áre, *1,* to change, alter, vary
várius –a –um, *adj.,* various, varied, divers
varus –a –um, *adj.,* diverse, different, deviating from the right line

vas, vadis, *m.,* surety
vas, vasis, *n.,* vessel, vase
vasa –órum, *n. pl.,* vessel
vasa psalmi, harps
vásculum –i, *n.,* a small vessel or dish
vastátio –ónis, *f.,* a devastating, laying waste
vastátor –óris, *m.,* a destroyer, waster
vastátrix –ícis, *f.,* a destroyer, waster
vaste, *adv.,* widely, vastly, extensively
vástitas –átis, *f.,* waste, desolation, emptiness, an empty space
vasto –áre, *1,* to spoil, destroy, lay waste
vastus –a –um, *adj.,* vast, empty, waste, desolate, deserted
vates –is, *m.,* a prophet
Vaticána, basílica, St. Peter's church in Rome
Vaticánus –i, *m.,* the Vatican
vaticínium –ii, *n.,* a prophecy, revelation
vaticíno –áre, *1,* to prophesy
vaticínor –ári, *dep. 1,* to prophesy
vecórdia –ae, *f.,* foolishness, folly
vecors –córdis, *adj.,* silly, foolish, senseless, mad
vectátio –ónis, *f.,* carrying
véctigal –ális, *n.,* revenue, rent
vectis –is, *m.,* a bolt, bar, lever, a large bolt for fastening a door
vecto –áre, *1,* to carry, convey
vector –óris, *m.,* a sailor, passenger, carrier, one who is carried
végeo –ére, *2,* to stir up, quicken, excite to rapid action
vegetábilis –e, *adj.,* vegetable
vegetátio –ónis, *f.,* new life
végeto –áre, *1,* to stir up, quicken, nourish, live
végetus –a –um, *adj.,* strong, vigorous
véhemens –éntis, *adj.,* mighty, violent, furious, vigorous
veheménter, *adv.,* greatly, exceedingly, very much, vehemently, violently
veheméntius, *adv.,* earnestly
vehículum –i, *n.,* a conveyance
veho –ere, vexi, vectum, *3,* to carry, bear, convey
velámen –inis, *n.,* a veil, cloak
velaméntum –i, *n.,* a veil or covering, protection, shelter
velle, vólui, to desire, will, wish, delight in, choose
vello –ere, velli *or* vulsi, vulsum, *3,* to pluck
vellus –eris, *n.,* fleece

velo –áre, *1,* to cover, veil, hide, conceal, blindfold

velóciter, *adv.,* swiftly, speedily, quickly, rapidly

velox –ócis, *adj.,* swift, rapid, quick, fleet

velum –i, *n.,* a veil, a covering for the ciborium or the chalice

velum humerále, a Benediction veil, the veil worn by the subdeacon while holding the paten during a solemn High Mass

velut, *adv.,* as, like, even as, just as, just as if

vena –ae, *f.,* vein, inclination

venális –e, *adj.,* for sale, to be sold

venans –ántis, *m.,* a fowler, hunter

venátio –ónis, *f.,* hunting, venison, game

vanátor –óris, *m.,* hunter, one who fights with wild animals in the arena

venátrix –ícis, *f.,* huntress

venátus –us, *m.,* hunting

vendítio –ónis, *f.,* selling

vénditor –óris, *m.,* a seller, vendor

vendo –ere –didi, *3,* to sell

venefícium –ii, *n.,* witchcraft, magic, sorcery

venéficus –i, *m.,* a sorcerer, wizard, enchanter

venenátus –a –um, *adj.,* venemous, poisonous

venéno –áre, *1,* to poison

venenósus –a –um, *adj.,* venemous

venénum –i, *n.,* poison, venom

véneo –íre –ii, ventum, *4,* to be sold

venerábilis –e, *adj.,* venerable, worthy of reverence, to be revered

venerándus –a –um, *adj.,* venerable, worthy of reverence, to be revered

venerátio –ónis, *f.,* veneration, honor

vénero –áre, *1,* to venerate, worship, hold in honor

véneror –ári, *dep. 1,* to respect, venerate, honor, worship, adore

vénia –ae, *f.,* pardon, indulgence, grace, favor

veniábilis –e, *adj.,* venial, pardonable

veniáliter, *adv.,* venially

vénio –íre, veni, ventum, *4,* to come

venor –ári –átus sum, *dep. 1,* to hunt, pursue, strive after

venter –tris, *m.,* womb, stomach

ventilábrum –i, *n.,* a fan

véntilo –áre, *1,* to fan, winnow, toss, scatter

véntio –ónis, *f.,* a coming

ventíto –áre, *1,* to come often

ventúrus –a –um, *adj.,* coming, to come

ventus –i, *m.,* the wind

venúndo –áre –dedi –datum, *1,* to sell

venústas –átis, *f.,* beauty

vepres –is, *m.,* briar, briar bush, thorn bush

ver, veris, *n.,* spring

veráciter, *adv.,* truly, truthfully

verax –ácis, *f.,* true, truthful, veracious

verber –eris, *n.,* lash, blow, stripe, lashing, scourging

verberátio –ónis, *f.,* chastisement, punishment

vérbero –áre, *1,* to beat, to strike

verbósus –a –um, *adj.,* wordy, verbose

verbum –i, *n.,* word, saying, speech

Verbum incarnátum, the Incarnate Word, the God-Man, the Word made Flesh, the Second Person of the Blessed Trinity

vere, *adv.,* truly, in truth, indeed, rightly, aright

verecúndia –ae, *f.,* shame, modesty, a feeling or sense of shame

veredárius –ii, *m.,* a messenger, letter carrier

véreor –éri, *dep. 2,* to fear, reverence

vergo –ere, versi, *3,* to be inclined, bend

verisimíliter, *adv.,* in all probability

véritas –átis, *f.,* truth, fidelity

vermiculátus –a –um, *adj.,* inlaid, checkered, adorned with inlaid work

vermículus –i, *m.,* crimson, scarlet

vermis –is, *m.,* a worm

vernáculus –i, *m.,* a homeborn slave, domestic

vernans –ántis, *adj.,* springlike

verno –áre, *1,* to flourish

vernus –a –um, *adj.,* pertaining to the springtime

vero, *adv.,* in truth, in fact, really

verro –ere, versus sum, *semi-dep. 3,* to sweep

versánia –ae, *f.,* wild rage, madness

versánus –a –um, *adj.,* furious, insane

versátilis –e, *adj.,* revolving

versátus –a –um, *adj.,* versed

versículus –i, *m.,* a short verse

vérsio –ónis, *f.,* translation, version

versipéllis –e, *adj.,* changeable

verso –áre, *1,* to change, turn

versus –us, *m.,* verse

versus clusor, a final verse

versútia –ae, *f.,* craftiness, subtlety

versútus –a –um, *adj.,* crafty

vertex –icis, *m.*, the top, crown of the head, pate

vertíbilis, *adj.*, convertible, liable to be turned back

verto –ere, verti, versum, *3*, to use, turn

verúmtamen, *adv.*, but, nevertheless, notwithstanding, surely, verily, in truth

verus –a –um, *adj.*, true, real

vescor, vesci, *dep. 3*, to eat

vesper –i *or* –is, *m.*, the evening star, the evening, eventide

véspera –ae, *f.*, evening, eventide

vésperae –árum, *f. pl.*, Vespers

vesperális –e, *adj.*, pertaining to Vespers

vesperásco –ere, *3*, to become evening

vespertínus –a –um, *adj.*, evening, belonging to an evening

vester –tra –trum, *adj.*, your, yours

vestiárium –ii, *n.*, a sacristy of vestry

vestiárius –ii, *m.*, a sacristan

vestíbulum –i, *n.*, a court, porch, vestibule

vestígium –ii, *n.*, foot, footstep, footprint, the sole, that part of the foot that makes an imprint

vestiméntum –i, *n.*, a garment, vestment, robe, raiment, vesture

vestítio –ónis, *f.*, investiture

vestítus –us, *m.*, clothing, vesture, apparel, raiment

veteránus –a –um, *adj.*, veteran

veterásco –ere –ávi, *3*, to grow old, become old, decay, vanish

veternósus –a –um, *adj.*, dull, lethargic

vétitus –a –um, *adj.*, forbidden

veto –áre –ui –itum, *1*, to forbid, prohibit

vetus –eris, *adj.*, original, old, former, ancient

vetus error, ancient enemy, the devil, former sins

vetústas –átis, *f.*, old age, old life, old man, former ways, former manner of life

vetústus –a –um, *adj.*, old, ancient

vexátio –ónis, *f.*, annoyance, ill-treatment

vexíllifer –eri, *m.*, a standard-bearer

vexíllum –i, *n.*, a banner, the standard. The Vexillum was the old Roman cavalry standard surmounted by a cross instead of the Roman eagle.

vexo –áre, *1*, to oppress, afflict, trouble, harass, vex, torment

via –ae, *f.*, the way, path, highway, road, manner of life

viárius –a –um, *adj.*, relating to highways

viáticum –i, *n.*, fare, money or provision for a journey, the Holy Viaticum

viáticus –a –um, *adj.*, pertaining to travel

viátor –óris, *m.*, traveler, wayfarer

vibro –áre, *1*, to brandish, shake

vicariátus –us, *m.*, a vicariate

vicárium –ii, *n.*, a vicariate

vicárius –ii, *m.*, a vicar

vice-párochus –i, *m.*, one supplying the place of a parish priest

vices –um, *m.*, punishment; *in* or *ad vicem*, instead of

vícia –ae, *f.*, the vetch, any of various leguminous plants, mostly climbing herbs

vicínus –a –um, *adj.*, nearby, neighboring

vicis (*gen.*, *no nom.*), change, alteration, time, return, interchange

vicíssim, *adv.*, in turn, by turns, in return

vicissitúdo –inis, *f.*, alteration

víctima –ae, *f.*, a victim

Víctima paschális, the Paschal Lamb

víctimo –áre, *1*, to offer as a victim

víctito –áre, *1*, to live upon

victor –óris, *m.*, conqueror

victória –ae, *f.*, victory

victrix –ícis, *adj.*, victorious, conquering

victuália –ium, *n. pl.*, victuals, sustenance

victus –us, *m.*, food, support, way of living

vicus –i, *m.*, town, district, lane, way, street

vidélicet, *adv.*, namely, forsooth, plainly, evidently, manifestly

viden (videsne?), seest thou?

videns –éntis, *m.*, seer

vídeo –ére, vidi, visum, *2*, to see, behold

vídeor –éri, visus sum, *dep. 2*, to seem

vídua –ae, *f.*, a widow

vidúitas –átis, *f.*, a widowhood

víduo –áre, *1*, to deprive of

víduus –a –um, *adj.*, separated from, bereaved of, destitute of

vígeo –ére –ui, *2*, to live, flourish, be raised to power

vigil, vígilis, *adj.*, watchful

vigilánter, *adv.*, vigilantly, watchfully

vigilántia –ae, *f.*, watchfulness, vigilance, wakefulness

vigília –ae, *f.*, watch, vigil, a night watch of a feast

vigíliae –árum, *f. pl.*, Matins

vígilo –áre, *1*, to watch, keep watch, be on guard, be awake

vigor –óris, *m.,* strength, vigor, force, activity, energy

vilésco –ere, *3,* to become valueless, become vile

vilis –e, *adj.,* cheap, vile

vílitas –átis, *f.,* baseness

villa –ae, *f.,* a village, farm, country place

villicátio –ónis, *f.,* stewardship

víllico –áre, *1,* to be a steward, manage an estate

víllicus –i, *m.,* a steward, overseer, keeper of an estate

vimpa –ae, *f.,* a silken veil worn by the miter and crosier bearers

vinárius –a –um, *adj.,* of wine

víncio –íre, vinxi, vinctum, *4,* to bind, fetter with chains

vincla –órum, *n. pl.,* bonds, chains

vinco –ere, vici, victum, *3,* to overcome, conquer

vinctus –i, *m.,* captive, prisoner

vínculum –i, *n.,* bond, chain, fetter

vindémia –ae, *f.,* vintage, wine, the season of vintage

vindemiátor –óris, *m.,* a grape gatherer

vindémio –áre, *1,* to gather grapes, to pluck

vindex –icis, *c.,* avenger

víndico –áre, *1,* to claim, avenge

vindícta –ae, *f.,* revenge, vengeance, punishment

vínea –ae, *f.,* vine, vineyard

vínitor –óris, *m.,* a vinedresser

vinoléntus –a –um, *adj.,* given to wine drinking

vinum –i, *n.,* wine

vio –áre, *1,* to go, travel, wander, travel about

violáceus –a –um, *adj.,* violet

violátor –óris, *m.,* a violator, profaner

violéntus –a –um, *adj.,* violent, furious, impetuous

víolo –áre, *1,* to violate, profane

vípera –ae, *f.,* viper, adder, snake

vir –i, *m.,* man, any human being, husband

virágo –inis, *f.,* woman, heroine

virátus –a –um, *adj.,* manly, valiant

viréctum –i, *n.,* a green place

virens –éntis, *adj.,* green

víreo –ére, *2,* to be green

virésco –ere, *3,* to grow green

virétum –i, *n.,* a glade, greensward, a green place

virga –ae, *f.,* a rod, scepter, staff, shep-

herd's crook, twig, bough, a vertical tail appended to a note

virginális –e, *adj.,* virginal, pure, relating to a virgin

virgíneus –a –um, *adj.,* virginal

virgínitas –átis, *f.,* virginity

virgo –inis, *f.,* virgin, maiden

vírgula –ae, *f.,* a small rod, a comma

virgúltum –i, *n.,* a plant, shrub, thicket, copse, brushwood

víridis –e, *adj.,* green

vírido –áre, *1,* to be green

virílis –e, *adj.,* manly, male, virile

viríliter *adv.,* manfully, courageously, vigorously

virítim *adv.,* individually

viror –óris, *m.,* verdure, freshness, vigor

virtuóse *adv.,* virtuously

virtus –útis, *f.,* virtue, power, ability, strength, excellence

virus –i, *m.,* poison, venom

vis vis, *f.,* force, violence, power, might, strength

víscera –órum, *n. pl.,* bowels, innermost parts, the flesh under the skin, the inmost part of anything

viscum –i, *n.,* a viscuous substance, birdlike

visíbilis –e, *adj.,* visible, outward

visibíliter *adv.,* outwardly, visibly

vísio –ónis, *f.,* vision, appearance, the act of seeing

visitátio –ónis, *f.,* visitation, visiting

visitátor –óris, *m.,* a visitor

vísito –áre, *1,* to visit, survey, to visit as a manifestation of Divine power, favor, or wrath

viso –ere, visi, visum, *3,* to behold, contemplate

visor –óris, *m. and f.,* one who sees

visum –i, *n.,* a dream, vision, appearance

visum sómnium, a dream

visus –us, *m.,* vision, sight

vita –ae, *f.,* life, eternal life, heaven

Vita, the Author of Life

vitális –e, *adj.,* life-giving, of life, vital

vitam trádere, to give life to men

vitiátor –óris, *m.,* a corrupter

vítio –áre, *1,* to injure, damage, corrupt, mar, spoil

vitióse *adv.,* viciously

vitiósitas –átis, *f.,* wickedness, viciousness

vitis –is, *f.,* vine, grapevine

vítium –ii, *n.,* vice, sin, defect, default, blemish

vito –áre, *1,* to avoid, shun, withstand

vítreus –a –um, *adj.,* transparent, of glass, of porcelain

vitrum –i, *n.,* glass

vitta –ae, *f.,* a ribbon, band, lace; the two bands pendant from a miter

vítula –ae, *f.,* heifer, calf

vitulámen –inis, *n.,* a shoot, sprout

vítulus –i, *m.,* bull, bullock, calf

vituperátio –ónis, *f.,* defamation, slandering, defaming, censuring

vituperátor –óris, *m.,* a blamer

vitúpero –áre, *1,* to blame

vivax –ácis, *adj.,* vigorous, long-lived

vívidus –a –um, *adj.,* healthy, living, animated

vivíficans –ántis, *adj.,* life-giving

vivificátrix –ícis, *f.,* vivifier, quickener

vivífico –áre, *1,* to bring to life, vivify, give life to, make alive, quicken

vivo –ere, vixi, victum, *3,* to live, have life, be alive

vix, *adv.,* scarcely, hardly, with effort

vobismetípsis (*dat. pl.*), you yourselves

vocábulum –i, *n.,* name, word

vocátio –ónis, *f.,* calling, summons, vocation

vociferátio –ónis, *f.,* jubilation, loud shaking

voco –áre, *1,* to call, summon, invite

voláticus –a –um, *adj.,* fleeting, ephemeral

volátile –is, *n.,* a fowl, bird

volatília –ium, *n. pl.,* winged creatures, birds

volátilis –e, *adj.,* winged, flying

volátus –us, *m.,* flight

vólito –áre, *1,* to fly about, fly, fly often, fly to and fro

volo –áre, *1,* to fly

volo, velle, vólui, to will, wish, desire

volúcer –cris –cre, *adj.,* flying

volúcris –is, *f.,* a fowl, bird

volúmen –inis, *n.,* book, volume, roll

voluntárie, *adv.,* voluntarily, of one's own free will, freely, gladly, willingly

voluntárium –ii, *n.,* a free-will offering

voluntárius –a –um, *adj.,* voluntary, gracious, generous, free

volúntas –átis, *f.,* will, wish, inclination

volúptas –átis, *f.,* pleasure, delight

volvo –ere, volvi, volútum, *3,* to ponder, meditate, roll

vomo –áre –ui –itum, *1,* to vomit

voráciter, *adv.,* greedily

vorágo –inis, *f.,* breach, chasm, abyss

vorax –ácis, *adj.,* gluttonous, voracious

voro –áre, *1,* to eat, devour

vosmetípsos (*acc.*), you yourselves

votívus –a –um, *adj.,* votive

votum –i, *n.,* vow, desire, prayer, petition

vóveo –ére, vovi, votum, *2,* to vow, promise solemnly, promise sacredly

vox, vocis, *f.,* voice, sound

vulgáris –e, *adj.,* common, coarse, plain

vulgo –áre, *1,* to publish

vulgo, *adv.,* commonly

vulgus –i, *n.,* people, multitude

vúlnero –áre, *1,* to wound

vulnus –eris, *n.,* wound

vulpes –is, *f.,* fox

vultus –us, *m.,* countenance, face

vulva –ae, *f.,* womb

X

Xánthicus –i, *m.,* the name of a month corresponding to April

xeniólium –i, *n.,* a small gift

xénium –ii, *n.,* a gift, present

xenodóchium –ii, *n.,* a hospice, a house for travelers

xerophágia –ae, *f.,* a dry fast, a meal of dry food

xylon –i, *n.,* the cotton tree

xystus –i, *m.,* a walk planted with trees

Z

Zábulon (Hebr.), *indecl.,* Zabulon

zábulus –i, *m.,* devil

Zacharías –ae, *m.,* Zachary, the prophet

zámia –ae, *f.,* loss, damage, injury

Zebee (Hebr.), *indecl.,* Zeb, a Madianite prince

zelátor –óris, *m.,* enthusiast, zealot

zelo –áre, *1,* to be envious of

zelor –ári, *dep. 1,* to be zealous for
zelótes –ae, *m.,* a zealot
Zelótes, *indecl.,* a surname of Simon the Apostle
zelotýpia –ae, *f.,* jealousy
zelotýpus –a –um, *adj.,* jealous
zelus –i, *m.,* jealousy, zeal
zetárius –ii, *m.,* a valet

zimárra –ae, *f.,* a cassock with a small cape
Zipháei –órum, *m. pl.,* Ziphites, the inhabitants of Ziph
zizánia –ae, *f.,* also used in *pl. n.,* cockle, tares, a sort of weed
zona –ae, *f.,* a sash, belt, girdle
zonárius –a –um, *adj.,* pertaining to a girdle

Liturgical Latin, obviously enough to anyone who has even a smattering of the language, is not the Latin of the classical writers. Liturgical Latin, for the most part, is the common Latin of the people with a vocabulary suited to its use. Some Latin words were "christianized" — i.e., given meanings not found in dictionaries of classical Latin. Variant spellings are also quite common in the ecclesiastical books.

Here are over 11,000 words — gathered from Scriptures (including the new Latin Psalter), the Breviary, the Missal, and other church books — a good percentage of which are not to be found at all in classical dictionaries, and almost all of which have a peculiar meaning in ecclesiastical use.